UNFOLDING STAKEHOLDER THINKING 2
RELATIONSHIPS, COMMUNICATION, REPORTING AND PERFORMANCE

Edited by Jörg Andriof, Sandra Waddock, Bryan Husted and
Sandra Sutherland Rahman

Unfolding Stakeholder Thinking

2

RELATIONSHIPS, COMMUNICATION, REPORTING AND PERFORMANCE

EDITED BY JÖRG ANDRIOF, SANDRA WADDOCK, BRYAN HUSTED
AND SANDRA SUTHERLAND RAHMAN

Greenleaf
PUBLISHING
2 0 0 3

© 2003 Greenleaf Publishing Limited

Published by Greenleaf Publishing Limited
Aizlewood's Mill
Nursery Street
Sheffield S3 8GG
UK

Printed and bound, using acid-free paper from managed forests, by
Bookcraft, Midsomer Norton, UK.

British Library Cataloguing in Publication Data:
   A catalogue record for this book is available from the British Library.

ISBN 1874719535

CONTENTS

FOREWORD

Dr Andreas Pohlmann
Chief Administrative Officer
Celanese AG

The relationship between business and society continues to change in new and significant ways. In 2002 the global economy was an intricate web of social, political and economic entities: advanced industrial nations, such as the United States, Japan and Germany; emerging economies that are rapidly developing in Asia and Latin America; Eastern European economies that are free after decades of political repression; and countries that are still struggling to devise economic strategies that help produce prosperity and an improved quality of life for their citizens. 2003 is a year in which businesses worldwide experience the economic aftermaths of events such as the Enron and WorldCom debacle, September 11th and the likelihood of a new 'Gulf War'.

In difficult times, stakeholder relationships have become increasingly important targets of examination, debate, research and strategy formation. Internationalisation and globalisation as openers of a firm's activity sphere; the formation of the new political economy towards a worldwide market economy ideology; the recession area as a period in which to concentrate more on business world details; the increased consciousness, demands and activities of different and sometimes new stakeholder groups in the mental and physical environment of companies—all these features imply huge new pressures to develop better frameworks and theories to understand comprehensive and complex business and society relationships.

In the midst of this social change, the realities of managing a business are also changing. Businesses have new roles and new responsibilities in the modern economy. Decisions are not made in the same way as they were 10 or 20 years ago. More people, in more ways than in earlier times, feel the impact of business decisions. And, because so many other things have changed in the new global economy, business leaders are required to think more carefully than ever about the effects of their actions on their companies' employees, customers, suppliers, investors and other stakeholders. The media, government officials and the communities in which business is conducted watch the actions of business carefully. In a very real sense, the world is watching as business executives chart their companies' future direction.

Celanese's stakeholder engagement efforts are built on a concept of sustainable development that balances the economic, environmental and social concerns of today's and future generations. Sustainability is, to Celanese, a precondition for economic success. Dealing with raw materials and energy efficiently is just as much a part of sustainability as good neighbourly relations to site communities and society in general. Only companies that work in harmony with society and manufacture environmentally friendly, safe products using efficient processes will enjoy lasting success in the marketplace.

Society—the whole complexity of stakeholders—provides companies with a so-called 'licence to operate': that is to say, it has confidence in the competence and will of a company to adhere to national and international legal requirements and to behave in accordance with the demands of a democratic society. In this context, sustainability means developing a common understanding of the safe, responsible and acceptable operation of our facilities by consulting others in our environment. Celanese seeks opportunities for active engagements with various stakeholders but in particular with its suppliers and customers, local authorities, the communities and, most importantly, with its employees and shareholders.

Stakeholder thinking as a framework for analysing these relationships or developing and implementing related strategies has become a known paradigm worldwide. This book enables practitioners, academics as well as students to understand various underlying theories and to gain insight into business cases. This approach opens up a new perspective; it enables the **unfolding of stakeholder thinking**.

In the 21st century business and society are moving closer together. For this reason, it is all the more important for companies to understand *stakeholder thinking*. In this context, therefore, this book provides crucial current impulses as to how companies can view themselves as corporate citizens and, as such, can fulfil their responsibility towards society. The book is also comprehensive reading for academics as well as students trying to unfold *stakeholder thinking*. This is a book with a vision. It is not simply a compendium of information and ideas.

INTRODUCTION

Sandra Sutherland Rahman
Framingham State College,
USA

Sandra Waddock
Boston College, Carroll School of
Management, USA

Jörg Andriof
Celanese AG, Germany;
Warwick Business School, UK

Bryan Husted
ITESM/Instituto De Empresa,
Mexico

This volume is the companion to *Unfolding Stakeholder Thinking: Theory, Responsibility and Engagement*, which examined many emerging theoretical and normative issues. It collects a series of essays focused on the practice of stakeholder engagement in terms of relationship management, communication, reporting and performance.

The stakeholder approach to the firm reframed the relationship between business and society in a fundamental way by explicitly recognising the embeddedness of the corporation into a *network* of stakeholder *relationships*. This more relational view of the firm, while initially corporate-centric (the common 'spoke-and-wheel' picture suggesting this centrality), began to shift scholarly understanding of the relationship of the firm to society toward more of a business *in* society framing, although the language did not shift accordingly.

The concept of stakeholders as in *relationship* to the firm has become a core element of the unfolding of stakeholder thinking as it stands today. By recognising the embeddedness of ethics in actions with impacts and assuming this network perspective, we could even argue that *relationship* is possibly the third 'R' that Frederick (1987, 1994) was seeking. Frederick attempted to show the development of the field of business in society moving from CSR1 to CSR3 (1994) by *integrating* ethics into corporate responsibility—a move unnecessary if we avoid the separation thesis (Freeman 1994) in the first place. Stakeholder partnerships as a specific form of stakeholder engagement represent another developmental shift (Andriof 2001). The implication of the relationship perspective is that companies are inherently connected to other institutions *in* society (business *in* society) and that they are inextricably linked in relationship with at least primary and secondary (Clarkson 1995) stakeholders.

Several shifts can be identified in recent years that highlight this relational approach in stakeholder thinking. First is the integration through empirical studies of corporate 'social' performance as manifested by stakeholder relationships, of which Waddock and Graves 1997 and Berman *et al.* 1999 are representative studies. Second is the emergence of corporate citizenship as new terminology to describe a company's behaviour in society (cf. Marsden and Andriof 1998; McIntosh *et al.* 1998; Waddock 2002), and the attendant recognition that business exists in, not alongside, society. Waddock (2002) makes clear the link between corporate citizenship or corporate responsibility (dropping the 'social' in the belief that responsibility is integral to practice as many practitioners, particularly in Europe, are doing today) and a company's treatment of its stakeholders as the way responsibility is evidenced in practice.

As the relational perspective on which stakeholder thinking is based has unfolded, it has become increasingly clear that identifying who stakeholders are is a key concern. There are two approaches to identifying who a stakeholder is and which claims are salient to management (Windsor 1992). The broad view of stakeholder identification focuses on a stakeholder's ability to influence the firm's behaviour, direction, process or outcome, and focuses on the urgency, power and legitimacy of the stakeholder in question (cf. Mitchell *et al.* 1997). The classic broad definition is Freeman's: 'those who affect or are affected by a firm' (Freeman 1984; see also Alkhafaji 1989; Freeman and Reed 1983; Jones 1980; Thompson *et al.* 1991).

The narrow view of stakeholder identification in an organisation focuses on a stakeholder's legal, moral or presumed claim (Mitchell *et al.* 1997) on the firm. The classic narrow definition is determined by the level of risk a stakeholder bears. 'Voluntary stakeholders bear some form of risk as a result of having invested some form of capital, human or financial, something of value, in a firm. Involuntary stakeholders are placed at risk as a result of a firm's activities. But without the element of risk there is no stake' (Clarkson 1994: 5, quoted in Mitchell *et al.* 1997: 856-57).

The narrow and broad definitions of 'stakeholder' merge on several important questions. First, which stakeholders have legal, moral or presumed claims on the firm and which stakeholders can influence a firm's behaviour, direction, process or outcomes (Mitchell *et al.* 1997; see also Savage *et al.* 1991; Brenner 1993; Starik 1994)? Second, can an entity (e.g. a competitor) be a stakeholder without being in an actual relationship with the firm (Mitchell *et al.* 1997; see also Ring 1994; Clarkson 1994; Post *et al.* 2002a)? Third, if the firm and a stakeholder have a relationship, what is the nature of that relationship (Mitchell *et al.* 1997)? A combination of theories contributes to understanding the dynamics of a firm–stakeholder relationship.

Stakeholder thinking unfolds: relationship, communication, performance and reporting

As stakeholder *relationships* and business in society have become increasingly central to the unfolding of stakeholder thinking, important new topics have begun to take centre stage in both the worlds of practice and academics. The chapters in this volume reflect several emerging themes that are now unfolding in the management of stakeholder relationships dealing with communication, performance and reporting.

Part I, 'Stakeholder communication and relationship management', makes it clear that simply engaging with stakeholders is insufficient to build successful stakeholder strategies. Companies, considered as the focal entity in a relationship, also need to actively communicate with stakeholders and actively manage their relationships. As the first chapter in this section by Sandra Rahman, 'Stakeholder discourse and critical-frame analysis: the case of child labour in Bangladesh' indicates, companies not only need to communicate with stakeholders but also to be aware of the messages that are being sent by stakeholders so that they can develop appropriate responses. Andrew Crane and Sharon Livesey put this theme into a critical lens in their chapter 'Are you talking to me? Stakeholder communication and the risks and rewards of dialogue'. In a practice-oriented paper, Jem Bendell provides new insight into what it takes to make stakeholder communication work in 'Talking for change? Reflections on effective stakeholder dialogue'.

It is essential to understand the role of power and influence in stakeholder engagement strategies if they are to become dominant modes by which companies interact with their stakeholders. This topic is tackled in two papers, in Aharon Factor's 'Stakeholder influences in developing a sustainability culture within the UK biotechnology sector' and Stephanie Welcomer, Philip Cochran and Virginia Gerde's 'Power and social behaviour: a structuration approach to stakeholder networks'.

Engagement strategies inevitably mean that partnerships or collaborations will emerge from the relationships that are engendered. In 'State of the union: NGO–business partnership stakeholders', Jonathan Cohen looks at a wide range of corporate–NGO collaborations to determine what makes them effective—and what makes them fail. In an interesting treatment of an interactive approach to an emerging industry, Bruce Clemens and Scott Gallagher assess 'Stakeholders for environmental strategies: the case of the emerging industry in radioactive scrap metal treatment'. Just what is involved in stakeholder (relationship) management and what makes such relationships effective is also the topic of Michael Johnson-Cramer, Shawn Berman and James Post's 'Re-examining the concept of "stakeholder management" '.

In the types of intensive interaction that stakeholder engagement involves, conflict is almost inevitable. Julia Robbins looks at how conflict is dealt with in collaborative stakeholder alliances in 'Stakeholders and conflict management: corporate perspectives on collaborative approaches'. The final chapter in this section by James Weber and David Wasieleski deals with the ways in which a company's exposure to its social environment interacts with its top-management philosophy, external affairs (stakeholder relationship) strategy and internal structure ('Managing corporate stakeholders: subjecting Miles's 1987 data-collection framework to tests of validation').

There is, however, one final and critically important element to be addressed, which has emerged in recent years. That element is covered in the second and final section, 'Stakeholder performance and reporting', which deals with emerging schemes for the assessment, measurement and reporting about business in society relationships involving stakeholders. Three chapters address this important topic. Michael King examines a variety of current approaches to stakeholder assessment and reporting in 'Approaches to stakeholder performance and reporting: an investor's perspective. Investigating how sustainable companies deliver value to shareholders'. The performance question is again addressed in 'Top managers and institutional stakeholders: a test of two models of adaptation and performance' by Michael Russo and Frank Schultz. Finally, Jane Zhang, Ian Fraser and Wan Ying Hill provide a comparative analysis of reporting schemes in 'A comparative study of stakeholder-oriented social audit models and reports'.

Conclusion

The evolution of stakeholder thinking has led to a new view of the firm as an organism embedded in a complex web of relationships with other organisms. This ecological model of the firm is consonant with recent advances in organisational theory (Hannan and Freeman 1989) and highlights the symbiotic nature of the relationship between firm and stakeholders. Consequently, this view moves beyond stakeholder management to emphasise new concerns such as firm engagement with stakeholders and stakeholder responsibilities.

The role of management becomes immeasurably more challenging, when stakeholders are no longer seen as simply the objects of managerial action but rather as subjects with their own objectives and purposes. This volume has begun to capture some of the complexity of managing relationships with stakeholders by discussing the practice of stakeholder engagement and dialogue and the consequences of this practice for both reporting and performance.

Part 1
STAKEHOLDER COMMUNICATION AND RELATIONSHIP MANAGEMENT

STAKEHOLDER DISCOURSE AND CRITICAL-FRAME ANALYSIS
The case of child labour in Bangladesh

Sandra Sutherland Rahman
Framingham State College, USA

The fundamental assumption in stakeholder theory (Freeman 1984) is that there exists a relationship between the firm and the stakeholder that is based on some mutual interest. The mutual interest in this study is the employment of underage children. Bangladeshi factory owners/managers are targeted by their stakeholders for hiring children, and US importers are targeted by their stakeholders for buying clothing that children participated in making. In both cases the firms generally believe that children benefit from being employed because it enables them to sustain life through a comparatively more attractive means. The Bangladesh/US child labour discourse exploded with controversy because of strong stakeholder activism in the US that led to the removal of those children from their job in Bangladesh. The purpose of this chapter is to untangle the complex set of local and international stakeholder messages that define the stakeholder environment to which firms are asked to respond. More simply stated, this chapter defines the message sent from stakeholders to US importing and Bangladeshi manufacturing firms regarding their use of child labour.

This research accepts that management scans the business environment to consider stakeholder interests in its strategic planning process. The issue at the core of the stakeholder maps is the concern for children being employed by garment factories in Bangladesh that produce goods for the US consumer market. This concern has become one of the largest international trade issues of the past several decades. For this reason, it has been discussed in a variety of public forums around the world between interested stakeholders. Management is able to gather critical stakeholder sentiment from the identified discourses. There is limited evidence that stakeholders are directly contacting either the Bangladeshi manufacturer or the US importer. Therefore, it is assumed that most of their information permeates the environmental scanning process through public stakeholder discourse.

Stakeholder discourse in the public arenas is critical in this research because it involves the general consumer public. Garments being imported from Bangladesh are targeted towards men, women and children. It is recognised that the consumer ultimately decides whether or not to buy a garment that was imported from Bangladesh. Therefore, stakeholders often target opportunities that will affect public sentiment towards the use of child labour. It is critically important to the business firm to track and understand discourse that affects consumer demand.

The issue of children working under the age of 14 has been debated in economic and human rights literature for decades. All developed countries today that have passed through the stage of industrialisation seem to have passed through a transition period where children moved from the farm, to the factory and then into the schools. In earlier times the issue was primarily dealt with on a local or a national level. The critical difference today is that multinational firms are trading with nations that are in different stages of economic development and stakeholders are objecting to certain business practices. This makes the international discourse on child labour particularly rich to analyse and critically important for international management and international stakeholders to understand.

1.1 Methodology

To identify and analyse the content of stakeholder frames of the Bangladeshi supplier and the American buyer that are interested in their use of child labour, I began by drawing two comprehensive stakeholder maps (Freeman 1984). Details of the maps can be found in Rahman 2000. Critical-frame analysis (Rein and Gamson 1999) was applied to the two stakeholder maps that were drawn for the purpose of sorting the stakeholder discourse on the use of child labour by the US importing firms and the Bangladeshi manufacturing firms. The stakeholder-frame model was then used to name/identify the messages being expressed and the stakeholder-objective model was used to classify the stakeholder groups based on their operating objective for the purpose of analysis. More simply stated, this methodology records the stakeholder messages, identifies the content of the messages based on their ethical foundation, and compares the content based on the operating objectives of the stakeholder. Thus, the methodology allows for an objective domestic and cross-cultural comparison of a highly controversial stakeholder issue. The organisation of this analysis is shown in Table 1.1.

1.2 Who are the stakeholders?

According to the definition, 'a stakeholder is any group or individual who can affect or is affected by the achievement of an organisation's purpose' (Freeman 1984). Therefore a map is the identification of such individuals or groups.

Question	Tool	Author
1. Who are the stakeholders?	Stakeholder map	Freeman 1984
2. What is the content of the messages being sent to the firm?	Critical-frame analysis	Rein and Gamson 1999
3. How do stakeholders frame the content of their messages?	Stakeholder-frame model	Cavanagh *et al.* 1981
4. What is the operating objective of the stakeholder?	Stakeholder-objective model	Defined by the stakeholder
5. Which stakeholder frames are used within and between Bangladeshi manufacturers and US importer stakeholder environments?	Critical-frame analysis matrix	Rahman 2000, based on Rein and Gamson 1999 and Cavanagh *et al.* 1981

Table 1.1   **Tools for analysis**

In order to identify the stakeholders of the Bangladeshi manufacturers, their interests in the firm, and how they attempt to influence firm behaviour, I conducted a thorough library search. From this effort, I was able to obtain a variety of written sources expressing a variety of opinions on the issue. I narrowed my stakeholder population to those stakeholders that actually expressed an opinion on (1) Bangladeshi manufacturers that are employing children; or (2) US importers that are sourcing from Bangladeshi factories employing children.

To obtain information on the Bangladeshi stakeholder environment, I visited the country to gather as many facts as possible. Since there are very few libraries in the country and the ones that exist are not equipped to offer a database of information, I chose to visit places to gather information and to elicit the assistance of a local student to gather information for me. I visited the BGMEA (Bangladesh Garment Manufacturers' Exporters' Association), the United Nations Children's Fund (UNICEF) office, the International Labour Organisation (ILO), Save the Children, the Export Promotion Bureau, several factories, a sales agent in the garment industry and an economics professor at the University of Dhaka. At these locations I was able to obtain government, industry, non-government and academic reports, articles, publications and opinions. Through a local contact I collected local print media coverage of the discourse regarding child labour in the garment industry. Articles were in both the English and the Bengali newspapers. A colleague translated articles that were printed in Bengali. For details of the stakeholder map, see Rahman 2000.

1.3 What is the content of the messages being sent to the firm?

Critical-frame analysis is a methodology for sorting discourse. 'Frames are coherent meaning-systems that provide a coherent story line for events and issues' (Rein and Gamson 1999). In this research, the frame refers to the primary and secondary interests/demands that the stakeholder levies towards the firm. Critical-frame analysis is used: (1) to establish a coherent structure that works to clarify the streams of thought in a discussion; (2) to facilitate a general understanding of the arguments; and (3) to eventually promote agreement. This methodology is ideally suited to clarify the cross-cultural complexity of stakeholder interests in firm behaviour regarding the best interest of the child in Bangladeshi garment factories.

Critical-frame analysis requires the identification of sponsors of frames and the forums in which they are discussed. The sponsors are the proponents of the message and the forum is the place where they make their message known. The sponsors in this research are the stakeholders and the forum is primarily a government arena such as public hearings on child labour and congressional debates on the Child Labour Deterrence Act. Other forums such as the media and industry research publications are also included. The period of discourse analysis extends from the early 1980s to 1999 both in Bangladesh and in the US. The stakeholder discourse from these forums is identified as a particular frame. The frames are then studied to create an organised picture of the stakeholder discourse.

1.4 How do stakeholders frame the content of their messages?

1.4.1 Stakeholder-frame model

To apply critical-frame analysis methodology to this study, two models were used to establish an underlying structure to accommodate the stakeholder frames and to allow for comparative analysis. The first model, identified as the stakeholder-frame model, was selected on the assumption that decisions have an ethical base. It is based on the ethical model of Cavanagh et al. (1981) and organised by Hellriegel and Slocum (1996). The language of the ethical model of decision-making was modified to fit the language of this study (see Appendix A).

Up to two critical frames were identified for each stakeholder group. The primary frame represents the most common frame supported by members of the stakeholder group. The secondary frame represents the second most common frame supported by members of the same stakeholder group. The primary and secondary frames were determined under the guidelines of critical-frame analysis (Rein and Gamson 1999). Rein and Gamson, researchers at the forefront of critical-frame analysis, require the researcher to identify the frames. They believe that, since the researcher has the most intimate knowledge of the stakeholder's language and intentions, he or she is in the best position to make a judgement as to which frame the stakeholder supports.

However, to add to the rigour of the frame identification, I conducted a reliability check. I chose one of my colleagues to identify a primary and a secondary frame that best represents the argument of each stakeholder. This colleague was selected because he is from Bangladesh, he holds an MBA from Harvard Business School and he has research experience. I gave my colleague the following information: (1) the name of the stakeholder; (2) their interest in firm behaviour; (3) their method of influencing firm behaviour; (4) the adapted model of ethical decision-making; and (5) the two comprehensive stakeholder maps. I asked my colleague to choose up to two frames that best represented the beliefs of the stakeholder. In a few weeks he gave me his list and I compared it with my original list. We matched primary frames 70% of the time and secondary frames 60% of the time. After discussing our differences, we agreed on some changes to the frame identification chart.

Table 1.2 lists the resulting stakeholder discourse frame identification. The ethical model codes used in this table are defined in Appendix A. However, to assist in the following explanation a few of the frame codes are defined as follows:

- **MRM:LAS.a:** Moral Rights Model: Life and Safety. Children have the right to a healthy (physical and emotional) childhood.

- **MRM:LAS.b:** Moral Rights Model: Life and Safety. Children have the right to a healthy (physical and emotional) work environment.

- **UM:RU.a:** Utilitarian Model: Rule Utilitarianism. Necessary stage in economic development according to economic theory.

- **UM:RU.b:** Utilitarian Model: Rule Utilitarianism. The written law does not allow children to work.

- **JM:FP.a:** Justice Model: Fairness Principle. Children should not be forced to work (i.e. be exploited).

- **S:** Silence

A brief glance at Table 1.2 reveals that the primary and secondary frame of a stakeholder sometimes differ in Bangladesh from those in the US. For example, the ILO supports the same two frames in Bangladesh and in the US but differs in which frame it presents first. In Bangladesh, the ILO first argues that 'children have the right to a healthy (physical and emotional) childhood' (MRM:LAS.a) and they therefore should not be working in garment factories in Bangladesh. Second, it argues that 'the written law does not allow children to work' (UM:RU.b). In the US the primary and secondary frames are reversed.

A second example is UNICEF/international. UNICEF/international supports the same frame in both Bangladesh and the US. Its primary argument is that 'children have the right to a healthy (physical and emotional) childhood' (MRM:LAS.a). However, on the secondary frame level, UNICEF/international differs on the frame it supports in the two different environments. In Bangladesh, UNICEF/international argues that 'the written law does not allow children to work' (UM:RU.b) and in the US argues that 'children should not be forced to work (JM:FP.a).

Stakeholder	BANGLADESHI MANUFACTURERS		US IMPORTERS	
	Primary frame	Secondary frame	Primary frame	Secondary frame
ILO	MRM:LAS.a	UM:RU.b	UM:RU.b	MRM:LAS.a
UNICEF/international	MRM:LAS.a	UM:RU.b	MRM:LAS.a	JM:FP.a
UNICEF/local	MRM:LAS.a	UM:AU.a	MRM:LAS.a	JM:FP.a
WTO	S	S	S	S
IMF	UM:RU.a	UM:AU.b	UM:RU.a	UM:AU.b
World Bank	UM:RU.a	UM:AU.b	UM:RU.a	UM:AU.b
Local subsidiary/Levi-Strauss	JM:NDP.b	JM:FP.b	S	JM:NDP.b
Retailers sourcing from Bangladesh	UM:RU.b	MRM:LAS.a	S	S
Economic development policy/ Bangladesh	UM:AU.a	JM:NDP.a	UM:RU.a	UM:RU.c
Child labour laws/Bangladesh	UM:RU.b	MRM:PP.a	UM:RU.b	UM:RU.c
Child Labor Deterrence Act/USA	MRM:LAS.a	JM:FP.a	MRM:LAS.a	JM:FP.a
Secretary of Labor (USA)	S	S	JM:DJM.b	JM:FP.a
BGMEA	JM:NDP.b	UM.AU.a	S	S
US Garment/Textile Association	S	S	UM:RU.b	S
Import and Export/Textile Association	S	S	JM:FP.a	S
Garment Workers' Federation and SKOP/Bangladesh	MRM:LAS.b	JM:FP.b	S	S
AAFLI/international union	MRM:LAS.a	UM:RU.b	S	JM:FP.a
US-based AFL–CIO union members	S	S	JM:FP.a	UM:RU.b
CLC/international NGO	MRM:LAS.a	JM:FP.a	MRM:LAS.a	JM:FP.a
SACCS/regional NGO	JM:NDP.b	UM:AU.a	JM:DJM.b	UM:AU.a
BASF/local NGO	JM:NDP.c	JM:NDP.b	S	S
Women and Children International/international/US	S	S	MRM.LAS.a	JM:DJM.b
Children's Rights Project/ international/US	S	S	JM:FP.a	UM:RU.b
Oxfam UK and Ireland/ international/US	S	S	JM:FP.a	UM:RU.b
Forgotten Children/international/US	S	S	JM:FP.a	MRM:LAS.a
Print media/international	UM:AU.a	JM:NDP.b	UM:AU.a	JM:NDP.b
TV media/USA	MRM:LAS.a	JM:FP.a	MRM:LAS.a	JM:FP.a
Print media/local	JM:NDP.b	MRM:PP.a	MRM:LAS.a	JM:FP.a
US consumers of ready-made garments	S	S	MRM:LAS.a	JM:FP.a
US importers of ready-made garments	JM:NDP.a	UM:AU.a	S	S
Factory owner/manager	JM:NDP.a	UM:RU.a	S	S
Child employee	MRM:PP.a	UM.AU.a	S	S

AAFLI = Asian-American Free Trade Labor Institute; AFL–CIO = American Federation of Labor–Congress of Industrial Organizations; BASF = Bangladesh Shishu Aadhikar Forum; BGMEA = Bangladesh Garment Manufacturers' Exporters' Association; CLC= Child Labor Coalition; ILO = International Labour Organisation; IMF = International Monetary Fund; NGO = non-governmental organisation; SACCS = South Asian Coalition on Child Servitude; SKOP = United Front of Workers and Employees; UNICEF = United Nations Children's Fund; WTO = World Trade Organisation.

For a description of codes, see Appendix A, page 36.

Table 1.2 *Stakeholder frame identification*

I consider the observation that one stakeholder group espouses a different frame in Bangladesh from that in the US to be a significant finding. This finding is not unique to the ILO and UNICEF/international and will therefore be more fully explored in the critical-frame analysis section of this chapter. However, at this stage in the analysis, the fact that stakeholders support different frames in different environments seems to indicate that the stakeholders may be adapting their message to appeal to their target audience.

1.4.2 Cross-cultural stakeholder-frame analysis

The first step in understanding the international child labour discourse is twofold. First, on a micro level, I looked at the frames that each stakeholder group is supporting and compared the stakeholder frames in the US environment and in the Bangladeshi environment. Do global stakeholders support the same frame in different environments? Second, on a macro level, I looked at the ethical models that represent the frames that stakeholders support. This provides both a detailed and a broad overview of the stakeholder group, their frame and the ethical (basis) model of their argument.

Table 1.2 presented the stakeholders and the primary and secondary frame that they support in the US and Bangladeshi child labour discourse. Comparing the US stakeholder environment with the Bangladeshi stakeholder environment revealed that the frames were either the same (i.e. identical or similar) or different (i.e. different frame or silent in one environment and active in the other). Table 1.3 lists the stakeholder groups that support identical and similar frames.

Identical frame in Bangladesh and in the US	Similar frame in Bangladesh and in the US
▪ WTO	▪ ILO
▪ IMF	▪ UNICEF/international
▪ World Bank	▪ UNICEF/local (Bangladesh)
▪ Child Labor Deterrence Act	▪ Child labour laws/Bangladesh
▪ CLC/international NGO	▪ Local subsidiary/Levi-Strauss
▪ SACCS/regional NGO	
▪ Print media/international	
▪ TV media/US	

CLC= Child Labor Coalition; ILO = International Labour Organisation; IMF = International Monetary Fund; NGO = non-governmental organisation; SACCS = South Asian Coalition on Child Servitude; UNICEF = United Nations Children's Fund; WTO = World Trade Organisation;

Table 1.3 *Identical and similar frames in Bangladesh and the US*

This chapter identifies 32 stakeholders that are participating in the child labour discourse in Bangladesh and in the US and are making claims on Bangladeshi manufacturers and/or US importers. Only eight stakeholders are identified as using the same primary and secondary frame in Bangladesh and in the US to argue their position on the use of child labour in Bangladesh for export to the US. This represents only 25% of the stakeholders in this study. This indicates that 75% of the stakeholders are varying their frame depending on whether they are participating in a US-based child labour discourse or a Bangladeshi-based child labour discourse.

Only five (16%) of the stakeholders support a similar frame in Bangladesh to that in the US. These stakeholders present the same primary or secondary frame in Bangladesh as that in the US. For example, the primary frame of the ILO in the US is that 'children have the right to a healthy (physical and emotional) childhood' (MRM:LAS.a) and the secondary frame is that 'the written law does not allow children to work' (UM:RU.b). In Bangladesh, the ILO presents those two frames but in reverse order. Perhaps the ILO recognises the cultural resonance of its message and arranges its frames to appeal more effectively to its target audience.

Although UNICEF/international supports the same primary frame in Bangladesh and in the US, it differs on the secondary frame. In Bangladesh, UNICEF/international argues that the written law in Bangladesh does not allow children to work (UM:RU.b) and in the US argues that children should not be forced to work (JM:FP.a). In Bangladesh the argument against child labour is embedded in the argument that the law prohibits children from working. In the US, however, the more persuasive argument according to UNICEF/international is to assume that children are being forced to work and to emphasise that they should not be. UNICEF/international also indicates that children deserve to have control over their lives and are deserving of a childhood.

The more telling segment of this comparison of stakeholder frames is to see where the frames espoused by the same stakeholder group actually differ in Bangladesh from those in the US. The 'differ' category is divided into three parts: (a) the stakeholder frames differ; (b) the stakeholder is silent in Bangladesh and active in the US; and (c) the stakeholder is silent in the US and active in Bangladesh. Table 1.4 lists stakeholder groups that support a different frame in each country.

Stakeholder	Bangladesh	US
AAFLI/international union	MRM:LAS.a* UM:RU.b**	S JM:FP.a
Economic development policy/Bangladesh	UM:AU.a JM:NDP.a	UM:RU.a UM:RU.c
Print media/local	JM:NDP.b MRM:PP.a	MRM:LAS.a JM:FP.a

AAFLI = Asian-American Free Trade Labor Institute
Note: primary frame is listed first (*), secondary frame is listed second (**)

Table 1.4 **Different frame in Bangladesh from that in the US**

Only three (9%) of the stakeholders in this study differ markedly in the frame they chose to argue the child labour issue in Bangladesh and in the US. AAFLI is the Asian branch of the AFL–CIO. It is headquartered in Washington, DC, and focuses on promoting safe labour conditions and the enforcement of child labour standards. Primarily, AAFLI remains silent (S) in the US. However, it does clearly argue that children should not be forced to work (JM:FP.a). In Bangladesh, AAFLI emphasises that children have the right to a healthy (physical and emotional) childhood (MRM:LAS.a) and that the law does not allow children to work (UM:RU.b). The silence can perhaps be explained by the fact that it focuses on the Asian region and therefore does not significantly enter the dialogue in the US.

The economic development policy of Bangladesh does not directly address the issue of child labour but the opinion of the policy-makers was captured in various official documents from their office. The economic development policy-makers in Bangladesh support the belief that to have children working in the garment sector is better than the available alternatives (UN:AU.a) for many children in Bangladesh today and they note the harsh reality that children need to work to survive (JM:NDP.a).

These frames clearly resonate with the general public of Bangladesh and therefore continue to perpetuate the acceptance of child labour. Comments from the economic development policy-makers in Bangladesh in the US emphasise to the American public that child labour is a necessary part of economic development (UM:RU.a) and that the unwritten law in Bangladesh allows children to work (UM:RU.c). The frames chosen in Bangladesh are practical and address the realities that the people of Bangladesh understand only too well. Americans, however, have difficulty in visualising such low economic standards. Therefore, the economic development policy-makers of Bangladesh seem to justify the existence of child labour as something unavoidable and uncontrollable in order to garner US support/sympathy.

The local print media in Bangladesh and in the US also differ on their messages regarding the use of child labour in Bangladesh garment factories that export to the US. In Bangladesh, the media emphasise the fact that children need non-hazardous work and a formal education (JM:NDP.b) and that human beings (i.e. children) have the right to have life's 'basic necessities' (food, clothing and shelter) (MRM:PP.a). In the US, the media emphasise that children have the right to a healthy (physical and emotional) childhood (MRM:LAS.a) and that children should not be forced to work (JM:FP.a). The media are identified in this study as being a mixed-objective stakeholder (i.e. in the pursuit of economic and non-economic gain). Their goal is to make money by selling newspapers/magazines and to inform.

It appears that the print media in the US and in Bangladesh have taken on the perspective of the country. They are both re-emphasising the views that resonate with the local environment so that they can more successfully exploit violations of the local norms and increase sales. In both Bangladesh and the US, the media play the role of sifting the discourse for the general public. Therefore, for firms to engage meaningfully in child labour discourse, it is significant for them to document the perspective of the print media and note that they are different in Bangladesh compared to the US.

The most striking variation in stakeholder frames in Bangladesh and in the US is when a stakeholder group is active in one country and silent in another. Table 1.5 lists stakeholder groups that are silent in Bangladesh and active in the US.

SILENT *stakeholder in Bangladesh, yet . . .*	**ACTIVE** *in the US*	
	Primary frame	*Secondary frame*
Secretary of Labor (USA)	JM:DJM.b	JM:FP.a
US Garment/Textile Importing Association	UM:RU.b	S
Import & Export Textile Association	JM:FP.a	S
US-based AFL–CIO	JM:FP.a	UM:RU.b
Women and Children/international/US	MRM:LAS.a	JM:DJM.b
Children's Rights Project/international/US	JM:FP.a	UM:RU.b
Oxfam UK and Ireland/international/US	JM:FP.a	UM:RU.b
Forgotten Children/international/US	JM:FP.a	MRM:LAS.a
US consumers of ready-made garments	MRM:LAS.a	JM:FP.a

AFL–CIO = American Federation of Labor–Congress of Industrial Organizations

Table 1.5 **Silent in Bangladesh and active in the US**

Of the 32 stakeholders in this study, nine (28%) are silent in Bangladesh and active in US child labour discourse. All nine stakeholders are non-profit stakeholders. Rein and Gamson (1999) note that understanding the silence is critical in understanding the true dynamics of a discourse. All nine stakeholders listed in Table 1.5 are involved in the child labour discourse regarding children working in Bangladeshi garment factories that are exporting to the US. However, all of the stakeholders mentioned are only voicing their frames in the US. First, the Secretary of Labor (USA) is only peripherally interested in foreign labour to the extent that it affects US workers. In the US the Secretary of Labor responds to the child labour issue in Bangladeshi garment factories by saying that the child is different from an adult and therefore should be treated differently (JM:DJM.b) and that children should not be forced to work (JM:FP.a). The silence of the US Secretary of Labor in Bangladesh could be because its main focus is on local workers in the US or because it is not perceived to be salient to Bangladeshi manufacturers.

The US Garment/Textile Importing Association and the Import and Export Textile Association believe that the written law does not allow children to work (UM:RU.b) and that children should not be forced to work (JM:FP.a), respectively. Both industry associations are not only silent in Bangladesh but are also relatively quiet in the US child labour discourse. Their frames are true statements and are not controversial in the US. This may perhaps be an attempt to avoid entering the international child labour argument. They may be silent in Bangladesh because they have no real interest. From their perspective, they work to support importers in bringing clothing into the US. If importers have difficulty importing from Bangladesh, they may begin to import from another low-cost producing country. There appears to be little thought given to the plight of children in Bangladesh.

The AFL–CIO, Women and Children/international, the Children's Rights Project and Forgotten Children/international are all US-based organisations that are organised to represent workers and/or children's rights. They appear in the child labour discourse regarding children working in Bangladeshi garment factories that are exporting to the US. However, they are silent in Bangladesh. Their focus appears to be on convincing the general public that children should not be forced to work (JM:FP.a), which will put pressure on retailers and regulators to demand that goods are not produced by children. The target of these stakeholders' frames is the US and therefore it appears unnecessary to enter the child labour discourse in Bangladesh.

Oxfam UK and Ireland has a strong presence in the US child labour discourse and is absent from the Bangladeshi discourse. Perhaps this is because Oxfam recognises that the buyer has the power and the buyers are in the US. Oxfam enters the US child labour discourse with non-controversial frames. It believes that children should not be forced to work (JM:FP.a) and that the written law does not allow children to work (UM:RU.b). These frames resonate in the US because it is widely assumed that child labour is forced labour and laws must be enforced. In Bangladesh, however, it is widely understood that children are not *forced* to work and that laws are often not enforced.

US consumers of ready-made garments are not making their voice heard in Bangladesh. Although threats of consumer boycotts are sometimes mentioned, there is no real presence of US consumer interests in Bangladesh. In the US, however, consumers clearly state that children have the right to a healthy (physical and emotional) childhood (MRM:LAS.a) and that children should not be forced to work (JM:FP.a). Both frames are not internationally controversial on the surface. However, Bangladesh and the US interpret the two frames differently. In the US, the parent(s) and/or the government generally provide for children. In some cases the grandparents or extended family may support the child. In Bangladesh, the child is totally dependent on the parent(s) for support. When the parent(s) is/are poor or the child is orphaned, the child must provide for him or herself. There is often no extended family that is financially able to help. Therefore without extra-hard-working parents, the means to a healthy childhood in Bangladesh is to work for sustenance and marketable skills. A formal education in Bangladesh is a luxury that many children cannot afford.

There are seven (22%) stakeholders that are silent in the US child labour discourse and active in Bangladesh. Three are for-profit stakeholders (US retailer, US importer, factory owner/manager), three are non-profit business-oriented (BGMEA, Garment Workers' Federation and SKOP, BASF), and one is mixed-objective (child employee).

The US importer and Bangladeshi factory owner/manager each represents the 'firm' in their own stakeholder environment. They are also stakeholders of each other. Their business relationship is the nucleus of this study. The US retailer is a significant stakeholder because it places the order with the importer so the importer must satisfy the retailer's demands. Also, the child employee in the garment factory is at the centre of this international child labour discourse. The stakeholders that are silent in the US and active in Bangladesh are shown in Table 1.6.

Bangladeshi factory owner/managers and US importers of ready-made clothing both agree that children in Bangladesh need to work to survive. Factory owner/managers believe that child labour is a necessary stage in the economic development of the country (UM:AU.a) and US importers believe that working at the garment factory is better than the alternatives (UM:AU.a). The frames that are supported in Bangladesh by these two stakeholders evidently resonate in Bangladesh because they are clearly spoken without ensuing controversy. These frames do not appear in the US.

SILENT *stakeholder in the US, yet . . .*	ACTIVE *in Bangladesh*	
	Primary frame	*Secondary frame*
Retailers sourcing from Bangladesh	UM:RU.b	MRM:LAS.a
BGMEA	JM:NDP.b	UM:AU.a/MRM:FOC.a
Garment Workers' Federation and SKOP/Bangladesh	MRM:LAS.b	JM:FP.b
BASF/local NGO in Bangladesh	JM:NDP.c	JM:NDP.b
US importer of ready-made clothes	JM:NDP.a	UM:AU.a
Factory owner/manager	JM:NDP.a	UM:RU.a
Child employee	JM:PP.a	UM.AU.a

BASF = Bangladesh Shishu Aadhikar Forum; BGMEA = Bangladesh Garment Manufacturers' Exporters' Association; NGO = non-governmental organisation; SKOP = United Front of Workers and Employees

Table 1.6 *Silent in the US and active in Bangladesh*

US retailers are active in the child labour discourse in Bangladesh and not in the US perhaps because of the attention and scrutiny it would generate. The media have proved to be relentless in their pursuit of sensationalising exploitative child labour situations in the garment industry. Perhaps to avoid being found out or misrepresented by the media, US retailers that purchase clothing from Bangladesh have remained silent in the US. However, in Bangladesh they say that the written law does not allow children to work (UM:RU.b) and that children have the right to a healthy (physical and emotional) child-hood (MRM:LAS.a). The two frames that the US retailers voice in Bangladesh are not controversial when defined in their own home environment. However, the controversy begins when the frames are interpreted across borders as discussed in the previous section.

The BGMEA is the only non-profit business-oriented stakeholder active in Bangladesh and not in the US. The BGMEA represents the interests of the manufacturing exporters as the industry struggles to grow. It worked closely with UNICEF, the ILO and the local government to draft the Memorandum of Understanding (MOU) that ordered all factories to remove workers who were under the age of 14. The BGMEA first argues that children need non-hazardous work and a formal education (JM:NDP.b). Second, it argues that factory work is better that the alternatives and that children have the right to willingly choose jobs that align with their moral and religious beliefs (MRM:FOC.a).

The BGMEA is the only stakeholder that has argued frames from all of the three ethical bases of decision-making at the same time. Rarely are these frames used in US child labour discourse. Occasionally stakeholders that are familiar with conditions in Bangla-desh or another developing economy will suggest these frames (see e.g. *Asghar* 2000). However, they do not resonate with the general American public. The BGMEA is only active in the child labour discourse in Bangladesh. This could be intentional, because its frames would only generate a negative response in the US, or unintentional, because its most salient stakeholders are only in Bangladesh.

The Garment Workers' Federation, the SKOP and the BASF are three local, non-profit, labour-oriented stakeholders that are active in Bangladesh and silent in the US. These non-profit, labour-oriented stakeholders in Bangladesh argue that children have the right to a healthy (physical and emotional) *work* environment (MRM:LAS.b), that children and employers must act in ways that are mutually fair (JM:FP.b), that factories are obligated to help children by allowing them to work in order to survive (JM:NDP.c), and that children need non-hazardous work and a formal education (JM:NDP.b). Again, as for the BGMEA, the silence in the US may be intentional or unintentional. These frames do not resonate with the general American public, particularly the idea that factories are obligated to help children by allowing them to work to survive. This is a notion that the US does not even consider for children but does demand fervently for adults. In fact the essence of stakeholder theory establishes relationships between the firm and its stakeholders. These relationships carry certain responsibilities such as providing work and wages that afford workers a means to live. In Bangladesh, this concept of responsibility to its employees seems to extend to the child whereas in the US it does not.

1.5 What is the operating objective of the stakeholder?

1.5.1 Stakeholder-objective model

The second model, identified as the stakeholder-objective model (see Appendix B), is designed based on the fundamental organisational objective of for-profit stakeholders, non-profit stakeholders and mixed-objective stakeholders. Given that it is widely assumed that a stakeholder's opinion on the use of child labour is determined by the economic benefit of their low cost, this model was selected because it is able to capture cross-cultural differences in frames supported by for-profit, non-profit and mixed-objective stakeholders.

To accurately identify the organisational objective of each stakeholder group, I collected the mission statement of each of the 32 stakeholder groups in this study. I created a stakeholder-objective identification chart, which presents the stakeholder group, its mission statement and the appropriate objective category. The list of stakeholders by their objective is shown in Table 1.7.

The 32 stakeholders have been divided into four for-profit (FP) stakeholders, 16 non-profit labour (NPL)-oriented stakeholders, seven non-profit business (NPB)-oriented stakeholders, and five mixed-objective (MO) stakeholders. Put another way, 12% of stakeholders identified by the literature as being salient to Bangladeshi manufacturers and/or US importers relevant to the child labour discourse are for-profit stakeholders. Eighty-two per cent of the stakeholders identified by the literature are non-profit stakeholders. Of the 82%, 50% are labour-oriented and 22% are business-oriented. Lastly, 16% of the stakeholders identified by the literature are mixed-objective stakeholders.

It is interesting to note that, of all the stakeholders identified in the literature as being active and important to the discourse on the employment of children in Bangladeshi garment factories, half (50%) are non-profit labour (NPL)-oriented stakeholders. The

Objective	Number of stakeholders	Stakeholder
For-profit (FP)	4	Local subsidiary/Levi-Strauss Retailers sourcing from Bangladesh US importers of ready-made garments Factory owner/manager
Non-profit labour-(NPL) oriented	16	ILO UNICEF/international UNICEF/local Child labour laws/Bangladesh Child Labor Deterrence Act/USA Secretary of Labor (USA) Garment Workers' Federation and SKOP/Bangladesh AAFLI/international union US-based AFL–CIO union CLC/international NGO SACCS/regional NGO BASF/local NGO/Bangladesh Women and Children International/international/US Children's Rights Project/international/US Oxfam UK and Ireland/international/US Forgotten Children/international/US
Non-profit business-oriented (NPB)	7	WTO IMF World Bank Economic development policy/Bangladesh BGMEA US Garment/Textile Association Import and Export/textile association/US
Mixed-objective (MO)	5	Print media/international TV media/USA Print media/local US consumers of ready-made garments Child employee
Total	**32**	**32 stakeholders are identified**

AAFLI = Asian-American Free Trade Labor Institute; AFL–CIO = American Federation of Labor–Congress of Industrial Organizations; BASF = Bangladesh Shishu Aadhikar Forum; BGMEA = Bangladesh Garment Manufacturers' Exporters' Association; CLC= Child Labor Coalition; ILO = International Labour Organisation; IMF = International Monetary Fund; NGO = non-governmental organisation; SACCS = South Asian Coalition on Child Servitude; SKOP = United Front of Workers and Employees; UNICEF = United Nations Children's Fund; WTO = World Trade Organisation

Table 1.7 **Stakeholder-objective model**

significance of NPL stakeholders in the child labour discourse will depend on how salient that stakeholder is to the firm. However, assuming that all NPL stakeholders are active in the child labour discourse may indicate that their interests will dominate the discourse and that the real child labour debate is held within the NPL stakeholder group itself.

A matrix will ultimately bring together the stakeholder frame with the for-profit, non-profit, mixed-objective stakeholder for both the Bangladeshi manufacturer and the US importer. The critical-frame analysis matrix allows for a cross-cultural comparison of the stakeholder-frame and the stakeholder-objective type. The objective of this matrix is to clarify the complex stakeholder environment created by local and international stakeholders interested in children working in garment factories in Bangladesh.

1.5.2 Cross-cultural stakeholder-frame and -objective analysis

A primary and secondary frame for all 32 stakeholders has been identified, representing a cumulative total of 64 frames. The frames were then grouped according to their ethical model (i.e. utilitarian, justice, moral rights and silence). The stakeholders were grouped according to their organisational objective (i.e. FP, NPL, NPB, MO). There are four for-profit stakeholders, 16 non-profit labour-oriented stakeholders, seven non-profit business-oriented stakeholders and five mixed-objective stakeholders identified in this study. Table 1.8 identifies the stakeholder type and the ethical model selected for the stakeholders of Bangladeshi manufacturers.

Ethical model	FP	NPL	NPB	MO	Total
Utilitarian model (UM)	3	7	7	2	19 (30%)
Silence (S)	0	12	5	2	19 (30%)
Justice model (JM)	4	6	2	2	14 (22%)
Moral rights model (MRM)	1	7	0	4	12 (18%)
Total	8	32	14	10	64 (100%)

Code: FP = for-profit; NPL = non-profit labour-oriented; NPB = non-profit business-oriented; MO = mixed objective

Table 1.8 **Bangladesh frame category and stakeholder objective**

The most popular frames for stakeholders of Bangladeshi manufacturers to argue their position on the use of child labour in the garment industry in Bangladesh are the utilitarian model (30%) and the silence model (30%). Evidently stakeholders participating in the local discourse on child labour feel it most convincing to stand behind the philosophy of doing the greatest good for the greatest number. The other popular frame is to simply remain silent and not participate in the local discourse. Third, stakeholders opt for an argument based on the justice model (22%). These stakeholders argue their position on the use of child labour in the garment industry on the principles of what is 'fair'. Lastly, the least popular ethical model from which to argue the position on child labour is a moral rights (18%) philosophy. Stakeholders in Bangladesh find it less persuasive to emphasise the fundamental liberties and privileges of children. Which type of stakeholder supports which ethical framework?

Fifty per cent of the stakeholder frames that were used by non-profit (NP) stakeholders of Bangladeshi manufacturers were based on the justice model and no stakeholders were silent. The most popular ethical model according to non-profit business-oriented stakeholders was the utilitarian model and the second most popular was silence. The interesting observation in this comparison is that these two related stakeholder groups do not share the same philosophical perspective on child labour. The common thread between these two stakeholder groups is that they both have a business interest although one is organised to make money and the other is organised to achieve a non-financial gain.

The most striking observation from Table 1.8 is how silent non-profit labour (NPL)-oriented stakeholders are in Bangladesh. Almost 40% (12/32) of the frames selected by NPL stakeholders are silent. The remaining frames are almost evenly divided between the utilitarian, justice and moral rights models. Why the silence? And why are all other models viewed as equally persuasive? It is beyond the scope of this research to answer the question conclusively. However, it is useful to have identified this behaviour among NPL stakeholders. It indicates that there is disagreement among them in terms of the philosophical reasoning behind child labour. All stakeholders in this category are organised to protect the interests of the child who finds him or herself labouring before the international legal age of employment, yet there is widespread disagreement as to why.

It is also curious why there is so much silence in Bangladesh among NPL stakeholders. Certainly the topic of children working in Bangladeshi garment factories that produce for export to America is relevant to their organisational objectives. Perhaps the reason for their silence is that their frame does not resonate in Bangladeshi society or that the stakeholder or their frame is not considered salient. The mixed-objective stakeholder type represents all the ethical models of decision-making and is not silent.

In the United States, stakeholders of US importers favour the justice model (30%). Of the 64 frames that are directed at US importers from their stakeholders, nearly one-third are based on the philosophy of justice. We can say that the argument that is considered most persuasive among stakeholders in the US is to do what is fair for the child. Silence is also a popular frame among stakeholders in the US. These stakeholders choose not to enter the local child labour discourse. The least popular ethical model of decision-making is the moral rights model (16%) (see Table 1.9).

Ethical model	FP	NPL	NPB	MO	Total
Silence (S)	7	5	6	2	20 (31%)
Justice model (JM)	1	13	1	4	19 (30%)
Utilitarian model (UM)	0	7	7	1	15 (23%)
Moral rights model (MRM)	0	7	0	3	10 (16%)
Total	8	32	14	10	64 (100%)

Code: FP = for-profit; NPL = non-profit labour-oriented; NPB = non-profit business-oriented; MO = mixed objective

Table 1.9 **US frame category and stakeholder objective**

For-profit stakeholders are silent in the US. Seven out of the potential eight frames are silent. Nearly half of the NPB stakeholders are silent in the US and the other half chooses the utilitarian model. The silences, once again, prove to be the intriguing mystery in interpreting the discourse. Why is there a significant level of silence among for-profit stakeholders in the US? The explanation seems to be either that the stakeholder's frame does not resonate in the US or that the stakeholder does not consider his or her frame to be salient in the US. The mixed-objective stakeholders in the US appear to emphasise the justice model. The NPL stakeholders are also attracted to the justice model to argue their position on child labour in Bangladesh. The other frames that were chosen by NPL stakeholders are almost evenly split between the remaining ethical models. Since the child labour discourse is between Bangladesh and the US, it is appropriate to look at the stakeholder's discourse in a global context.

Table 1.10 brings together the ethical model with the stakeholder-objective type in Bangladesh and in the US. In general, the stakeholder that operates in Bangladesh and in the US most often chooses the *same* ethical model in both environments. Note that the table does not show that the stakeholders choose the same frame or the same interpretation of the frame. This micro level of interpretation will occur in the next section. Table 1.10 simply points out that the ethical model of decision-making is almost identical in most cases as the same stakeholder operates in different environments. There are, however, a few exceptions, noted in bold.

Ethical model	BD/US	FP	NPL	NPB	MO	Total
Utilitarian model (UM)	BD	3	7	7	2	19 (15%)
	US	0	7	7	1	15 (12%)
Silence (S)	BD	**0**	**12**	5	2	19 (15%)
	US	**7**	**5**	6	2	20 (16%)
Justice model (JM)	BD	4	**6**	2	2	14 (11%)
	US	1	**13**	1	4	19 (15%)
Moral rights model (MRM)	BD	1	7	0	4	12 (9%)
	US	0	7	0	3	10 (8%)
Total		16	64	28	20	128 (100%)

Code: BD = Bangladesh; FP = for-profit; NPL = non-profit labour-oriented; NPB = non-profit business-oriented; MO = mixed-objective

Table 1.10 **Bangladesh and US ethical model and stakeholder objective**

The most startling difference is how for-profit (FP)- and non-profit labour (NPL)-oriented stakeholders choose to remain silent in one country and participate actively in another. Note that all the FP stakeholders are active in the discourse. There are no stakeholders that choose to remain silent. Yet, in the US, most of the FP stakeholders are silent. The NPL stakeholder category shows the opposite. In Bangladesh the NPL stakeholders are silent yet they are active in the US. In the US, they base their opinions regarding the use of child labour in Bangladeshi factories on the philosophical principles of justice. Perhaps the NPL stakeholders choose to remain silent in Bangladesh because the justice frame does not resonate in Bangladesh as it does the US. Therefore, it is possible that the NPL stakeholders feel that they should be silent in Bangladesh in order to avoid any negative impact in the US where they are more active.

When the same stakeholder-objective type chooses a different ethical model in a different cultural environment, it indicates that the stakeholder is strategising his or her goal. The FP stakeholders and NPL stakeholders shifted their ethical model to enable them to achieve their organisational objective. They carefully interpreted their audience and altered their frame appropriately to maximise their power to influence their target (i.e. the firm or another stakeholder to leverage their power, legitimacy or urgency). Let us now take a closer look at the content of the frames that the stakeholders of the same objective type are supporting.

1.6 Which stakeholder frames are used within and between Bangladeshi and US importer stakeholder environments?

1.6.1 Critical-frame analysis matrix

The supplier–buyer relationship between the Bangladeshi manufacturer and the US importer has been affected by the international child labour discourse. What is missing is an understanding of the stakeholder discourse that influenced the firm's decision to dismiss children from the factory. So far this chapter has looked at the frame and the stakeholder and the frame and the stakeholder-objective type in both Bangladesh and the US. The critical-frame analysis matrix will provide an overview of the discourse as it is sent from the stakeholder-objective type to the firm.

Table 1.11 provides an overview of the frames that are being sent to the Bangladeshi manufacturer and to the US importer grouped according to the organisational objective of the stakeholder. Although the content of these frames has been discussed in the previous section, this table presents a consolidated overview of the frames for the purpose of establishing a conceptual understanding of the dialogue. As Table 1.11 shows, the frames used by stakeholders to argue their position on whether Bangladeshi manufacturers and US importers should utilise the labour of children are quite complex, particularly when stakeholders in both countries agree on the ethical frame but disagree on its interpretation.

FOR-PROFIT (FP) STAKEHOLDER OVERVIEW

BD	25%	Children need to work to survive
	75%	Combination 'it is better than the alternatives' and other related frames

US	13%	Children need to work to survive
	87%	Silence

NON-PROFIT LABOUR-ORIENTED (NPL) STAKEHOLDER OVERVIEW

BD	19%	Children have a right to a healthy (physical and emotional) childhood
	6%	Children should not be forced to work
	6%	Children need non-hazardous work and a formal education
	6%	The written law does not allow children to work
	6%	It is better than the alternatives

US	31%	Children should not be forced to work
	22%	Children have a right to a healthy (physical and emotional) childhood
	16%	Silence
	12%	The written law does not allow children to work

NON-PROFIT BUSINESS-ORIENTED (NPB) STAKEHOLDER OVERVIEW

BD	21%	Silence
	21%	Necessary stage in economic development according to economic theory
	21%	The unwritten law allows children to work
	14%	It is better than the alternatives

US	29%	Silence
	29%	Necessary stage in economic development according to economic theory
	21%	This is the way to a better life

MIXED-OBJECTIVE (MO) STAKEHOLDER OVERVIEW

BD	20%	Silence
	20%	Children have a right to a healthy (physical and emotional) childhood
	20%	Children need non-hazardous work and a formal education

US	30%	Children have a right to a healthy (physical and emotional) childhood
	30%	Children should not be forced to work
	20%	Silence

Table 1.11 *Organisational objective and messages being sent to Bangladesh (BD) manufacturers and to US importers*

1.6.2 Cross-cultural critical-frame analysis matrix

As complicated as the discourse is, the arguments regarding the use of child labour often appear as two simple positions. The nucleus of the argument seems to rest on whether a stakeholder justifies the use of child labour or disagrees with children working under any circumstances. Therefore, because of the nature of the argument I found it necessary to interpret the frames along those same lines. From Table 1.11, I deduced the underlying position of the stakeholder-objective type as it participates in the child labour discourse in Bangladesh and in the US (for details of this analysis, see Rahman 2000). Table 1.12 shows the resulting critical-frame analysis matrix.

	Bangladesh	*US*
FP	Need to work	Silence/need to work
NPL	Need to work	Should not work
NPB	Silence/need to work	Silence/need to work
MO	Silence/need to work	Should not work

Code: FP for-profit stakeholder; NPL = non-profit labour-oriented stakeholder; NPB = non-profit business-oriented stakeholder, MO = mixed-objective stakeholder

Table 1.12 **Critical-frame analysis matrix**

In Bangladesh, all four types of stakeholder (i.e. for-profit, non-profit labour-oriented, non-profit business-oriented and mixed-objective) support, with various frames, the view that children need to work to survive. Therefore, in Bangladesh there is no disagreement between stakeholders that poor children with few alternatives for a means of survival must work to live. The local discourse in Bangladesh surrounds what type of work children should be allowed to do and how to make sure that children are treated fairly in the workplace. It appears that, in Bangladesh, children are perceived by other stakeholders as a stakeholder of the Bangladeshi manufacturing firm. And, in most cases, the firm considers their interests along with the interests of the other stakeholders.

It is noted, however, that the primary frame used by non-profit business-oriented stakeholders and mixed-objective stakeholders in Bangladesh is silence. I have often stated that one reason for the silence of a stakeholder is that they may choose to remain silent if their frame does not resonate with the local environment. In this case their frame does resonate with the local environment. The most likely explanation for the silence of NPB and MO stakeholders in Bangladesh is that there are stakeholders in this category that are simply just active in the US and not in Bangladesh. When this occurs their frame would be identified as silent because their organisational objective is simply US-centric.

In the US, there is disagreement among stakeholder types over whether a child should be allowed to work or not. Interestingly, the two stakeholder types that recognise that a child needs to work to survive are primarily silent. After the noticeable silence of FP and NPB stakeholders, they humbly speak about the need for children to work in Bangladesh in order to live. NPL stakeholders and MO stakeholders openly and aggressively support the argument that children should not work. NPL and MO stakeholders are not silent. In the US, these finding indicate that perhaps the NPL stakeholders are organised, confident and powerful in their position and that their message does resonate with their local environment. It may also indicate that MO stakeholders are influenced by the NPL stakeholders.

The MO stakeholder group is made up of local print media, US TV media, international print media, the child employees and US consumers of ready-made clothing. The under-age workers are silent in the US discourse regarding their work. NPL stakeholders heavily target the remaining MO stakeholders. Consumers are organised by NPL stakeholders to boycott US importers/US retailers who have purchased goods from Bangladesh, a country known for using child labour. NPL stakeholders appear to be accessing the media in their attempt to leverage their influence on firm behaviour. Bangladeshi manufacturing firms and US importers are sensitive to negative publicity about their business practices. In the garment industry, negative publicity concerning the exploitative use of child labour could end an importer's or a supplier's career. Therefore, it is critical for firms in the US to recognise the media position on the use of child labour in foreign factories.

A comparative look at the same stakeholder type in Bangladesh and in the US reveals some disagreement. For-profit stakeholders in Bangladesh and in the US agree that children need to work. However, in the US they are silent. Notice the position of the US importer and the Bangladeshi manufacturer doing business in both stakeholder environments. In Bangladesh, the source of the debate, firms witness and are free to acknowledge the plight of poor children. Factories that successfully attract US buyers and provide jobs are viewed as a responsible stakeholder in the effort to eradicate poverty and hunger. For-profit and non-profit stakeholders seem to agree that garment factories have a responsibility to help grow the economy, eradicate poverty and improve the lives of the children and adults in society. In the US, however, the garment factory is viewed as the reason why poverty is perpetuated. The reasoning is that when children are lured to work they do not go to school, and education is the true catalyst of economic change. Therefore, how do Bangladeshi manufacturers and US importers, operating in an international environment, satisfy both stakeholder interests?

NPB stakeholders agree in both stakeholder environments. In Bangladesh and in the US, NPB stakeholders are primarily silent but do support the perspective that children need to work to survive when there are limited alternatives. In Bangladesh, business is considered to be a means to improve one's life because: (1) there are not enough schools to accommodate all children; (2) parents cannot afford to send their child to school (i.e. opportunity cost of not working and/or the cost of materials); (3) there is little market demand for a formal education between very basic literacy and advanced college education; (4) work provides training and teaches marketable skills; and (5) most poor parents want their child to work because it brings in an income and it is considered a viable means to a better life. These reasons are not generally accepted in the US.

The NPL stakeholders in Bangladesh and in the US clearly disagree. In Bangladesh, NPL stakeholders understand that, given the alternatives available to poor children, they often must work and garment work is a better choice. In the US, NPL stakeholders support the opposite view. In the US, NPL stakeholders argue that children should not work. Hence the vacillation of NPL stakeholder frames—depending on the country in which it enters the discourse—creates a quandary for firms operating in an international environment to satisfy global stakeholder demands. Sethi (1997) identifies this dilemma for international firms by noting:

> it is the same corporation that receives public accolades for exemplary behaviour in one aspect of its business and is simultaneously hauled into the court of public opinion and judicial arena for acts of moral reprobation and illegal behaviour in other aspects of its business.

However, in this study, the firm is being judged differently for the same behaviour.

The MO stakeholders in Bangladesh and in the US disagree on their argument on whether children should work or not. In Bangladesh the MO stakeholders are primarily silent but then report that children need to work. In the US, the MO stakeholders emphasise that children should not work. Again, given the power of the media, it is difficult for firms to satisfy local MO stakeholder interests when they operate cross-culturally. Deciding on the right business behaviour is particularly hard when the home country (i.e. Bangladesh) and the host country firm (i.e. US importer) agree but the US stakeholders disagree.

1.7 Conclusion

The results of critical-frame analysis, as it was applied to the stakeholders of Bangladeshi manufacturers and to the stakeholders of the US importers, have provided a cultural picture of the child labour discourse within and between the US and Bangladesh. In some level of detail this chapter identifies the primary and secondary frame that the stakeholder supports. The frames were organised for the purpose of analysis using the ethical model for decision-making and the stakeholder-objective model. It should be noted that critical-frame analysis does not criticise the content of the frames. This methodology simply organises the discourse so that it may be better understood.

Critical-frame analysis of the child labour discourse pertinent to Bangladeshi manufacturers and to US importers indicates: (1) a strong agreement of frames among stakeholder types in the Bangladeshi environment; (2) a strong disagreement of frames among stakeholder types in the US environment; and (3) a strong disagreement of frames within the same stakeholder type in a different cultural environment. Although children working in garment factories in Bangladesh met to a large degree with local approval, it did *dissatisfy* non-profit labour (NPL)-oriented stakeholders in the US. History informs us that the NPL stakeholders in the US, much to the disappointment of for-profit stakeholders, successfully pressured Bangladeshi manufacturers to release all of their underage garment workers from the factory.

Because of the strategic positioning of the NPL stakeholder argument, this result is in keeping with Donaldson and Dunfee's (1999) Integrative Social Contracts Theory (ISCT). One of the clauses of the ISCT is that 'in order [for a norm] to become obligatory (legitimate), a microsocial contract (i.e. agreement of ethical norms between stakeholders), must be compatible with hypernorms (i.e. "the root of what is ethical for humanity")'. The NPL stakeholders primarily argued that children should not be forced to work and it is against the law for children to work. These norms are congruent with the hypernorms of children working and therefore they overpowered the norm set by the Bangladeshi stakeholder environment and relevant parts of the US importer stakeholder environment. NPL stakeholders were clever in their strategic positioning of their frame to match the hypernorm. For, if it didn't, the local ethical norm established by the local community would have been recognised according to the theory.

What is perplexing is that the hypernorm that the NPL stakeholders stood behind did not describe the children working in garment factories in Bangladesh. It appears that the NPL chose their frame to purposely align their argument with the hypernorm so as to achieve their organisational objective. For example, there is no documented forced child labour in the garment industry in Bangladesh and, with a glance down *any* street in Bangladesh, one witnesses a profusion of child labourers in all capacities. This finding indicates that all stakeholders (i.e. FP, NPL, NPB and MO) are institutions with goals and are capable of risking the interests of fellow stakeholders in the pursuit of their own organisational objectives.

This chapter has provided a comprehensive cultural picture of the child labour discourse within and between the Bangladeshi manufacturing stakeholder environment and the US importing stakeholder environment. This represents, however, only half of the discourse equation. This chapter identified what message stakeholders are sending to the firm. Given the rich stakeholder discourse in Bangladesh and in the US on child labour in Bangladeshi garment factories that export to the US, it would be interesting to know which stakeholder frames management considers important. See Rahman 2000 for an analysis of what message the Bangladeshi manufacturer and the importing firms consider salient.

Appendix A

I. Utilitarian Model (UM)

1. Act Utilitarianism (UM:AU)

     a. It is better than the alternatives (**UM:AU.a**).

     b. This is the way to a better life (**UM:AU.b**).

2. Rule Utilitarianism (UM:RU)

     a. Necessary stage in economic development according to economic theory (**UM:RU.a**).

     b. The written law does not allow children to work (**UM:RU.b**).

     c. The unwritten law allows children to work (**UM:RU.c**).

II. Justice Model (JM)

1. Distributive Justice Model (DJM)

    a. The child must be paid and treated the same as an adult (**JM:DJM.a**).

    b. A child is different from an adult and therefore should be treated differently (**JM:DJM.b**)

2. Fairness Principle (FP)

    a. Children cannot be forced to work (i.e. be exploited) (**JM:FP.a**).

    b. Child and employer must act in ways that are mutually fair (**JM:FP.b**).

    c. When Bangladesh uses child labour, it gives them an unfair competitive advantage, and ultimately disadvantages labour in the US (**JM:FP.c**).

3. Natural Duty Principle (NDP)

    a. Children need to work to survive (**JM:NDP.a**).

    b. Children need non-hazardous work and a formal education (**JM:NDP.b**).

    c. Factories are obligated to help children by allowing them to work in order to survive (**JM:NDP.c**).

III. Moral Rights Model (MRM)

1. Life and Safety (LAS)

    a. Children have a right to a healthy (physical and emotional) childhood (**MRM:LAS.a**).

    b. Children have a right to a healthy (physical and emotional) work environment (**MRM:LAS.b**).

2. Truth (T)

    a. Children have the right to know the truth about their rights as a child and their opportunities for a better life (**MRM:T.a**).

3. Privacy (P)

    a. Children have the right to know what information is being recorded in their personnel file (**MRM:P.a**).

4. Freedom of Conscience (FOC)

    a.   Children have the right to willingly choose jobs that align with their moral and religious beliefs (**MRM:FOC.a**).

5. Free Speech (FS)

    a.   Children have the right to speak out against their employer without fear of retribution (**MRM:FS.a**).

6. Private Property (PP)

    a.   Human beings (i.e. children) have the right to have life's 'basic necessities' (food, clothing and shelter) (**MRM:PP.a**).

IV. Silence (S)

Appendix B

The definition of each segment, based on the fundamental organising objective of the entity, is as follows:

1. **For-profit (FP) stakeholder:** a stakeholder who is in the pursuit of economic gains.

2. **Non-profit labour (NPL)-oriented stakeholder:** a stakeholder who is in the pursuit of non-economic gains and supports the interests of labour.

3. **Non-profit business (NPB)-oriented stakeholder:** a stakeholder who is in the pursuit of non-economic gains and supports the interests of business.

4. **Mixed-objective (MO) stakeholder:** a stakeholder who is in the pursuit of economic and non-economic gains. In this research the primary mixed-objective stakeholder is the media since its dual objective is to generate wealth and to educate/inform. This category is unique because it is one of the most public sifting tools for stakeholder discourse on child labour, it is viewed as neutral and therefore credible, and it therefore yields significant power to influence firm/stakeholder behaviour.

2

ARE YOU TALKING TO ME?
Stakeholder communication and the risks and rewards of dialogue

Andrew Crane
University of Nottingham, UK

Sharon Livesey
Fordham University, USA

Recently, significant attention has been directed to the relations between corporations and their stakeholders. A growing number of academic studies have proposed that corporations should consider the interests of their stakeholders, whether for ethical reasons (Freeman 1984; Donaldson and Preston 1995; Evan and Freeman 1988) or for the achievement of strategic/economic objectives (Jones 1995; Frooman 1999; Maignan *et al.* 1999). As a result, corporations have experienced pressure to provide a broader range of information (e.g. data on environmental and social performance, equal-opportunity employment practices, consumer protection) to a wider range of stakeholders. Several high-profile multinational corporations such as Shell, Levi-Strauss and Nike have joined the ranks of progressive niche companies such as The Body Shop to argue vigorously that they have listened and responded to their various internal and external stakeholders, including their critics (see McIntosh *et al.* 1998). At the same time, non-governmental organisations (NGOs) such as Greenpeace, WWF, Environmental Defense, Amnesty International, Oxfam and Save the Children have also embraced a more collaborative approach to their relations with business (see Murphy and Bendell 1997; McIntosh *et al.* 1998; Bendell 2000). The pressure to communicate more proactively and more frequently with stakeholders suggests that firms need to, and perhaps do, engage a newly diverse range of stakeholders through enhanced inclusiveness, partnership and dialogue. This trend has significant implications for methods and responsibilities entailed in stakeholder communication that to date are not well understood.

In this chapter, we examine the potential effects of more sophisticated concepts of stakeholder relationships on stakeholder communication. We consider first the impacts of a complex understanding of stakeholder relations on one-way communication models that offer alternatives of standardising or tailoring messages. Then, we deal with more interactive forms of communication, focusing specifically on the issue of stakeholder dialogue. In our view, this is a notion that has been touted by consultants (e.g. Elkington 1997) and become common parlance among corporations (e.g. Shell), but has been rather little explored in terms of its practical organisational benefits and risks. Hence, in order to set out what might constitute 'responsible' stakeholder communication (both for businesses and for other organisations), we attempt to develop a critical understanding of the meaning and consequences of dialogue.

To accomplish our purpose, we draw on stakeholder and communication theory literatures to identify both the benefits and the drawbacks of different forms of stakeholder communication and their implications for organisational action. Our analysis leads us to two conclusions:

- One-way models of communication not only require intense efforts of co-ordination and management but may be illusory in so far as they suggest an ability by firms to instantiate and control particular meanings among and within stakeholder groups.

- Contrary to the accepted wisdom of the current stakeholder management literature, while the more involved and interactive modes of stakeholder dialogue can offer significant advantages, they also surface important and, as yet, unexamined risks. Specifically, stakeholder dialogue may be either:
  - Instrumentally and superficially employed, thus producing cynicism and distrust, with concomitant negative effects on organisational image; or
  - If genuinely adopted, may lead to cacophony and contradiction, thus producing inaction or fragmentation within the organisation itself (see e.g. Westley and Vredenburg 1991; Livesey 1999).

2.1 Understanding stakeholder relationships

The stakeholder model of the firm has been highly influential in management theory and practice (Stoney and Winstanley 2001). In a descriptive sense, stakeholder theory offers a more complex and interactional model of the firm than the traditional stockholder model. Rather than suggesting that the firm is a 'black box', which processes inputs to produce certain outputs (primarily for the benefit of shareholders), stakeholder theory proposes that the firm exists at the nexus of a series of interdependent relationships with groups that can affect or are affected by the firm (Freeman 1984). This is illustrated in Figure 2.1.

Clearly, the different stakeholder groups envisaged in this model (Fig. 2.1) will have their own unique set of claims, demands and objectives which they are likely to communicate to the firm. The problem for the company in this situation, therefore, is how to successfully manage these interdependences and, most particularly, the conflicts of interest that they may engender. A number of frameworks and models have been proposed in the literature. They generally stress the need for companies to understand the relative power and influence of the different stakeholders, as well as their interest in a particular issue (Hill and Jones 1992; Meznar and Nigh 1995; Frooman 1999).

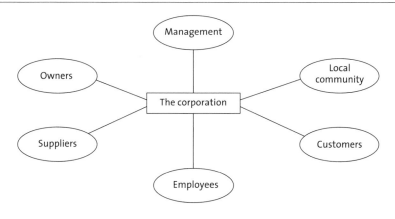

Figure 2.1 **A stakeholder model of the corporation**

Source: Freeman 1984

More complex conceptualisations of stakeholders and stakeholder interactions, how-ever, have begun to emerge to address our developing understanding of the dynamics entailed by stakeholder interdependence. Significant among these are: (1) the network perspective on stakeholders (Rowley 1997); and (2) the 'differentiated' stakeholder con-cept (Crane 1998). Under the **network** model, stakeholders are understood not to be just related to the firm but are also recognised to be related in many ways to each other, whether by exchange, communication or whatever other form of interaction. Thus, just as firms have relationships with diverse stakeholders, so too do those stakeholders have relationships with *their own* stakeholders, and these stakeholders in turn have relation-ships with a further set of stakeholders and so on. For example, we might consider that General Motors has relationships with its employees (among other stakeholders), but these employees also have relationships with other constituencies such as their families, communities, religious groups, retailers, financial institutions and so on, who all have a 'stake' in the employees' relationships with their company. The network conception of stakeholder relationship decentres, or displaces, the firm as the central node in the stake-holder model, since the network can be entered simultaneously from many different perspectives. This point, as we shall see, becomes critical in so far as communication and decision-making in the firm is enacted by and through individuals or groups of individ-uals, each tied into particular networks of relationship.

The **differentiated** stakeholder perspective acknowledges intra-stakeholder differ-ences (see Crane 1998; Winn 2001). Thus, while a focal organisation may act *as if* stake-holder groups share interests in a single issue, the interests of any one stakeholder group may not in fact be identical, and the group itself may not be homogeneous (Winn 2001). From this perspective, an organisation (or any constituency) is unlikely to be charac-terised by complete uniformity, whether in terms of behaviours, strategies, values, beliefs or even identity. A particular firm may interact with a particular stakeholder but this interaction may be located and experienced (and even perhaps recognised) in only one or a few departments or divisions of that firm and stakeholder. Similarly, where an organisation is dealing with multiple stakeholders, these may be handled by a single team or by completely different teams within that organisation (see Crane 1998).

In the case of McDonald's revamping of its waste programme, for example, an environmental task force, comprising members of various departments within McDonald's and representatives from the Environmental Defense Fund (an NGO), worked to make the company's waste practices more environmentally friendly. Problems occurred, however, when the task force decided that it would be advantageous to abandon McDonald's traditional clamshell hamburger packaging. Other groups within McDonald's, who had long-standing relationships with the company's plastic packaging suppliers and who valued the heat-retaining and convenience features of the packaging, had different interests from those of the task force and opposed the move (see Livesey 1999).

Figure 2.2 presents an illustrative example of a differentiated network model of stakeholder relations. The direct stakeholders from the original stakeholder model are unshaded, and labelled stakeholders 1–6. The shaded stakeholders 7–14 are indirect stakeholders with which the focal organisation does not have a relationship, but which, as part of the larger network, might influence the direct relationships in some way. The differentiated aspects are illustrated with the labels A, B, C and D, which represent different organisational teams or departments. Relationships (denoted by the lines) are thus established at the level of individual teams—and indeed between such teams, as well as between organisations.

Under previous models, the primary issue was to identify which particular constituencies (e.g. customers, competitors, regulators, social advocacy groups) were legitimate stakeholders and to determine what levels of power and influence they possessed *vis-à-vis* the focal organisation (see Grunig and Hunt 1984; Meznar and Nigh 1995). Recent

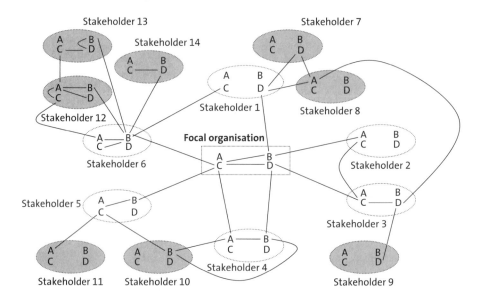

Figure 2.2 **A differentiated network model of stakeholder relationships: an illustrative example**

organisational research, however, has begun to question the empirical status of stake-holders, suggesting variously: that stakeholders are socially constructed (Fineman and Clarke 1996; Winn 2001); that managers strategically mobilise the claims of external constituencies to support particular interpretations (Child 1972); and that stakeholder groups themselves are composed of those with shifting roles and interests (Winn 2001).

These new understandings have put an increased emphasis on analysing the fluidity of situational contexts. Consider, for example, employee stakeholders in downsizing and merger situations. In the first case, the employee stakeholder group, which might in other situations be considered homogeneous, would be bifurcated into those who remain and those who are laid off; and lay-offs might again be separated into voluntary and involuntary severance. Even as the firm separates those laid off from the firm, it must seek to maintain aspects of the old relationship—namely, its concern for its employees, and employee loyalty to the firm—in order to minimise the disruptive effects of the lay-off on remaining employees and on the firm as a whole. In cases of merger, the opposite effect would be found: disparate employee groups from the merging organisations would, over time, be integrated within the merged entity, while threads of the old culture and identity inevitably remain.

In the differentiated network model, stakeholder relationships must therefore be understood as a complex interplay of shifting, ambiguous and contested relationships between and within diverse organisations. This highlights the central role of communi-cation in constituting, managing and maintaining stakeholder relationships, as we consider next.

2.2 Stakeholder communication

Early communication theory described communication within and by the firm in terms of a simple linear model, wherein the firm's stakeholders constituted 'receivers' or 'audiences' for particular messages (Axley 1985; Redding and Tompkins 1988). In this perspective, the focus was on the information itself, a commodity that needed to be transmitted, rather than on communication as a social process that brought meaning to life through negotiation and consensus (Smircich and Stubbart 1985). The essential challenge lay in effectively coding messages and reducing any 'noise' that might distort audience decoding. More sophisticated communication models moved from an exclusive emphasis on information transmission to concern with message effects (Berko *et al.* 1997; Ruben and Stewart 1998). This new focus required audience 'feedback', which then might be used by senders to adapt and refine their messages. Ultimately, feedback helped the sender to learn whether the message had been correctly decoded (see Fig. 2.3).

Public relations theory (e.g. Grunig 1984; Grunig and Hunt 1984; Grunig and Grunig 1992) provided a more complex understanding of corporate communication which is useful for understanding stakeholder relations. Grunig and Hunt's (1984) well-known corporate public relations model distinguished between one-way and two-way forms of communication and between the communicator's purpose in communicating: to manip-ulate/persuade or to educate/facilitate understanding. In its more genuine forms, one-way communication was designed to persuade its audiences through honest, if rhetorically

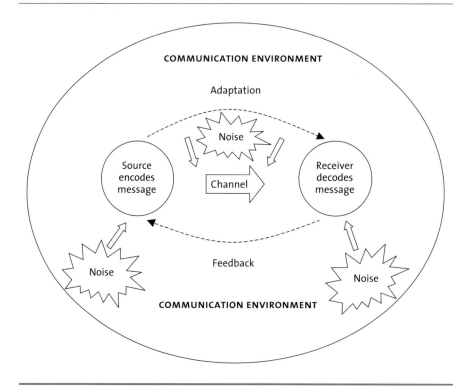

Figure 2.3 **Traditional communication process model**

slanted, messages. Two-way asymmetrical models were designed to gather information from the corporation's public in order to identify messages most likely to produce the attitudes and behaviours that the corporation desired. In contrast, symmetrical models were designed to facilitate understanding and communication between the parties.

Grunig's (1975) second important contribution from the perspective of stakeholder theory was his recognition of the complexity of monitoring and managing corporate environments. He advocated a systems approach that highlighted the multiple-publics perspective of corporations. These contributions from public relations theory provide a base from which to build and extend our understanding of stakeholder communication.

2.2.1 One-way models: standardised versus customised messages

In top-down and firm-to-stakeholder communication in multi-stakeholder environments, a key strategic decision for marketers and corporate communication departments is whether to customise or standardise communication to their stakeholder audiences (see e.g. Doherty and Ennew 1995; Weddle 1995). The standardised approach suggests that firms adopt a uniform message strategy with stakeholders which emphasises a core set of corporate values, a distinct (and distinctive) organisational 'voice' and a coherent message or 'story', explaining and justifying organisational actions. The purpose of this is to maintain a strong and consistent brand image across the firm's interactions with its multiple constituencies such that interpretations of the firm are controlled and directed towards a specific identity that the firm hopes to project. A standardised approach may also help to prevent accusations of hypocrisy should the firm be seen to be rolling out different stories to different audiences. Increasingly then, the **integration** of communications is being advocated as an appropriate response to diverse and conflicting demands (Schultz *et al.* 1993; Shimp 1997).

Communicating a uniform message to stakeholders may be particularly important when a corporation is attempting to orchestrate change and/or protect a firm's image. Thus, when Shell revised its general business principles to reflect its growing commitment to the natural environment and human rights, the overarching message of its communication campaign was that profits and principles (responsible behaviour) had to go hand in hand. In the context of our model of stakeholder relationships in Figure 2.2, however, this controllability of meaning must inevitably recede: different departments or divisions of the firm may communicate different things to their stakeholders; stakeholders may talk to each other; and so on. It is virtually impossible for any one participant to seize control of communication and meaning within the complex web of stakeholder relations. Shell has been unable to 'sell' its profits and principles message in Nigeria, where environmental and human rights activists continue to challenge the corporate image (Wheeler *et al.* 2002). The experiences of Nike are also apposite. A firm that allocated a multi-million-pound annual advertising budget to the development and enhancement of a carefully crafted brand image has been rendered powerless to prevent the undesirable image of sweatshop labour irrevocably tainting its products.

The need for tailored messages, on the other hand, become particularly acute when the focal organisation is dealing with multiple publics with different needs or conflicting interests. The benefit of a customised approach for the corporation is that it may facilitate improved stakeholder understanding of the corporation's position and behaviour; and, since (in theory at least) stakeholders are being spoken to in something approximating their own voice, it may also enhance their empathy and trust for the corporation. Here, we are likely to see the corporation relating different interpretations of the same events in order to support the different impressions that it wishes to present to different stakeholders. A simple example is the case of a company attempting to market its products in a global market, where customer needs and perceptions may vary significantly by national context (e.g. Sciulli and Taiani 2001). Similarly, an NGO such as the Environmental Defense Fund, which is interested in business–government partnerships but at the same time needs to preserve its reputation as an aggressive environmental advocacy organisation, is likely to create different messages for foundation funders from those for its membership (see Livesey 1999).

A dramatic example which represents the challenges involved in custom messaging is represented by Union Carbide's crisis communication after its plant in Bhopal, India, leaked toxic gases that killed thousands of workers and village residents. As Ice (1991) demonstrated, Carbide made several blunders in attempting to tailor messages to stakeholders as different as the Indian government, victims, Carbide employees in the United States, consumers and shareholders. Carbide's claim, for instance, that its Indian facility was not substandard and was the same in design and safety standards as its US facilities, led to fears about safety risks among its US employees and public. Its attempts to assuage its shareholders by claiming that the firm's profits would not be seriously impacted by the accident, on the other hand, interfered with its negotiations with the Indian government, which was representing the victims who sought compensation rather than just the humanitarian aid that Carbide had offered .

There is a seductive (and hard to dislodge) appeal in the suggestion that the communicator (e.g. senior managers or corporate communications departments) can control the message: what the organisation says, and how it is perceived by its public. Nevertheless, however attractive 'one-way' communication to stakeholders may seem, the fundamentally dialogic nature of meaning-making is in fact implicit in every act of communication, whether it is explicitly recognised or not. In the case of Union Carbide, for example, antagonistic stakeholder audiences transposed meanings from one context to another, producing interpretations that the corporate communicator did not intend. Even the corporate annual report, as an example of an apparently self-contained, one-way, firm-to-stakeholder communication product is born out of internal dialogue within the company and anticipates ongoing dialogue with analysts and shareholders who have to interpret it.

In summary, one-way stakeholder communication obviously demands careful analysis of stakeholder needs and co-ordination of messages across stakeholder groups in multi-stakeholder environments. More importantly, the communicator (message crafter) in the focal organisation must be sensitive to: (1) the role of stakeholders as nodes in their own stakeholder networks; (2) the active role of stakeholder audiences in meaning-making; and (3) the resulting provisional and ambiguous qualities of the meaning made (see Winn 2001). They must also consider the dynamic aspects of stakeholder environments, as provided in the Carbide example above, when the Indian government shifted its role from regulator (interested in the safety features of the plant) to litigator (interested in victim compensation).

We turn next to a consideration of these implications and of the role of various forms of dialogue in stakeholder relationships.

2.2.2 The dialogic model: 'genuine' and instrumental forms

From the corporate public relations perspective, Grunig and colleagues have argued consistently that symmetrical forms of communication are superior because they are more ethical and also because they achieve public relations goals more effectively (e.g. Grunig and Grunig 1992; Grunig, et al. 1992). Similarly, Cheney and Christensen (2001) have concluded that, in Western democratic society, ongoing, genuine, two-way dialogue between organisations and their stakeholders, a goal perhaps difficult or impossible to achieve, nonetheless represents the best possible solution for the management of complex issues confronting contemporary society. Dialogue has also been forcefully advocated in the practitioner literature, particularly as an instrument in the paradigm shift from conflictual modes of relationship towards partnership and collaboration in complex problem-solving (e.g. Long and Arnold 1995; Elkington 1997). Dialogue, however, is a concept that has been little examined or theorised in the stakeholder literature. Indeed, as Grunig and Grunig (1992) pointed out from a communications perspective, exactly what is meant by 'symmetrical' communications is problematic. Moreover, neither public relations theory nor stakeholder theory considers the constitutive effects of language and their consequences for stakeholder identity.

Andriof (2001: 228) has defined stakeholder dialogue in terms of a 'conversation' between business and stakeholders where information is exchanged and knowledge acquired. Similarly, Gao and Zhang (2001: 243) emphasise that dialogue should be a two-way process where stakeholders are not merely consulted or 'listened to' but also responded to. However, Gao and Zhang (2001: 242) also acknowledge that 'a dialogue may merely be a form of information gathering that does not allow feedback or interactive two-way communication'. Indeed, what an organisation considers 'active listening' and responsiveness might be considered advocacy or unobtrusive control by a third party (Hellweg 1989, cited in Grunig and Grunig 1992: 311). Moreover, listening and responding do not necessarily rule out self-interested persuasive efforts. For Cheney and Dionisopoulos (1989), symmetrical communication is achieved so long as the parties' interests are represented in such a way that both persuade and allow the other to persuade. In this instance, dialogue might be conceptualised as a process whereby persuasiveness and persuasibility are maximised for all parties (Grunig and Grunig 1992).

Clearly, then, in-depth understanding of dialogue demands further elaboration of motive. In order to cut through some of these complexities and ambiguities surrounding dialogue, we distinguish here between dialogue as two-way communication designed for asymmetrical persuasive and instrumental purposes (compliance gaining), and 'genuine' or 'true' two-way symmetric practice.

Dialogue of the first kind can be thought of as a way of communicating *to* rather than *with* stakeholders. It is then a monologic dialogue, centred on communicating self-interest and aligning the other's interest to one's own. In contrast, 'genuine' dialogue is geared towards mutual education, joint problem-solving and relationship-building. It can be thought of as a high-quality form of engagement between organisations which occurs as part of a wider process of relationship formation and maintenance (see Andriof 2001; Gao and Zhang 2001).

Of course, in reality, these two alternative forms of dialogue more likely represent points on a continuum, and the distinctive forms are unlikely to be purely engaged. As in other forms of bargaining (see Wilson and Putnam 1990), parties to dialogue might well have mixed motives of co-operation and self-interest. Nevertheless, dialogues as conceptualised from these two different perspectives lead to overlapping yet distinct sets of problems for stakeholders.

2.2.2.1 Monologic dialogue

We acknowledge that the monologue that poses as dialogue undoubtedly represents a somewhat superficial application of stakeholder dialogue. Nevertheless, we do not feel it can be easily dismissed, not least because such an approach clearly prevails in contemporary theory and practice (see Grunig and Grunig 1992). Shell's interactive web forum represents one example of this form of 'dialogue'. Stakeholder contributors to the forum discussion, who range from customers, to NGO activists, to corporate consultants, take a position that tends either to praise or attack Shell's policies and behaviours (e.g. support of Kyoto guidelines, commitment to social and environmental reporting, support of human rights in developing countries). Where stakeholder responses are critical, Shell most often explains or defends its action. The stakeholders in this dialogue apparently have no more at stake than airing their views. From a corporate image perspective, the fact that the communication takes place, and that Shell airs its stakeholders' views, negative and positive, is probably as significant as the content of the discussion itself.

Where dialogue is engaged for instrumental and rhetorical purposes, it is susceptible to the problems of discursive control that we discussed above in relation to one-way communication in multi-stakeholder environments. If it is perceived as an attempt at manipulation, co-optation or control, it puts at risk organisational attempts to demonstrate sincerity and consistency. Moreover, the choice of partners, even where the purposes for dialogue are symbolic, has political ramifications for the participating parties that influence image and credibility. Including some stakeholders in a dialogue inevitably leads to excluding others, who may become critical (for an example, see Westley and Vredenburg 1991).

2.2.2.2 Genuine dialogue

In contrast to compliance gaining, asymmetrical forms of dialogue, Cheney and Christensen (2001: 260) characterise genuine dialogue as: 'a dialogue in which questions of interest and representation are constantly negotiated'. It is a means for managing stakeholder interdependence and problem-solving. Thus, it often occurs where stakeholders are regarded as having significant degrees of power and influence and/or where relationships have been developed into an alliance (see Hartman and Stafford 1997). In these contexts, it is often employed in order to resolve or anticipate and avoid conflict. In discussing the defining characteristics of business–environmental partnerships, Long and Arnold (1995) specifically rule out dialogue 'intended only as a forum to share ideas'. Dialogue of the sort relevant to partnerships must lead to 'discrete action' and '[p]arties should be prepared to change if the results . . . demand it' (1995: 7). In other words, parties to genuine dialogue should be open to the transformative effects of their communication.

As Cheney and Christensen (2001) noted, the interdependence of firms and stakeholders is starkly evident: for example, in the expansion of the marketing perspective. This entails firms engaging consumers in a responsive process that influences business decision-processes; accordingly, we find leading firms such as IKEA, Procter & Gamble, Toyota and others defining themselves and their business strategies as customer-driven (see Kotler et al. 2001). Similarly, practitioner-oriented writers have advised companies to '[b]e a partner, not a teacher' to newly emergent constituents, such as environmental groups (Bennett et al. 1993: 95). Hence, practices such as product-related consumer dialogues and panels that had been earlier instituted have been expanded to include issue-oriented dialogues with a range of other interest groups (Pires 1988). This potentially brings stakeholders into the decision-making process of the firm itself.

The literature deals with these questions almost exclusively from the perspective of the firm—understandably, given the focus on the organisation in management literature and the centring of the firm in the traditional stakeholder models. Nevertheless, by decentring the firm in our approach, it is possible to see concomitant effects among other stakeholder groups, whose identity and decision processes may be equally affected.

We can understand the mutually transformative effects of communication in stakeholder dialogue by conceptualising communication processes not as involving *exchange* of information but rather the constitution of meaning itself. In this respect, dialogue implicates stakeholders in the joint negotiation of meaning, as demonstrated in Figure 2.4.

COMMUNICATION ENVIRONMENT

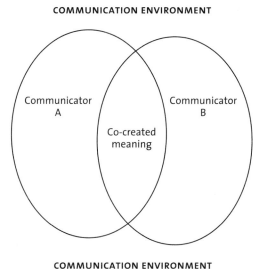

COMMUNICATION ENVIRONMENT

Figure 2.4 *Communication as co-creation of meaning*

From a social constructionist perspective, then, dialogue leads stakeholders to co-create shared realities (see Cheney and Christensen 2001; Winn 2001). Dialogue can thus be seen as closely related to, if not a form of, relationship management described in the literature on conflict and negotiation (e.g. Gray 1989; Wilson and Putnam 1990). In the context of collaborative problem-solving, dialogue becomes the means of 'unfolding of a negotiated order' (Gray 1989: 233) and jointly mapping problem domains (Westley and Vredenburg 1991).

Clearly then, the very process of dialogue has potentially radical effects on participants. Therefore, firms, NGOs and other stakeholders who are moving to adopt modes of communication that emphasise dialogue need to better understand the distinctions between traditional approaches to communication and the dialogic practice that is now being increasingly espoused. Crucially, while the potential advantages of dialogue as discussed earlier have been vigorously promoted, firms and stakeholders need also to consider the potential risks to dialogue that these changes might also generate.

2.3 The risks of dialogue:
cacophony, fragmentation, paralysis

Because it draws by analogy from conversation between individuals, the metaphor of 'dialogue' as applied here tempts us to think of stakeholders maintaining something akin to a private conversation. The complex environment as represented in Figure 2.2, however, requires us to consider such dialogues as a profusion of simultaneous, often contradictory and cross-firing interactions. Clearly, dialogue in this context requires simultaneous communication with multiple groups and subgroups, some of whom have conflicting interests. Moreover, stakeholder groups themselves cannot be assumed to be either homogeneous or stable because the individuals who constitute them belong to and interact with more than one group (Winn 2001).

With so much dialoguing among such diverse (and divided) entities, one drawback we are faced with, it seems, is a high potential for **cacophony**. Hence, while the promotion of dialogue partly rests on its ability to aid in the 'informing' and 'educating' of stakeholders (e.g. Andriof 2001), it may also serve to confuse and obfuscate understanding. While cacophony may not be evident at the micro level of individual dialogues, such confusion generated at the macro level may be counterproductive to effective decision-making and action, which demand clarity and consensus (Brunsson 1989).

Dialoguing organisations also need to recognise that the engagement of their various and variegated external stakeholders is likely to affect how those inside the organisation act and identify with the organisation. As Scott and Lane (2000) suggest, there are strong strategic reasons for managers to choose differing organisational images for presentation to stakeholders. However: 'Making public commitments on the part of an organisation influences people to change their self-perceptions and act consistently with the presented self-image' (Scott and Lane 2000: 47). Thus, in a sense, 'external' communications are also autocommunicative in that they are often equally viewed and responded to by organisational members (Christensen 1995; Gilly and Wolfinbarger 1998).

At a deeper level, then, these multiple conversations, where genuinely engaged, present serious identity risks to participants. More than an exchange of words, dialogue involves taking on discursive regimes that potentially embody very different histories, different ways of thinking, different values and beliefs, languages and world-views. All the while, dialoguing parties have to remain recognisable to their other constituencies, with whom they are also in dialogic relationships. In such circumstances, the focal organisation may present to its stakeholders a number of apparently different 'identities' depending on the situations and the dialogue partner(s) involved. For Shell to participate in parallel conversations with General Motors, Greenpeace, the Nigerian government and the EPA (just some of its many 'audiences') about very different yet very complex issues, it is required to reframe and negotiate its previously held 'certainties' within each discursive context. Sometimes the identity strains are simply too great. Pollution Probe, for instance, was accused of forgetting its role as advocate for the public interest as it identified with the needs and interests of the Canadian supermarket chain Loblaws that sought its eco-endorsement (see Stafford and Hartman 1996).

While some models of organisational identity stress its enduring and distinctive nature (e.g. Gray and Balmer 1998; Hooghiemstra 2000), the notion that identity is socially constructed—and hence that organisations may not actually 'have' an identity but rather construct multiple identities through communication—is becoming prevalent (see Czarniawska 2000). According to Czarniawska (2000: 274), 'such a view on identity would see it not as found or exhibited, but as produced and reproduced in interactions' and thus: 'What becomes clear is that identities are performed in conversation' (2000: 275). In conventional one-way communication, the identity of organisations and their stakeholders may therefore remain relatively unchallenged and unquestioned, given the low level of interaction. However, in genuine dialogue, the increased level and number of conversations is likely to surface such identity **fragmentation** again and again.

The 'schizophrenic' nature of the dialoguing organisation should not then be seen simply as a risk to avoid but rather as an inevitable and wholly predictable aspect of organisational talk. Sometimes, maintaining a consistent and coherent identity presentation may not only be highly challenging but even ultimately futile. This does not mean, though, that a plausible identity presentation becomes impossible. While consistency of belief and action may be unlikely, a convincing explanation of identity inconsistency may be necessary to support and sustain stakeholder relationships (see Czarniawska 2000: 276).

The acceptance—even embracing—of uncontrollability and inconsistency poses a significant challenge for the dialoguing organisation. Dialogue, by its nature (when it is genuine at least), takes time, is not efficient, cuts against hierarchical control, and does not assume a predetermined fixed understanding of how things (the world) are or what should be done. Modern organisations, however, are typically dominated by a decision-making model that depends on opposite ideas of consistency and control (Brunsson 1989). Dialogue may therefore, on the one hand, have **paralysing** effects on organisations and their stakeholders, preventing them from reaching consensus and action; or, on the other hand, may result in them splitting and falling apart.

2.4 Implications and conclusions

The preceding discussion raises a number of significant implications, not only for how we conceptualise stakeholder communication but also for what might constitute 'responsible' stakeholder communication, both for businesses and for other organisations. In the first case, stakeholder communication is clearly complex and multifaceted. Issues of process (one-way versus two-way), content (tailored versus standardised), motivation (persuasive versus informative versus transformative) and outcome (benefits versus risks) have been addressed here, leading to a richer and more variegated picture of stakeholder communication. This suggests that it is no longer sufficient to simply promote and propound the development of stakeholder communication per se, at least not without a clear understanding of what kind of stakeholder communication is implied. Moreover, it should be clear that stakeholder communication cannot be realistically considered in isolation from wider issues of organisational relationships, identity and meaning.

The side-effects, or unintended consequences, of stakeholder communication that have been uncovered are particularly important, not least because they have been so rarely acknowledged in the past. What is interesting is that there are potential risks associated with *all* forms of attempted communication between and within stakeholders, even the more 'genuine' forms of dialogue. And, by risks, we do not mean merely the costs in terms of time and resources that such dialoguing demands but rather the fundamental challenges to organisations of maintaining the discursive coherence necessary to establish organisational identity and action (see e.g. Westley and Vredenburg 1991; Livesey 1999). This is the case for both firms and their stakeholders—each is fundamentally challenged by its commitments to dialogue. Hence, those currently advocating the universal benefits of stakeholder dialogue (including corporations, NGOs, consultants, academics and the business press) might do well to address more fully the implications of their advocacy. Indeed, until further research detailing the potential consequences is forthcoming, simply acknowledging and addressing with one another the problematic nature and effects of different forms of communication and dialogue is probably the closest organisations and their stakeholders can get to being genuinely responsible.

Any implications for practice suggested by our analysis therefore focus not on what organisations and stakeholders should do to effect genuine, effective and responsible dialogue but rather on how they can prepare themselves for dialogue. First, stakeholders must realise that they will end up 'doing dialogue' very differently, from situation to situation, and possibly even within the same relationship and discussion. Though it is clearly desirable to transfer learning from one situation to the next, attempts to apply a cookie-cutter approach in the name of consistency may result in cutting down the potential for innovation and learning that new situations have to offer.

Second, organisations and their stakeholders need to anticipate identity threats, accept complexity, plan for diversity and limit their expectations of controllability. Communication, and especially asymmetrical dialogue, *produces* change, just as much as it is *constitutive* of a change in approach to stakeholder relationship management. While many of those involved in stakeholder relationships may entertain the possibility that their stakeholders will be changed by the dialogic process—indeed, this may even be one of their initial intentions—they should also recognise the changes and challenges that their own organisations will face.

Planning for such change, however, is extremely demanding, particularly when so little is known about the possible consequences. However, some avenues are being explored. For example, one potential way to deal with internal contradiction and conflict is to create 'subsidiaries' or departments to handle business dialogues and partnerships, as some NGOs (e.g. Greenpeace and Environmental Defense) have done. This makes possible some degree of accommodation of their mixed dialogic and advocacy modes. Likewise, many corporations have contracted external consultants to deal with stakeholder relations. Such actors can play the role of cultural mediators, a buffering role which involves the translation of cultural knowledge between different stakeholder groups and the construction of shared meanings across stakeholders (Crane 1998). On the other hand, organisations need to beware of contradiction so extreme that it threatens their ability to respond adequately to stakeholders (see Cheney and Christensen 2001: 261).

Finally, however, we would like to make it clear that, despite these risks, we still see stakeholder dialogue as a potentially positive and important development in stakeholder management. Our concern though is that, if it is embraced superficially, it may simply lead to further mistrust and cynicism; if it is embraced more deeply and genuinely, but without the critical lens that we have applied here, it may lead to some unexpected and (for some parties at least) potentially undesirable outcomes. Greater attention to stakeholder communication, in all its forms, is clearly vital.

3

TALKING FOR CHANGE?
Reflections on effective stakeholder dialogue[*]

Jem Bendell
Lifeworth.com

This chapter presents reflections on the practice of stakeholder dialogue, based on the author's participation in dialogue processes in the UK (the WWF 1995 Group and the Marine Stewardship Council) and Costa Rica (pre-ETI banana pilot work), as well as eight years of research, much of which is drawn on in my book *Terms for Endearment: Business, NGOs and Sustainable Development* (Bendell 2000). This chapter focuses as much on the concepts of stakeholder dialogue as it does on examples and principles of best practice, as the intention is to stimulate innovative thinking on the reasons for engaging in stakeholder dialogue. Focusing on personal or corporate intentions is important as this helps us to understand what stakeholder dialogue will or won't achieve. I hope that the arguments and visioning that follow will stimulate your own thinking so that we can meet the challenges and seize the opportunities being presented to today's corporation by ongoing changes in society.

3.1 Talking to whom?

The first step in effective stakeholder dialogue is to determine who one's stakeholders are. The idea that companies have stakeholders has become commonplace, in both the academic literature and business practice, and relations with stakeholders are considered key to the strategic planning process (Starik *et al.* 1996). Freeman (1984: 52) suggests that stakeholders include 'any group or individual who can affect or is affected by the achievement of an organisation's purpose'. This definition is too broad for some as it

*   This chapter © New Academy of Business; it was originally published by the New Academy of Business in 2000 (www.new-academy.ac.uk).

includes interested parties as well as affected parties, and therefore an argument has been made for restricting the term to those 'who have a "stake", or vested interest, in the firm' (Carroll 1993: 22). In much management practice, however—for instance, in stakeholder reporting and social auditing—Freeman's approach holds, and stakeholders are defined as primary or secondary, depending on an assessment of whether they are immediately affected by, or can immediately affect, a firm's operations.

Social Accountability International (SAI), which operates the labour practices auditing scheme SA8000, defines stakeholders in this way, and requires accredited auditors to conduct a stakeholder mapping exercise. This is a simple process, involving a pictorial representation of primary and secondary stakeholders with relations drawn between them, to depict which group influences or is influenced, or which has an interest. This is intended to help in the identification of key stakeholders in order to speed the process of consultation undertaken during an audit.

Identifying stakeholders is therefore a subjective process, despite the creation of systems such as AA1000 by the Institute of Social and Ethical Accountability (now called AccountAbility). This standard simply requires that a management system includes documentation of the way stakeholders were identified, how they were classified and what their relationship is to the company. This chapter focuses on dialogue between corporations and non-financial stakeholders, i.e. not company shareholders. These stakeholder groups may include, but are not limited to: employees (managers, staff, trade unions), customers, suppliers and other partners, competitors, government and regulators, non-governmental organisations (NGOs) and interest groups, and local and international communities. In addition, stakeholders without a voice, such as the environment and future generations, can be included. The AA1000 standard stresses the principle of inclusivity, so that organisations should seek to include as wide a collection of stakeholder groups as possible.

NGOs are often regarded as useful chunks within the stakeholder stew. However, as companies have increasingly sought to talk to and work with NGOs, a number of problems have arisen. In many cases NGOs assume a mandate from members of society that is not backed up by processes of accountability with those people. Different NGOs have different levels of embeddedness in local communities, North and South, and some are therefore more worthwhile representatives of stakeholder groups than others.

3.2 Why talk?

In this chapter, dialogue is understood to be a flow of information between two or more entities, whether they are groups or individuals. Stakeholder dialogue occurs all the time, as managers communicate with staff, suppliers and consumers during the normal course of business. Dialogue continues in an organic fashion after-hours in the communities, clubs and families of company managers. However, more proactive and structured **stakeholder dialogue initiatives** have become an increasingly important management issue in the last five years, to the extent that traditional ideas about public relations are being redefined. Now there are specialist agencies offering consultancy and training in the field of stakeholder dialogue, such as the Environment Council (Box 3.1).

THE ENVIRONMENT COUNCIL RUNS COURSES TO HELP ORGANISATIONS FACILITATE stakeholder dialogue, as well as working with organisations to aid them with specific initiatives. One well-known example was the contract the Council had with Shell, to discuss the various options for the disposal or re-use of the Brent Spar oil platform. The Council stresses the difference between consultation and dialogue, arguing that the latter uniquely involves:

- A search for win–wins
- An exploration of shared and different interests, values, needs and fears
- A focus on process rather than issues
- Strengthening and building relationships

Box 3.1 *The Environment Council's approach to stakeholder dialogue*

Source: Environment Council 1999: 8

The increase in interest in stakeholder dialogue is due to both the shifting perceptions within society and the private sector about the role of the modern corporation, and management's growing awareness of the importance of intangible assets to corporate value and profitability. There is a range of approaches towards stakeholder dialogue, some of which seem to be limited by their downplaying of ethical and emotional considerations. For example, there have been a number of books published that seek to help corporations to defend themselves when 'under siege' from stakeholders (Neal and Davies 1998: 1), and advise them on 'Managing Outside Pressure' (Winter and Steger 1998) by providing a 'practical roadmap to protecting [a] company's reputation' (Peters 1999: 1). Indeed, models of effective stakeholder relations management can be proposed, which focus on:

1. Defending the organisation's position against stakeholders that represent a high threat and a low potential for co-operation

2. Collaborating with stakeholders that represent a high threat and a high potential for co-operation

3. Involving stakeholders that represent a low threat and a high potential for co-operation

4. Monitoring stakeholders that represent a low threat and a low potential for co-operation (Savage *et al.* 1991).

In the first instance this analysis might seem helpful to business. However, it is a utilitarian approach, and somewhat 'anti-ethical', in the sense that it deems ethical considerations to be unprofessional and irrelevant to good management practice. In *Terms for Endearment* (Bendell 2000) I adopted a different approach and did not seek to advise business on how to manage stakeholder pressure to corporate advantage, because:

> much stakeholder pressure is motivated by belief in the principles of social justice and environmental sustainability, and so to try to analyse this pressure

from a utilitarian management approach both misunderstands these principles and denies the humanity of both managers and students of business. Therefore this book examines cases where business can work *with* stakeholder pressure for sustainable development (Bendell 2000: 15).

Therefore my research suggests that when one is seeking or managing dialogue with stakeholders it is important and helpful to reflect on one's own intentions, as well as those of colleagues and competitors. It is to this I now turn.

3.3 Talking levels

The definition of stakeholder dialogue set out by the Environment Council (Box 3.1) is important because it focuses on the intentions of the participants. However, intentions differ widely and affect the extent to which dialogue is a mechanism for stakeholder participation in the shaping of policies and practices of companies. Sociological analyses of dialogue and participation in the decision-making of governmental organisations in the 1960s and 1970s, inspired by an interest in direct democracy, identified various levels or types of dialogue (Arnstein 1969). These levels were based on the motivation of organisations seeking dialogue; we could call them 'dialogue intention levels'. The characteristics identified at that time can be translated into the modern context of corporate stakeholder dialogue, to help us to see how the motives for seeking stakeholder dialogue actually shape the type of dialogue. In the modern context, eight different 'dialogue intention levels' can be identified:

1. **Dialogue as manipulation**. This form of dialogue is based on a motivation to disarm particularly critical stakeholders who are, nevertheless, prepared to talk with a company. Evidence of this type of interaction with civil society still arises from time to time, such as a leaked document about the Sony Corporation. This was a proposed action plan for counteracting the efforts of several domestic and international environmental groups—including Friends of the Earth and Greenpeace. The plan suggested a 'detailed monitoring and contact network' to track the activities of these groups as well as 'pre-funding intervention' (*Inside* EPA 2000). This intervention could take the form of co-sponsoring research in order to influence its conclusions.[1]

2. **Dialogue as therapy**. This is also a non-participatory approach, although with more positive intentions. The aim is to educate critical stakeholders. For example, plans for items such as new product lines or environmental management systems are believed by the company to be justified and the job of dialogue is to achieve stakeholder support. Managers of biotechnology companies held this

---

1   Infonics, the company recommended to Sony to monitor activists on the Internet, worked with Shell. They picked up discussion of INTRAC's proposed research on Shell on an e-mail list and offered to co-fund the research. Now that the researcher has published his moderately critical findings, his contacts in Shell are reportedly no longer interested in discussing issues with, or involving, him further (R. Shah, personal communication, September 2000).

view of dialogue during their early exchanges with critics, believing that their critics needed to understand the science better and have their unfounded fears assuaged. This proved inadequate for the biotechnology industry, which has since adopted a different approach. In the reticent words of the then head of Monsanto, Bob Shapiro, 'because we thought it was our job to persuade, too often we forgot to listen . . . We're now publicly committed to dialogue with people and groups who have a stake in the issue' (quoted in Bendell 2000: 106).

3. **Dialogue as information.** This is the type of dialogue in which the company aims to be transparent about its activities and policies and to inform stakeholders about them. It is 'dialogue' only in so far as the stakeholders are able to respond by asking questions of clarification. There is no expectation on behalf of the company to learn from stakeholders, and little or no expectation to manipulate or educate stakeholders' views. Although largely one-way, it is an important first step towards real dialogue. Most early corporate environmental, and then social, reports have been in this mould, with minimal stakeholder dialogue over the relevance (materiality) of the information provided.

4. **Dialogue as consultation.** This type of dialogue involves the accessing of stakeholder opinions through techniques such as attitude surveys, neighbourhood, consumer or staff meetings. Similar to market research, it is largely a one-way flow of information, in the opposite direction of 'dialogue as information', so opportunities for learning are also limited. The role of the company in interpreting the information and then determining actions is reinforced in consultation exercises, rather than being challenged and reshaped.

5. **Dialogue as placation.** Some companies seek to placate stakeholder concerns by establishing close dialogue with a few key critics—in limited ways. For example, well-known critics or experts can be invited onto advisory committees. This allows these critics or advocates to advise, review and plan ad infinitum but the corporation retains the right to judge the legitimacy or feasibility of the advice given.

6. **Dialogue as partnership.** The term 'partnership' is now so widely used that its meaning has been somewhat clouded. However, as opposed to placation, real partnership implies that the power of the partners is redistributed between them through negotiation. Dialogue through partnership means that planning and decision-making responsibilities are shared through joint committees, for example. As Uwe Schneidewind (2000) argues in *Terms for Endearment*, business–NGO alliances can create new forms of power to change social, economic and cultural 'structures' that shape our choices and actions.

7. **Dialogue as delegation.** I have found it hard to find examples of corporates involved in the delegation of responsibility for making decisions to stakeholders. This could take the form of delegating certain decisions to committees where stakeholders had a clear majority of seats, thereby ensuring that stakeholders had the power to assure the accountability of a project or initiative. This form of relationship with stakeholders has been used by non-corporate organisations such as development agencies and local governments, and is some-

times used in corporate community involvement (CCI) initiatives, where charitable foundations are run by key representatives of stakeholder groups. Its use for core business issues may have occurred, but, if so, this author is unaware of it.

8. **Dialogue as democracy.** For certain companies, key stakeholders, often the staff and/or the customers, are also the owners of the company: these are called co-operatives. In some cases each individual with a relationship to the company has an opportunity for an equal say in the direction of that company, through mechanisms of direct and representative democracy (i.e. participation in committees and election of directors). At this stage there are structural impediments preventing privately and publicly owned corporations from pursuing stakeholder dialogue at the democratic level: namely, the duties of directors to stockholders. Here we reach a paradox, as the corporation of 2020 may need to be a democratic organisation if it is to have legitimacy, and succeed in the market place.

Reality is not as neat as any typology, but this has been offered as a tool for self-reflection. In practice, different organic or structured stakeholder dialogues can take place for a mix of intentions, and no organisation is internally undifferentiated; some managers may have a vision for higher levels of dialogue and struggle with those who do not. As Seb Beloe of the management consultancy firm SustainAbility points out:

> Today the battle has moved on . . . in many companies the battle is within . . . Much comment has been made on the internal struggles within Monsanto, Shell and other TNCs between those who have understood the strategic importance of many environmental and sustainability concerns and those who have yet to be convinced (Beloe 1999: 48).

There is also a temporal aspect to stakeholder dialogue, with confrontational dialogue often preceding other forms. Energy and natural resource companies around the world have learned from Shell's experience with Brent Spar and Ogoniland, and biotechnology companies have resonated with the fall of Monsanto.

Once the dialogue moves beyond confrontation, the participants are likely to focus on the areas of common ground and cherry-pick. After some time dialogue can progress to involve the consideration, appreciation and even acceptance of the interests of others. And so intentions behind the dialogue may evolve, although most companies appear to have hit an evolutionary ceiling at the fourth consultation, fifth participation or sixth partnership levels. Whether this is a result of their organisational DNA—the form of incorporation and ownership—or something that can be changed, is open to debate.

3.4 Talking drivers

The experience of business–NGO relations demonstrates that the nature of dialogue with stakeholders is not determined entirely by the intentions of corporates and their staff. Two key factors include the stance and campaigning strategy of stakeholder groups, and the type of economic activity the company is involved in.[2] However, here I want to discuss the intentions of managers who actively seek dialogue, or aim to reshape it. The level of dialogue, from manipulation to democracy, that is sought by managers depends on their interpretation of the drivers for corporate citizenship or corporate social responsibility, which in turn shapes their understanding of the business case for being corporate citizens.

The win–win argument that doing good is also good for business is now widely endorsed. However, the empirical evidence relating financial and ethical performance in positive correlation is still partial, and for many it is a leap of faith and intuition. A number of attempts have been made to distil the ways in which positive stakeholder relations and, in turn, business–NGO partnerships help business (Table 3.1). One of the most visible drivers that translates positive social and environmental performance into market signals and corporate financial gains is the emerging pattern of 'civil regulation' (Murphy and Bendell 1999). Civil regulations are pressures exerted by processes in civil society to persuade, or even compel, organisations to act differently in relation to social and environmental concerns. This effect is created by the gamut of civil-society groups pursuing confrontational campaigns that damage corporate reputations, on the one hand, to groups supporting and endorsing corporations in their change processes on the other (as indicated in Table 3.1). Civil regulation is not clearly defined but is an organic, perhaps anarchic, process involving different actors. At a minimum, civil regulation acts through the mechanisms of consumer preference, applicant interest, staff motivation, investor concern, regulatory body concern and even force (the costs of dealing with direct actions).

In addition to those drivers associated with civil regulation, there are other drivers such as the financial benefits of identifying eco-efficiencies, or hands-on supply chain management, as well as the personal ethics of managers.

Based on their interpretation of these drivers, managers build their understanding of the business case for corporate citizenship. Many business managers' perspectives on good corporate citizenship can be argued to fall into four broad categories.

1. **Traditional business perspective.** This view of corporate citizenship regards it as a non-core issue, something of an add-on to help lubricate the wheels of commerce, rather than help to define them. Therefore managers undertake specific activities where there are relatively tangible and demonstrable financial gains from the activities. These can involve targeted community involvement actions to help gain planning permission, or resource management and forest or mineral exploitation rights. This view of corporate citizenship leads to low-level dialogue intentions.

2. **Reputational defence perspective.** This view of corporate citizenship gives it more weight than the traditional business perspective but focuses on threats rather than opportunities. Thus the business case focuses on the avoidance of potential financial losses rather than financial gains. As with the first perspective, this can lead to relatively low-level dialogue intentions.

---

2   See Chapter 18 of *Terms for Endearment* (Bendell 2000) for a typology of NGO approaches towards corporations.

Corporate goal	NGO function
Risk management and reduction	Providing stakeholder views as early warning of possible risks
	Integrating business and community goals
	Creating and enforcing popularly supported standards, codes, etc.
Cost reduction and productivity gains	Negotiating community benefits and role
	Supporting transparent processes
	Leveraging non-tax status
	Educating publics
	Accessing altruistic energy
New product development	Providing knowledge about communities and their resources
	Lobbying for regulatory change
	Providing knowledge about technical issues
	Providing linkages to non-commercial creativity
New market development	Aggregating small and poor markets to profitable size
	Extending trusting public image
	Creating demand through new business development
	Providing delivery support
	Educating communities about new approaches
Human resource development	Teaching and training about specific communities
	Providing inspirational outlets for employees and boosting morale
	Monitoring standards
Production chain organising	Organising all the chain players for total quality improvement strategies
Building barriers to entry	Building a distinctive image
	Linking to a distinctive market
Creativity and change	Providing alternative viewpoints to reveal unrecognised assumptions and develop new integrative strategies

Table 3.1 **NGO functions in business strategies**

Source: Waddell 2000

3. **Strategic business perspective**. This view of corporate citizenship places it as a central element of a company's approach to long-term success. Consequently, managers actively examine the social and environmental impacts of products and service delivery, seeking to move to more sustainable modes of generating revenue (from non-renewable to renewable resources, or sales to service rentals, for example). This view also suggests that business takes a leadership role in promoting institutional frameworks for human rights and sustainable development. The strategic business perspective suggests higher-level dialogue intentions, such as 'dialogue as partnership' and perhaps even 'dialogue as delegation'.

4. **Innovation systems perspective**. This final view of corporate citizenship sees it as the key to future organisational value, through its ability to bring together diverse stakeholders in systems of innovation and feedback. This perspective regards 'citizenly organisations' as the best mode for accessing, collating and acting on high-quality information to anticipate market trends and thereby to effectively innovate and deliver goods and services. Donar Zohah (1997: 136) believes that it is important to 'rewire the corporate brain' and that dialogue is 'a powerful means by which we can grow new neural connections'. It could be argued that this view of corporate citizenship suggests the highest level of dialogue intention: dialogue as democracy.

Hearing new economy entrepreneurs at seminars or in magazines such as *Fast Company* talk about the future of business has inspired some to think of an 'innovation systems' approach to corporate citizenship. The changing worlds of work, product and service delivery, and branding that are promised by the digital revolution makes the establishment of effective innovation systems through good corporate citizenship a crucial strategic issue for business. The necessary actions to implement an innovation systems corporate citizenship strategy are unclear at this stage, but issues as central as corporate governance would need to be considered, with major implications for stakeholder dialogue. A deeper exploration of the possibilities for democratising corporate governance is beyond this chapter, but is covered in the chapter by Rob Lake and this author in *Terms for Endearment* (Bendell 2000).

3.5 Talking reporting

Social or environmental reports are key stages in any stakeholder dialogue process, while a stakeholder dialogue process is a key stage in any valuable social or environmental report. The first corporate social report that recognised this fact was *The Body Shop Social Statement 95*. The approach taken by that company was to focus on the interests and perspectives of stakeholders and thereby measure the company's performance from that vantage point. An attempt was made to let the stakeholders speak for themselves, so the report was punctuated with stakeholder quotes that were selected by the NGO helping them with the report, the New Economics Foundation (NEF). Since that time there have been efforts to integrate social and environmental reporting into 'sustainability reports', culminating in a major, multi-stakeholder, international undertaking called the Global Reporting Initiative (GRI). Its mission is to develop and disseminate globally applicable sustainability reporting guidelines for voluntary use by organisations reporting on the economic, environmental and social dimensions of their activities, products and services. Since its inception in 1997, the GRI has worked to design and build acceptance of a common framework for reporting on sustainability. Facilitating dialogue with all stakeholders is a key aim of the GRI, as it promotes reporting that 'provides stakeholders with reliable information that is relevant to their needs and interests and that invites further stakeholder dialogue and inquiry' (GRI 2000: 1).

GRI reinforces the link between stakeholder dialogue and reporting in its 'underlying principles of GRI reporting', where it sets out a definition of the materiality required by sustainability reports: 'Materiality in economic, environmental and social reporting is dependent on what is relevant either to reporting organisations or to their external stakeholders' (GRI 2000: 15). The GRI goes on to recognise that different stakeholders may not agree on what is material, so that the reporting organisation needs 'continuing interaction with stakeholders' (GRI 2000: 15). The role of stakeholder dialogue is reinforced in the section on 'qualitative characteristics for GRI reporting', which emphasises that reporting must be relevant, and that 'the issue of what is or is not relevant may best be gauged through various forms of stakeholder engagement conducted by reporting organisations or by external parties' (GRI 2000: 16).

With major funding from the UN Foundation, widespread interest from the business community and input from civil society, the GRI is a key leadership initiative that will shape the future of reporting-oriented stakeholder dialogue (www.globalreporting.org). One company that piloted the reporting guidelines was TXU-Europe. In one sustainability report TXU states on the opening page its philosophy that 'by talking regularly with our stakeholders, we have learned not only how best to include them in our decision-making process, but also how to account for our behaviour' (TXU-Europe 2000: 1).

TXU started a stakeholder engagement programme with the Environment Council, and then continued this itself. In co-operation with the Environment Council, TXU established key environmental issues and, at a later stage, key social issues. In the field of environmental management, the number one issue was global warming/CO_2 emissions, and, in response, TXU came up with its 20% reduction target. The number one social issue was fuel poverty. TXU is now in a process of determining key indicators. Information about TXU stakeholder engagement was presented in a paper summary report, and more fully in the online report. This represents a trend towards different reporting on paper and web media. TXU no longer prints its entire report, only a summary. The online version allows for those with an interest to seek out further information. Over time these web reports could become more interactive and further facilitate stakeholder feedback. With this in mind a number of communications companies are beginning to specialise in online sustainability reporting, such as C21, which worked with TXU (www.C21.co.uk).

3.6 Talking measuring

Whether standards for stakeholder dialogue will play a major part in future developments in corporate citizenship is unclear. The move away from technical, industry-defined standards for acceptable social and environmental performance towards a recognition that stakeholders have a right and a role in determining what is acceptable, has been rapid in the UK. Whether this leads to widespread uptake of standardised processes for stakeholder dialogue at the level of individual company, or industrial sector, is uncertain at this stage.

It is also unclear whether more companies will seek to use an off-the-shelf guide to what they should be measuring and reporting on (the aim of the GRI) or whether they will recognise the benefit of a systematic process of stakeholder dialogue—and seek to measure and report on that. Any stakeholder management system, and any benchmarking or quality assessment of such a system, should consider the following four dimensions:

1. **Inclusiveness**: who is included in the dialogue

2. **Procedures**: the basis on which the dialogue is designed and implemented

3. **Responsiveness**: the degree to which the various parties respond to the dialogue

4. **Outcomes**: what actually happens and who reaps the associated costs and benefits

The stakeholder dialogue management system standard of AccountAbility (the Institute of Social and Ethical Accountability [ISEA]) is called AA 1000. This standard focuses particularly on the issues of inclusiveness and procedures. AA 1000 advocates the centrality of 'stakeholder inclusivity', by which it means:

> Inclusivity concerns the reflection at all stages of the SEAAR [social and ethical accounting, auditing and reporting] . . . the views and needs of all stakeholder groups. Stakeholder views are obtained through an engagement process that allows them to be expressed without fear or restriction. Inclusivity requires the consideration of 'voiceless' stakeholders including future generations and the environment (ISEA 1999).

The standard goes on to explain that quality engagement needs to:

1. Allow stakeholders to assist in the identification of other stakeholders

2. Ensure that stakeholders trust the social and ethical accountant (internal or external) who is collecting and processing the findings of the engagement

3. Be a dialogue, not a one-way information feed

4. Be between parties with sufficient preparation and briefing to have well-informed opinions and decisions

5. Involve stakeholders in defining the terms of engagement. The terms will include, but are not limited to, the issues covered, the methods and techniques of engagement used, the questions asked, the means of analysing responses to questions and the stakeholder feedback process

6. Allow stakeholders to voice their views without restriction and without fear of penalty or discipline. However, stakeholders must be aware that, if their

opinions are taken seriously and acted on, this will have consequences for them and other stakeholder groups.

7. Include a public disclosure and feedback process that offers other stakeholders information that is valuable in assessing the engagement and allows them to comment on it (ISEA 1999)

The standard therefore focuses more on process than the actual techniques of dialogue. This is important, as the Environment Council recognises that techniques are relatively simple, but 'the complexities and subtleties come in *how* to use which technique at what moment and with what group of people' (Environment Council 1999: 17). In my research on social auditing practices on banana plantations (Bendell 2000), I found that, whereas a variety of techniques such as focus groups and interviews were being used, the key requirements for quality dialogue, set out in points 2–7 above, were being overlooked. For example, critics argued that workers did not always trust the auditors as they were seen to be working for the management (point 2). Second, I found that workers did not know of their rights or what terms such as 'sexual discrimination', when used in an abstract sense, actually meant (point 4). Another concern was that stakeholders were not involved closely in determining the issues to be studied by the social auditor (point 5). In addition, interviews were conducted on-site in view of supervisors so that workers might not feel relaxed about talking (point 6). Finally, there is only a weak feedback system to the workers about the findings of the audit (point 7). AA 1000 therefore serves a useful purpose in focusing on process principles and bringing these issues to the fore. However, it does not deal so well with the other two aspects of quality stakeholder dialogue, responsiveness and outcome, and more work will be required on these issues.

3.7 Talking agreements and certifications

There are a number of other initiatives that provide innovative approaches to meaningful and effective stakeholder dialogue. Partnerships between businesses and NGOs focusing on specific products, management systems or social/environmental projects have been outlined in books such as *In the Company of Partners* (Murphy and Bendell 1997). The dynamics of dialogue within these partnerships has been explored further in subsequent research, some of which is presented and analysed from a business perspective in *Terms for Endearment* (Bendell 2000) and from an NGO perspective in *NGOs Engaging Business* (Heap 2000). One important organisational form that has evolved to manage outcome-oriented stakeholder dialogue is the multi-stakeholder accreditation council. These organisations bring together stakeholders to determine social and/or environmental standards for a particular economic activity and then operate systems of endorsement for companies and products meeting the agreed criteria. No two of these organisations are the same—they have different ways of involving different stakeholders—but they share some characteristics. They include the Forest Stewardship Council, The Marine Stewardship Council, Fairtrade Labelling Organisation and Social Accountability International, among others. They have recently formed an alliance to help determine best practice and ensure high-quality standards setting, accreditation and certification processes (Box 3.2).

Another form of stakeholder dialogue is being innovated by global business and international confederations of trade unions. These dialogues involve the negotiation of 'framework agreements' which establish basic principles relating to labour rights and how labour disputes should be resolved by members of the union confederation and subsidiaries of the multinational corporation. The framework agreements recognise the validity of unions as groups that should be negotiated with by employers, in order to resolve conflicts. On 7 March 2000 the General Secretary of the International Union for Food and Agricultural Workers (IUF), Ron Oswald, and Vice President for Del Monte Latin America, José Antonio Yock, signed a framework agreement. The agreement affirms, among other points, the right of all the illegally sacked workers on a plantation to return to their jobs and guarantees the Guatemalan union, SITRABI, to organise and represent the workers for collective bargaining.[3]

The IUF–Del Monte example shows how stakeholder dialogue between global groups can lead to agreements that facilitate further stakeholder dialogue (and potentially agreement) regionally and locally. Collective bargaining between free trade unions and companies is a form of stakeholder dialogue that has existed for decades and the ground rules of which have been established by the International Labour Organisation (ILO) in Conventions and the ILO *Declaration on Fundamental Principles and Rights at Work*. Collective bargaining can be understood as 'dialogue as partnership', as the intention is to ensure a balancing of power in the negotiations between employer and employed.

A more detailed exploration of industrial relations, union rights and collective bargaining processes is beyond the scope of this chapter, but many UK companies are currently involved in a learning process about these issues through their involvement in the Ethical Trading Initiative (ETI). This tripartite grouping—business, unions and NGOs—is a novel forum to facilitate dialogue and learning between the sectors, on the issue of labour standards throughout the supply chains of UK companies. The complex dynamics of the process of establishing the ETI and agreeing the base code of labour standards has not been documented as yet, but will be presented in my forthcoming PhD thesis.

3.8 Talking success factors

A number of research projects have been undertaken to look at corporate attempts at stakeholder dialogue. Most of these, such as that of the Centre for Innovation in Corpo-

---

3   The conflict had its origins in the dismissal last year of 900 workers employed on three Bandegua-owned plantations (subsidiaries of Del Monte) in Guatemala's Morales district and the subsequent assault by 200 heavily armed men on the union leadership which was organising a mass protest against the illegal dismissals. Since the 13 October conflict, the SITRABI leadership, which was forced to flee to Guatemala City, has been under police protection. The IUF contacted the Guatemalan government to demand that the organisers and perpetrators of the assault be brought to justice, and continues to pressure the new government to take appropriate action.

IN A GROUND-BREAKING MEETING ON 7 DECEMBER 1999 IN BRUSSELS, THE MAJOR international environmental and social organisations involved in standards setting, accreditation and labelling put in place a strategy for more formal co-operation and mutual support. The objective of the meeting, facilitated by Falls Brook Center, a Canadian environmental NGO, was to prioritise the common issues that the participating organisations want to work on together and to decide on a framework for moving forward.

The six participating organisations are forming an alliance in order to safeguard and promote environmental and labour concerns within international trade as well as to pursue continuing professional improvement. Participants were clearly excited by the potential to build the capacity of their systems and to strengthen their common priorities. Their organisations had already confirmed the desire and intent to work together by signing an Agreement in Principle in September that commits them to seek a framework for collaboration.

These organisations have come together because they share a number of common features—most importantly, that they have their origins in civil society. Each of these systems was developed as an initiative of advocacy and producer organisations in collaboration with businesses, and is characterised by a concern for human rights, sustainable livelihoods and environmental health. They have developed global standards and promote third-party independent certification to ensure compliance with these standards for a wide range of products. Certification standards are based on the process or production methods used in the development of these products.

Participants in the meeting were enthusiastic about the significant potential for collaboration between their organisations, based on common experiences. Among the issues that participants prioritised as key areas for further collaboration are an analysis of accreditation procedures leading to a common framework; a peer review process for accreditation that will enhance the transparency of these organisations; research on the overlap of standards between systems and a strategy for increasing compatibility; development of joint training programmes; and further discussions on trademark use and logo proliferation.

This alliance includes all of the major international systems currently in place and has the potential to benefit producers of all sizes in both developed and developing countries. The standards, certification programmes and accreditation systems being implemented by these organisations are all truly global in nature and address the worldwide concern for social and environmental issues in trade and development. This collaboration is a significant movement to promote the interests of workers, communities and the environment in world trade.

The international organisations participating in this alliance include:

- Council on Economic Priorities Accreditation Agency (CEPAA)
- Fairtrade Labelling Organisations (FLO) International
- Forest Stewardship Council (FSC)
- International Federation of Organic Agriculture Movements (IFOAM)
- International Organic Accreditation Service (IOAS)
- Marine Stewardship Council (MSC)
- Sustainable Agriculture Network (SAN)

Box 3.2 *International Social and Environmental Labelling and Accreditation (ISEAL) Alliance*

Source: ISEAL 1999

rate Responsibility (Greenall and Rovere 1999), assume a low-level intention for dialogue: manipulation, therapy, information, consultation or placation. Nevertheless, some of the findings are relevant for deeper forms of dialogue with more radical objectives, and complement the recommendations of the AA 1000 standard discussed above. The main points are summarised below.

1. **Identification of the important stakeholders.** Failing to identify the key stakeholders central to the process means that the company agrees to joint priorities with the wrong people. The identification of stakeholders is sometimes influenced by guidelines provided by local governments and funding agencies such as the World Bank, which can either misguide or help corporate efforts in this area, depending on the case. As mentioned above, systems for identifying stakeholders are not well established, and questions about the representativeness of different NGOs and community groups remain. (Michael Edwards [2000] suggests that a code of conduct for NGOs may help to resolve this problem.)

2. **Development of trust.** Developing understanding of one another and trust between business and stakeholders is the foundation for co-operation. 'Our goal is intimacy. Being on a first-name basis with everyone in the community. Making sure every person has had a chance to air their questions and concerns' (Greenall and Rovere 1999).

3. **Flexibility.** Most businesses note that it is important to establish flexible relationships and, when necessary, agreements where all parties agree that changes would be made as time progressed. 'We won't get the equation right, right away' (Greenall and Rovere 2000).

4. **Open sharing of information.** It is important that there is a good two-way flow of knowledge and information so that dialogue can be well informed. For the company, having access to as much local information as possible is vital to various processes from environmental impact assessments to the implementation of labour rights codes of conduct, to the funding of community projects. A company needs to understand the important issues and concerns in order for it to work together with the local community to address them. At the same time, it is vital that there is an exchange of information from the company to the community. This interchange is central to achieving proper understanding so that both sides can move beyond rhetoric and posturing.

5. **Having appropriate time-frames to converse.** Stakeholder dialogue is normally related to specific objectives, such as an agreement or a decision on a project. A lack of adequate time for dialogue (particularly at the outset) before an agreement or decision is reached can mean that an adequate level of trust will not be established. Consequently, there may not be clear understanding and appropriate expectations by the corporate or the stakeholders.

6. **Building realistic expectations.** On a number of occasions, managers have indicated that initial stakeholder expectations were far beyond the means of the company (Greenall and Rovere 1999). Adequate time and resources must be

invested in managing those expectations and coming to mutual agreement with stakeholders as to what is realistic and what is not, in the short, medium and long term. Just because something is not workable in the short term does not mean it should be left out of the agenda for future work. There must also be agreement on what the respective company and community responsibilities are for agreed-upon goals.

To these, as a proponent of higher-level dialogue intentions, such as partnership, delegation and democracy, I would add a seventh important factor:

7. Sharing the agenda

The agenda for stakeholder dialogue should be open, with nothing ruled in or ruled out. Although it is an approach recommended by the Environment Council (Box 3.1) a focus on immediate win–wins can actually limit the agenda. The situation with biotechnology provides one example. In Bob Shapiro's speech to the Greenpeace Business Conference, he set out where he sought win–wins with stakeholders:

> The underlining premise of dialogue is pretty straightforward. In this case, it is that there are both real benefits to the use of biotechnology and at the same time there are real concerns about its use. If you don't believe that there are real benefits, then there is no room for dialogue (Shapiro 1999 quoted in Bendell 2000).

Setting the rules in this way is not really workable. Given the various concerns with biotechnology (see Bendell 2000: ch. 6), many in civil society do not believe there are any net sustainable development benefits to be gained from it. A win–win resolution therefore appears elusive. Even those NGOs that might recognise the potential of biotechnology could dispute the potential of its application in the hands of companies seeking rapid commercialisation and profit maximisation. The issues that need to be discussed are therefore probably broader and more complex than the industry would initially desire, such as commercially viable alternatives to the patenting of life-forms and even the need for a moratorium on the current commercialisation of GM crops.

In addition there are fundamental political problems which need to be resolved in any dialogue. The bottom line for the biotechnology companies appears to be that their stock valuation is based on the investors' belief that the companies will increasingly control the system of food supply in a biotech future worth billions. The bottom line for NGOs might just turn out to be democracy: a belief that no one organisation or group of organisations should have the final say over our future. The 'dialogue' should not be over biotechnology, then, but the role of business in society. Effective stakeholder dialogue needs to be able to open up and explore agendas in this way.

3.9 Conclusion

Effective stakeholder dialogue is a critical element of good corporate citizenship. Done well, with progressive intentions, it can underpin a powerful change process that benefits all. Badly handled or initiated with bad intentions, however, it can be an expensive, time-consuming and counterproductive activity, which neither builds trust, facilitates collaboration nor enhances the value of the corporate organisation. For stakeholder dialogue to be worthwhile it must not be seen in isolation from real outputs and outcomes, and must involve a tangible sharing of power.

STAKEHOLDER INFLUENCES IN DEVELOPING A SUSTAINABILITY CULTURE WITHIN THE UK BIOTECHNOLOGY SECTOR

Aharon Factor

Aarhus School of Business, Denmark

As a response to a growing recognition of the benefits of good corporate governance a minority of highly proactive multinational corporations have wittingly responded to the challenge of sustainable development. Reportedly, a similar response to sustainable development by the small and medium-sized enterprise sector has been contrastingly sluggish (Hillary 1999). An important feature enhancing this behavioural trait has been the difficulties for SMEs to tackle broader stakeholder issues.

Inherently, actions taken towards promoting sustainable management procedures are closely affiliated with the requirements of, mainly, primary stakeholders. Thus, stakeholders of higher salience are better positioned to instigate sustainability practices within the SME sector. Rarely, however, do 'green' stakeholder pressures carry significantly high salience (Fineman and Clarke 1996).[1] Consequently, stakeholder influences in the SME sector generally promote a 'business-as-usual' approach. As a result, calls for improved environmental performance and sustainable development practices by SMEs necessitate acceptance that environmental issues are an important and relevant business criterion (Ulhøi and Madsen 1997; Merritt 1998).

Empirical investigations describing environmental characteristics of SMEs have, generally, focused on firms across manufacturing and industrial sectors (Christensen 1997; Smith *et al.* 1998). Current investigations within a group of emergent UK biotechnology companies may enrich our understanding of the development of sustainability processes within SMEs. Uniquely, this study reveals cultural barriers and catalysts affecting sustain-

---

1 The level of salience possessed by a stakeholder is categorised by the three principle factors: urgency, power and legitimacy. The ownership of a greater degree of all three factors will enhance the prioritisation of the stakeholder's demand by the firm (Mitchell *et al.* 1997).

ability practices within high-technology companies. Managerial responsiveness to stakeholder pressures is shown to play an important role in the greening of the firm. Thus, in reporting stakeholder influences through a managerial lens this chapter demonstrates why managers prioritise issues, and explores possible ramifications for sustainable development.

4.1 Background

In broadening the scope of traditional stakeholder theory, a growing body of academic literature has developed (Freeman 1984, 1999; Gioia 1999). It describes how bi-directional influences may exist not only between groups and individuals who are instrumental in ensuring the success of the firm (**primary stakeholders**) but crucially between groups who are not engaged in transactions with the corporation and are not essential for its survival (**secondary stakeholders**). Essentially, the latter group includes literature pertaining to sustainable development and corporate social responsibility (Clarkson 1995; Mitchell *et al.* 1997; Ulhøi and Madsen 1997).

The literature itself may be categorised by academics that identify a possible augmentation of existing dominant strategic management theories to simply incorporate environmental and social parameters by adding sustainability principles They ask, for example: Can Porter's three generic strategies, which consider market positioning in terms of strategic bundles of objectives, be made 'ecologically sustainable'? Such normative strategies, however, are criticised by Malandri (1999) and Steger and Meima (1998) for safeguarding competitiveness through exploitation of cost-reduction opportunities. They claim that successful companies need a guiding vision and recognise the broader external environment within which the company operates. Thus, they identify three essential objective bundles, **performance**, **market** and **profit**, to determine the long-term survival of the firm. Hence, environmental issues are accordingly placed alongside health and safety and quality issues as performance objectives (Steger and Meima 1998), thus managing the 'good corporate governance' demanded by a wide array of stakeholder groups and individuals.

Ambiguities associated with stakeholder identification, though, have provoked a wider conflict within the academic community. The dominant camp is grounded within a Western dualistic philosophy (as discussed above and represented by a 'code of conduct' within Table 4.1). Derived from this perspective, **stakeholder** and **sustainable development** terminology segregate human from non-human interests. An opposing camp, however, identifies the non-human environment as 'if' a stakeholder (main proponent Starik 1995). This approach has been criticised by the dominant camp for providing human status to a non-human environment (Jensen 2000; Philips and Reichart 2000; Windsor 2002). Does this rift represent a non-commensurability between the two paradigms? If so, then these terms can only serve human interests (Rachels 1999). Thus, the environment is not a stakeholder and accordingly stakeholder interests become inclusive of sustainable development concepts.

Adherence to the notion that the environment is a stakeholder is not, however, prominently expressed within the new world-view (see Table 4.1). This paradigm, in contrast to

Code of conduct	State of being
Dominant world-view	New world-view
Shallow ecology	Deep ecology
Conventional ethical discourse	New ethical discourse
Hierarchical	Systemic
Individualistic/atomistic	Holistic/Gaian/Spiritualist
Anthropocentric	Eco-centric

Table 4.1 *The divergence of ecological philosophy*

Source: Adapted from Tilley 2000

the dominant approach, enriches the concept of sustainability in recognising future generations. This emphasis on time separates this paradigm from the dominant focus on present generations. It additionally makes all non-human and human entities interdependent. Within this spatially holistic approach the concept of defining stakeholders loses all significance.

Newton and Harte's (1997) illuminating paper describes how the code of conduct (dominant camp) approach has become the victim of 'green evangelism'. This is portrayed as a rhetorical strategy by which businesses are able to justify a shift from regulatory to market-based incentives for organisational eco-change and to use environmental excellence and corporate environmental strategies to place the responsibility of environmental protection with the market. In essence this reduces the influence of state control.

More radically, Cramer (1998) urges businesses to escape from the present 'black box' in which they reside and to **stretch environmental** strategy towards a sustainable paradigm. In this context, Bhargava and Welford (1996) view corporate environmental strategy as relatively underdeveloped and thus requiring broadening to incorporate principles of sustainable development (and subscribe to the 'state of being' approach of Table 4.1). They believe that few companies are truly enthusiastic. Therefore they state, 'the strategic approach does not challenge the traditional model of the profit-centred industrial organisation'; it is a 'business-as-usual' paradigm. Thus, ignoring environmental threats and opportunities instigated by stakeholder relationships could endanger the overall objective of long-run survival because the freedom of a corporation to act autonomously would be eventually limited if the interests of stakeholders were violated in a repetitive and intolerable manner (Steger and Meima 1998).

Stakeholder theory has developed as a response to the growing recognition that the survival of a corporate company may reside in the delicate relationship established with those with a stake in the firm. Although this may be of equal relevance to the survival of an SME, the organisational context may differ greatly. Critically, sustainability issues are inherently long-term problems (Welford 1995). Whereas the organisational arrangements within a corporate company may permit long-term planning and the development of sustainability policy, the SME may be woefully lacking. It is therefore hardly surprising that a host of surveys have indicated that SMEs are reluctant to address these issues (Yoxon 1997; Smith et al. 1998).

Instead, demands by regulatory bodies for compliance with tight H&S legislation and responsiveness to market demands for improved quality standards have provided a spur for SMEs to accept that H&S and quality considerations are real business issues. Therefore, investment in time and costs may be viewed as acceptable. Increasingly stringent environmental regulations and market demands for adherence to environmental standards are also, albeit slowly, promoting the uptake of sustainability practices within the SME sector (Hillary 1999). Broader environmental issues, however, although recognised as important in a 'general' sense, are not seen as relevant to the business. The SME is chiefly concerned with survival 'today' and thus the perception is that the long-term environmental considerations are costly and time-consuming 'today'. Consequently, in Cramer's (1998) terms, SMEs attempt to 'fit' rather than 'stretch' the sustainable development agenda.

Uniquely, the biotechnology SME features certain characteristics, which may favour the development of a sustainability culture. In contrast to reported ignorance towards environmental issues (Smith *et al.* 1998), SMEs in this sector comprise a highly educated workforce and highly astute stakeholder groups. Thus, good corporate governance practices are viewed as a given. This chapter discusses how a small group of companies within the UK sector respond to the sustainability challenge.

4.2 Method

The interview questions were based on the concluding hypothesis emerging from a growing number of quantitative studies (Madsen and Ulhøi 1996; Madsen *et al.* 1997; Smith *et al.* 1998; Hillary 1999, 2000). These suggested that there exist significant barriers towards the implementation of environmental initiatives within SMEs. Emanating from this hypothesis, a set of propositions was developed, the key tenet being that **stakeholders influence SME sustainability behaviour**.

In digging more deeply into this sustainability paradox, 'how' and 'why' questions are more fruitful in providing 'information-rich' qualitative data (Tilley 2000). As the investigator has little control over events, and the focus is on a contemporary phenomenon within a real-life context, this invites a case-study approach (Yin 1994).

The use of multiple cases permits a **replication logic** allowing for the convergence among multiple operations by which we can increase confidence in our findings (Brinberg and McGrath 1985; Yin 1994). Hence, the case-study design has been strengthened to provide a greater robustness of validity of data through methodological triangulation, combining interviews, archival analysis and observational techniques. The use of a triangulated sampling procedure has yielded a group of seven UK biotechnology companies from an initial pool of 120 SME UK companies. Selection criteria required that all companies were geographically clustered within southern and central England.

Additionally, it is recognised that there is a general perception that high technology and clean production are synonymous. Selected companies also needed to demonstrate early growth dynamics, critical for studying the perception of environmental affairs of supply chain stakeholders, outsourcing being common at this stage of development. An indication of at least some element of the phenomena of study (allowing for a reactive/proactive group of companies to be established) was also sought.

4.2.1 *Data sources*

Interviews lasting between 60 and 90 minutes were conducted with a founding manager from within each of the seven companies. To improve data reliability, the interview questions (see Appendix) pertaining to business affairs were segregated from environmental elements. This allowed for the repetition of the same underlying phenomena throughout the interview period. The interview questions were semi-structured to simultaneously exert better control over the data collection and to support a richer exploration of the research phenomena.

4.2.2 *Data analysis*

Following the transcription of interview tapes and hand-written notes, coded clustering selectively reduced the data and aided the construction of a pattern-matching matrix. The matrix data was consequently analysed for commonality and discrepancy both within and across cases. Analysis using pattern matching has been used to link repeated cause-and-effect sequences together and increase the validity of the results. Prior knowledge and experience, techniques, matrices and arrays will combine to provide robustness to the validity of the analysis.

4.3 **Results and discussion**

This section reveals the findings of the research interviews. Qualitative data is represented as managerial quotes. The selection of the reported data is based on the methodological approach described above. This data is, subsequently, used to develop a tentative framework and discussion.

The case-study interviews revealed two interesting features among the firms (labelled α, β, χ, A, B, C, D for confidentiality purposes). The first corresponds to the categorisation of key stakeholders and their influence on firm strategic intent.[2] The second

---

2 **Shareholders**. The majority of companies are seeking to fund their biotechnology research and development activities through stakeholder engagement. Initially, the company goal, witnessed throughout the group, is for the attainment of IPO (initial public offering) status, thus rendering shareholders critically important stakeholders. Early-stage strategic development is heavily dictated by shareholder involvement, usually venture capital (α, β, χ, B). Interestingly, through personal funds (A, B) public finance (A, B, C) and collaborative partners (A, β, C), four companies in the group have, to some extent, diminished investor influence. Nevertheless, as companies C and χ illustrate, investors provide invaluable consultancy advice.

  Legislation. Throughout the sector, stringent health and safety (H&S) legislation, standard operating procedures (SOPS), good laboratory practice (GLP) and good manufacturing practice (GMP) regulations are an important driver in formalising management procedures.

  Employees. An organic culture that engages employees (α), allows an 'open way of thinking' (A) and an effective communication platform (χ) is reportedly critical to developing employee motivation. Inherently, though, as companies develop and knowledge flows, increased project management becomes essential to manage complexity and formalisation. The dilemma, thus, is that increasing formalisation may threaten the problem-solving culture (β, A, D) essential in maintaining a motivated workforce. As the innovation capacity resides within

indicates to what degree these influential stakeholders act as sustainable development drivers. In this chapter, the influence on sustainable development of these three important stakeholders—shareholders, regulators and employees—is discussed. The sustainable development concept itself encapsulates a multitude of disciplines (e.g. natural environment, poverty, human rights, etc.). More specifically, therefore, this study limits itself to those components of sustainable development that pertain to the natural environment and its relationship with business ethics.

4.3.1 Stakeholder influences on standardisation implementation

Table 4.2 encapsulates some of the important characteristics that will dictate the level of influence that stakeholders will have in 'greening' the firm. It was found that the companies have differing organisational arrangements. Standardisation practices theoretically favour formal 'command-and-control' practices. Nevertheless, the data demonstrates a greater linkage between the number of employees and standardisation in response to regulatory (and industry association) pressures; the development of health and safety and quality standards in the group has been strong. Observably, companies β and C show a high degree of formalisation in this process. Further, company β publishes a compliance statement within its annual report. Working towards standards is a learning process which small companies nurture through more organic/semi-formalised organisational structures and channels. Thus, the majority of companies report a high degree of semi-formalisation[3] in their approach to developing standards ($\alpha > \chi > D > A > B$). In terms of stakeholder relationships, this has an important role for employee engagement (as discussed above). The real drivers for standards, though, emanate from legislative pressure. This is observed generally throughout the group.

Company (no. of employees)	α (54)	β (147)	χ (22)	A ($\cong$ 20)	B ($\cong$ 10)	C (<5)	D ($\cong$ 10)
Standards							
H&S	✔	✔	✔	✔	✔	✔	✔
Quality	✔	✔	✔				
EMS	✔						

Organisational structure: ■ Hierarchical   ▨ Collective   ▢ Semi-formalised

Table 4.2 **Corporate profile of seven UK biotechnology companies**

highly educated employees, the cultivation of such a culture within a biotechnology company is paramount. Thus, all seven companies stress the importance of employee engagement.

3   The terminology 'semi-formalisation' represents a growth stage of the firm whereby organic organisational arrangements (characteristic of small firms) are not adequate in coping with increasing business complexity. Standards and procedures are subsequently in the early phase of development and not representative of truly formalised 'command-and-control' practices as observed in larger organisational settings.

In terms of ISO 14001- and EMAS-type standardisation, the sample lacks proactive members. Nevertheless, one member of the sample can be distinguished as an 'environmental champion'. Company α reports that it exceeds environmental best practices such as ISO 14001. In this company it is the employees and ethical shareholders who are pushing the environmental agenda. Company β is more favourable to ISO 14001 and takes a similar line as company χ in observing rate of uptake in the sector. Companies A, B, C and D do not see environmental standards as relevant to their operations, unless compelled by law.

4.3.2 Stakeholder influences and the uptake of specific environmental schemes

Stakeholder influences on the implementation of specific practices to protect the environment are outlined in Table 4.3. As a biological research-dependent sector, managerial perceptions towards environmental issues are, not surprisingly, indicative of an aware-

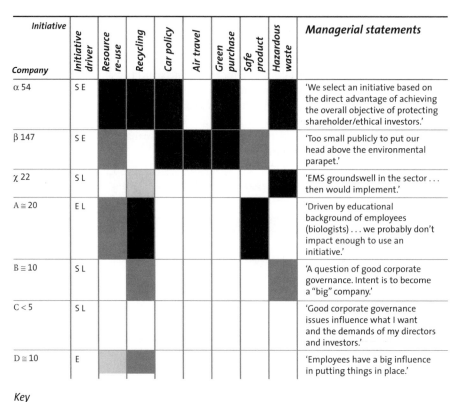

Initiative Company	Initiative driver	Resource re-use	Recycling	Car policy	Air travel	Green purchase	Safe product	Hazardous waste	Managerial statements
α 54	S E	■	■	■		■		■	'We select an initiative based on the direct advantage of achieving the overall objective of protecting shareholder/ethical investors.'
β 147	S E	▨		■	■	▨			'Too small publicly to put our head above the environmental parapet.'
χ 22	S L		▨					■	'EMS groundswell in the sector . . . then would implement.'
A ≅ 20	E L	▨	■				■		'Driven by educational background of employees (biologists) . . . we probably don't impact enough to use an initiative.'
B ≅ 10	S L							▨	'A question of good corporate governance. Intent is to become a "big" company.'
C < 5	S L								'Good corporate governance issues influence what I want and the demands of my directors and investors.'
D ≅ 10	E	▨	▨						'Employees have a big influence in putting things in place.'

Key

Numbers (first column):	employee members
Stakeholder driver:	S, shareholder; L, legislation; E, employees
Level of activity (darkest = highest):	

Table 4.3 **Environmental initiatives uptake within seven UK biotechnology companies**

ness of the broader context of the terminology and meaning of 'sustainability' and 'environment' (α, β > A > D, χ, B).

Nevertheless, certain members of the group related environmental issues to the local level (C > χ > B). Thus, although not observable in an operational sense, generally, a 'green' thinking culture pervades the group. Insights into how this grass-roots culture interacts with the interests of stakeholders and develops a sustainability culture may be revealed through further analysis of the interview data.

Perceptions are demonstrated to be an important part of the stakeholder-influenced decision-making process; some companies state that environmental affairs are relevant to their business activities (α > β > χ). In contrast, they probably do not have enough impact to use an initiative (A, C > B, D). Such a division within the group reveals an interesting feature. The larger companies in the group (α, β) demonstrate a greater tendency to implement initiatives. They, too, are the only firms to indicate that a combination of shareholder and employee pressures has (and will in the future) influenced their environmental decision-making. Thus, in these two companies and similarly in company A, employee engagement has, to some extent, sown the seeds for a greening culture (α > β > A).

Alternatively, shareholder and legislative pressures combine in companies B and C and employees and shareholders in A and D. Importantly, among these four companies, greening pressures are greatly determined by legislative demands. Finally, χ and A may be observed to foster a middle ground between reacting to legislative pressures (B, C, D) and taking a proactive role in environmental affairs (α, β).

4.3.3 *Stakeholder influences and sustainability*

Analysis of Table 4.3 supports the general hypothesis that companies in a sector will demonstrate varied behavioural patterns towards environmental affairs. It also shows that companies may be actively implementing specific schemes related to environmental considerations. The results of Table 4.4, however, indicate a slower progress and hesitancy in coming to grips with the concept of sustainability and their firm.

The sustainability agenda is generally portrayed to be weak. Only one company, driven by employees, truly acts to integrate sustainability features into the business (α). Company β is unsure about the desires of its shareholders, while χ will only respond to legislative and shareholder pressures to do so. Company A has implemented one sustainability feature related to its products. The pressure, again, is emanating from employees. Companies B and C view the issue as a concern of corporate governance, which may become more relevant as they grow. Finally, company D views sustainability as irrelevant to its operations but would act if pressurised by employees and legislation.

4.3.4 *Tentative framework*

The management literature is rich in the terms **proactive** and **reactive**, which are equally widely used in the environmental management literature. These terms, however, are static and not representative of all company environmental stances. Several authors have therefore introduced terms and metaphors to categorise intermediate firm behaviour (Hunt and Auster 1990; Clarkson 1995; Rugman and Verbeke 1998). Here the term 'semi-

Company	S D	Level of activity	Managerial statements
α 54	S E	▓▓	'The firm has a global sustainability purchasing/ supply-chain programme.'
β 147	E L	▓▓	'Increasingly, I think this has an ethical component.'
χ 22	L		'Similar forces (to the environmental initiatives) would also conspire to push sustainable development.'
A ≅ 20	L		'Employee pressures through the sector may instigate a sustainability push if it were linked to a wider societal dimension . . . we have a very high level of ethics.'
B ≅ 10	S		'Sustainability pops up if we start bulk-manufacturing . . . had not thought of this.'
C < 5	S		'Ethics are important . . . sustainability . . . a huge train of events occurring first.'
D ≅ 10	E		'Well we don't see a problem with sustainability with what we do . . . we are Internet-based.'

Key

Numbers (first column):	employee members
Stakeholder driver (SD):	S, shareholder; L, legislation; E, employees
Level of activity (darkest = highest):	▢▢▓▓██

Table 4.4 ***Practices contributing towards sustainable development within seven UK biotechnology companies***

proactive is used to define this position. Illustratively, a stratification of management response to stakeholder influences is, thus, permissible (see Table 4.5).

The framework demonstrates that managers prioritise stakeholder salience. Thus, where environmental considerations are stipulated by ethically motivated investors, proactive strategies towards sustainable development ensue. In contrast, absence of environmental pressures diminishes the magnitude of firm response. Nevertheless, there is evidence from the interviewed companies that investors, regulatory bodies and animal rights organisations exert significant influence on firm behaviour. By conjuncture, therefore, it may hold that latent sustainability drivers recede within the confines of business ethics. At societal level, these dormant traits may subsequently become activated through increased environmental concern.

Observably, employee engagement is critical in developing, albeit limitedly, both semi-proactive and proactive stances towards sustainability, and may be the sole influence of reactive companies. This latter group will respond to regulations only if mandatory. In general they fail to recognise regulators as a stakeholder and may only incorporate environmental features as a component of good corporate citizenship—a pressure not exerted by present shareholder demands.

In short, only companies that engage and respond to all stakeholders in the left-hand column of Table 4.5 will be capable of instigating a proactive stance towards sustain-

STAKEHOLDER DRIVERS/ SUSTAINABILITY STANCE	*Reactive* (companies with **one** of the following pressures)	*Active* (companies with **all** of the following pressures)	*Proactive* (companies demonstrating significant stakeholder influence)
Environmental conditions attached with shareholder investment			✔
Shareholders with alternative ethical requirements	✔	✔	✔
Regulatory compliance	If mandatory	If mandatory	✔
Employee engagement	✔	✔	✔

Table 4.5 *A tentative framework demonstrating the influence of three key stakeholders in developing proactive sustainability practices within UK SME biotechnology companies*

ability. Those without shareholders stipulating environmental conditions, which 'accommodate' (Clarkson 1995) regulatory requirements and engage employees on environmental matters can be said to take an active stance. Reactive companies can be seen to be 'laggards' (Welford 1995): that is, they may respond only if forced to do so either by environmental regulatory requirements or by environmental initiatives taken by employees.

4.4 Conclusion

An interaction of legislative, employee and shareholder pressures conspire to stratify firms in the sample into those that are reactive (will only respond to legislative and shareholder demands), active (χ and A) or proactive (employee- and shareholder-driven) companies. Interestingly, therefore, shareholders' influences vary between groups. Thus, shareholders' interests may diverge between those of traditional and ethically inspired investors. Whether this is a response to good corporate governance among investors may be worth further investigation. If so, the intangible benefits may surpass the time and cost implications suggested to exist, generally, within the SME sector. Certainly two reactive companies have reported that they may become more proactive on the sustainability issue if pressurised by shareholders promoting good corporate governance practices. Interestingly, the one environmental champion of the group demonstrates such shareholder–firm characteristics. Important, too, in this company are the roles of employees in driving the sustainability agenda.

In general, employee motivation is viewed as critical throughout the group. Crucially, it is maintained through 'open' organic/semi-formalised organisational arrangements and promotes innovation within the firm. This management approach has allowed the environmental champion of the group to, reportedly, take its first steps towards managing a sustainability culture—a truly proactive stance. Consideration of company size, however, is important. Many of the firms are small (between 20 and 50), and as they grow they will face increasing complexity and regulatory pressures.

Formalised systems were witnessed in only two companies of the sample group (including company β). This approach provides an organised framework through which companies are able to manage increasing complexity. Such organisational arrangements may upset presently 'loose' systems and threaten the development of creative solutions required to drive sustainable development. Nevertheless, company β produces a compliance report with its annual report and indicates commitment to developing its environmental programmes. Clearly the organic/semi-formal behavioural characteristic witnessed by some members of the sample indicate that some organisations are attempting to balance both demands.

Although a varied response to implementing specific environmental schemes suggests potential for further progress, the development of a sustainability culture by companies in the group is slow. The key to successfully nurturing a sustainability culture within a biotechnology SME may reside within a balance between shareholder and legislative demands for companies to 'fit' environmental parameters into their strategic planning and for employees to 'stretch' the sustainability agenda.

Based on a sample size of seven companies, the findings of this study can be described as valid only within the confines of the uniqueness of small UK biotechnology companies. This follows the general logic of Yin (1994), who refers to the analytical generalisation of case studies. Hence it is to the theory that one generalises not to a population. Thus, if companies are from a similar sector (with the same characteristics) a comparison can be said to be valid.

What these findings imply for managers in this sector is that as company size increases it appears to become more susceptible to environmental pressures by investors, regulators and employees. This may be due to an integrated mix of demands stimulated by increased public exposure and the need to protect investors, and a greater internalisation of manufacturing functions (and the need for direct regulatory control). These demands could also be compounded by a workforce well versed scientifically and environmentally. Pressures from these stakeholders may increase as their numbers swell.

It is those managers that pay attention to areas such as good product stewardship (assess and reassess their product mix, nature of processes and resultant emission toxicity) that will determine the firm's ability to respond to stakeholder demands accordingly. Effective action by reactive and semi-reactive companies will place a new demand on currently proactive companies to remain competitive (not just in terms of profitability but in ability to engage stakeholders). This may require a growing need to be responsive to stakeholders calling for improved practices regarding sustainable development. It may also have implications for the development of good governance and citizenship strategies.

At present, the biotechnology sector remains heavily research-oriented. As commercialisation develops, the sector is likely to come under greater scrutiny concerning environmental affairs. This is exemplified by the well-publicised problems of commercialising genetic modification in plants. In terms of business ethics, too, the sector has featured heavily in the press over issues such as animal rights and embryo cloning. Subsequently, some managers in this sector have learned the importance of stakeholder engagement, beyond the confines of 'normal' business practice. In this study it is indicated that environmental and sustainability affairs emanate through stakeholder pressures. But why and how SME biotechnology companies seek to engage stakeholders more proactively needs further investigation. A useful start may be to understand the role of the British Biotechnology Industry Association as the central node within the stakeholder network.

Appendix

Interview guide

Section A: Business affairs

1. I would like to give you an opportunity to outline the company's mission statement.

2. What, in general terms, interests the company?

3. And how do you actually designate routine tasks?

4. Do you have a vision as to where the company is going?

5. Are there any stakeholders who may affect your strategic development?

6. What difficulties has your company come up against in implementing initiatives within the firm?

7. Have you come up against any specific hurdles? Perhaps you can explain how you overcame them?

8. What do you understand by the term 'accreditation to specific standards'?

9. And how have these standards been implemented?

10. What do you think your organisation learns from the above?

11. How do you think employee motivation and aspirations affect the implementation process?

Section B: Environmental affairs and sustainable development

12. What does the term 'environment' mean to you?

13. Why do you yourself think that the environment has become such a topical issue in society?

14. How will this affect your own quality of life?

15. Why do you think that, in general, businesses regard environmental issues as irrelevant to their activities?

16. What would you say are the most relevant environmental issues to the biotechnology industry?

17. And what do you understand by the term 'environmental initiative'?

18. Can you perhaps provide an example where you were unsuccessful or maybe had problems implementing environmental initiatives?

19. What is your understanding of environmental management?

20. How would you differentiate between sustainable development and environmental management?

21. What would you understand by the term 'sustainable development'?

22. Do you ask your suppliers about their environmental and social activities?

23. Why do you think firms rarely associate global sustainable development with their activities?

24. How would external pressures affect the introduction of environmentally sustainable practices within firms?

25. How would the supply chain affect the introduction of environmentally sustainable practices? And do you exert any pressure along the supply chain? Does this affect your business?

26. How would ethical issues in the company drive forward strategic thinking in terms of sustainable development?

POWER AND SOCIAL BEHAVIOUR
A structuration approach
to stakeholder networks[*]

Stephanie Welcomer
University of Maine, USA

Philip L. Cochran
Smeal College of Business, USA

Virginia W. Gerde
University of New Mexico, USA

The metaphor of a web has commonly been used to represent the relations between an organisation and its stakeholders. In this web of relations, actors can exchange information and resources, seek each other for advice and exert pressure. Essentially, the content of these exchanges embodies the myriad of possibilities inherent in human relations. Comprising links and actors, networks form from interactions, and in turn exert influences on actors via the resulting structure (Barley 1986, 1990; Monge and Eisenberg 1987; Brass 1995). From Giddens's structuration (1976, 1982) perspective, both subject (individual/organisation) and object (society/social network) are 'constituted in and through recurrent practices' (1982: 8). Thus, neither the forces that bring actors together, nor the effects of the structure on subsequent interactions have primacy—both are important in understanding organisational behaviour.

Influences on the structuring of relations and influence of structure are central to stakeholder theorists and practitioners. Begun as simple interactions between, say, supplier and firm, and between firm and competitors, the network of an organisation in turn structures the information received by the firm, resources available, reputation, community relations, etc. Though the firm is always an active participant in maintaining, creating and severing relations, it is also ever subject to pressures arising from this structure.

* We appreciate the comments of John K. Ford, Virginia R. Gibson, Ivan Manev and Harold Daniel on earlier versions of this chapter. Also, a portion of this research was funded by the Nicholas E. Salgo summer research grant.

Firm networks arise, according to stakeholder theory, because firms attend to survival and to ethical norms (Donaldson and Preston 1995; Freeman 1984). Survival can depend on firms securing key resources. If stakeholders have power over those key resources, the firm must attend to stakeholder interests. Ethical norms may dictate that firms demonstrate social responsibility or social responsiveness, once again involving interaction with stakeholders to address their issues. Stakeholder theory therefore would predict that, in general, those firms that perceive stakeholder power over a key resource to be high and emphasise social responsiveness will try to build networks in which they have many strong ties to stakeholders.

What effects might such networks have on firms? Network studies call attention to the effects of structure on actors' communicative activity, reputation, conflict and innovation. Specifically, a firm's networks dictate its access to others, independence from others, information quality, new information and speed of access to others.

To explore the impacts of stakeholder power and firm social responsiveness on network characteristics, we use a case-study approach, surfacing the networks formed between forest product firms and non-governmental stakeholders facing a contentious forest policy referendum. The specific questions we examine are: Does stakeholder power affect a firm's network? Does firm social responsiveness affect its network? And, what are the implications of specific network position on firm access to, and transmission of, information, conflict management and generation of innovation?

5.1 Social structure using the stakeholder perspective

Social structure is the pattern of interrelationships between social actors, specifically measured as a social network. A social network's basic unit of analysis is the relation, for a social network is a collection of units (or nodes) and the relations that tie, or do not tie, these nodes together (Alba 1982). Relational data:

> are the contacts, ties and connections, the group attachments and meetings, which relate one agent to another and so cannot be reduced to the properties of the agents, but of systems of agents; these relations connect pairs of agents into larger relational systems (Scott 1991: 3).

The results of network analysis, like maps, measure and depict the connections between nodes (individuals, groups, organisations). Whole networks reveal connections between all actors, showing the network as a system, such as structural equivalence, clusters and the overall density of the network.

Egocentric networks illuminate one actor's structural position, which is, 'The way a particular node is embedded in a pattern of ties' (Lincoln 1982: 4). Egocentric networks illuminate the extent to which an actor is central in the network, the actor's type of relations (e.g. working relation, advice relation, friendship), and the relations' strength (e.g. strong, weak), direction (e.g. reciprocated, one-way) and duration (e.g. short-term, long-term).

Network analysis, the intellectual heir to Moreno's social configurations (1934) and Konig's graph theory (1936), as developed in the work of Cartwright and Harary (1956), and Harary (1959), uses graphs to represent data. Graphs represent points connected by lines. The lines can capture directional data, denoting whether a relation is reciprocated, and can denote a positive (e.g. friendship) or negative (e.g. conflict) relation. Graph theory thus enables mapping paths between nodes. A path is defined as 'a connected sequence of lines, by which one can move from one point to another. A path has a length equal to the number of lines it contains' (Alba 1982: 52). Paths are effectively the social distance between one node and another. Depending on the types of link being measured, paths illustrate patterns of relationships, such as friendship, communication and influence, and indicate the extent to which an actor is central in the network. For example, one measure of centrality is closeness, or how easily a particular node can reach, and be reached by, other network members. For instance, a firm that communicates directly with a stakeholder organisation is, in network terms, closer to that organisation than a firm that indirectly communicates with a stakeholder through another firm. Applying social distance to stakeholder theory, firms can therefore range in closeness to their stakeholders, leading to varying abilities to obtain information, understand interests, solve problems and build trust.

Perhaps the most intuitive measure of an actor's centrality is its number of direct connections, called degree. Links directly to others are considered to be a measure of activity. One is considered to be more central or peripheral based on the relative number of connections with others in the network.

For forest products firms working on forest policy, stakeholder and network perspectives suggest that firms would have different types of structural positions, depending on stakeholder power and firm social behaviour.

5.2 The case: Maine's referendum to ban clear-cutting

The Maine forests have long provided a significant portion of the state residents' economic and recreational opportunities (cf. Coolidge 1963; Smith 1972; Judd 1988; Lansky 1992). Smith, in his history of the Maine woods, explains, 'The "northeast corner" of the United States is concerned primarily with one raw material and its manufacture. For that reason the central fact about Maine throughout its history is that Maine is lumber and lumber is Maine' (1972: 1). The importance of Maine's timber as a state economic base has continued into the late 20th century. As the Maine Forest Service states, 'Forests are Maine's most important natural resource—providing jobs, clean water and air, wildlife habitat and recreational opportunities. Maine's forests are key to the quality of life and economic prosperity of the citizens of the State' (Maine Forest Service 1995: 1). The forests, through recreation and manufacturing, account for an annual payroll of US$888 million and, overall, the 'contribution of the forest resource to Maine's economy exceeds US$7.5 billion' (Maine Forest Service 1995: 1).

Maine has 7.0 million hectares of 'commercial timberlands'—87% of the state's total land area (Maine Forest Service 1995: 1), which is the highest proportion of forest to land in the United States. Of these commercial timberlands, 96% are privately owned (Center for Research and Advanced Study 1987, quoted in Lansky 1992), an amount and dominance of private ownership unmatched elsewhere in the United States.

Northern Maine contains most of the forest harvested for timber. Because of its sparse population, much of northern Maine has been state-designated as the 'unorganised territories'.[1] The state agency that oversees land-use decisions in this area is called the Land Use Regulation Commission (LURC). Most of the 4.2 million hectares composing the unorganised territories has been owned and managed for timber or paper production by private and public forest products companies.[2] As the forest products industry has evolved, technological changes in harvesting, such as the introduction of herbicides and whole-tree cutters, and changes in market forces, such as firm ownership shifting from state-based ownership to multinational ownership, altered the nature of forest practices. To the public, one of the most obvious changes was an increase in the practice of 'clear-cutting'. Clear-cutting is 'a harvest greater than 5 acres in size that leaves less than 30 square feet basal area of residual trees per acre' (Maine Forest Service 1995).[3] With the increased use of clear-cutting came increased public concern about its effects on the forest ecosystem, and corresponding calls for a ban on clear-cutting. In late 1995, a group of citizens collected enough signatures to put a citizens' initiative on the ballot for a public state-wide vote in November 1996.

This referendum, 'The Citizens' Initiative to Promote Forest Rehabilitation and Eliminate Clear-cutting' (or, the Citizens' Initiative), pertained to the state's northern 4.2 million hectares, the unorganised territories. The referendum attempted to change the regulation of forest practices, most notably eliminating the practice of clear-cutting.[4]

This initiative had a number of stakeholder supporters, including state and nationally based organisations.[5] Its opponents included the state's governor, Angus King, prominent members of Maine's legislature, the forest products industry (represented by the Maine Forest Products Council) and some state and national stakeholders. They argued that, in general, the referendum would cause the state to lose a significant amount of jobs, income and revenue from taxes.

1   The unorganised territories are an official state-designated assignation used in locales that do not have a population base warranting local municipal organisation. Therefore a state agency, the LURC, oversees the ordinances and administration of the unorganised territories.

2   The LURC states, 'To visitors, much of this area may seem like wilderness compared to most of the rest of the Northeast; for those living or working in or near the mainland portion of the jurisdiction, however, logging roads and active timber harvesting clearly identify the region as a managed forest important to the forestry industry and segments of the recreation industry in the state (Maine Department of Conservation Land Use Regulation Commission 1997: 1).

3   Basal area refers to 'the area of cross-section of a tree stem, measured at 4.5 ft above the ground. The total basal area of trees per acre is a commonly used measure of stand density and stocking, and is directly related to stand volume' (Maine Forest Service 1995).

4   In brief, its major proposals included (Maine Forest Service 1996b: 1-2): the elimination of clear-cutting; limits on the amount of timber that may be harvested in a specified period of time and minimum residual stand volume, based on forest type, following harvesting operations; in a 15 year period, timber harvesting operations may not result in the removal of more that one-third of the volume on any acre, on a basal area basis of trees of commercial species greater than 4.5 inches in diameter at 4.5 feet above the ground; prohibits creation of openings in the forest canopy, by timber harvesting, larger than 0.5 acre; and requires that, after timber harvesting, a healthy, well-distributed stand of trees must remain with minimal damage to individual trees. The diversity of tree species, tree sizes and tree age classes in the residual stand must be maintained to the maximum extent possible.

5   These stakeholders included those with interests intersecting forestry: environmental, land conservation, recreation and property rights.

More specifically, the projected economic impact for 1997 on Maine's forest-related industries was estimated to be approximately 30,000 jobs and US$965 million in wages (Maine Forest Service State Planning Office 1996a: iii). In northern Maine, forest industries produce 62% of Maine's timber harvest. The Maine Forest Service estimated that the Citizens' Initiative would reduce the annual harvest of spruce-fir by 57% for the first 30 years and reduce harvest of northern hardwoods by 60% from current harvest levels (Maine Forest Service State Planning Office 1996a: ii). Key economic impacts included the loss of 15,600 jobs (2% of Maine economy), and a decline in wage and salary of US$439 million (4% of state total). Total state output was estimated to drop by US$1.3 billion (3% of state total) (Maine Forest Service State Planning Office 1996a: iii).

The impacts of the Citizens' Initiative were gauged by the forest products industry to be large, and mostly negative. (For instance, forest products newsletters in North Carolina, Pennsylvania and New Hampshire all carried articles detailing the issue.) The large landowners acted to try to counter the Citizens' Initiative with one less onerous. To do this, many formed networks with non-governmental state and national stakeholders to formulate alternatives to be placed on the ballot to compete with the Citizens' Initiative. Working with non-governmental stakeholders was especially important in this case, as the competing referendum needed to have the legitimacy of representing 'the people', not the government or solely industry.

The networks formed during that time are the subject of this chapter's examination. Stakeholder theory suggests that the network of each forest products firm would be influenced by the amount of power held by the stakeholders and by the social responsiveness of the firm. These ideas are more formally developed in the following sections.

5.3 Power and structural position

Resource dependence theory suggests that stakeholder power is based on external actor control over a key resource. That is, organisations will address a stakeholder's interests only if that stakeholder has some kind of control over key non-substitutable resources. Otherwise the firm can gain access to its resources without giving up control of its processes.

There are three factors that gauge the interdependence of a firm and stakeholder: the primacy of the resource, the amount of control the interest group has over the resource and the substitutability of the resource for the firm. These three factors indicate the degree to which stakeholders may have power over a firm. The primacy is 'the relative magnitude of the exchange and the criticality of the resource' (Pfeffer and Salancik 1978: 46), or how central the resource is to firm operations. The second characteristic is substitutability, 'the extent to which input or output transactions are made by a relatively few, or only one, significant organisations . . . the important thing is whether the focal organisation has access to the resource from additional sources' (Pfeffer and Salancik 1978: 50). The third characteristic is the firm's perception of the stakeholder's discretion over the key resource. This is 'the extent of discretion over the allocation and use of a resource possessed by another social actor' (Pfeffer and Salancik 1978: 47-48). This discretion comes through ownership, access and use, and from 'the ability to make rules or otherwise regulate the possession, allocation, and use of resources' (Pfeffer and Salancik 1978: 49). Because stakeholders often attempt to influence firm access to resources by imposing regulations, or other legislated forms of control, this is one of the main avenues stakeholders have to gain power.

Resource dependence theory predicts that, when there is interdependence, there will be increased firm efforts to work with the interest group:

> an organisation will comply with the demands of interest groups in accordance with its dependence on them. Failure to comply with the demands of an important interest group may lose an organisation the support of the group and disable its continuing operations (Salancik 1979: 376).

Interdependence stems from an external actor's ability to 'at present, or . . . potentially, provide or affect those [critical] resources' (Pfeffer and Salancik 1978: 84). When an external actor can provide or restrict availability of a critical resource, the firm's access to this critical resource is uncertain, possibly jeopardising firm survival. Because of this interdependence and uncertainty, the firm is predicted to make efforts to work with this important resource channel. These efforts to work together have implications for the firm's network.

> Those coalition participants who provide behaviours, resources, and capabilities that are most needed or desired by other organisational participants come to have more influence and control over the organisation, for one of the inducements received for contributing the most critical resources is the ability to control and direct organisational action (Pfeffer and Salancik 1978: 27).

Those firms that perceive stakeholders to have power will attempt to reduce the uncertainty generated by resource dependence by forming ties with these stakeholders in order to gain control over the resource. Also to reduce uncertainty, it is expected that firms perceiving stakeholders' power will generate stronger ties, as such ties provide more assurance of future relation (Granovetter 1982). Firms perceiving high stakeholder power will also attempt to minimise the distance between themselves and all other stakeholders, as this ensures more efficiency in passing information between the two (Bavelas 1948; Freeman 1978/79).

Hypothesis 1

For firms with high levels of resource primacy and non-substitutability, stakeholder discretion over a resource is positively associated with the number of direct ties between the firm and stakeholders.

Hypothesis 2

For firms with high levels of resource primacy and non-substitutability, stakeholder discretion over a resource is positively associated with strong ties between the firm and stakeholders.

Hypothesis 3

> For firms with high levels of resource primacy and non-substitutability, stake-
> holder discretion over a resource is negatively associated with the distance from
> the firm to each stakeholder.

5.4 Social behaviour and structural position

The stakeholder perspective suggests that firms address stakeholder interests not only because of stakeholder power but also because, from a normative perspective, stakeholders have an intrinsic right to be heard: 'The interests of all stakeholders are of *intrinsic value*. That is, each group of stakeholders merits consideration for its own sake and not merely because of its ability to further the interests of some other group' (Donaldson and Preston 1995: 67). In general there have been two approaches to the normative component of the stakeholder perspective. The first is to prescribe a particular ethical theory. Ethical theories such as the Kantian theory of value (Evan and Freeman 1993) and the pluralistic theory of property rights (Donaldson and Preston 1995) have been advanced. However, these approaches have been fraught with logical pitfalls (cf. Verstegen Ryan 1995). For instance, the pluralistic property rights approach of Donaldson and Preston draws from multiple ideas of distributive justice, including utilitarianism, libertarianism and social contract theory (Donaldson and Preston 1995: 84). Applying these theories to stakeholder interactions proves to be logically indefensible, as 'each of the three theories of distributive justice noted above rests on competing—and mutually exclusive—metaphysical, epistemological, and ethical foundations' (Verstegen Ryan 1995: 144).

A second approach attempts to describe managers' moral obligation by measuring firm moral obligation via top-management values and firm actions. The values of top management affect strategy formulation (Miles 1987; Freeman and Gilbert 1988), the degree to which managers formalise issues management activities (Greening and Gray 1994) and the evaluation of social issues (Sharfman *et al.* 2000). However, though top-management values play a part in the firm's behaviour, research also suggests that there can be a disconnect between top-management values and firm actions. Organisations may change their structure to meet the legitimacy requirements of industry, thus signalling conformity to outside expectations but not necessarily meeting them (Meyer and Rowan 1977; DiMaggio and Powell 1983). Organisations often use carefully chosen verbal communication to manage impressions (Brown 1994; Elsbach 1994; Salancik 1984). Therefore firms might espouse a credo of social responsibility but not follow through with corresponding actions (Wartick and Cochran 1985; Wood 1991; Wood and Jones 1995).

Stakeholders do not necessarily trust corporate pledges of upstanding citizenship and sensitivity (Welcomer *et al.* 2000) and so focus on firm processes, checking for the resemblance of firm pronouncements to actions (see Wondolleck 1996; Moore 1998; Banerjee 2000). This research suggests that what a firm *does*—the processes in which it engages to anticipate or respond to social issues—is important. These managerial and organisational processes of response have frequently been viewed as constituting a firm's corporate social responsiveness (Ackerman 1973; Ackerman and Bauer 1976; Frederick 1978; Rands 1991; Wood 1991).

Firms that emphasise responsive processes thus offer more forums for stakeholders to participate in firm processes (Deetz 1995). With social responsiveness, stakeholders have opportunities for 'institutional dialogues' (Calton 1996). Yuthas and Dillard (1999) suggest that, by providing mechanisms for stakeholder discourse, there will be more interaction. This leads to the following hypotheses:

Hypothesis 4

Firm emphasis on receptivity, stakeholder legitimacy and awareness of stake-holders is positively associated with the number of direct ties between firm and stakeholders.

Hypothesis 5

Firm emphasis on receptivity, stakeholder legitimacy and awareness of stake-holders is positively associated with strong ties between firm and stakeholder.

Hypothesis 6

Firm emphasis on receptivity, stakeholder legitimacy and awareness of stake-holders is negatively associated with the distance between the firm and stake-holders.

5.5 Method

To ascertain the influences of stakeholder power and firm social responsiveness on structural position, 12 forest products firms and 11 stakeholders were interviewed using a questionnaire. Such a single industry case-study design helped to ensure that organisa-tions faced similar resource constraints, and that interest-group pressure for policy changes affected all organisations (Wartick and Mahon 1994). Restricting the sample to only one industry controlled for organisation response differences due to contingencies intrinsic to industry characteristics (Dess and Beard 1984).

Firms were identified through archival and interview sources. Of the 15 large land-owners in Maine, 12 agreed to be interviewed. The procedure to identify the sample's stakeholders was a modified fixed list technique (Doreian and Woodard 1992), by which stakeholders were identified through a series of interviews with professionals knowledgeable about the industry and its ties specific to Maine. This list was presented to each informant, and checked for its completeness. If stakeholders were missing, they were added to the list. Therefore, the fixed list served as a base from which respondents could add additional stakeholders.

Two different questionnaires were used, one for firms and one for stakeholders. Both surveys were administered through verbal interviews, either on the telephone or in person. In total, 20 interviews were conducted with 12 firm members, and 20 interviews with 11 stakeholder members. The duration of the interviews ranged between half an hour and three hours.

5.6 Independent variables

Power was measured through four questions all on a 0–5 point Likert scale. The four questions gauge the criticality of the resource to the firm, the resource's substitutability, and the positive and negative discretion the firm rated each stakeholder as having over the resource. The firm's responses for each stakeholder's positive and negative power were then averaged (making 10 the maximum possible for each stakeholder), and summed across all stakeholders, for a possible maximum of 110.

Each organisation's social responsiveness was measured via three questions with a 0–5 Likert scale. These questions used a combination of firms' and stakeholders' reports of firm receptivity, awareness and legitimacy. In operationalising the response of companies to other actors in their social environment, Miles tested constructs developed in Sonnenfeld's (1981) analysis of the forest products industry. In Miles's study of the insurance industry, insurance commissioners rated the responsiveness of the 25 largest corporations in the United States. The three measures that were the strongest discriminators of social responsiveness were: the extent to which company executives listen and are **receptive** to information flowing from outside the company; the extent to which company executives are **aware** of potential public policy issues; and the perceived **legitimacy** of outsiders—the extent to which company executives respect the purposes of outside critics (Miles 1987: 76). Accordingly, stakeholder respondents were asked for their perception of the firm's receptivity to their organisation, and the degree to which they perceived the firm as seeing their organisation's interests as legitimate. Preparedness was measured as the firm's assessment of each stakeholder's openness to the firm. These three items were summed for a maximum of 15.

5.7 Dependent variables

A firm's number of direct ties, its degree, was measured as the sum of ties from stakeholder to firm or firm to stakeholder. Ties were counted if either firm or stakeholder said there was a relation (possible maximum of 11).

Strength of the tie was measured as the average responses to four questions, gauging the intensity of the tie. These questions were based on studies of communication between parties with overlapping interests. Relations of overlapping interests are often characterised by a series of successive conflicts and negotiations. Studies of such relations (e.g. Crowfoot and Wondolleck 1990) suggest that ties between parties that have multiple overlapping and conflicting interests often have a sequence of developmental stages in working together. In the first stage, the parties make some attempt to work together. Following this attempt, they try to listen to the concerns and interests of the other party, In the third stage, they work towards joint solutions, perhaps not achieving them, but more importantly working towards them. The last stage represents the degree to which the relationship has established a foundation of trust, thus predisposing the parties to work together in the future. Corresponding to these developmental stages, a set of four questions was constructed to assess the strength of the tie between firm and stakeholder. This is commensurate with previous network measures of strength using 'multiplexity': that is, multiple contents (e.g. information, advice, planning) that are exchanged (Kapferer 1969: 213). The more types of contents exchanged, the higher the tie's multiplexity.[6] Both stakeholders and firms were asked the same four questions regarding their tie, and these four questions were averaged (potential average maximum of 5). Therefore each tie strength had a potential maximum of $5 + 5 = 10$, and a total network tie strength potential maximum of $10 \times 11 = 110$. Closeness was measured as the number of links between the firm and all stakeholders.

5.8 Results

To consider the study's findings, three types of data are provided: graphs of power and social responsiveness versus firm structural position characteristics (degree, strength and closeness); networks of firms that perceived the highest and lowest amounts of stakeholder power, networks of firms that had the highest and lowest social responsiveness; and multivariate regression analysis of firm characteristics and network structural position.

Figure 5.1, the plot of power and degree, shows no visible pattern between stakeholder power and firm degree. Nor is there a discernible pattern in Figures 5.2 and 5.3, the plots for power and strength, and power and closeness, respectively. We expected that, as power increased, so too would degree and strength. We also expected that as power increased, closeness would decrease. From these graphs, no such relation is apparent.

The firm–stakeholder networks provide another illustration of these relationships. These networks depict the firms that perceive the highest and lowest amounts of stakeholder power and those firms with the highest and lowest amount of social responsiveness. Summary statistics and correlations are presented in Table 5.1.

The firm perceiving the lowest amount of stakeholder power is company 1, with a score of 44. Two networks (Figs. 5.4 and 5.5) show company 1's network. Figure 5.4 shows company 1 and all stakeholder ties. Figure 5.5 shows company 1 with only its direct ties. Company 1 has direct ties to 9 stakeholders (out of 11); has an average closeness of 13

---

6 Sometimes, the strength of a tie has been measured as the frequency of contact, following an argument that the longer the time of contact, the stronger the tie. Network research suggests, however, that frequency is a dubious indicator of tie strength (Marsden and Campbell 1984; Marsden 1990). Also, in his study of forest products firms, Sonnenfeld (1981) found that, when measuring the sensitivity of interactions between forest products firms and stakeholders, 'those companies spending more time with outside sources may not necessarily use that time to develop potential information sources. Rather, that time may perhaps be used to set up channels for one-way communication from the firm outward' (1981: 152).

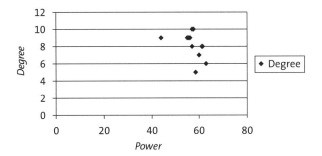

Figure 5.1 **Power versus degree**

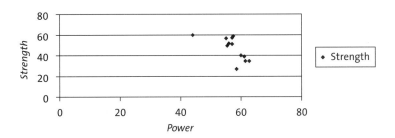

Figure 5.2 **Power versus strength**

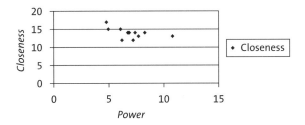

Figure 5.3 **Power versus closeness**

Variable	N	Mean	Standard Deviation	Power	Responsive-ness	Degree	Strength	Close-ness
Power	12	57	4.8	1.00 (0.0)	−.708 (.009)	−.312 (.323)	−.363 (.245)	.354 (.259)
Responsive-ness	12	7	1.6	−.708 (.009)	1.00 (0.0)	.624 (.03)	.773 (.003)	−.633 (.027)
Degree	12	8	1.5	−.312 (.323)	.624 (.03)	1.00 (0.0)	.785 (.003)	−.943 (.0001)
Strength	12	47	11.2	−.363 (.246)	.773 (.003)	.785 (.003)	1.0 (0.0)	−.792 (.002)
Closeness	12	14	1.4	.354 (.259)	−.633 (.027)	−.943 (.0001)	−.792 (.002)	1.00 (0.0)

Table 5.1 **Summary statistics**

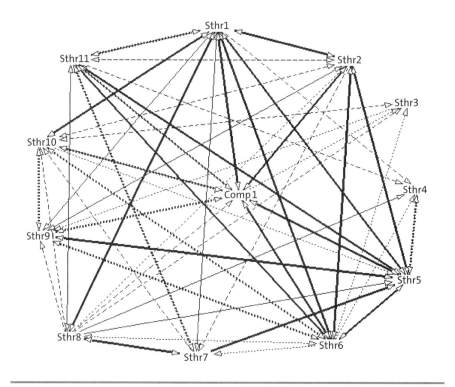

Figure 5.4 **Company 1 with all stakeholders**

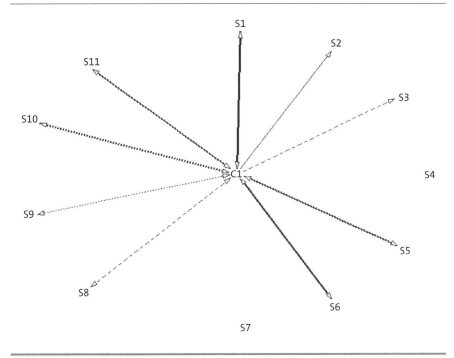

Figure 5.5 *Company 1 with only its direct connections to stakeholders*

links to reach all 11 stakeholders; and totals 60 for its tie strength (recall that the maximum is 110). In contrast, company 8 perceived the highest level of stakeholder power (62.75). Figures 5.6 and 5.7 show that it has five direct ties to stakeholders, a closeness of 17 links to reach all 11 stakeholders, and total strength of ties at 26.88. Thus the company perceiving the lowest power is actually more tightly connected in terms of degree, closeness and strength than the company perceiving the highest amount of stakeholder power.

Multiple regression analysis, with stakeholder power as the independent variable, and degree, closeness and strength as dependent variables, also suggests a weak relation between stakeholder power and firm structural position. Regarding the effect of social responsiveness on structural position, as firms' social responsiveness increases, structural position changed as well. The graphical plots illustrate firm social responsiveness versus number of direct links, strength of ties and closeness. For instance, Figure 5.8, social responsiveness versus degree, shows that, as social responsiveness increases, the number of direct ties does as well. In Figure 5.9, social responsiveness versus strength, the same trend is apparent. As social responsiveness increases, so too does the strength of the ties between firm and stakeholder. The plot of social responsiveness versus closeness, in Figure 5.10, shows the projected negative relation. As social responsiveness increases, the distance from each stakeholder to each firm decreases.

Regarding the networks of high and low social responders, companies 1 and 6 had the highest social responsiveness, with 10.8 and 8.27, respectively. In company 1's network

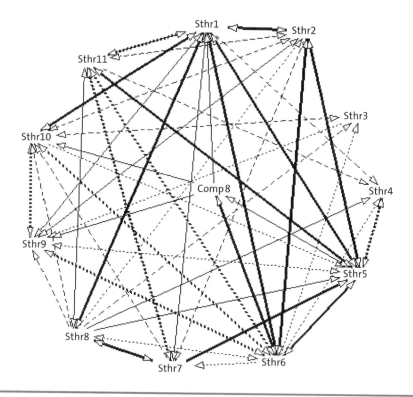

Figure 5.6 **Company 8 with all stakeholders**

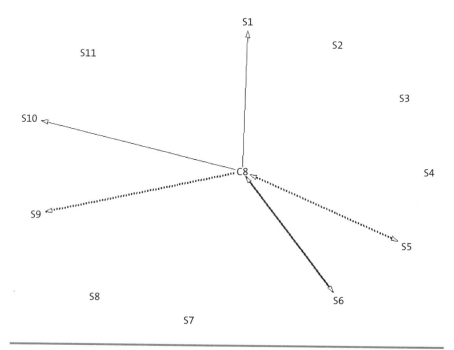

Figure 5.7 **Company 8 with only its direct connections to stakeholders**

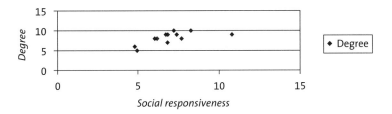

Figure 5.8 *Social responsiveness versus degree*

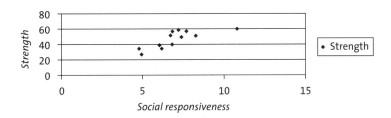

Figure 5.9 *Social responsiveness versus strength*

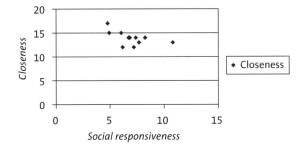

Figure 5.10 *Social responsiveness versus closeness*

(see Figs 5.4 and 5.5), the number of direct ties is 9, the average strength of ties is 60 and the closeness is 13. Company 6 (Figs 5.11 and 5.12), a firm also high in social responsiveness with 8.27, had 10 direct ties, with tie strength of 6 and closeness of 12. In contrast, the two lowest social responders, firms 8 and 12, show different structural positions. Firm 8, seen in Figures 5.9 and 5.10, with a social responsiveness of 4.95, had direct connections to five stakeholders, strength of ties of 26.88 and closeness of 17. Firm 12 (Figs 5.13 and 5.14), another low social responder at 4.8, had direct ties to 7 stakeholders, tie strength of 34.25 and closeness of 15.

Multiple regression provides another indicator of these trends, suggesting that a firm's social responsiveness may have an effect on firm structural position in stakeholder networks (see Tables 5.2, 5.3 and 5.4). For degree and social responsiveness, the model was significant at the 0.1 level, and for social responsiveness at the 0.05 level. For strength and social responsiveness, the model was significant at the 0.01 level, and for social responsiveness at the 0.01 level. For closeness and social responsiveness, the model was significant at the 0.1 level and social responsiveness was significant at the 0.1 level.

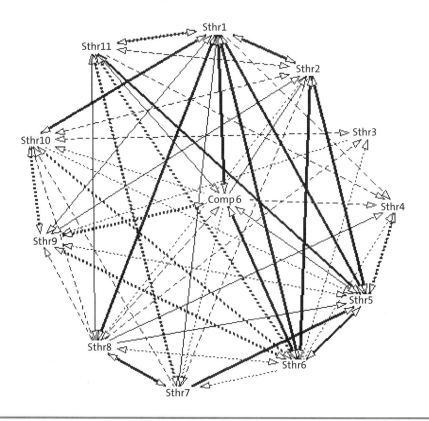

Figure 5.11 **Company 6 with all stakeholders**

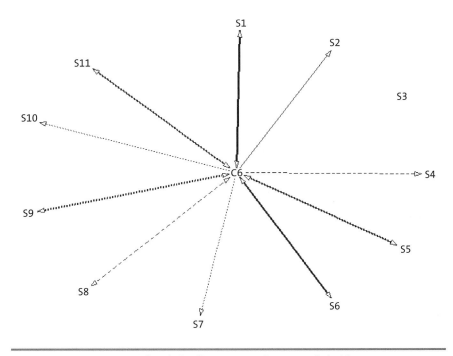

Figure 5.12 *Company 6 with only its direct connections to stakeholders*

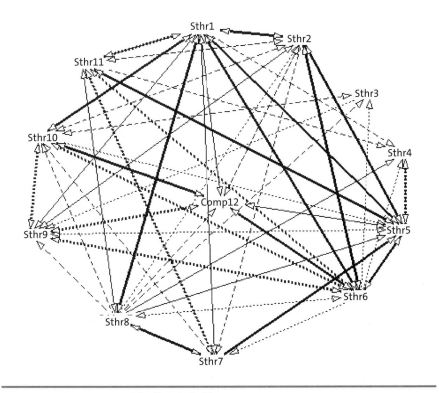

Figure 5.13 *Company 12 with all stakeholders*

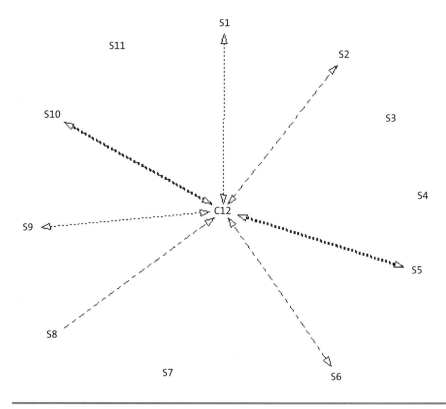

Figure 5.14 **Company 12 with only its direct connections to stakeholders**

Source	DF	SumSqs		Mean Square		F Value Prob > F			
Model	2	11.0102	5.5051	3.305		.0839			
Error	9	14.9898	1.6655						
C Total	11	26.0000							

Root MSE	1.2905	R-square	.4235	
Dep Mean	8.0000	Adj R-sq	.2954	
C.V.	16.1319			

Parameter estimates

						T for HO:			
Variable	DF	ParEst		Std Err		Parameter = 0	Prob > |T|		VIF
Intercep	1	-2.2460	8.4345		-0.266		.7960	.0000	
Power	1	.0831		.1141		0.728	.4850		2.0076
Respons	1	.7871		.3488		2.256	.0505		2.0076

Table 5.2 **Degree, power and social responsiveness**

Source	DF	SumSqs	Mean Square	F Value Prob > F			
Model	2	923.9242	461.9621		9.009		.0071
Error	9	461.4939	51.2771				
C Total	11	1385.4181					
Root MSE		7.1608	R-square	.6669			
Dep Mean		46.5008	Adj R-sq	.5929			
C.V.		15.3993					

Parameter estimates

				T for HO:			
Variable	DF	ParEst	Std Err	Parameter = 0		Prob > |T|	VIF
Intercep	1	–54.2193	46.8006	1.159		.2765	.0000
Power	1	.8627	.6332	1.363		.2061	2.0076
Respons	1	7.3609	1.9357	3.803		.0042	2.0076

Table 5.3 **Strength, power and social responsiveness**

Source	DF	SumSqs		Mean Square		F Value Prob > F			
Model	2	8.7498		4.3749		3.236		.0873	
Error	9	12.1668	1.3518						
C Total	11	20.9167							
Root MSE		1.1627		R-square	.4183				
Dep Mean		13.9166		Adj R-sq	.2991				
C.V.		8.3547							

Parameter estimates

						T for HO:			
Variable	DF	ParEst		Std Err		Parameter = o	Prob > |T|		VIF
Intercep	1	21.6912		7.5990		2.854	.0190		.0000
Power	1	–.0542		.1028		–0.527	.6107		2.0076
Respons	1	–.6695		.3143		–2.130	.0620		2.0076

Table 5.4 **Closeness, power and social responsiveness**

5.9 **Structure's effect on companies**

The structuration approach (Giddens 1976, 1982) suggests that structural context influences individual behaviour. In the networks presented in this study, firms' degree, strength and closeness have implications regarding power, information, conflict and innovation. Structure has an impact on operations through the 'avenues' of information, communication, conflict and innovation. For managers, the implications are that stakeholder relationships are important and can impact firms' potential to exchange information or exert influence.

Firms high in degree (i.e. having a higher number of direct ties) are more central in their networks than those firms low in degree. Measured as the number of direct connections between the firm and stakeholders, high-degree firms have the potential to communicate with a variety of stakeholders:

> As the process of communication goes on in a social network, a person who is in a position that permits direct contact with many others should begin to see himself and be seen by those others as a major channel of information. In some sense he is a focal point of communication, at least with respect to the others with whom he is in contact, and he is likely to develop a sense of being in the mainstream of information flow in the network (Freeman 1978/79: 219-20).

Firms high in degree are also likely to have access to more information and, therefore, to participate in more interactions.

With greater centrality, firms are more likely to have greater access to information, ability to communicate the firm's position or interests to its stakeholders, and potentially less conflict. Attitudes are also likely to be similar through repeated interaction. Erickson (1988) brings attention to the influence of connections in forming individuals' attitudes, noting that with interaction often comes attitudinal similarity. For instance, Kilduff's (1992) study of MBA decision-making found that MBA students' perceptions about job decisions were influenced by the attitudes of their close peers. Organisations central in a network will be in close proximity to stakeholders; thus attitude similarity is likely to be higher than in those firms on the network's margins. For firms that are peripheral in terms of degree, there are fewer opportunities to participate in this sense-making.

Closeness, the sum of the number of links it takes for an actor to reach all other actors in a network, also influences access to information. Firms close to many others are independent from reliance on other actors. For instance, in Figure 5.4, stakeholder 7 is dependent on stakeholder 6 or stakeholder 8 to reach company 1. If stakeholder 7 needs to communicate with company 1, stakeholder 7 is dependent on these actors not only to relay information, but to relay it accurately and in a timely manner. 'Short distances mean fewer message transmissions, shorter times, and lower costs' (Freeman 1978/79: 225).

Greater closeness enables more efficient information processing and co-ordination. Therefore, it is generally advantageous for the firm to improve the level of closeness within its network. If a resource is easily substitutable or the firm feels that stakeholders have little power over resources, it may choose to have fewer direct ties with stakeholders. Similarly, if there is strong competition within an industry or if a firm chooses to isolate itself, fewer direct ties may be desirable. For instance, if a firm is developing a new technology and it has the resources internally (research and development), it may choose to 'distance' itself from stakeholders to maximise its competitive edge.

A firm with strong ties is subject to positive and negative constraints. Positive effects of strong ties are that there may be less conflict in such networks. Nelson (1989) found that high numbers of strong ties between different groups were lower in conflict than those groups tied with weak ties. In engaging with stakeholders, firms strongly tied may have less conflict. Also, information flow and decision-making differ for those with strong ties. Strong ties transmit information more quickly and credibly. Particularly notable is the finding that 'Most of the influence is carried through strong ties' (Weiman 1980: 12). In a network, those with strong ties are most likely to be 'the players' in decision-making. 'The influence on the decision making is done mainly by the strong ties network within each group' (Weiman 1980: 21). For policy-making, the strongly tied firm would appear to have an advantage over the weakly tied firm.

Granovetter suggests that strong ties have a downside, in that those that form strong ties are most likely to be similar in attitudes, therefore relaying redundant information, 'empirical evidence that the stronger the tie connecting two individuals, the more similar they are' (Granovetter 1973: 1362). Innovative ideas are likely to come not from a strong tie but from a weak one. And, there is some empirical evidence that innovations spread more through weak ties than strong (Tushman 1977; Freidkin 1980; Granovetter 1982).

Structure can influence individual and organisational behaviour. With bounded rationality, an individual will see a limited number of options. Those options may be defined by the structural position. Stakeholder coalition building may not be an option, or a very expensive option in terms of resources, if firms have weak ties with specific stakeholders. The costs, risks and benefits of various options may vary depending on structural positions as well.

5.10 Social responsiveness

As stakeholders' perception of the firm's social responsiveness increases, the strength of ties and the degree, or number of ties, also increases. In addition, the closeness of the firm within the network seems to increase. Firms that stakeholders perceive to be socially responsive may have stronger and more direct ties and be more central in the network. Because stronger ties may help a firm to influence its stakeholders, this means it can be a competitive advantage for managers to improve stakeholder relations through inclusion in decision-making, sharing information or resources, or other firm behaviour designed to foster relations.

This research indicates that firm behaviour is likely to influence its structural position. Firms that are considered more socially responsive have stronger and more direct ties to stakeholders. The firm's behaviour is likely to influence that perception, so the organisation's policies, decisions and actions have an impact on the firm's centrality and perception of social responsiveness. For managers, this implies that programmes designed to reach out to stakeholder groups, to communicate and work with stakeholder groups, are likely to improve relations between the firm and its stakeholders.

The effect of these programmes may be seen in a variety of ways. An increased number of direct ties with stakeholder groups will provide more open channels of communication and possibilities for information-sharing and potential collaboration. Stronger ties indicate less conflict between the stakeholder and the firm, which may result in attitudinal similarity, thus increasing the overall influence of the firm. For example, if a regulation was proposed by a government organisation, and the firms and the special-interest groups had similar goals, they would be more able to form a coalition and work together if there were more direct and stronger ties. With weak, indirect ties to the special-interest groups, the firms and the interest groups may lobby for the same position but would not be as powerful as a coalition of stakeholder groups.

Stakeholder power may also influence structural position, although it was not found in this study. While a firm may perceive a stakeholder as having power over a resource, it may not behave in such a way to balance that power with a direct tie, closeness or strong tie. An intermediate 'variable' may be strategic actions taken by the firm. Further study controlling for strategy may provide additional insight.

Overall, the research supports Giddens's (1976) structuration theory that behaviour may influence structure and vice versa. Even if the causality is not clear, there is certainly a relationship or reflexive interaction within the network. A firm can take action to improve its position in its network.

5.11 Stakeholder theory

Stakeholder theory has become a core concept in management theory (Harrison and Freeman 1999). Understanding a firm's relationships with its stakeholders and their connections with each other may provide insight into firm behaviour and performance. Network analysis provides a framework for such study with an emphasis not on the individual groups as separate entities but on the relationships or interactions within the network.

This study reinforces that what firms do is important: what stakeholders perceive is important in the firm's success by influencing the network. Berman et al. (1999) concluded that stakeholder relationships and resource allocation decisions were inseparable. Managerial attention to the concerns of stakeholders, whether for instrumental or normative motivations, could influence the strength of ties with the stakeholder groups and the closeness with which a firm could obtain information and influence to promote the firm's interests.

Relationships with stakeholders can have a direct impact on a firm's ability to access information and the speed and quality of such information as well as to exert influence. The perception of social responsiveness is critical in the quality of stakeholder interaction, such that transparency of the firm's consideration of stakeholder concerns may increase the strength of the tie (Berman et al. 1999).

This study builds on resource dependence theory as well. Although stakeholder power was not shown to be significant in relation to a firm's structural position, there may be alternative models that include the variables of strategy, effectiveness, communication and effects of reputation. Theoretically, there is an increased effort to work together if there is interdependence, so an analysis of power from the outside in, or analysis of stakeholder perceptions of their saliency to the firm, may be helpful.

This study furthers our understanding of stakeholder relations and the roles of power, ties and social responsiveness in maintaining that web of relations. In this particular study, network theory is used to describe the networks and structural positions of 12 firms. Although stakeholder power, as part of saliency (Mitchell *et al.* 1997), was thought to be influential in a firm's network and structural position, this was not supported by these results. However, there may be other factors mediating the influence of stakeholder power, such as implementation of a firm's strategy or reputation.

5.12 Conclusion

In this chapter, we have used a structuration approach to explore the genesis of firms' networks with stakeholders, and we have explored the impact of network structure on firm operations. A firm's structural position can have significant impacts on its ability to attain and disseminate information, generate innovations, manage conflict and maintain long-term relations, suggesting that structural position has performance implications. The forces that influence firm structural position were the central target of this study. Our case study of 12 firms and 11 stakeholders suggests that stakeholder power does not play the role thought in positioning the firm as a central actor. Firm social responsiveness does, however, seem to be a notable influence in determining its network position.

Of course, from our study, with its small sample, only the most tentative of conclusions can be drawn. Also, the study was of one industry; other industries may behave differently. Further studies may examine other industries or include longitudinal assessments to research the influence of structural position on performance and the impact of behaviours and perceptions on the network structure. We hope that this study encourages further exploration of the structure and evolution of firm–stakeholder networks.

STATE OF THE UNION
NGO–business partnership stakeholders

Jonathan Cohen
AccountAbility, UK

In the post-Cold War era, globalisation of the marketplace has outstripped the ability of national governments to exert effective authority over business. Progressive non-governmental organisations (NGOs) have acted as a check to the negative aspects of global business expansionism (*Ecologist* 1993; French 2000). As NGOs grew in prominence their role transformed from calling for regulation of the private sector to resolve societal problems to actively seeking such solutions, at times in partnership with their former adversaries (Murphy and Bendell 1997).[1] A fundamental difference between NGO–business partnership interaction in the past decade and the limited interaction based on fundraising and project sponsorship that came before is that the focus is now on strategic relationships concerning the internal, operational side of core business practices (Murphy and Bendell 1997; Heap 2000). The past decade of NGO–business partnerships offers potential for new ways of tackling global problems.[2]

The purpose of this study is to examine a diverse group of NGO–business partnership case studies to learn from best and worst practices that can inform future partnerships. The partnership field remains new and fragile. The challenge ahead lies in creating a body of knowledge that stakeholders can easily reference before embarking on the path to partnership.

1 The definition of NGOs used here, as cited by Jem Bendell (2000), is 'organisations whose stated purpose is the promotion of . . . social goals rather than the achievement or protection of economic power in the marketplace or political power through the electoral process'.
2 Socially responsible business (SRB) can be characterised as encompassing a triple bottom line linked to financial, environmental and social indicators. Laurie Regelbrugge (1999) defines SRB as the practice of business's direct responsibilities to employees, shareholders, customers, suppliers and to the communities where it conducts business and serves markets. Stakeholders are defined as 'any group or individual who can affect or is affected by the achievement of an organization's purpose' (Freeman 1984) as cited by Bendell (2000) in *Terms of Endearment*.

What are the key characteristics—interpersonal and organisational—of partnerships between non-governmental organisations, businesses and their stakeholders? How do they affect success or failure? In order to achieve success, partners with the same interests join together, involve all with a relative stake, communicate effectively concerning partner interests, build trust, forge mutually agreeable goals, invest in building the relationship, respect partners' needs and interests, share partnership success, evaluate results against goals and alternatives, and then consider sustaining progress by institutionalising arrangements (Long and Arnold 1995). Partners can hail from diverse geographic locations, possess differing orientations and purposes, come in various shapes and operate under different codes. Partnership requires patience, commitment and the willingness to learn, but is not always the answer.

Different types of partnerships offer contrasting ramifications. Cases concerning codes of conduct, for example, offer more long-term engagement versus finite, project-oriented partnerships. How will the outcome of partnerships between NGOs and businesses be impacted if the stakeholders involved are different sizes, from different countries, different industries or focus on different issues?

6.1 The Long–Arnold matrix of partnership success factors

Frederick Long and Matthew Arnold's matrix of environmental partnership success factors, as delineated in their book *The Power of Environmental Partnerships* (1995), will serve as the theoretical framework for analysing 25 case studies of NGO–business partnerships (see Fig. 6.1). The framework is applicable to partnerships that cover issues other than the environment. Also, characteristics beyond those in the framework will be taken into account.

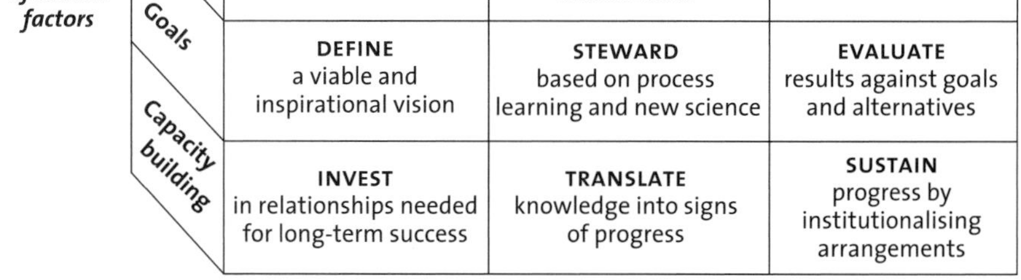

Phases of the partnership life-cycle

Categories of success factors		Initiation	Execution	Closure
	People	**INCLUDE** all critical stakeholders	**RESPECT** players' needs and interests	**SHARE** success and credit
	Goals	**DEFINE** a viable and inspirational vision	**STEWARD** based on process learning and new science	**EVALUATE** results against goals and alternatives
	Capacity building	**INVEST** in relationships needed for long-term success	**TRANSLATE** knowledge into signs of progress	**SUSTAIN** progress by institutionalising arrangements

Figure 6.1 *The Long–Arnold matrix of partnership success factors*

An additional characteristic of successful partnerships that will be examined is trust. Trust is a precondition for peaceful human relationships. Trust can mean absence of fear or, in a much stronger sense, the foundation of community and self-fulfilment. Without trust the 'other' can become an enemy instead of a potential ally or partner.

The Long–Arnold matrix of partnership success factors consists of three phases, initiation, execution and closure/renewal, and three categories within each of the phases, people, goals and capacity building (Long and Arnold 1995).

6.2 Phases of the Long–Arnold partnership life-cycle

6.2.1 Initiation

Initiation of a partnership entails including stakeholders that can bring relevant competences to bear on the task at hand, create credibility for the partnership process and communicate with the public at large. Participants with the authority to deliver their institutions are an important part of the process. Maintaining flexibility during this stage is helpful, as activities will become more defined in the subsequent execution phase (Long and Arnold 1995). The following are characteristics of the initiation phase:

- Partnership opportunity needs to be defined
- Participants should be identified
- The basis for working together must be formed
- The agenda needs to be created

6.2.2 Execution

Execution means translating the goals of the initiation phase into action. Effective communication is key to sustaining peaceful relationships between partners. It involves listening to and respecting partners, which can be difficult owing to diverse institutional cultures and values. This becomes all the more important as stakeholders have to adapt to the inevitable changes in a living partnership (Long and Arnold 1995). The following are characteristics of the execution phase:

- Ground rules need to be established and observed.
- Disputes must be resolved.
- Sufficient financing should be secured.
- Timetables need to be followed.
- Individual interests and relationship building must be developed.

6.2.3 Closure/renewal

Closure/renewal entails sharing success and credit for partnership activities as part of the relationship-building process. The level of sharing relates to the level of work and sacrifice contributed. Publicity of partnership documents plays an important role in this regard. In addition, learning from the evaluation of results in relation to goals is essential to the continuation of a partnership. The following are characteristics of the closure/renewal phase:

- Written agreements should be produced.

- Actions and policies must be implemented.

- Partnership activities need to continue or conclude.

6.3 Long–Arnold categories of success factors

6.3.1 People

People, more than any other aspect of NGO–business partnerships, will influence the chances of success. Strip away the theory and the rhetoric, and the concept of partnership is all about people from different backgrounds working together on a common goal. More specifically, the 'people' category encompasses those involved with creating a sense of ownership in the partnership on the part of stakeholders, forging relationships between stakeholders, and carrying out the nuts-and-bolts work to turn ideas into reality (Long and Arnold 1995). While it is institutions that will expend credibility and resources in a partnership, it is the people that make up those institutions that will or won't make it work. The following are Long–Arnold success factors related to people:

- Commitment to issues involved in partnership is needed.

- Commitment to establishing the relationships necessary to ensure the partnership's success is needed.

- Participants must be invested with the authority to make decisions.

- Participants should act as partnership champions within their organisation.

6.3.2 Goals

Goals to achieve socially responsible ends 'are the driving force for partnerships' (Long and Arnold 1995). The drive to accomplish that which a partner cannot accomplish on its own, without the skills of another sector, gives rise to the partnership process. Goals are the glue that binds together partners with different missions. Translating goals to strategy and then to action are crucial links in the life of a successful partnership (Long and Arnold 1995). The following are success factors related to goals:

- Viable goals need to be jointly defined.

- Effective goals must be realistic.

- Clear work plans need to be established that are based on agreed principles.

- Strategies that match the particular objectives of the partnership are needed.

- Action that can be planned, held accountable and evaluated in order to determine success must take place.

6.3.3 Capacity building

Capacity building entails building the means to carry out progress in realising partnership goals. It is the tangible and intangible bricks and mortar that hold together the people and goals of a partnership. Key to this is ensuring that partnership activities can be carried out in a sustainable manner over time (Long and Arnold 1995). The following are success factors related to capacity building:

- Resources need to be mobilised.

- An equitable management structure must be established.

- Each partner's competences should be brought to bear on achieving the agreed goals.

The categories of success factors are inextricably intertwined with the phases of the partnership life-cycle. 'People', for example, forge relationships in the initiation phase that will mature and evolve, which will help to avoid process breakdowns in the execution stage. Such breakdowns can take place in any of the three partnership phases. Another example would be when all relevant people are not involved in a partnership, and crucial viewpoints are not included in the development of an appropriate organisational structure. This can ensure failure in later phases (Long and Arnold 1995).

Long and Arnold argue that 'the matrix enables practitioners and students to quickly assess what is needed to make a partnership a viable, functional and, ultimately, durable solution to a particular problem' (Long and Arnold 1995). The matrix embodies an ideal partnership. Consequently, even successful partnerships will not necessarily fit neatly into all nine primary success factors. The cases examined below possessed enough of these characteristics to be considered worth the investment by partners in all save one instance. Partially successful cases exhibited fewer of these characteristics, which is helpful in analysing beyond the simple notion of success or failure.

6.4 Case sample

The sample of partnership case studies examined was chosen based on the following categories:

- Numbers: 25 cases will be examined.

- Geography: each region of the world will be represented.

- Issues: cases involving the environment, economic development, labour and human rights will be chosen.

- Partners: only NGO–business cases will be chosen.[3]

- Industry: companies from a variety of industries will be represented.

The 25 partnership case studies include pairings of transnational businesses and transnational NGOs, local businesses and local NGOs, transnational businesses and local NGOs, and even transnational NGOs and local businesses, reflecting the complexity of the partnership phenomena. The range of partners and pairings offers stark contrasts in goals, operating styles, culture and process versus outcome orientations among stakeholders. The sample solely covers partnerships with NGOs and businesses as the principals, and offers a representative snapshot rather than an exhaustive inventory of cases.

The two most frequent reasons for cases not being included among the 25 were the involvement of government in the operational side of the partnership and the lack of quality information in descriptions of the partnerships. The lack of a common definition for what constitutes a case study resulted in vastly different levels of quantity and quality in available partnership information.

Sources of partnership cases included:

- Organisations that research NGO–business partnerships, such as the International Business Leaders' Forum, Japanese Center for International Exchange, New Academy of Business and the United Nations

- NGOs involved in partnerships, such as the World Resources Institute

- Academics that research NGO–business partnerships

One case study, 'Environmental NGO–Business Collaboration and Strategic Bridging: A Case Analysis of the Greenpeace–Foron Alliance', was obtained by responding to an offer of a limited supply through an e-mail discussion list. An issue of *Greener Management International* devoted to partnership case studies was obtained through a colleague's reference. Other cases were obtained by a response from a keynote speaker—Interface CEO Ray Anderson at the first New Jersey Sustainable Business Conference—to a question by the author.

The names of the participants involved in one of the cases—a failed partnership—will not be disclosed in the study because of the NGO's sensitivities concerning the business partner. The NGO maintains relations with the business, and would like to keep it that way, in order to possibly engage in a partnership in the future, or at least not be negatively impacted by an entity with vast resources at its disposal.

Representative cases among the 25 will be explored in the context and order of the three phases and categories of the partnership life-cycle, with accompanying analysis encompassing the remaining cases.

---

3   Only NGO–business partnerships were chosen for study owing to the recent emergence of both as powerful global forces in the context of a decline in government. Due to the changing nature of NGO–business interaction, from a largely adversarial history to one of increasing co-operation, co-operation proved to be particularly compelling subject matter.

Section 6.5 provides an overview of the partnership initiation phase by examining five very different cases. The cases encompass a global multi-stakeholder partnership surrounding the timber industry; a local, one-to-one approach in India concerning human resources in an NGO; a sub-national multi-stakeholder case in Venezuela's tourism industry; a US multiple-location and multi-stakeholder effort regarding the apparel industry; and a local, one-to-one Thai case focusing on grass-roots economic development.

Section 6.6 examines the partnership execution phase through the lens of four cases. Examples include a pair of national, one-NGO-to-many microcredit business cases in Bangladesh; a US–Ecuador multi-stakeholder effort regarding sustainable biodiversity products; and a one-to-one US case between a media conglomerate and a one-person NGO concerning human rights education.

Section 6.7 explores the partnership closure phase by looking at six cases. The section views cases involving a US–Dominican Republic multi-stakeholder effort in the apparel industry; a US–Guatemalan multi-stakeholder case concerning the energy sector; a one-to-one US case in the fast-food industry; a one-to-one German case in the manufacturing sector; a national multi-stakeholder case in Vietnam addressing healthcare; and a global multi-stakeholder example surrounding the fishing industry.

The pairing of real-world NGO–business partnership examples with concepts that point to success or failure aims to help future practitioners. An examination of a large number of diverse partnership cases in terms of geography, issue, industry, as well as size and number of partners, attempts to combine factors that have been explored piecemeal previously.

6.5 Initiation phase

The initiation phase of the Long–Arnold matrix of the partnership life-cycle includes three categories: people (the inclusion of all stakeholders), goals (defining a viable and inspirational vision) and capacity building (investing in relationships needed for long-term success) (Long and Arnold 1995).

6.5.1 People: the inclusion of all stakeholders

Two questions will be explored: (1) To what extent are all stakeholders included in partnerships; and (2) What role, if any, do partnership brokers play in the inclusion of all stakeholders?

(1) The Forest Stewardship Council exemplifies the challenges involved in attempting to include all stakeholders in a partnership. The creation of the Forest Stewardship Council stemmed from the willingness of the UK-based WWF (formerly known as the World Wide Fund for Nature), the world's largest independent conservation NGO with more than 5 million supporters, to work with the timber industry at the same time that other NGOs were engaged in direct-action tactics against them. Starting in the early 1990s, NGO direct action aimed at changing timber industry policy and consumer choice drove business to the negotiating table. In fact, WWF sought out wood product retailers and suppliers—led

by the do-it-yourself retailer B&Q—following failed attempts to change the policies of timber companies that did not interface directly with consumers (Murphy and Bendell 1997).

A multi-stakeholder founding group engaged in 18 months of preparatory work to forge the Forest Stewardship Council (FSC). An international NGO was established that could serve as a standard-setting body with a system for verifying good forest management claims worldwide. Following protracted negotiations, the first FSC board featured two representatives from the private sector and seven from NGOs, certifiers and individual experts. Five of the nine board members hailed from the Southern Hemisphere and four from the Northern Hemisphere (Murphy and Bendell 1997).

The FSC logo and labelling system would not be launched until early 1996, however. Part of the delay stemmed from the commitment to involving a wide range of stakeholders, which made for a lengthy and often contentious decision-making process due to the wide range of different opinions that had to be synthesised into agreement (Murphy and Bendell 1997). Stakeholders need to strike the ideal balance between including all stakeholders, as the Long–Arnold matrix of partnership success factors suggests, and slowing progress towards later phases of the partnership life-cycle.

(2) As the business and NGO sectors have been traditional adversaries and have only been working together in partnership relatively recently, a third party that can facilitate co-operation between the two would seem to play a crucial bridging role. Partnership brokers, who will be defined as an intermediary between different parties to facilitate interaction between them, can play such a role (Tennyson and Wilde 2000). Approximately one-third of the 25 partnership cases utilised a broker (see Table 6.1). Perhaps the most important role of a broker is to foster trust among stakeholders in a partnership. For these reasons, a broker that commands respect, can bring stakeholders together and moves the proceedings forward can be key to success (Winer and Ray 1994; Tennyson and Wilde 2000). The for-profit sector clearly needed more help in this regard than NGOs. Every case save one that featured a broker involved business as the initiating stakeholder.

A.T. Kearney, an international US-based consulting firm, began operations in India in 1997 and sought an NGO with which to partner. A.T. Kearney asked a public relations company for help in becoming involved in a socially responsible project, and was referred to Partners in Change (PiC), an Indian NGO that brokers NGO–business partnerships. A meeting was set up between the two at which it was determined that the consultancy could provide the greatest contribution by sharing its expertise in developing human relations strategies. The NGO Deepalaya works with poor children in the slums of New Delhi, India. Deepalaya had explored partnership possibilities with corporations, but was stymied by the lack of staff and board connections with the corporate world, and the business stereotype that NGOs were unprofessional and inefficient (Action Aid 1999).

PiC knew that Deepalaya needed help because of rapid growth and an increase in services that had led to higher attrition rates among staff, increased morale problems and even a strike. PiC set up a meeting between A.T. Kearney and Deepalaya which resulted in an agreement on the scope of the partnership. PiC and Deepalaya gave a joint presentation to all of A.T. Kearney's staff and, subsequently, the latter gave a presentation explaining the process of consulting to the NGO. A.T. Kearney also kept its own staff informed of the project's progress via informal briefings, as the inclusion of indirect stakeholders

Primary stakeholders NGO/business	Location	Initiators/ brokers	Media	Codes of conduct
1. Deepalaya/ A.T. Kearney	India	Business/yes	No	No
2. Katha Khazana/ Taj Mansingh Hotel	India	Business/yes	No	No
3. Integrated Rural Development Trust/ Titan Industries	India	Business/yes	No	No
4. International Resource for Fair Trade/B&Q	UK– India	Business/yes	Yes	Yes
5. Fair Labor Association (multiple stakeholders)	US– multiple	Government/yes	Yes	Yes
6. Oxfam/ Levi-Strauss	US– Dominican Republic	Business/yes	No	Yes
7. Grameen Bank/ microbusinesses	Bangladesh	Individual/no	No	No
8. Grameen Telecom/ microbusinesses	Bangladesh	Individual/no	No	No
9. Paria Project Foundation/ Corpomedina	Venezuela	Business/no	Yes	No
10. Winrock International/ Monsanto	US– Africa	NGO/no	No	No
11. Appropriate Technology Association/Panmai Group	Thailand	Business/no	No	No
12. Fundación Café Forestal/ Coocafe	Costa Rica– Germany	Business/no	Yes	Yes
13. Rainforest Alliance/ Platanera Rio Sixaola	US– Costa Rica	NGO/no	Yes	Yes
14. Rainforest Alliance/ Chiquita	US– Costa Rica	NGO/no	Yes	Yes
15. Greenpeace/ Foron Household Appliances	Germany	NGO/no	Yes	No
16. Dana Mitra Lingkungan/ Aqua Golden Mississippi	Indonesia	Business/no	No	No
17. World Wide Fund for Nature/ B&Q (FSC)	UK– multiple	NGO/no	Yes	Yes
18. World Wide Fund for Nature/ Unilever (MSC)	UK– multiple	NGO/no	Yes	Yes
19. Environmental Defense Fund/ McDonald's	US	NGO/no	Yes	No
20. Conservation International/ multiple businesses	US–Ecuador	NGO/no	No	No

Table 6.1 *Location/initiators and brokers/media/codes of conduct* (continued over)

Primary stakeholders NGO/business	Location	Initiators/ brokers	Media	Codes of conduct
21. Conservation International/ McDonald's	US– Costa Rica– Panama	Business/no	Yes	No
22. World Resources Institute/ Applied Energy Services Corporation	US– Guatemala	Business/yes	Yes	No
23. World Resources Institute/ Applied Energy Services Corporation	US– Latin America	Business/no	Yes	No
24. Save the Children/BP	UK–Vietnam	NGO/no	No	No
25. Small human rights NGO/ large media conglomerate	US	Individual/yes	Yes	Yes

TOTALS:

Location	Initiators/ brokers	Media	Codes of conduct
US–Latin America 7	Business . . . 12	Yes 14	Yes 8
Asian Subcontinent . . 5 (India and Bangladesh)	NGO 9	No 11	No . . . 17
UK–multiple 2	Individual 3		
US 2	Government . 1		
Asia 2			
US–multiple 1	*Brokers*		
US–Africa 1	Yes 8		
Latin America 1	No 17		
UK–India 1			
UK–Vietnam 1			
Costa Rica–Germany . 1			
Germany 1			

Table 6.1 (continued)

also proved to be important (Action Aid 1999). The business was clearly committed to achieving partnership success, although the commitment of the NGO's board was questioned. Without total commitment by both sides, partnership success was not guaranteed. This case was also notable in that it focused on the internal operations of the NGO, rather than the business. The Long–Arnold matrix of partnership success factors applied to cases that involved the internal operations of both businesses and NGOs. Also, including all stakeholders occurred across businesses and NGOs as well as within them.

6.5.2 Goals: defining a viable and inspirational vision

The establishment of goals must take place in the initiation phase of the partnership life-cycle, as these agreed ideas serve as the basis for the success or failure of subsequent phases. Goals of successful partnerships spell out both purpose and process (Long and Arnold 1995). They also involve the inclusion of stakeholders to develop goals that represent the interests and aspirations of those impacted by a partnership. Fourteen of the cases in this study involved the media as a stakeholder, and all of those cases featured consumers as a stakeholder. The goal on the business side was to publicise the social responsibility of products or services, enhance business image and of course boost sales. While NGOs may not necessarily share the latter two business goals, they coincide with the first in terms of translating consumer concern and pressure into business action in support of an aspect of their mission. This intersection of goals between direct stakeholders forges the basis for a partnership.

Partnership stakeholders include the NGO and business partners directly involved in carrying out a partnership as well as other, indirect stakeholders, which exert influence of a different kind on the direct partners. Such influence can change or limit the behaviour of direct partners, as with the FSC case, when pressure by indirect NGO stakeholders led timber companies to agree to meet with WWF concerning their operations. That convergence of direct and indirect partner action lies at the heart of the partnership paradigm, which is represented by a partnership stakeholders Venn diagram (Fig. 6.2).

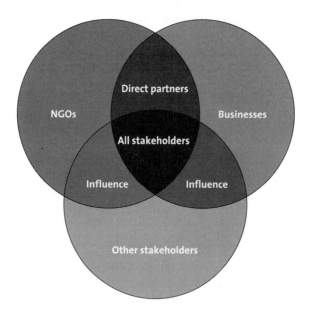

The intersection of stakeholder goals forges the basis
for the partnership paradigm.

Figure 6.2 **Partnership stakeholders**

Examples of partnership goals include: (1) training the poor; and (2) establishing codes of conduct for business behaviour.

(1) The challenges of goal setting between the divergent objectives of an NGO, a business and other stakeholders are exemplified in the case of the Paria Project Foundation (PPF) and the tourism and real estate business that founded it, Corpomedina. At issue was the proposed size of an ecotourism project in Venezuela. Corpomedina established and funded PPF to separate its community relations function due to the anti-business climate in the region (WRI 1994).

The company planned a large ecotourism development project that would act as a catalyst to improve the socioeconomic conditions of the Paria Peninsula's communities (some of the poorest in the country), preserve its environment and enhance the company's business as well. Corpomedina had garnered positive press for a pilot project it launched to test the market, the attitude of the local people, and the capacity and receptivity of the local labour pool. As part of the larger project Corpomedina invested in the ongoing education of its employees, many of whom were illiterate (WRI 1994). In addition to creating employment from the ecotourism development, PPF began rural micro-enterprises, or very small businesses, such as handicrafts, fishing, carpentry and sweet shops.

Consequently, Corpomedina had difficulty understanding how its offspring could disagree on the size of the proposed 360-room project, which the latter felt the Paria communities were unprepared to handle. Corpomedina almost went so far as to exclude those that did not agree on the project size from involvement with PPF. Eventually the business and the NGO met 'without preconditions', discussed the project, and agreed on scaling back its size to 250 rooms, the size of a similar project in Cuba. The control that Corpomedina possessed over the partnership's ground rules almost derailed the Long–Arnold matrix of partnership success factors. The negative media Corpomedina would have engendered had it purged dissenters from PPF could have soured an already sceptical local population concerning the company's intentions. The media also played a role in cases with codes of conduct (WRI 1994).

(2) Eight of the 25 cases in this study featured goals that dealt with certifications or codes of conduct to which business partners submitted (see Table 6.1). Seven of the eight certification cases also featured the media as a stakeholder (see Table 6.1). Goals in these cases developed as a response to the failure of effective governmental action (Murphy and Bendell 1997; Elkington and Fennell 1998).

Apparel companies, labour unions and other NGOs met in the aftermath of the Kathie Lee Gifford sweatshop scandal in April 1996 to discuss the need for labour standards that could combat sweatshops. The apparel industry was represented by businesses such as Liz Claiborne, L.L. Bean and Nike. Unions and groups such as the National Consumers' League and the Lawyers' Committee for Human Rights were involved along with academia. The partners released an agreement in April 1997 that included a 'Workplace Code of Conduct' and 'Principles of Monitoring' for the apparel industry (Hemphill 1999).

Issues addressed in the code included forced and child labour, workplace discrimination, health and safety, freedom of association and collective bargaining, hours of work, and of course salary and benefits. The principles called for companies to establish written standards for the workplace, monitor compliance with the standards, collect data on and audit the monitoring, ask for information concerning compliance from interested stakeholders, and set up a remediation process. Independent external monitors were to conduct inspections of a sampling of company and contractor facilities with total access, and report on the findings as well as recommendations (Hemphill 1999).

In 1998 the case partially broke up, however, due to a fundamental disagreement over a key aspect of the negotiations concerning goals. Key players—the garment workers' union UNITE and the Retail, Wholesale and Department Store Union, as well as the Interfaith Center for Corporate Responsibility—dropped out of the partnership negotiations following a disagreement. It was over the idea of a living wage, or a wage that meets basic human needs as opposed to a minimum wage, a higher percentage of factories that would be externally monitored, and operations in countries with poor labour rights records. A more moderate but less representative group survived. The remaining partners established an NGO, the Fair Labor Association (FLA), to carry out the earlier agreements that would allow companies in good standing to use the FLA symbol on products and in advertising (Hemphill 1999).

Non-industry stakeholders considered some aspects of the goals that dealt with monitoring to be weak. Only 10% of manufacturing facilities, for example, are monitored annually for the first three years, with as little as 5% thereafter. Questions have also been raised about the acceptable number of hours worked in a week, as well as overtime allowed (Benjamin 1999). The partners that left over the living wage issue did not achieve all of their goals, but did succeed in obtaining recognition of the right to freedom of association and collective bargaining under the code. The limits of shared partnership goals between stakeholders with competing interests had been reached. Understanding the goals and aspirations of the various partnership stakeholders is key to building the capacity to achieve them.

6.5.3 Capacity building: investing in relationships needed for long-term success

Partners laid the groundwork for capacity building in the initiation phase by making presentations to key stakeholders about organisational structure and decision-making processes, and investing in staff time, research and training. Communication between partners and with stakeholders that have the capacity to implement or prevent partnership results proved to be a crucial element of success.

The Appropriate Technology Association (ATA), a development NGO, and the Panmai Group, a rural Thai community business group formed by women, created a partnership in 1985. The partners worked together to determine an activity around which the women could organise themselves. The main objective throughout the development of the Panmai Group was to instil the concept of self-reliance in the community. Members were to be involved in all levels of activity and decision-making. ATA and the women organised a series of discussions, study visits and training sessions. Consultations were held with various stakeholders, including the women's husbands, in order to analyse the problems of the community and their causes. A feasibility study indicated that the weaving of traditional materials, an activity in which the women were already involved, was an activity around which the women could organise themselves (Japanese Center for International

Exchange 1999). The partners clearly demonstrated the commitment needed to establish the relationships necessary to ensure the partnership's success.

Effective communication in capacity building also entails reaching out to other members of the same sector. During partnership initiation Murphy and Bendell recommend that businesses 'inform contacts in trade associations and other professional bodies' about the partnership. They also recommend that NGOs 'inform counterparts in [other] groups working on similar issues' about the partnership (Murphy and Bendell 1997).

Including all stakeholders required a representative constituency that incorporated the views of indirect stakeholders. Partnership brokers played a role in making this happen in approximately one-third of cases by bringing stakeholders together and fostering trust between them. The intersection of interests between stakeholders defined viable and inspirational partnership goals, although this was not always without difficulty owing to the fundamental differences in mission. Patterns concerning goals featured the prominent role of media and consumers in increasing the market for socially responsible products in 14 cases, as well as in seven of the eight codes of conduct cases (see Table 6.1). Media pressure fuelled the process of partnership formation in addition to consumer purchases. Local actors, however, were often conspicuously absent from goal-setting processes. Building capacity involved communication with key stakeholders about partnership structure and process, and investment in staff time, research and training. The partnership initiation phase required a notable investment of resources and time, but it was necessary to progress to the execution phase, and was well spent in the end (Alliance for Environmental Innovation 1999; Regelbrugge 1999).

6.6 Execution phase

Where the participants were identified, the basis for working together and the opportunity defined, and the agenda created in the initiation phase, the execution phase represents the concrete activity that carries out those plans.

The execution phase of the Long–Arnold matrix of the partnership life-cycle entails three categories: people (the respect of players' needs and interests), goals (stewardship based on process learning) and capacity building (translation of knowledge into signs of progress) (Long and Arnold 1995).

6.6.1 People: the respect of players' needs and interests

Opportunities for communication between stakeholders, more than any other characteristic, were required in order to achieve successful partnerships. Communication in this sense meant taking into account the views of stakeholders that were not normally consulted, and respecting the potential of unproven partners. The trust built up by efforts taken in this category laid the groundwork for moving from establishing the basis for working together in the initiation stage to building the relationship in the execution stage.

The Grameen Bank, and consequently the Grameen Telecom case, turned on the respect that its founder, Professor Muhammad Yunus, had for the capability of poor, rural villagers in Bangladesh to take the responsibility of collateral-free credit and learn new skills starkly at odds with traditional customs.[4] Grameen came about as a result of informal communication between Professor Yunus and villagers. It was also viable because of informal communication he had with established banks. The banks did not respect the needs and interests of the poor, rural Bangladeshi women and refused to loan them money, despite larger and larger successes by Professor Yunus in doing exactly that. The Grameen Bank case featured a mechanism whereby poor, rural women formed groups of five from the same village with joint liability for repaying loans. Disbursement of loans took place only after approximately one month of training meetings dedicated to learning about Grameen and memorising its 16 decisions concerning social conduct. The Grameen method has resulted in increased respect by the women for themselves and each other. The star success stories in the Grameen Bank went on to receive respect and further credit, literally, when chosen as candidates for retailing phone services by Grameen Telecom based on their demonstrated ability to learn new skills and on past borrowing records (Hashemi 1997). While viable goals were not jointly defined between borrowers and Grameen, as the Long–Arnold matrix of partnership success factors recommends, partnership activity was held accountable and evaluated in order to determine success.

6.6.2 Goals: stewardship based on process learning

Stewardship refers to a model of behaviour in which partners place a higher value on being supportive of the partnership than on acting self-servingly (Davis *et al.* 1997). Trust between partners is needed in order to follow agreed processes and carry out strategic goals as a partner relationship moves forward. Goals that provide benefit to each partner can come about through the establishment of jointly defined, realistic work plans based on agreed principles. Plans drawn up by one partner without the input of another risk not allowing each to have a stake in the process.

Conservation International (CI), a Washington DC-based transnational NGO that works to conserve global biodiversity, and Fundación de Capacitación e Investigación para el Desarrollo Socioambiental (CIDESA), a national community development organisation based in Ecuador, worked with residents of the 15,000 person 52 village Comuna Rio Santiaga Cayapas to develop business opportunities. The Communa, among Ecuador's poorest areas, stands adjacent to the Cotocachi Cayapas Ecological Reserve, one of the most biologically diverse and endangered ecosystems in the world. CI's Sound Environment Enterprise Development (SEED) programme was started in 1990 to address the reality that poor people living around biologically sensitive areas need economic incentives not to develop that land in an unsustainable manner. SEED's first project was the Tagua Initiative to market a biodiversity product made from the sustainable harvest of the ivory-like nut of the tagua plant, a tropical rainforest tree. The partnership had a goal of transferring full management responsibility and ownership to the local community (UNEP and Prince of Wales Business Leaders' Forum 1994).

CI, CIDESA and the target communities worked together on a system for collecting and selling tagua to Ecuadorian processors through the establishment of 20 buying centres. A second stage of the partnership aimed to increase diversification in products and

---

4 Microcredit businesses represent local business partners, with Grameen being the larger, NGO partner with all of the leverage in the relationship.

markets, with the help of the NGO Aid to Artisans. Communication and learning in the form of training for 16 community members in accounting, management and product sales, sought to fulfil the goal of enabling them to run the enterprise. In the end, CI and CIDESA experienced difficulty in transferring full management responsibility and ownership of the programme to the local community (UNEP and Prince of Wales Business Leaders' Forum 1994). The failure to include local community members in jointly defining the partnership's goals, as suggested by the Long–Arnold matrix of partnership success factors, foreshadowed the difficulties that threatened its capacity building.

6.6.3 Capacity building: translation of knowledge into signs of progress

Capacity building acts to concretise goals through the mobilisation of resources and the establishment of a management structure that can bring each partner's competences to bear. Partners must first agree on goals such as an education campaign before they can build the means to carry them out.

A mammoth media corporation and a small, human rights NGO formed a partnership to create recordings by pop music stars that would be paired with curricula to teach children about human rights. Content from various parts of the conglomerate would be integrated into the classroom material. The human rights knowledge of the NGO would be matched with the product development, public relations and vast distribution network of the media conglomerate. A national advisory board was to be created consisting of experts in music and human rights from business and NGOs to provide advice concerning the content. The projected budget of more than US$15 million spoke volumes for the capacity envisioned for the partnership.[5]

Problems arose, however, while drawing up a grant proposal—the first time any ideas or ground rules were written down. Some issues were resolved, others deferred. Consequently, control over the partnership's content became the central issue. The advisory board reserved the right to dissociate itself from the project if the corporation ignored its advice. The NGO, however, felt its role in this regard to be viewed by the corporation as one of controlling rather than engaging the human rights community. The NGO was to be housed within the corporation, which wanted to exercise a veto over its hiring of staff. Final decision-making responsibility was implied to belong with the corporation. The partnership would amount to the corporation being in charge of implementation and the NGO acting as a subcontractor, able to be terminated at any time. The NGO proposed the development of a letter of agreement to resolve the differing views of the partnership's shape. The partners spent six weeks attempting to forge it, but the NGO refused to sign in the end.[6]

The NGO needed the corporation to widely disseminate its human rights message, and the corporation needed the NGO to provide the knowledge and credibility to further its interests. Tension resulted from the conflicting missions and operating styles, which in turn strained the innate trust issues between the two. The lack of agreement on the decision-making process for carrying out goals in the initiation phase of the Long–Arnold matrix of partnership success factors resulted in failure in the execution stage.

5 Personal interview with the author, 12 May 2000.
6 Ibid.

Respecting the needs and interests of partnership stakeholders required communication opportunities—often between stakeholders that possessed vastly different resources. The absence of such communication, stewardship and translation of knowledge into partnership progress pointed to problems that developed in the closure phase. The fact that the cases in the execution phase occurred between Bangladeshi credit institutions and poor villagers, transnational and national NGOs and poor villagers in Ecuador, and a transnational communications corporation and small NGO in the US points to the flexibility of the Long–Arnold matrix.

6.7 Closure phase

The beginning and end of relationships often leave the greatest impressions. The degree to which an NGO–business partnership can be considered successful reflects whether expectations were met, recognition awarded, goals implemented, strategy followed and efforts continued or concluded. The closure phase of the Long–Arnold matrix of the partnership life-cycle includes three categories: people (share success and credit), goals (evaluate results against goals and alternatives) and capacity building (sustain progress by institutionalising arrangements) (Long and Arnold 1995).

6.7.1 People: share success and credit

Partnership success and credit were shared in three ways: (1) between partners; (2) by partners with those outside the partnership; and (3) by outside entities recognising partners. Of these three types, sharing success and credit by partners with those outside the partnership occurred most frequently. The media played the dual role of spreading partnership credit and success, while having exerted pressure on business and consumer decisions to help foment them in the first place. By sharing success and credit, goals were reaffirmed and partners more likely to walk away with a positive feeling that could lay the groundwork for participating in future partnerships.

An NGO partner with Levi-Strauss expressed one of the few examples of sharing success and credit between partners. The head of the Research Centre for Feminist Action praised the company's contractors for not requiring pregnancy tests for female job applicants. Such practice is common among many other contractors in the Dominican Republic. Fewer cases featured examples of credit shared by partners with each other than sharing with those outside the partnership, or outside entities recognising partners (Amnesty International *et al.* 2000).

Sharing of success and credit by partners with those outside the partnership promoted public relations and communicated the image of social responsibility, which at times contrasted with the reality. The World Resources Institute (WRI) worked with the NGO CARE and the power supply company AES, formerly the Applied Energy Services Corporation, to offset the latter's carbon dioxide emissions from a coal-fired power plant in Connecticut through a reforestation project in Guatemala. WRI announced the establishment of the project in a press release that garnered positive attention in the media including *Time* magazine, gaining the then small company international recognition, which aided its eventual expansion overseas (WRI 1992).

An NGO stakeholder not involved in the partnership, Greenpeace, called the case a classic example of 'greenwashing', citing no evidence that reforestation will actually affect long-term atmospheric concentrations of CO_2. They pointed out in a report that once the trees die and decompose or are chopped down and burned, the CO_2 they captured returns to the atmosphere. Additionally, the report noted that the environmental externalities of a fossil-fired power plant go far beyond its CO_2 emissions, and include exploration and mining for the fuel, transport of the fuel, as well as acid rain and smog from burning the fuel (Greenpeace 1995). The media played a more prominent role in success and credit being shared by outside entities recognising partners.

Recognition of partners by those not directly involved with the partnership came primarily in the form of awards and media attention. McDonald's, the world's largest fast-food company with annual global sales in excess of US$30 billion, and the 200,000 member Environmental Defense Fund, now Environmental Defense, signed a formal agreement on 1 August 1990 after a year of discussions to address McDonald's solid waste issues. In January 1991 McDonald's swept an Advertising Age/Gallup poll as the most environmentally responsible fast-food chain. The partners released a Waste Reduction Task Force report in April 1991 that contained 42 recommendations concerning policy, pilot projects and testing to change the operational side of McDonald's (Murphy and Bendell 1997).

Conversely, problems developed when success and credit were not shared. The Environmental Defense Fund (EDF) was initially criticised by an early campaigner against McDonald's practices in the late 1980s, the Citizens' Clearinghouse for Hazardous Waste, for being a sell-out and later for not giving grass-roots campaigners enough credit for making McDonald's realise it had a solid waste problem in the first place. On a different note, McDonald's seemed much more concerned about higher profits and lower costs than any larger sense of social responsibility when it sued five Greenpeace-UK activists who distributed a pamphlet called 'What's Wrong with McDonald's' for libel at about the same time it engaged with EDF. In December 1995 the trial became the longest civil case in British history (Murphy and Bendell 1997).

The question of whether an NGO–business partnership is more or less likely to occur if it takes place in a forest with no one around is answered by the fact that success and credit were shared by partners most frequently with those outside the partnership. While a partnership may be a factual reality on the ground, what makes it news is its dissemination to other stakeholders (Ellul 1973). Examples of sharing success and credit that laid the groundwork for participating in future partnerships include AES, which went on to forge another partnership with WRI, and McDonald's, which entered into additional partnerships with CI and others following its relationship with EDF. Not surprisingly, success and credit in the Long–Arnold matrix of partnership success factors came about when goals were met.

6.7.2 Goals: evaluate results against goals and alternatives

A shared goal between partners in the initiation phase of one particular partnership ended up being evaluated quite differently in the closure/renewal phase.

Foron Household Appliances, a former East German manufacturer, was put up for sale on the privatisation block following German reunification. It was an inefficient company close to bankruptcy following its entry into the Western marketplace, and consequently faced dissolution if investors could not be found. Greenpeace Germany proposed using hydrocarbon technology—which was an energy-efficient refrigeration advance that did not destroy the ozone layer or add to global warming—to Foron as a way to achieve competitive advantage, and avoid being sold and losing jobs. The German refrigeration industry favoured using hydrofluorocarbons, which did not harm the ozone layer, but did add to global warming. Greenpeace believed that Foron's use of hydrocarbon technology could lead the industry to adopt product standards consistent with an international agreement on the ozone layer, the Montreal Protocol (Stafford *et al.* 2000).

Following extensive talks about a partnership, Greenpeace provided a grant of DM 27,000 to the company in July 1992. Greenpeace guided the partnership process through the launch of a grass-roots campaign that had three goals: (1) to generate publicity; (2) to educate consumers about the environmental benefits of the new refrigerator; and (3) to dissuade the Treuhand, a holding company established by the German government to privatise thousands of former East German state-run enterprises, from going through with its plans to eliminate Foron (Stafford *et al.* 2000).

Foron's 'Clean Cooler' refrigerator debuted in March 1993, much to the consternation of the German chemical and refrigerator industries, who launched their own campaign of misinformation warning that the new product was dangerous, unproven and inefficient. Greenpeace's grass-roots campaign and product endorsement resulted in over 70,000 orders for the 'Clean Cooler' within three months of its launch. Also, the 'Clean Cooler' won a prestigious award from the German Environment Ministry. By 1994, all German refrigerator manufacturers switched or planned to switch to the hydrocarbon technology (Stafford *et al.* 2000).

Greenpeace achieved its goal of ridding the German refrigerator industry of a technology that harmed the environment, and replacing it with a benign alternative. Foron, on the other hand, lost its competitive advantage following the German refrigeration industry's adoption of hydrocarbon technology, and subsequently lost market share. Without Greenpeace's support Foron lacked the money and ability to stand on its own. The company declared bankruptcy in 1996. A Dutch company then bought its refrigerator division. Greenpeace was said to have abandoned Foron in order to concentrate on spreading hydrocarbon technology to developing countries such as China and India before they adopted more harmful alternatives (Stafford *et al.* 2000). Foron's demise illustrates the need for partners to engage in long-range strategic planning, as well as clearly state the desired length of their participation in a partnership from the outset of the Long–Arnold partnership life-cycle.

6.7.3 Capacity building: sustain progress by institutionalising arrangements

Two characteristics of NGO–business partnership capacity building that indicated success and sustainability were (1) extension of a project started by a partnership; and (2) replication of a project by one of the partners or another organisation. Imitation demonstrated the start of a trend, which could be the most important characteristic of all in sustaining progress by institutionalising arrangements, because little causes can become contagious and have vastly larger effects (Gladwell 2000).

In the case of Save the Children, a well-established NGO with operations in 35 countries, and BP, one of the world's largest oil and petrochemical companies, partnership extension revolved around a programme begun in Vietnam in 1991. Save the Children worked with local women's unions, farmers' unions and people's committees, which are said to be the Vietnamese equivalent of NGOs, to reach consensus on alleviating mounting hunger by the poorest of the poor—particularly children—as the first priority for the partnership. The Poverty Alleviation and Nutrition Program (PANP) was to be in line with BP's criteria for community projects, in that it be sustainable with regard to local resources, rather than foster dependency (Japanese Center for International Exchange 1999).

Children who were identified as malnourished were invited to attend a two-week Nutrition Education Rehabilitation Program, in which their mothers or caregivers were taught by health volunteers to prepare a calorie-sufficient meal using shrimp, crab and greens, which were abundant but not traditionally fed to young children. The PANP then focused on preventing malnutrition and understanding the importance of women's health as a personal and community asset. The training of local citizens is believed to be one of the critical factors in the success of the programme. BP offered advice and recommendations to Save the Children based on the NGO's periodic programme reports and the company's occasional site visits. In addition, BP and Save the Children developed a common programme for their staff development (Japanese Center for International Exchange 1999).

The NGO established what it called a Living University in 1994 to enable health volunteers, government officials and other groups to replicate a hunger alleviation programme on their own. By May 1998, more than 2,600 health volunteers and 750 government staff from 15 provinces had attended the Living University and are now implementing the programme themselves in more than 200 communities across Vietnam (Japanese Center for International Exchange 1999). Successful continuation not surprisingly had the capacity to relate to replication as well.

If imitation is the sincerest form of flattery then the Forest Stewardship Council's stakeholders should be flattered. The Marine Stewardship Council (MSC) is in fact modelled on the FSC, which was also formed in part by WWF. Unilever, one of the world's largest buyers of fish with about 25% of the frozen fish market in Europe and the US, represented the initial private-sector partner. The basis for the partnership was the shared objective of ensuring the long-term viability of global fish stocks, approximately 60% of which were overfished or fished to the limit, by building a new institution to generate market incentives for sustainable fishing. Like the FSC, direct action by other NGOs aimed at changing industry policy and consumer choice drove business to the negotiating table. The structure and decision-making process of the MSC, however, originated from WWF and Unilever, who then consulted with stakeholders concerning the formation of standards of sustainable fishing. This contrasts with the FSC model of direct involvement by a wide range of stakeholders in the democratic formation of partnership goals and processes (Murphy and Bendell 1997).

Formal establishment of the new NGO occurred in 1997, with the FSC-like purpose of independently certifying qualified fishing enterprises with an MSC logo, giving consumers an identifiable way to support socially responsible business practices. The MSC's initial board largely comprised WWF and Unilever, although this set-up was disbanded in 1998 following MSC's independence. Subsequently, Unilever was no longer involved with the MSC's day-to-day running in order to establish its credibility as a neutral body to both competitors and NGOs (Heap 2000).

The MSC has already been considered a success by some stakeholders, because it has made progress in protecting the marine environment via a market-led initiative, whereas governments and the United Nations have not. The origin, structure and governance of the MSC, however, differed from the FSC in that it eschewed a wide and time-consuming consultation in exchange for a cheaper process and a quicker impact on the industry. The lack of democratic stakeholder participation at the start also pervades MSC's governance, which accounts for some of the challenges to its credibility within the international NGO community (Heap 2000). Once again, the categories of success factors demonstrated their inextricable link with the phases of the Long–Arnold partnership life-cycle.

6.8 Conclusion

The NGO–business partnerships examined in this study ranged from harmonious to contentious, and temporary to institutionalised. The partnerships encompassed stakeholders that were diverse in numbers, size, mission, geography, issue and industry. The Long–Arnold matrix of partnership success factors provided a useful and effective conceptual framework through which practitioners can forge partnerships between NGOs and business. The issue of trust proved to be an important additional characteristic of partnership success. Perhaps the greatest challenge to the success of NGO–business partnerships was the need to establish a balance between stakeholder goals that overlapped and those that conflicted. Partnerships must provide enough benefits for all partners and stakeholders without compromising their essential beliefs, otherwise the relationship becomes less appealing than not having one, and becomes an end in and of itself.

The initiation phase of the partnership life-cycle displayed the need to balance the tension between NGO desires to include all stakeholders with the business imperative of acting in a timely manner. Including local stakeholders in partnerships posed a challenge, whereas the media and consumers were well represented. While most partnerships focus on the internal operations of business, the possibility exists for partnerships to focus on the internal operations of NGOs as well. Partnership brokers played a key role in fostering trust and building bridges between NGO and business stakeholders. The establishment of mutually agreeable goals proved to be perhaps the most difficult aspect of the partnership process. Communicating partnership goals was also a key ingredient of success. The initiation phase proved to be more fragile and demanding than the subsequent phases, but essential to their success.

The execution phase of the partnership life-cycle featured the empowerment of local partners, which turned on respect for their capacity to learn given the opportunity, as well as a realistic scope of responsibility when translating respect into the execution of goals. Goals established without the input of crucial stakeholders slowed partnership execution and caused delays in the closure phase. Lack of agreement on goals also caused struggles over partnership resources during capacity building. Communication proved to be cumulative in that the respect between partners fostered earlier in the partnership became building blocks for concrete achievement and closure later in the partnership.

The closure phase of the partnership life-cycle looked at sharing success and credit, which pointed towards motivations behind NGO and business interest in partnerships. Shared goals by partners and stakeholders in the initiation stage were capable of being evaluated quite differently in the closure phase. The extension and replication of partnership projects were the clearest indication of sustained partnership progress through institutionalised arrangements. Partnership imitation, the extension of projects as well as project skills, and partnership continuation all built the capacity to sustain and institutionalise progress. Trends started by the imitation of partnerships often proved contagious, resulting in much larger effects.

The Long–Arnold matrix of partnership success factors proved flexible enough to provide direction for a sizeable number of cases from around the world that involved a variety of issues, industries and sizes of partners. The ideal partnership embodied by the Long–Arnold matrix did not exist among the 25 cases in this study. Stakeholders in future partnerships, however, have a better chance at achieving the ideal partnership, with the matrix and partnership history as a guide.

In order to effect positive change in the status quo, new methods of solving societal problems are needed. Partnerships between NGOs and businesses offer one possible way forward. Each partnership has the ability to transform its stakeholders into participants in the drive for positive change. The sustainability of the partnership paradigm depends on the ability of NGOs and businesses to build on the cumulative body of best practices forged during the past decade so that stakeholders in future efforts do not repeat the mistakes of the past.

7
STAKEHOLDERS FOR ENVIRONMENTAL STRATEGIES
The case of the emerging industry in radioactive scrap metal treatment*

Bruce W. Clemens and Scott R. Gallagher
James Madison University, USA

Stakeholder management has attracted considerable attention from organisational scholars since its introduction to strategic management (Freeman 1984). Both considerable theoretical development work (Clarkson 1995; Donaldson and Preston 1995; Mitchell *et al.* 1997; Jones and Wicks 1999; Jawahar and McLaughlin 2001) and successful efforts at broad empirical investigation (Hillman and Keim 2001) have occurred. However, one area left relatively unexplained is the idea of stakeholder responsibility: how claims of one stakeholder affect the ability of other stakeholders to attain their goals. We begin this chapter with a theoretical overview of central stakeholder theory concepts as a basis for evaluation. We then apply existing theories of stakeholder development to the radioactive scrap metal (RSM) industry. While stakeholders are known to be extremely important to the success of the individual firm, we highlight the role of stakeholder responsibility by arguing that stakeholders are also important to an industry, particularly an emerging industry. As a result, our level of analysis is the industry rather than the firm. This allows a special emphasis on the issue of reciprocal stakeholder responsibility rather than on the more popular corporate social responsibility issues (Carroll 1979).

* This effort was partially funded by the US Environmental Protection Agency and the US Department of Energy but does not constitute an endorsement. The survey data would not have been possible with the help of Ed Parton, owner of Knox Metals, Michael Mattia of the Institute of Scrap Recycling Industries (ISRI), and James Dacey of Auburn Steel and the Steel Manufacturers' Association (SMA). We are extremely thankful to Jörg Andriof and the anonymous reviewers. Christine Oliver, Michael Gresalfi, Val Loiselle and Thomas McGalliard provided advice and helpful comments.

7.1 **Theoretical overview**

Freeman (1984) posited the central question for stakeholder theory: Who or what really counts in an organisation? A considerable body of research has flowed from this simple question. Subsequent efforts have categorised the field into domains (Clarkson 1995), attempted to unify different domains (Jones and Wick 1999; Jawahar and McLaughlin 2001) and further refined important elements of the theory such as stakeholder identification (Hill and Jones 1992; Mitchell *et al.* 1997).

Because a central focus of this chapter is stakeholder responsibility, we adapt the exchange perspective of stakeholders developed by Hill and Jones (1992). Under this perspective organisations must continually strive to offer sufficient inducements to balance the contributions of their stakeholders (Hill and Jones 1992). We couple this exchange perspective with three attributes of stakeholders—power, legitimacy and urgency—which were developed by Mitchell *et al.* (1997). This combination of theories helps to explain the results of competing demands between relevant stakeholders.

We characterise power as the ability of a stakeholder group to absorb the impact of uncertainty from the organisation as a result of our focus on the exchange nature of stakeholders (Hickson *et al.* 1971). This conceptualisation allows us to examine the source of stakeholders' power rather than simply the end result of being able to compel another to action that would not otherwise occur (Dahl 1957; Pfeffer 1981) while still remaining parsimonious and consistent with dependency perspectives of power (Emerson 1962). We adopt the Mitchell *et al.* (1997: 869) definitions of legitimacy as '[The] . . . perception . . . that the actions of an entity are desirable, proper and appropriate' and urgency as 'the degree to which stakeholder claims call for immediate attention'.

Our attention is focused on addressing stakeholder responsibility and its potential for creating competing demands between stakeholders rather than studying just the dynamics between the organisation and stakeholders. Introducing a fourth stakeholder attribute, durability, adds a temporal component that complements stakeholder urgency analysis. This addition is necessary because most existing stakeholder analysis frameworks are centred on the firm and stakeholder dynamic. However, stakeholder responsibility encompasses a broader scope including mutual dependence between the demands of stakeholders on the claims of others. Indeed, Mitchell *et al.* (1997) highlighted the importance of the temporal and dynamic nature of stakeholder analysis though they did not explicitly include it.

Webster's Dictionary defines durability as 'highly resistant to wear, decay; capable of lasting or enduring'. In the context of stakeholder attributes durability represents the continued ability of the stakeholder to demand inducements from the organisation that occur because of legal, institutional or other reasons. For example, shareholders in market economies (i.e. owners) are remarkably durable stakeholders regardless of the contributions they offer to the organisation. Therefore, while stakeholder urgency is the ability to make immediate demands on the organisation, durability is the likelihood of a stakeholder being able to continue to make future demands on the organisation.

For example, consider an oil spill. In this situation, a firm would reach out to external stakeholders such as environmental groups to access their legitimacy to protect its reputation. These environmental groups would presumably demand some form of inducement, such as time from the top-management team or financial resources that would otherwise go to employees or stockholders, in exchange for their contribution. While the environmental groups presently have high power (they are absorbing the uncertainty of how to protect a firm's image/reputation), high legitimacy (they are devoted to the environment) and high urgency (their help is needed NOW!), they are not durable. The firm will revert to focusing on their stockholders, top-management team and other, more durable, stakeholders as soon as the public portion of the crisis is past. This example shows the need for an additional attribute in examining the ongoing mutual influence of stakeholders on other stakeholders.

These four stakeholder attributes coupled with the exchange model of stakeholder theory provide the theoretical basis for our examination of the RSM industry. The next section describes the industry, including its stakeholders. Then we discuss four major initiatives in the industry. In our analysis section, we use the results of these initiatives on the disparate stakeholders identified to illustrate the significance of our theoretical framework. In our conclusion we discuss the significance of this model for stakeholder theory and responsibility, centring on how claims made by various stakeholders can adversely impact other stakeholders. We expect the success or failure of firms in the industry, as well as the industry itself, to be heavily influenced by the competing claims of stakeholders and their shifting levels of power, legitimacy, urgency and durability.

7.2 The radioactive scrap metal industry

Radiation is the process in which energy is emitted in either particles or waves. Radiation occurs both in nature and from man-made sources. Environmentalists, citizens and industrialists have long viewed radioactive contamination with alarm despite the fact that radiation is a fundamental part of nature (Stoel 1981). This concern is well founded because radioactive materials can result in the inhalation of bone-seeking particles, such as caesium, which pose a significant health threat including death. Beyond the more publicised environmental[1] problems, such as the Three Mile Island and Chernobyl incidents, radiation offers a particular challenge for a wide range of industries. Human-made radiation can contaminate film, photographic equipment and medical equipment such as computerised axial tomography (CAT) scanners, in addition to the well-known problems of nuclear power plant equipment and materials. Furthermore, naturally occurring radioactive material (NORM) contaminates oil drilling equipment and pipelines. Proper disposal of this contaminated metal is an important issue.

Metal recycling has a long and extensive history. In the Middle Ages, blacksmiths were some of the first to recycle metal. A major reason for the growth of the metal industry was the ability to recycle and re-use metals. The popular novelist, Tom Clancy, offers that your flatware might have been part of Pharaoh Rameses II's double-crown or Napoleon's royal sceptre (Clancy 2000). Recycling rapidly accelerated with the rise of the 'mini' steel mill, first in Japan and later in the US (in the 1960s), which relies on scrap metal as its primary

---

1   A potential source of confusion may exist for some readers between the natural environment and the business environment. In order to minimise the potential confusion, in the remainder of this effort, environment will mean the natural environment. The more specific business environment will be called the business environment.

feedstock (Ghemawat and Stander 1999). Scrap metal comes from a plethora of sources ranging from large scrapyards to recycling efforts by local scout troops.

Mini-mills experience significant exposure to RSM. Radioactive contamination can severely impact mini-mills because the introduction of a small amount of radioactive waste into the furnace can contaminate large quantities of baghouse dust, the particulate waste from steel production. Individual mini-mills have had to spend tens of millions of dollars for the remediation of baghouse dust contaminated with radiation (Kuster 1994).

Figure 7.1 illustrates the potential flow of scrap metal, including RSM and potential RSM, in the steel industry. Estimates suggest that a total of up to 3,000,000 tons of RSM from all sources exists. In comparison, a typical steel mini-mill produces 150,000–300,000 tons of steel per year.

Major sources of RSM in the US include the Department of Energy (~20%), nuclear utilities (~20%) and the petroleum industry (~60%) (Frisch *et al.* 1998; Gresalfi 2001). The Department of Energy (DOE) controls approximately 400,000 tons of RSM in inventory

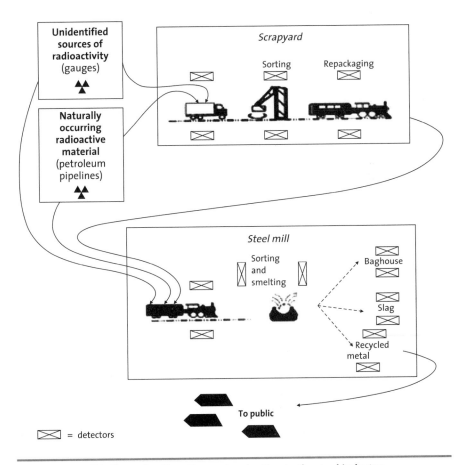

Figure 7.1 ***Possible flow of radioactive contamination in the steel industry***

and an additional 600,000 tons of RSM that will eventually be created from the destruction of the Department's three gaseous diffusion plants (Sanford Cohen & Associates 1992; Quadrex 1993).[2] Once clean, the metal is worth billions of dollars at conservative estimates of the spot metal prices.

RSM from nuclear utilities is often generated during outages, turnarounds and scheduled maintenance at nuclear power plants. Radioactive gauges used in a wide range of industrial and household applications, such as smoke detectors, also account for a very small amount of waste. Most RSM comes from the petroleum industry and is classified as NORM (*Environment Reporter* 1993). NORM arises because petroleum deposits contain radium, a naturally occurring radioactive element. As the petroleum flows in pipelines, radium deposits onto the lining of the pipes. Steel mills can run into problems if they receive radium-contaminated pipes as scrap.

The problem of radioactive steel emerged in the early 1980s when radioactive steel entered the scrap metal product stream (Lubeneau and Yusko 1995). Before this, radioactive metals had not been scrapped because they had not yet reached the end of their useful life (e.g. DOE facilities and nuclear power plants) or the levels of radiation they contained were not yet perceived as a health risk (e.g. oil industry pipe). Since then, RSM has been a growing national and international problem (IAEA 1992; *Environment Reporter* 1993).

This study examines the emergence of an industry including 20 US and multinational firms that treat the radioactive contamination problem in metals. This industry is particularly interesting because it offers insights at the intersection of environmental policy and business strategy, and therefore it involves a wide range of stakeholders including government regulators, industry groups, environmental groups and private citizens. For example, a myriad of international, federal and state rules govern radioactivity. Many conflict with each other, which results in a complicated regulatory web. Specifically, differences between the Nuclear Regulatory Commission and the Environmental Protection Agency at the federal level have indefinitely deferred the promulgation of national standards (Werner and Reicher 1992).

The RSM industry substitutes for two others: metals and waste disposal. The clearest substitute for recycled metals is virgin materials. The market price of carbon steel from virgin materials is similar to the cost of steel from a mini-mill of US$0.07 per pound (Hassler 1999). Due to the costs of treatment, the cost of radioactively decontaminated steel is between US$0.60 and US$1.50 per pound (Gresalfi 2001). However, the benefit of disposal enters here. The radioactively contaminated metals, if not recycled, must be disposed of in a safe manner. This would cost approximately US$0.60 per pound. Thus, the cost of recycled radioactive steel becomes more competitive, working out at US$0.00–0.90 per pound.[3] The potential for this type of market accounts for the attractiveness of firms that appear to have a cost-effective way to treat RSM, as illustrated by the stunning rise and fall of molten metal technology (Hoffman *et al.* 1999).

The problems from radioactive metal are great. First, the steel industry is very concerned about potential liabilities from radiation in metal and its potential risks to workers (ISRI 1992). Second, evidence from the 11 states that monitor these incidents has

---

2   These plants were used to enrich uranium in the production of nuclear weapons.
3   Radioactive treatment price of US$.60–1.50 per pound minus US$0.60 for disposal = US$0.00–0.90.

documented several hundred cases of scrap metal contamination. In February 1994, Nuclear Regulatory Commission (NRC) Chairman Ivan Selin emphasised the potential impact of the situation in a meeting with the Steel Manufacturers' Association (SMA). Dr Selin explained that the number of instances has increased rapidly over the past decades. Undocumented cases, however, could number in the thousands. This is best summed up by James Collins, the president of the SMA, which is the largest trade association for firms with electric arc furnaces, i.e. mini-mills, 'For some companies there is a crisis already, for others, it's still a crisis in the making' (Kuster 1994: 31).

Working with representatives from the SMA and the Institute of Scrap Recycling Industries (ISRI) we surveyed mini-mills and scrapyards in 1993 and 1997.[4] We found that all steel mills and 63% of all scrapyards had installed radiation-detection equipment. This measure is despite the absence of any federal environmental regulations requiring their installation, providing an excellent example of an innovative and voluntary environmental initiative.

7.3 Radioactive metal recycling industry stakeholders

We classify the stakeholders in this industry into three distinct groups. The first group consists of traditional internal stakeholders including workers, managers and owners. To facilitate our analysis we segment external stakeholders into two distinct groups, customers and regulators, based on the nature of their relationship with the industry.

7.3.1 Internal stakeholders

Workers. Workers in this industry are more highly trained than in the traditional steel industry. Their training includes health physics in addition to the health and safety typical of the steel industry. The power, legitimacy, urgency and durability of any single worker are low. While workers in some firms are organised into unions, the financial precariousness of the industry minimises the unions' potential to increase the workers' legitimacy and power. The potential for lay-offs and the turnover rate of waged employees decrease their durability.

Managers. Professional managers serve as executive officers in the larger firms. Most of the managers have a background in health physics and engineering. Understanding the regulatory processes increases managers' power by lessening the impact of the uncertainty of regulatory modifications. We recognise that managers do not directly reduce the uncertainty. However, effective management can decrease the *impact* of the uncertainty, consistent with Hickson *et al.*'s (1971) definition of power. The technical complexity of the processes in many of the firms increases the managers' legitimacy. As the decision-makers in each firm, the managers have a significant degree of urgency, especially regarding resource allocation. Management turnover has yet to be a problem in the industry. As such, managers are relatively durable.

4   The surveys are available from Bruce Clemens (clemenbw@jmu.edu).

Owners. The industry includes a mix of publicly and privately held firms. The largest firms are subsidiaries of multinational, publicly traded firms. Other participants are joint ventures between public and private firms. Shareholders range from private individuals to institutional investors.

Shareholders generally lack the ability to decrease the impact of uncertainty leading to low power. As owners of the venture, shareholders enjoy significant legitimacy. Consistent with agency theory, as their distance from management increases, their urgency decreases (Jensen and Meckling 1976). However, shareholders have high durability. Even if any one shareholder sells, collectively shareholders continue to be important over time.

7.3.2 *Customer stakeholders*

Department of Energy. DOE is a member of the executive branch in the US federal government. DOE's mission is to foster a secure and reliable energy system that is environmentally and economically sustainable, to be a responsible steward of the US's nuclear weapons, to clean up their own facilities and to support the US's efforts to foster effective science and technology development. DOE's role in the clean-up of facilities deals with radioactive metal. Indeed, DOE is responsible for more than 7,000 radioactively contaminated buildings including hundreds of thousands of metric tons of radioactively contaminated metal (National Research Council 1998).

As a customer, DOE has high power because it supplies a large portion of the scrap for decontamination. DOE has the potential to decrease the uncertainty of the industry dramatically through the letting of clean-up contacts. This leads to high power. As a potential consumer and significant supplier of radioactively contaminated metal, DOE also enjoys a high degree of legitimacy. Since DOE's business is offered on the basis of low-bid contracts, it can also command considerable urgency. DOE stockpiles provide for durability. However, as the finite stockpile is treated and reduced, DOE's durability will decline.

Nuclear utilities. The US is home to approximately 100 nuclear power utilities. They produce approximately 20% of the nation's electricity. The industry generates radioactive metal during routine maintenance and decommissioning. The utilities generate contaminated metal at a relatively constant rate leading to low power. If the utilities could generate RSM at differential rates, they would enjoy considerable power. The legitimacy of the nuclear power industry is low because it is a supplier rather than a consumer of radioactively contaminated metal. The routine nature of the supply of radioactively contaminated metal from the nuclear power industry produces low urgency. The degree to which the nation continues to rely on nuclear power and the lifetime of the existing plants cause high durability. Of the traditional sources of energy, nuclear power imparts the lowest impacts on global warming and greenhouse gases. As our awareness and concern for greenhouse gases and global warming increase, the nuclear utilities will increase in durability.

Petroleum industry. One of the largest industries in the United States, the petroleum industry generates large quantities of radioactively contaminated metal. Certain petroleum deposits contain radium, a naturally occurring radioactive element. Over time, the radium contaminates petroleum pipelines. The routine and predictable nature of the supply of radioactively contaminated metal from the petroleum industry leads to low power. As with the nuclear power industry, the legitimacy of the petroleum industry is low because it is a supplier rather than a consumer of radioactively contaminated metal. The routine nature of the supply of radioactively contaminated metal from the petroleum industry produces low urgency. The degree to which the nation will continue to rely on petroleum and pipeline transmissions provides high durability.

Metal customers. Metals are a significant part of the US economy. The 300 US steel mills shipped US$56 billion-worth of steel in 1997 (US Census Bureau 1999). Metals are traded as a commodity behaving as a quasi-perfectly competitive market. As such, it is difficult for metal customers to decrease uncertainty, leading to low power. As the ultimate consumer of metals, metal customers are legitimate. Unless environmental concerns appear, metal customers will not enjoy urgency. The continuing use of metal will sustain the durability of metal customers.

7.3.3 *Regulator stakeholders*

United States Environmental Protection Agency and Nuclear Regulatory Commission. The US Environmental Protection Agency (EPA) sets environmental standards for radioactivity. The US Nuclear Regulatory Commission (NRC) oversees the nuclear utility industry.

The potential to influence standards for radioactivity provides EPA and NRC with significant power. As the watchdog for the general public, both agencies also enjoy high degrees of legitimacy. The general public belief in environmentalism (EPA 1998) provides EPA and NRC with high degrees of urgency. As federal agencies, both organisations enjoy considerable durability. However, the potential volatile political climate lessens EPA's and NRC's durability to some extent.

The states. Individual states implement most of EPA's environmental programmes. The states also have other responsibilities to oversee DOE and the nuclear power industry. Because they implement rather than promulgate the standards, the states have at least the same significant levels of power, legitimacy and urgency as EPA and NRC. As public-sector entities, the states enjoy similar high levels of durability as EPA and NRC.

Interest groups and citizens. Individual citizens and US public-interest groups have gained power in the environmental movement over the past decades. The US citizen right-to-know legislation, passed in the previous decade, significantly increased the importance of citizens' and interest groups in the environmental arena. Unless empowered, interest groups and citizens generally respond to the initiatives of the regulatory agencies. As such, they are not powerful. As the definitive users of metal and the potential victims of environmental problems, citizens have the highest levels of legitimacy. As the voice for environmental advocates, interest groups are also highly legitimate. While their levels of urgency have increased with the advent of right-to-know legislation, most citizens and interest groups react to the regulatory agencies and do not enjoy high levels of urgency. As the ultimate consumers, citizens and interest groups have high levels of durability.

7.3.4 Relationships between stakeholders for radioactively contaminated metals

The relationships between the individual stakeholders are complex, interesting and potentially important. In general, the regulating stakeholders oversee both internal and customer stakeholders. As another common rule, customer stakeholders provide the market for internal stakeholders. Here we highlight the most important relationships:

- **Workers and managers; workers and shareholders.** The classic relationship includes confrontations on wages and working conditions. Employee ownership of a few of the firms clouds this classic relationship. Further, the cost of training and the additional safety concerns in the industry strengthen the relationships between workers and management and shareholders.

- **Workers and DOE/nuclear utilities/petroleum industry.** As suppliers of radioactively contaminated metal, DOE, nuclear utilities and the petroleum industry provide jobs. For this reason, workers could see DOE, nuclear utilities and the petroleum industry as allies.

- **Workers and EPA/NRC/states.** EPA/NRC and the states set safety standards for the job. Typically, workers are exposed to higher levels of environmental contamination than the general public. As such, workers rely on the public-sector agencies for protection.

- **Managers and shareholders.** Agency theory describes the potential conflicts between owners and managers. This industry provides little exception.

- **Managers and customers.** Managers must ensure the supply of radioactively contaminated metal from DOE, the nuclear power and petroleum industries. Managers must also react to the demand for clean metal from metal customers.

- **Managers and regulators.** Recent environmental legislation threatens managers with civil and criminal penalties for environmental problems. In addition, regulators rely on self-enforcement in many cases. Environmental groups have viewed the relationship between management and regulators as an unholy alliance.

- **DOE and nuclear utilities.** DOE provides enriched uranium for fuel for nuclear utilities and advocates nuclear power. DOE is also responsible for the eventual disposal of the industry's high-level radioactive waste.

- **DOE and metal customers/regulators.** Certain metal customers are concerned about contamination caused by metals released from DOE stockpiles. Customers have both health and industrial concerns. Under Section 107 of the Comprehensive Environmental Response, Compensation, and Liability Act (CERCLA) of 1980, EPA must treat DOE as any other private-sector entity. As such, EPA regulates the treatment of the DOE stockpile.

- **Nuclear utilities and the petroleum industry.** This is one of the more interesting relationships. Both compete to provide energy to the public. Their highly regulated business environments diminish potential competitive activities.

- **Nuclear utilities and the NRC.** NRC also has a potentially conflicting relationship with the nuclear industry. NRC is viewed as both a regulator and an advocate of nuclear power.

- **Metal customers and the regulators.** Metal customers rely on the regulators to provide safe metals free from significant amounts of radioactive contamination.

- **EPA/NRC and the states.** EPA and NRC have delegated the implementation of their programmes to most states. Other states have developed parallel radiation protection programmes. In those instances, EPA and NRC must certify that the state's programme is at least as protective as the federal programme.

- **EPA/NRC and interest groups.** Interest groups attempt to influence EPA and NRC to promulgate rules to support the interest group's agendas. For example, environmental interest groups try to push EPA and NRC to adopt more stringent regulations. Business-oriented groups typically push EPA and NRC to adopt regulations more attuned to business concerns.

Table 7.1 summarises the relationships between the stakeholders.

This section has provided a general overview of the RSM industry and many of its stakeholders. We will now examine how four major activities/initiatives were played out, illustrating competing stakeholder interests.

7.4 Government and industry initiatives: four initiatives resulting in competing stakeholder claims in a politically sensitive environment

7.4.1 Initiative 1: attempts at collective action

In 1994 the University of Tennessee, with financing from DOE, convened the firms dealing with radioactive clean-up. The meeting hosts encouraged the firms to establish a trade association. The trade association incorporated as the Association of Radioactive Metal Recyclers (ARMR). ARMR's first objective was to influence public policy on RSM to benefit members.

ARMR includes 20 firms, ten of which have been consistent and significant financial contributors. Long-standing member firms include GTS Duratek, SEG Westinghouse, British Nuclear Fuels, Alaron and US Ecology.

Hillman and Hitt (1999) examined two general approaches to political action (transactional and relational), two levels of participation (individual and collective) and three types of generic political strategies (information, financial incentive and constituency building). These studies present a comprehensive taxonomy of political strategies. ARMR members found it extremely difficult to affect federal policies. One of ARMR members' original objectives was to obtain environmentally lenient standards to allow cost-effective recycling. However, more important than lenient standards, the industry cam-

		Internal			Customer				Regulator		
		Workers	Managers	Shareholders	DOE	Nuclear utilities	Petroleum	Metal customers	EPA and NRC	States	Interest groups
Internal	Workers	×									
	Managers	Classic confrontations	×								
	Shareholders	Agency theory predicts conflicts.	×	×							
Customer	DOE	DOE, nuclear utilities and petroleum provide jobs.	Managers must predict and react to demand.		×						
	Nuclear utilities				DOE advocates nuclear energy.	×					
	Petroleum			Unclear	Unclear	Competitors in energy field	×				
	Metal customers	Unclear					Potential buyers	×			
Regulator	EPA and NRC	EPA, NRC and States attempt to protect workers.	EPA, NRC and States provide oversight. Managers help self-regulate.		EPA and States regulate DOE.	Mixture of regulations and nuclear advocacy.	Petroleum industry prefers State oversight.	Metal customers want strict regulations.	×		
	States					States regulate nuclear utilities.			States implement most EPA regulations.	×	
	Interest groups	Unclear			Interest groups drive DOE.	Interest groups drive environmental clean-up.	Interest groups drive environmental clean-up.	Share similar objectives	Interest groups drive EPA, NRC and States.		×

DOE = US Department of Energy; EPA = US Environmental Protection Agency; NRC = US Nuclear Regulatory Commission

Table 7.1 *Stakeholder relationships in the radioactive scrap metal industry*

paigned for specific, national standards. First they tried individually, then as a trade association, thereby combining both of Hillman and Hitt's (1999) two levels of participation. ARMR was generally unable to affect the policy process favourably due to environmental interest groups, the steel and petroleum industries, and the entire federal political process.

ARMR permanently closed its offices in the summer of 2001. While ARMR was far from a failure, it was not able to accomplish its primary objective of establishing cost-effective national standards for radioactive metal. This shows how easily external stakeholders can effectively make competing and rival claims in an industry. In subsequent sections we will describe how the petroleum industry was extremely effective in this way.

7.4.2 Initiatives 2 and 3: national standards and Recycle 2000

The primary agencies involved in regulating radioactive metals are NRC, DOE, EPA and the 50 state environmental regulatory bodies. Other interested parties include local governments, Native American tribes and environmental groups. Generally there has been little co-operation between these agencies, but two efforts stand out. The first was an effort to define national standards for RSM. The second was to develop a market for RSM that has been successfully recycled, Recycle 2000.

One major issue in the RSM debate is the lack of enforceable, national standards for all types of RSM (Clemens and Lin 1995). These standards would include maximum safe levels for various isotopes. This is especially important because of interstate commerce and federal environmental liabilities that can supersede state law. In such situations, DOE and government at all levels are increasingly committed to involving stakeholders early and often (English et al. 1993).

Although DOE, NRC and EPA are aware of the issue and initiated studies in the 1970s, only minimal information currently exists on the levels of radioactive contamination in metals (O'Donnell et al. 1978). In the absence of federal standards, the Conference of State Radiation Control Protection Directors has proposed guidelines to address the situation.

NRC and EPA, at the request of the SMA, have attempted to develop a regulatory strategy to address this growing problem for the past decade. Despite several years of work with full and extensive co-operation from the RSM industry, neither NRC nor EPA has disseminated any standards. The lack of federal standards has seriously hampered the development of the radioactive scrap decontamination industry. Without clear standards it becomes impossible for firms in the industry to recycle material for anything other than disposal purposes.

The industry is frustrated with the situation. Some comments, quoted directly, from our surveys of the steel industry follow:

> . . . The problem 'shows up' at the gate—it is not ours; however, the regulators want us to devote the manpower, machinery and time to find the source. We do not see the value of alerting them any longer . . . The fact that we put up monitors should not make us enforcement agents of the state. If the state would actually help, i.e. pay for the costs and handle the matter, it would be worth co-operating. Instead, the attitude of the state is to put blinders on and focus on a 'non-compliance'/'enforcement' mentality.

... In my market, all contaminated materials come from the oilfields. I have a problem with the fact that when I check EVERY load coming into my yard for radiation and a piece of pipe for example measuring 2' diameter and 6' long is missed ... Why don't they [the people] pay for this problem by providing disposal at my yard or at the mills? ... I have turned away many loads of scrap: where it ends up, who knows? There is NO doubt the severity of this problem; however, the costs for control to my very small business is high.

We have installed scale monitors ... We also have hand-held equipment. We double-check each shipment before it leaves the yard. The steel mills are continually changing their requirements and they give this information as they change it ... We understand [their problems] and are very co-operative with their people to help them [avoid contamination]. We educate our customers. We feel we are better able [than the state or municipal government] to control the problem.

The primary reason that standards have not been determined is the opposition of the petroleum industry. The petroleum industry is concerned about the amount of NORM-contaminated steel in its possession. Apparently, firms in the petroleum industry believe that they are better positioned in the absence of national standards. The political power of the petroleum industry is considerably greater than the emerging RSM industry.

The Recycle 2000 initiative was the DOE plan to fabricate waste containers from radio-active scrap metal (Clemens and Lin 1995). In the past, DOE had purchased clean waste containers to use for the transport and disposal (burial in a landfill) of radioactively contaminated materials. Instead of throwing the contaminated metal in a landfill in clean containers, Recycle 2000 proposed re-smelting the contaminated metal and fabricating containers. The containers produced from the RSM could then be used to store and dispose of other radioactively contaminated materials. It seemed to be a win–win strategy.

Consistent with stakeholder theory, DOE realised the importance of involving a broad range of potential Recycle 2000 stakeholders. DOE worked to obtain agreements for Recycle 2000 from a diverse group of stakeholders.

English et al. (1993) found that DOE stakeholder strategies have included anything from 'information elicitation' to 'decision-making'. By incorporating stakeholders, deci-sion-makers within DOE demonstrated a willingness to listen to a broad range of constit-uents. This is consistent with a relational political strategy under the Hillman and Hitt (1999) framework. Proponents theorise that stakeholder involvement may prove to be a more effective method of establishing policies and regulations in highly controversial areas such as RSM recycle and re-use strategies.

The steel industry quickly became the most vocal and strongest stakeholder. The steel industry convinced DOE not to allow any release of previously contaminated metal that was cleaned, even though the metal was cleaned to existing standards.

7.4.3 Initiative 4: recent regulatory events

DOE is especially important for the industry because it acts as a supplier, buyer and a quasi-regulatory body. Surprisingly, pressure for regulatory action in this industry has not come from environmental interest groups but rather from the steel and petroleum industries. The steel industry wanted national standards to safeguard their processes.

The petroleum industry did not want standards because of the large amounts of NORM contamination in pipelines. This resulted in the petroleum industry pushing for regulation of the metal recycling industry to occur at the state level. The oil industry is considerably stronger politically than the steel industry, and it has been largely successful in tying up efforts to create national regulations for RSM.

In their frameworks of firm-level strategies, Oliver (1991) and Hillman and Hitt (1999) presume that industry has the ability to influence the rule-making process. This has also been true of other political strategies such as information, financial and constituency-building strategies. In our case, the petroleum industry drove the regulatory process. Against this stakeholder group, the RSM and steel industries were not able to exert much influence on the rule-making process.

While they were unsuccessful at securing national regulations, DOE recently published two policies dealing with RSM at the steel industry's initiative. In February 2000, DOE put a moratorium on the release of any volumetrically contaminated metal (Richardson 2000). In July 2000, through an order prohibiting the release of any metal from a radiological area, DOE suspended the release of all potentially contaminated metals (DOE 2000). However, while these are potential successes for the industry, they do not address the danger of contamination from NORM, the primary concern of the oil and gas industry.

Firms are generally presumed to be well positioned to monitor changes and influences in their own industries. However, in this case regulations, or more precisely the lack of regulations, occurred because of the potential intervention of the oil industry. Not only does the petroleum industry dwarf the metals industry, it enjoys considerable power based on its critical role in the economy. Arguably, petroleum's lobbying power will grow in the current Bush administration.

7.5 Analysis

This case has described the RSM industry and four major initiatives that occurred since 1994. Each of the initiatives presented competing claims and challenges to various stakeholder groups. Table 7.2 recapitulates these stakeholder groups and our efforts to broadly categorise them into our modified Mitchell *et al.* (1997) typology. Below we discuss each of the three stakeholder groups we identified and how they fared under each of the four initiatives.

Given that the industry was generally frustrated, the internal stakeholders of workers, shareholders and firm managers generally did not fare too well. While internal stakeholders usually have considerable power and legitimacy, this industry is regulatory- as well as market-driven and the internal stakeholders ended up not meeting their goals and objectives from the four initiatives.

The customer stakeholder groups draw their power from the market, and, in the case of DOE, from regulatory actions. DOE is clearly one of the most influential customers as it provides a significant portion of metal for recycling and grants for initiatives such as Recycle 2000. The petroleum industry provides a majority of the recycled steel used and also possesses considerable influence over regulatory rule-making procedures. Therefore, it is no surprise that in initiatives related to the petroleum industry (1, 2 and 4) they

Type	Stakeholder	Power	Legitimacy	Urgency	Durability	Initiative 1 ARMR	Initiative 2 Standards	Initiative 3 Recycle 2000	Initiative 4 Current
Internal	Workers	*	*	*	*	L	L	L	L
Internal	Firm managers	**	**	**	**	L	L	L	L
Internal	Owners/shareholders	*	**	*	***	L	L	L	L
Customer	Department of Energy	***	***	***	**	–	L	L	L
Customer	Nuclear utilities	*	*	*	***	W	L	L	L
Customer	Petroleum industry	*	*	*	***	W	W	–	W
Customer	Metal customers	*	**	*	***	–	–	W	L
Regulator	EPA and NRC	***	***	***	**	W	W	–	L
Regulator	States	***	***	***	**	W	L	–	L
Regulator	Interest groups/citizens	*	***	*	***	W	L	–	L

Key

*** high level of attribute   ** medium level of attribute   * low level of attribute   L = loss   W = win   – not involved with initiative

ARMR = Association of Radioactive Metal Recyclers; EPA = US Environmental Protection Agency; NRC = US Nuclear Regulatory Commission

Table 7.2 *Stakeholder summary and evaluation*

achieved their aims at the expense of other stakeholder groups, especially the internal stakeholders. In our framework the customer groups also represent the 'tyranny of the market' and as a result are quite durable. Consequently, the metals buyers were able to defeat the Recycle 2000 initiative despite the backing of seemingly more powerful stakeholder groups.

The regulatory stakeholders offered the greatest range of different characteristics in our three stakeholder groups. Along with NRC, EPA shared in the considerable potential rule-making activities that governed industry operations, giving it high power and legitimacy as well as urgency when it chose to act. However, like DOE, EPA's influence was not as durable because of the highly variable nature of its political climate. State regulatory agencies enjoyed less urgency. Concerned citizens were even less powerful and urgent. A threatening state agency could be sidestepped via strategic siting. While citizen activity could be effective, it was also reactive, contingent on the organisation's siting process and decisions.

7.6 Conclusions

This chapter offered an overview of an existing framework for stakeholder analysis and added a fourth dimension of durability. We then examined four initiatives in an emerging industry to see how various stakeholder groups reacted to them. We tried to view the outcomes from these incidents as results of competition between stakeholders for organisational resources. Generally, the initiatives taken by the industry group were foiled by the actions of a subset of its stakeholders. This suggests not only that stakeholders do compete but that this competition in any one time-period may be a zero-sum game, such that a positive result for one stakeholder group comes at the expense of other stakeholders. This question of the 'pie to be shared by stakeholders' goes to the heart of considerable stakeholder theory: Are the inducements available for sharing by all stakeholders fixed or elastic? For example, does the considerably higher pay given to American executives result in greater returns for the remaining stakeholders, such as workers, shareholders and the community, because it attracts exceptionally capable executives, or does it come at their expense? Our cursory examination of the radioactive recycled metals industry suggests that, at least for any single given period, it is a zero-sum game and large benefits for one stakeholder come at the expense of another.

7.6.1 Durability of stakeholders

Our primary theoretical explanation for how some stakeholders are able to dominate others is based on the construct of durability. We offer that existing stakeholder theory does not adequately address the temporal dimension of stakeholder interaction. While power, legitimacy and urgency are important attributes, they do not adequately address long-term stakeholder management issues. We found that durability was especially important to shareholders, nuclear utilities, the petroleum industry, metal customers, interest groups and citizens. Durability may also help to explain the continued dominance of shareholders as stakeholders. While not a component of this chapter, we suspect that shareholders' successful linkage with top-management teams via stock option compensation has made them quite durable.

The idea of durability is especially helpful in the light of practitioner frustration (Gioia 1999) with corporate social responsibility research. Gioia (1999: 228) specifically complains that 'Managers simply do not find them [stakeholder theory frameworks] credible because they do not adequately represent the complex social, economic, and organisational realities managers face.' We view durability as insightful because it helps to highlight the stakeholders that managers must continually confront as well as considering other important stakeholder attributes. Viewing the attributes as a range, rather than simply being present or absent, also seems more consistent with managerial experience.

7.6.2 Uniqueness of US governmental agency stakeholders

Even though government stakeholders possess considerable power, legitimacy and urgency, they were not completely durable in the RSM context. This may be due in part to the changing nature of the US political process. DOE Secretary Richardson made major decisions affecting the RSM industry while balancing competing demands within an outgoing Democratic administration. Direct involvement of the government from DOE exerted a considerable amount of influence in the industry. Further, the entry of DOE into the market required a general reconfiguration of the resource and capability bases of many participants.

8

RE-EXAMINING THE CONCEPT OF 'STAKEHOLDER MANAGEMENT'

Michael E. Johnson-Cramer
Boston University School of Management, USA

Shawn L. Berman
Santa Clara University, USA

James E. Post
Boston University School of Management, USA

'Stakeholder management' is a broad and nebulous term. At first glance, it encompasses just about everything a company does, for each activity or decision has direct or indirect effects on a range of relevant constituencies. Every transaction has material effects on the partner as well as the focal firm, and most affect additional parties as well. For example, a decision to locate a plant in a particular town most obviously affects the landowner, who will sell the land on which the plant will be built. Yet the same decision affects the local community, the employees who will have new job opportunities at the plant (or those who will relocate from a previous site), the stockholders who will benefit from a successful decision (or suffer from a poor one), and various others. This complexity prompts the question at the heart of this chapter: Which aspects of these activities and decisions ought to be considered as 'stakeholder management'?[1] This chapter answers this question by re-examining the concept of stakeholder management and offering: (a) an integrated framework that describes the key aspects of stakeholder management; (b) theoretical logic that explicitly links stakeholder management to important outcomes; and (c) future directions for thinking about stakeholder management.

---

1 Some have suggested that 'stakeholder relationship management' may be the more appropriate term, since companies primarily manage their relationships rather than the stakeholder itself. This is a useful distinction that may, in the future, point towards an additional dimension along which stakeholder management approaches can be distinguished. For the moment, however, we have chosen the phrase 'stakeholder management' not only for its historical purchase but also because it includes efforts to manage relationships as well as efforts (admittedly less frequent) to control stakeholder behaviour.

This chapter is necessary because existing research has made only partial attempts to summarise the important dimensions of a firm's stakeholder management. These efforts fall into three categories.

- **Activities.** From the earliest perspective, stakeholder management is a bundle of related activities by which a company manages a stakeholder group and its relationship with that group. Freeman (1984), for example, lists a handful of activities such as communication, monitoring and explicit negotiation. Morris (1997) specifies particular structures and practices through which these activities take place. Thus, companies that engage in these boundary-spanning activities with various constituencies can be said to have a certain level of competence in stakeholder management.

- **Orientations.** A second perspective suggests that stakeholder management is not a set of activities but a general 'orientation'. This orientation can be assessed either in terms of cognition (Which stakeholders does a firm pay attention to?) or in terms of values (Which stakeholders does a firm give priority to?). Mitchell *et al.* (1997), for example, envision stakeholder orientation in terms of salience. On the other hand, Brenner and colleagues (Brenner and Cochran 1991; Hosseini and Brenner 1992) see stakeholder management as the stable pattern of values held by management.

- **Ethics.** A third perspective sees stakeholder management in ethical terms. It is not the behaviour itself but its moral quality that is the essence of a company's stakeholder management. Jones (1995) elaborates this perspective more clearly in proposing that the morality of a firm's actions, defined as honesty and fairness, affect its financial performance. Others have elaborated notions of stakeholder management as ethics, rooted in the rightness, justness and equity of a firm's actions (Evan and Freeman 1993; Phillips 1997; Gerde 2000).

The evolution of the stakeholder research domain has been driven by the constantly shifting attention of stakeholder researchers, who have turned their gaze, over time, from one aspect of stakeholder management to another. Thus, there is a logical progression underlying the advance of these diverse viewpoints. 'Activity' theorists have, for the most part, focused on the behaviours of firms in managing each relationship separately. Their insights are best implemented in parallel within each stakeholder relationship. The 'orientation' viewpoint arose, at least implicitly, out of a desire to understand how firms assess the relative importance of multiple stakeholder groups at the same time. The 'ethics' approach arose out of the fundamental insight that stakeholders are moral agents, and, where 'activities' thinking pointed towards the processes by which companies engaged with stakeholders, it is equally important to consider the impact of the ethical quality of a firm's behaviours and decisions. In the final analysis, these thinkers have drawn our attention to important if manifestly different aspects of stakeholder management, and, like the proverbial Hindu story of the five blind men and the elephant, these stakeholder theorists have focused on different parts without divining the overall shape of the beast.

Stakeholder theorists are in the business of generalisation. Their central claim has been that companies with good stakeholder management achieve better financial performance. In defining 'good stakeholder management', these theorists have been comfortable substituting the part—be it activities, orientation or ethics—for the whole. This is methodologically flawed, as testing the effect on performance of only a subset of stakeholder management practices will upwardly bias the results.[2] It is also dangerous from a practical standpoint as managers engaging in effective communication practices with stakeholders but ignoring the ethical quality of their policies will wonder why 'good stakeholder management' is not having the expected effect.

Ultimately, if the goal of stakeholder thinking is to generalise about a company's approach to stakeholder management, stakeholder theorists require a more comprehensive notion of the concept that integrates these diverse perspectives. Simply put, theorists and practitioners alike must begin to see the whole picture. From our perspective, this integration starts with a clearer notion of stakeholder management as both the pattern of giving and receiving corporate benefits (and costs) and the processes by which such actions are undertaken. It starts with an awareness that firms must engage directly with stakeholder groups while still thinking about how decisions affect multiple constituencies simultaneously.

8.1 The stakeholder management matrix

Putting the insights from the introduction more formally, we summarise the primary aspects of a company's stakeholder management along two dimensions (see Fig. 8.1).

- On the first axis of the figure is the **locus of action**. A company's stakeholder management includes both managing within each of its stakeholder relationships (**within**-relationship management) and managing across stakeholder relationships (**across**-relationship management).

Some firm activities are directed at managing within a single stakeholder relationship. Frequently, these activities take place in functional sub-groups that span organisational boundaries. For example, human resources managers handle the relationship with employees, and public affairs managers manage the relationship with government. The actions taken by boundary-spanning departments constitute **within**-relationship stakeholder management. In contrast, managers (frequently general managers) also confront the difficult task of integrating firm decisions concerning multiple stakeholders; they attempt, for example, to balance the interests of stockholders, employees and customers. This form of action, which mediates among multiple stakeholder interests, is **across**-relationship stakeholder management.[3]

---

2 Students of strategic human resources (HR) management have been particularly attuned to this effect. Huselid (1995) argues that, since organisations frequently adopt more than one strategic HR practice, a significant relationship between a single practice and overall performance will probably reflect upward bias.

3 While helpful as an illustration, the distinction between general and functional management can be misleading, as functional managers may engage in across-stakeholder actions even as general managers frequently concern themselves with within-stakeholder action. At issue is not the *subject* of the company's actions but the *object*.

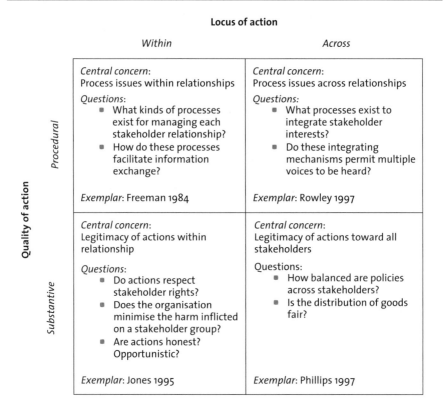

Figure 8.1 **The four aspects of stakeholder management**

- On the second axis of Figure 8.1 is the **quality of action**. Company behaviour towards stakeholders can be understood in either **procedural** terms (i.e. how managers formulate and implement stakeholder-directed policies) or **substantive** terms (i.e. the moral quality of those behaviours and policies).

Distinguishing between these two qualities means looking at the same activities in two different lights. The procedural aspect of stakeholder management deals with the social or behavioural character of a firm's actions. The substantive aspect of stakeholder management deals with the moral character of the firm's actions. Thus, for example, Ford Motor Company's response to reports of problems with Firestone tyres may be described in behavioural terms such as reactive or proactive, communicative or incommunicative. Its treatment of customers may also be characterised in relation to moral standards: responsible or irresponsible, just or unjust, fair or unfair. Of these two categories (procedural and substantive), the latter is more difficult to ascertain, for if the moral quality of company behaviour involves the degree to which that behaviour conforms to principles of good, or ethical, action, then there is a clear need for systematic descriptive and ethical theory.

Together, these axes define four components of stakeholder management: **procedural-within**, **procedural-across**, **substantive-within** and **substantive-across**. By simultaneously evaluating a company's engagement in each of these components, it becomes possible to assess a company's stakeholder management approach as a whole. Later, this chapter will explore the impact that different approaches to stakeholder management can have, but, before moving on to that subject, we devote the remainder of this section to describing specific variables that indicate a company's engagement in each of these components of stakeholder management.[4]

8.1.1 Procedural-within

A company manages its relationship with any given stakeholder group—be it a segment of employees, customers, stockholders or local community—through specific processes and structures. Its managers communicate decisions through newsletters and meetings. They implement hotlines and surveys to monitor satisfaction. They negotiate directly over issues with direct impact on the stakeholder group. In practice, these activities take different forms in different relationships, but, taken together, these constitute the company's procedural stakeholder management within a relationship. The essence of these procedures is the exchange of information between managers and the members of the stakeholder group. Assessing these 'procedural-within' activities requires the stakeholder analyst to assess: (a) the degree to which management creates and maintains these channels; and (b) the degree to which managers use these channels to send and receive information across the company–stakeholder boundary. There are, then, at least two important variables at play.

Participation. The first element of a company's 'procedural-within' stakeholder management is the degree to which open channels exist for stakeholders to express their concerns, voice their interests and, thus, participate in the processes by which their company formulates policies that, in turn, affect the particular group. At the very least, these participation opportunities inform management of stakeholder interests, but, in some companies, they represent highly empowering structures. Such is the case, for example, at Saturn, where employees can voice concerns about quality control by immediately halting the assembly line (Kochan and Rubenstein 2000). Companies vary in the number of participation avenues they offer. Interestingly, when a company deprives its stakeholder groups of participation channels, such groups increasingly turn to external avenues to voice their concerns (and their frustrations). Today's companies are learning that Yahoo chat sites are fertile grounds for stakeholder voice.

Dialogue. Of course, while the existence of participation channels is important, equally important is the quality of exchange that occurs in these channels. Thus, 'procedural-within' stakeholder management also includes the degree to which a company engages in genuine dialogue with the stakeholder group. The essence of stakeholder dialogue is the co-creation of shared understanding by company and stakeholder. Dialogue is, itself, a multi-dimensional construct. First, it entails an interactive dimen-

---

4 As explained in greater detail elsewhere (Johnson-Cramer 2001), we have selected these variables because they bear directly on those political processes by which managers enact stakeholder-directed policies. We believe that the metaphor of organisation as political system is particularly apt for describing stakeholder management.

sion. Partners must engage in active listening as well as constructive exchanges that acknowledge one another's positions. Dialogue exists in the micro-level structures of interaction such as turn-taking patterns and category use (Tulin 1996). Thus, a company evaluating the degree of dialogue within its communication channels must closely examine the structural patterns of interaction there. At the same time, dialogue includes a second dimension, characterised by emotional dynamics such as safety and sincerity. Managers may never agree fully with stakeholders, but the parties must achieve a mutual sense of emotional safety if the exchange is to continue.

There is still much to learn about recognising dialogic behaviours in the context of stakeholder interactions, but, to date, stakeholder theorists are growing increasingly able to discern between instances of dialogue and instances of 'serial monologue' (Isaacs 1999). If the essence of procedural-within stakeholder management is the exchange of information, then dialogue is the quality that ensures: (a) that the information has a similar meaning for both parties; and (b) that the exchange is satisfying to both the stakeholder group and the company's managers.

In sum, the first set of questions to ask about a company's stakeholder management approach concerns the structures and processes that its managers implement within stakeholder relationships. Has management built sufficient communication channels? Do these offer possibilities for stakeholders to voice relevant concerns? To what degree are the exchanges occurring within these channels characterised by dialogue?

8.1.2 Procedural-across

Where the previous section discussed those processes by which a company engages with individual stakeholder groups, this section examines those processes by which the company considers multiple stakeholder groups simultaneously. In short, it describes the integrating mechanisms by which decisions across stakeholder groups are made; we term this across-stakeholder management. At least two factors play a role here.

Representation. The first important piece of procedural-across stakeholder management is the extent to which multiple stakeholders have some degree of representation when decisions that affect multiple groups are being made. In top-management teams, this may involve the presence of boundary-spanning personnel capable of articulating stakeholder interests (Freeman 1984). At the board level, it may involve the participation of actual stakeholder representatives. Clearly, companies vary in the degree to which they enable diverse representation. For example, Luoma and Goodstein's (1999) study of 224 companies demonstrates a high degree of variance among American firms in the degree to which stakeholders are represented on boards of directors. Representation is not, of course, a panacea for lop-sided policies. However, it marks a necessary condition for effective procedural-across stakeholder management.

Contest. Of course, representation is of little use if a company's decision-making procedures evidence little dissent, or contest, among varying viewpoints. Eisenhardt and Bourgeois's (1988) study of strategic decision-making processes in high-tech firms demonstrates the varying quality of discourse within top-management teams. Where some companies encouraged a fairly high degree of disagreement in decision-making meetings, others stifled debate, equating silence with cohesiveness. The degree of contest—Eisenhardt and Bourgeois call it 'conflict'—between multiple points of view is a second necessary condition for across-stakeholder management. Indeed, it is more than a coincidence that, historically, those organisations that stifle contest at key junctures—recall the key discussions concerning the *Challenger* launch (Vaughan 1995)—have tended to make decisions that fail to consider multiple stakeholder perspectives. A company's procedural-across stakeholder management is visible in the degree to which multiple stakeholder interests are both represented and strenuously advocated during decision-making sessions. This integration process, thus, involves a combination of representation structures and informal norms encouraging contest.

8.1.3 Substantive-within

Describing the substantive dimensions of stakeholder management involves more than the social, or behavioural, character of a company's behaviour. Instead, it addresses the substance, or content, of a company's policies towards stakeholders. In particular, it involves the congruence between a company's treatment of stakeholders and ethical models of behaviour. Thus, the central question is: How fairly does the company treat each of its stakeholder groups? The underlying assumption here, a fundamental assumption in stakeholder theory, is that corporate morality matters when explaining the quality of stakeholder relationships and their ultimate outcomes (e.g. financial performance). Learning to diagnose the degree to which a company engages in effective substantive-within stakeholder management is the focus of this section. In describing a company's substantive-within stakeholder management, one must consider two alternative ethical concerns. On the one hand, one must determine whether a company's behaviour infringes basic standards of fairness and honesty. On the other hand, it is important to consider the balance of costs and benefits offered to a stakeholder group for engaging with the company.

Fairness. The most fundamental standard for the moral treatment of stakeholder groups is the level of fairness exhibited by the company within each relationship. In positive terms, such general standards of fairness include honesty, reliability, and the recognition of legal and moral rights (Clarkson Centre for Business Ethics 1999). Another way of phrasing this standard—popular among agency theorists (Eisenhardt 1989)—is the avoidance of opportunism. In practice, opportunism takes many forms and, in terms of judging the impact of opportunistic management, the perception of wrongdoing can be enough to sour stakeholder management. For example, chief executive officers (CEOs) who negotiate abnormally large compensation packages may signal to stakeholder groups that they are opportunistic and cannot be trusted. This opportunism can have a significant impact on: (a) whether the company forms trusting relationships with stakeholder groups; (b) whether these stakeholders offer the company attractive terms in contracting negotiations; and (c) whether companies can, in turn, achieve sufficient returns (Berman 1998). Other behaviours that figure within stakeholder relationships may signal opportunistic behaviour; these include mechanisms involved in corporate control, such as greenmail, poison pills and shark repellents, as well as employee surveillance (Jones 1995).

Munificence. The second critical element of substantive-within stakeholder management involves the absolute value of the benefits returned to individual stakeholder groups for their engagement with the company. At issue, here, is a cost-balance analysis of the returns and harms generated by interaction with a company. Since this balance is generally under the control of the company's management, we refer to this utility measure as the company's munificence. Here, munificence refers to the ability of a firm to sustain stakeholder groups. This reverses the traditional use of the term munificence in organisation theory, where environmental munificence refers to the ability of an environment to sustain firms (Dess and Beard 1984).

As with procedural-within stakeholder management, this aspect is best evaluated in each relationship separately, though it can be meaningful to evaluate the average munificence as an overall company-level measure. Thus, a company can be said to be munificent towards its employees if it offers above-market compensation and benefits while imposing few harms (e.g. health risks, workplace safety concerns, etc.). It seems obvious that a company's munificence towards a stakeholder will have a significant effect on the quality of its relationship with that group but, as explained below, the theoretical relationship may be more complicated.

In sum, this section introduces the idea that the substance of stakeholder management can have as powerful effects on relationship quality as management procedures. In particular, offering sufficient utility and treating a stakeholder group with an overall sense of fairness distinguish a company that has developed a substantive-within stakeholder management competence from one that has not.

8.1.4 Substantive-across

The final component of stakeholder management is the substantive nature of a company's behaviour as it affects multiple stakeholders simultaneously. This is termed 'substantive-across' stakeholder management. As with the substantive-within component, the moral quality of managerial action has an observable effect on stakeholder relationships and, in turn, on second-order outcomes such as organisational performance. Yet the question arises: How do organisations vary in their distributive stakeholder management?

A fine-grained understanding of a company's substantive-across stakeholder management might analyse each decision in terms of the specific trade-offs between stakeholder interests. For example, a given policy may privilege employee rights over stockholder interests and, over time, companies adopting such a policy may develop allocative patterns that can be described as pro-employee, based on a consistent trade-off in favour of employees. Such trade-offs are the central element of substantive-across stakeholder management. Of course, thinking about the substance of company decisions as they apply to multiple stakeholders, it would be easy to get mired in the details of specific allocations and miss the broader patterns. What remains is to describe this component of a company's stakeholder management in more general terms, as they exist over time and across multiple issues.

The most prominent variable in describing substantive-across stakeholder management is **equity**, the degree to which multiple stakeholders receive benefits proportionate to their involvement with an organisation (Adams 1965). Equity is a defining feature of normative stakeholder theory. In its more soundly developed forms, this argument does not require equal distribution of benefits or burdens among stakeholders. Instead, since firms as co-operative schemes exact different levels of involvement and investment, the obligation to stakeholders must be proportional to the investment (Phillips 1997). Philosophers will debate whether or not equity is the essence of moral stakeholder management, but, for our purposes (i.e. describing those aspects of stakeholder management that have tangible impacts on a company's outcomes), equity is a compelling variable indeed.

Of course, calculating the equity implications of a company's treatment of its stakeholders is no simple task. For one thing, the benefits allocated to stakeholders need not be of a tangible nature, i.e. dividends and incentive pay. They may also consist of intangible value, rights and risks. For example, most companies regulate employee use of internal e-mail systems and Internet portals. In doing so, they allocate access privileges and privacy rights to employees, balanced by the burden of risks allocated to stockholders—the company assumes the risk of lawsuits arising out of illegal uses of e-mail for harassment or offensive communications—and to potential victims of harassment. Here, a financial calculation of the allocation is difficult, for, though it is possible to quantify the expected risks of legal liability, it is more difficult to ascertain the value of intangibles such as privacy rights. Indeed, a strictly quantitative analysis of what employees receive in this bargain would amount to a costing of the demands that personal e-mail places on the company's computer system. Another complication in determining how equitable a company's stakeholder management is, is the need to consider the time-value of stakeholder benefits and costs. Ogden and Watson (1999) have studied the apparent trade-offs involved in investment decisions by managers in British water supply authorities. Their conclusion suggests that, taking short-term investment costs in balance with long-term returns, such decisions aren't really trade-offs at all. Despite the complexities, the description of a company's stakeholder management is incomplete without considering the substantive-across components and, to date, the most compelling factor in that component is equity.

8.1.5 Summary

To this point, this chapter has demonstrated that stakeholder management has four main components, and it has described several important variables that relate to each of these components. This matrix advances stakeholder theory by specifying a previously underdeveloped construct. The matrix offers an actionable tool with which managers can assess gaps in their company's stakeholder management approach, and diagnosing these gaps can be a useful first step towards improving stakeholder management. Yet, in order to know which gaps truly matter, stakeholder theory must link these variables (i.e. these elements of stakeholder management) to outcomes that matter to companies. We turn our attention to this issue in the next section.

8.2 The impact of stakeholder management

Today's general manager has a threefold task: (1) to prevent and resolve instances of conflict with primary and secondary constituencies; (2) to co-ordinate the co-operative efforts of internal and external constituencies engaged in the achievement of firm goals; and (3) to manage resources in such a way as to achieve competitive advantage in the marketplace. A company's approach to stakeholder management has demonstrable effects on the quality of stakeholder relationships and, in turn, second-order effects on each of these important outcomes. For managers, it is important not only to recognise the key elements of stakeholder management (outlined above) but also to understand the relationships between these elements and the firm's effectiveness. Thus, these essential theoretical relationships bear some elaboration by stakeholder theorists.

The purpose of this section is to take a first step towards relating the aspects of stakeholder management presented above to outcomes of interest to the stakeholder theorist and the general manager alike. Because the development of research hypotheses is not the central aim of this chapter and because the four cells represent a great deal of theoretical ground to cover, these propositions are sketched out in a rather basic form, suggesting for each outcome a fundamental logic and simple propositions. Much debate exists over how to measure these constructs, but for the sake of theory development we assume that these constructs can be adequately measured.

8.2.1 Conflict

First, it is necessary to confront the problem of conflict. Protracted conflicts, played out in lawsuits, boycotts, protests and strikes, can be extremely costly to companies, and the lasting damage to a company's operations and its reputation can prove fatal. Conflict prevention and management figure heavily in the thoughts of managers, and the narrative history of the business and society field centres on such disputes (Frooman 1999): *Shell v. the Ogoni people of Nigeria, General Electric v. the Environmental Protection Agency,* etc. It is natural for us, as stakeholder theorists, to look to some aspect of stakeholder management, as elaborated in the matrix above, to explain such conflicts.

In so far as conflict involves a difference of opinion between two or more parties regarding goals, interests or means (Wall and Callister 1995), conflict between a company and its stakeholders is a natural, everyday occurrence. The critical moment in conflict with stakeholders is the escalation from **latent** conflict, i.e. differences that are perceived but not acted on, to **manifest** conflict, in which one or more parties actively opposes the behaviour of the other (Pondy 1967). In stakeholder relationships, the moment of escalation is particularly critical as it represents that moment when constituencies turn from company-mediated channels of conflict resolution to external channels such as the courts, regulatory agencies or the media, in order to oppose the company. This moment of escalation accounts most for the direct and indirect costs of conflict.

Here, then, is the fundamental role of stakeholder management in conflict prevention: to offer robust channels for mediating conflict within stakeholder relationships. While the expression of opposition and latent conflict may prove more, rather than less, vocal within these channels, escalation outside of them will occur less frequently. What would these robust channels look like? They would exhibit the two key characteristics of procedural-within stakeholder management: high levels of participation and dialogue.

First, it is important to acknowledge that opening participation channels will not decrease the likelihood that the interests of a given stakeholder group will differ from those of a company's management. Neither is participation likely to diminish the probability that stakeholders will voice those concerns, often quite vocally. Indeed, offering opportunities for stakeholders to participate in the company's decision-making process will usually produce a more messy process than top-down management. However, it will also increase the likelihood that the stakeholder group will support the eventual outcome of the process; moreover, that stakeholder group will be less likely to seek outside avenues in order to voice their concerns and seek redress. Thus,

P1

> The more avenues for participation a company provides, the more likely it will see signs of conflict.

Yet

P2

> The more avenues for participation that exist within a stakeholder relationship, the less likely conflict will escalate.

Second, as stated above, it is important to regard the quality of discourse within the stakeholder relationship. Calton (1996, 2001) has pursued work in the area of stakeholder dialogue most fruitfully among stakeholder theorists. From his work, it is our conjecture that real dialogue, the construction of a 'flow of meaning' as Isaacs (1999) characterises it, will amplify the benefits of more participative stakeholder management. Dialogic engagement ensures that stakeholder group members will have a more meaningful opportunity to voice their interests and concerns. Further, when such participation approximates dialogue, rather than 'serial monologues', stakeholders will be more likely to view managers as operating from a position of honesty and fairness (Jones 1995). Therefore, stakeholders will be more likely to use company-mediated channels for resolving conflict. The result, when a company's avenues for participation are plentiful and approximate dialogue, is that it will experience reduced conflict escalation, relative to companies with less-well-developed modes for procedural-within stakeholder management. Thus,

P3

> The more that avenues for participation have dialogic characteristics, the more likely conflict will be resolved through company-mediated channels.

Of course, stakeholder conflict often originates in substantive differences within the stakeholder relationship, and the surest way to prevent conflict is to ensure that the firm's substantive-within stakeholder management is fair and mutually beneficial. The relationship between organisational munificence and conflict is relatively straightforward. Akin to arguments made by resource dependence theorists (Pfeffer and Salancik 1978; Dess and Beard 1984), the more resources the firm is able to allocate to any given stakeholder group, the more satisfied they are likely to be with their relationship with the firm. Of course, the ethical motivations for such largesse may be questionable (e.g. attempts by corporations to co-opt politicians), and it is equally important to consider the other moral qualities of the company's approach to that stakeholder, i.e. the levels of honesty, integrity and fairness. When munificent resource allocations are made in a situation where stakeholders are being treated with integrity, they will have a far greater effect in reducing the likelihood of conflict escalation, for even slightly less munificent allocations (even outright reductions in benefits) may be offset by the accumulated goodwill created by fair and honest conduct. Thus,

P4a

> Munificence towards a given stakeholder will be positively associated with stakeholder satisfaction.

P4b

> Munificence towards a given stakeholder will be negatively associated with conflict escalation within that relationship.

P5

> Firms that deal with stakeholders from a standpoint of respect and honesty will exhibit lower levels of conflict escalating outside company-mediated channels.

8.2.2 Co-ordination

General managers must also overcome the problems of co-ordination, marshalling and aligning stakeholder contributions towards firm goals. As organisational economists have argued, the challenge of co-ordination is the reduction of transaction and agency costs accruing to the firm (Jensen and Meckling 1976; Williamson 1981). Of course, market transactions are embedded in social relationships (Granovetter 1985), and much of the effort directed at co-ordination entails maintaining functional relationships with parties contributing to the achievement of company goals, such as suppliers, employees and customers.

How does stakeholder management contribute to (or detract from) a firm's ability to overcome co-ordination problems and minimise the costs associated with them? One starting point is to treat co-ordination as a function of procedure; efficient co-ordination requires the efficient management of the interface between multiple stakeholders. Put simply, co-ordination is a function of a company's procedural-across stakeholder management, inasmuch as the company's managers must serve as a conduit between diverse groups. From this perspective, one of the main effects of representation is to allow information to be shared across the stakeholder network (Rowley 1997). Whether achieved through direct stakeholder representation (e.g. on boards of directors) or by the apportionment of responsibility to functional area heads, representation enables the integration of stakeholder efforts and perspectives. In the short term, these integrating mechanisms make collaboration possible, making stakeholders aware of their roles in the network. Over the long term, integrating mechanisms increase mutual awareness of opportunistic behaviours—they foster the development of reputations—thereby reducing agency costs and eliminating the need for costly formal monitoring efforts. Thus,

P6

> Firms that have clear organisational responsibility for integrating decision-making across stakeholder groups will exhibit lower levels of co-ordination costs than firms where such mechanisms do not exist.

The moral quality of stakeholder management also has an impact on a company's ability to reduce co-ordination costs. Jones (1995) has elaborated on the effects of substantive-within stakeholder management on effective co-ordination. While acknowledging the usefulness of Jones's model, we advance another argument: that substantive-across stakeholder management also plays a role in enabling or hampering co-ordination. While companies may conform to ethical standards in dealing with specific stakeholder groups, there is also an ethical quality attached to the way stakeholders are dealt with as an entirety or relative to each other. Ethics-based stakeholder theorists, particularly Phillips (1997), have argued that firms deal equitably with stakeholders. That is, the benefits that accrue to a particular group should be proportional to either the amount of risk borne by that group (Clarkson 1995) or the value they help to create for the organisation (Hill and Jones 1992). Firms that violate the norm of equitable treatment will suffer decreased support from the stakeholder groups receiving inequitable treatment. The question of fair and equitable treatment closely approximates the social-psychological notion of distributive justice; at the individual level, studies have demonstrated the motive powers of perceived distributive injustice (Adams 1965; Sheppard *et al.* 1992). In emphasising the importance of equitable substantive policies, we maintain that the equity of a company's approach to its multiple stakeholders will have similar affects on individual members of stakeholder groups and, by aggregation, to groups as a whole. The decreased support of stakeholder groups will necessitate many of the co-ordination efforts that Jones attributes to firms with low levels of within-stakeholder fairness. Thus,

P7

> Firms with inequitable allocation patterns across stakeholders will exhibit lower stakeholder satisfaction and higher co-ordination costs than those with equitable patterns.

Of course, the procedural and substantive factors are not entirely independent. Following the logic developed within common agency (cf. Bernheim and Whinston 1986), when information asymmetries are reduced, a company will be in a position that makes large imbalances in stakeholder resource allocation less tenable. When stakeholders are more able to compare relative resource allocations, those receiving relatively fewer resources will be more likely to withdraw support from the organisation (Hill and Jones 1992), forcing the organisation to minimise such differences. Thus,

P8

> Firms with highly developed integrating mechanisms will exhibit less variance in stakeholder satisfaction and co-ordination costs.

8.2.3 Competitive advantage

The final two propositions in this section focus on how stakeholder management can help general managers to overcome the most important of the three challenges: the need to achieve sustainable competitive advantage (Barney 1991). A complete stakeholder theory of competitive advantage is well beyond the scope of this chapter. Indeed, stakeholder theory may never have as clear a link to competitive advantage as other dominant theories of strategic management (Post *et al.* 2002a). Yet stakeholder management clearly has implications for a firm's performance. The procedural–substantive split, which lies at the heart of this chapter's integrated view of stakeholder management, places equal emphasis on the flows of information facilitated by stakeholder management processes and the impact of moral characteristics of firm behaviour. Both aspects play a role in achieving competitive advantage.

The information gained through within-relationship channels translates directly into added value while also building goodwill among stakeholder group members. The effect of procedural-within stakeholder management becomes more evident in the light of recent efforts to redefine performance in broader terms of corporate, or stakeholder, performance (Berman *et al.* 1999; Harrison and Freeman 1999), as competition transcends the traditional notion of product-market competition for customers. A firm can reap benefits from establishing multiple, high-quality communication channels not only within the customer relationship but also within all transactional relationships in which it competes for scarce resources, such as human capital and raw materials. A firm's performance, *vis-à-vis* each of these stakeholders, hinges on its ability to collect accurate information about stakeholder needs (Porter and Millar 1991). Achieving this objective depends on the firm's ability to establish open channels of information within relationships. Thus,

P9a

> Firms with more developed avenues for participation will exhibit higher levels of stakeholder satisfaction.

P9b

> Firms with more developed avenues for participation within stakeholder relationships will have higher corporate performance than those that do not have such avenues.

Moreover, the substantive nature of a firm's dealings with individual stakeholder groups will also help it to reap competitive performance advantage. The link between the action of treating stakeholders fairly and enhanced performance is that stakeholders treated with moral consideration will exhibit higher levels of satisfaction, leading to enhanced performance in areas critical to firm success (e.g. produce more efficiently, contract with the firm in more favourable terms, etc.). Indeed, as marketing scholars have discovered, the moral character of a firm's behaviour within and across stakeholder relationships influences its ability to engender identification and commitment among members of key stakeholder groups (e.g. Glynn *et al.* 1995). Thus,

P10

> Firms with higher levels of stakeholder satisfaction will exhibit higher levels of stakeholder performance.

8.3 Future directions

A single chapter can only take us so far in elaborating a clear conception of stakeholder management. The foremost measure of success for a conceptual piece is the degree to which it serves as the basis for empirical research, and this chapter advances a series of testable propositions that should help to guide empirical studies. Yet, in keeping with the goal of 'unfolding stakeholder thinking', this final section focuses on the conceptual problems that deserve more sustained attention from those who think about the stakeholder management concept. We discuss three of these issues and, in doing so, hint at the future directions in which our own model may advance.

8.3.1 Extended profiles

The multiple aspects of stakeholder management clearly have direct implications for the performance (social and financial) of the focal organisation. This chapter, examining each component in isolation, has illustrated the main effects of each of these components on important firm outcomes. The next logical step is to consider the higher-order interactions of these components. As a first step, for example, one might assume that companies can be evaluated as either having low or high engagement in each of these components. Adopting a simple notation whereby low engagement is represented by small letters and high by capital letters, one can define 16 distinct stakeholder management profiles. Thus, for example, a company that has highly developed procedures for both within- and across-stakeholder management (**PW** and **PA**), fairly munificent substantive policies within some relationships (**SW**), but relatively inequitable distribution across relationships (**sa**) would fit a **(PW)(PA)(SW)(sa)** profile.

In developing this idea further, we suspect that, of the 16 possible profiles, only a handful of profiles commonly occur. Discovering which profiles are most common is beyond the scope of this chapter but might be the product of both deductive and inductive work. For example, by making a simple assumption—companies with well-developed procedures will tend to have well-developed substantive policies—one could deduce that most companies fall into one of four types. An inductive reasoning process might arrive at a different set of possibilities. Having thus arrived at a satisfactory taxonomy, future researchers could ask why companies assume one approach over another and whether there are performance implications associated with such profiles. Finally, as one anonymous reviewer of this chapter noted, there is also the potential for a developmental logic implicit in these profiles. After all, might we not say that a company with highly developed approaches in all quadrants (i.e. all capital letters) might have a higher degree of stakeholder competence than companies with other profiles? We agree that such a logic may exist. Further, we speculate that this developmental process may relate to the organisation and industry life-cycles, though this speculation is better left for future research.

8.3.2 The aggregation problem

This chapter rests on the assumption that the within-stakeholder factors can be safely aggregated across relationships. Thus, a firm that encourages participation among most but not all of its stakeholders can be said, on average, to have a high level of participation. In our desire to diagnose stakeholder management as a company-level characteristic, this assumption is convenient and, at first glance, it also seems reasonable. Yet others have rightly criticised this assumption as untenable (Rowley and Berman 2000). For example, how communicative is a firm that offers daily briefings to institutional investors about a proposed merger but fails to mention it to employees? To what degree does the presence of a trait (e.g. participation or dialogue) within specific stakeholder relationships indicate a general disposition towards procedural-within stakeholder management? Future work on stakeholder management must offer a more persuasive logic justifying some pattern of aggregation (across relationships and issues) in order to achieve a company-level measure for each component of stakeholder management. This is not as easy as it sounds, as generalisation across stakeholder relationships is a stumbling block. The difficulty of aggregation is readily apparent and deserves much more attention.

8.3.3 The issue of fit

A third conceptual problem that remains to be solved is the question of environmental contingency. To this point, this chapter has elaborated the components of stakeholder management in a vacuum. Companies engage in various levels of each type of stakeholder management, and this engagement affects prospects for avoiding conflict, co-ordinating stakeholder contributions and achieving competitive advantage. As posited, these are direct, unmoderated relationships. Yet all environments are not alike, and stakeholders act and react in different ways depending on their structural position, resource dependence and sense of identity (Rowley 1997; Frooman 1999; Rowley and Berman 2000). Until now, this stakeholder behaviour has outstripped theory concerning stakeholder management. Now, having elaborated the most relevant features of stakeholder management, future theorists must conceive of the interactions between stakeholder management, on the one hand, and stakeholder behaviour on the other. In some cases, stakeholder management efforts work because of the behaviours that they incite on the part of stakeholders. For example, based on existing findings about how people respond to distributive justice (and injustice), this chapter proposes a relationship between equitable management and favourable stakeholder responses. Yet, in many other cases, the interactions between stakeholder management and stakeholder behaviour remain unexplored. The next step towards this understanding is to conceive of a contingent stakeholder theory probing the degree to which a company's stakeholder management approach *fits* with the features of the stakeholder set with which it interacts.

8.4 Conclusion

This chapter began with two questions: What do stakeholder theorists mean by 'stakeholder management'? And, How can the diverse approaches to stakeholder management be synthesised in a meaningful way for both stakeholder theorists and managers? To answer these, we have (a) developed a stakeholder management matrix to synthesise existing contributions; (b) detailed some of the most relevant variables involved in each of the four aspects of stakeholder management; and (c) formulated a set of testable propositions relating to the important problems confronting general managers. The propositions developed above should prove useful in guiding future empirical work; however, the main objective in writing this chapter was to offer a useful conceptual framework to synthesise and advance research on stakeholder management. By highlighting the need to view stakeholder management holistically—as having procedural and substantive aspects within and across stakeholder relationships—we hope to enable future researchers to articulate their questions and their contributions more clearly within the stakeholder management framework, embedding their work firmly in existing lines of enquiry. The intricacies of stakeholder management offer fertile ground for future stakeholder thinking. Hopefully, this chapter will serve as a useful pathway for directing some of that work.

STAKEHOLDERS AND CONFLICT MANAGEMENT
Corporate perspectives on collaborative approaches

Julia Robbins
Independent consultant, Canada

This chapter explores how collaborative approaches to conflict management have become part of sustainable and responsible business practices. It presents the results of a study in which companies' views were sought on why they decided to participate in or initiate collaborative conflict resolution processes to address disputes and on the effects that experience had on ongoing stakeholder relations.[1] The research addressed, from a Canadian corporate perspective, the question of whether it is possible to avoid or minimise the use of adversarial approaches and instead use collaborative approaches as a first tactic, not a secondary 'alternative' to be tried after all adversarial approaches have failed to address conflict with external stakeholders.

9.1 Collaborative approaches to conflict

There is a variety of collaborative approaches to addressing disputes between companies and outside stakeholders. 'Collaborative approaches' to conflict management encompass a range of methods 'in which those parties with a stake in the problem actively seek a mutually determined solution' (Gray 1989: xviii). Collaboration is not the same as compromise, in which 'neither side gets what it wants, and hence the conflict will occur again

---

1 The term 'stakeholder' is defined here as any 'persons or groups who have an interest in or could be affected by an issue or situation . . . [and those] who perceive themselves affected' (Forrest and Hix Mays 1997: 32).

and again in some other form' (Svendsen 1998: 145). There is a focus on problem-solving in collaboration, and an attempt to get the parties to focus on identifying the issues underlying their disputes. Parties are asked to treat such issues as a mutual problem to be solved collectively (Weitzman and Weitzman 2000: 195).[2]

Many experts in the field of conflict analysis argue for or predict a greater use of collaborative (rather than adversarial) approaches to resolving conflict (Hair 1984; Gray 1989; Swanson 1995; Driscoll 1996; Svendsen 1998). Driscoll (1996) argues that, as competitive conflict over natural resources increases, 'consensus-based, collaborative initiatives are increasingly being chosen as an alternative to traditional confrontational approaches to conflict resolution and problem solving of complex social issues'. While Pellow (1999: 189) concludes that non-governmental organisations should continue to employ some confrontational tactics, his study of environmental activists' experience with consensus-based decision-making argues that collaboration will continue to expand. Reilly (1986: x) argues that such methods to address environmental disputes appear 'to be on the verge of expanding into new areas of formalised decision-making'.

Much of the study on collaborative methods arises from the environmental dispute resolution field. In 1984, Gilbreath noted that 'a decade ago the urgent task of awakening people to the dangers posed by a lack of environmental policies may well have required intransigence and direct conflict' and noted a greater recognition of 'the need to embrace more constructive and cooperative tactics' (1984: 445). Dorcey and Riek (1989: 8) also see an increasing tendency towards what they call negotiative modes of decision-making in which individuals or organisations make trade-offs among themselves and adopt agreements. Collaboration, therefore, is presented as the inevitable successor to violence and rights-based systems of conflict management (Cormick 1989; Dorcey and Riek 1989; Hoffman 1993).

The need for sustainable development has added pressure to increase participation in business decisions. In 1987, the United Nations-sponsored Brundtland Report noted that, in order to ensure long-term survival, changes to existing ways of managing resources were required, and that such a reorientation was considered beyond the reach of existing decision-making structures (WCED 1987: 46). Shared decision-making is linked with the concept of sustainable development because meaningful public participation is 'essential to incorporating very different values when formulating sustainable land use and resource management plans' (Wilde 1998: 40). Hardi and Barg (1997) undertook a comprehensive review of methods used to measure sustainable development. Participation in decision-making was important in several of them.

2 Multi-stakeholder problem-solving groups composed of stakeholders with the authority to implement decisions are one of the more concrete examples of collaborative processes encountered in this study. Other examples include community advisory bodies that have some power to see their recommendations acted on. Canada's National Round Table on the Environment and the Economy, through an extensive consensus process, identified the essential elements of successful consensus building (a type of collaborative approach), and developed ten principles to guide its use (Cormick et al. 1996). The principle of self-design allows for the parties themselves to design the process, thereby increasing their sense of ownership and acceptance of its outcomes (Cormick et al. 1996: 41). Susskind et al. (1999: 6) argue that consensus building 'involves a good-faith effort to meet the interests of all stakeholders'; the Round Table's principles also require parties to make their best efforts to address the issues in good faith (Cormick et al. 1996: 35). Collaborative methods may vary, but the overall approach stresses joint efforts at negotiation and problem-solving.

Another major reason cited for this prediction is a trend towards greater participation in decision-making in general throughout society (Gilbreath 1984; Reilly 1986; Hoffman 1993; Driscoll 1996; Forrest and Hix Mays 1997). Businesses are a key part of this societal movement which parallels a trend towards greater use of team approaches as 'communities and businesses are moving from discussions of rights to interests, and from forcing to negotiation. The significance of the shift grows as . . . highly diverse communities seek to reduce violence, and companies attempt to deal with change' (Isenhart and Spangle 2000: xiii). As Gray (1989: 130) notes, 'the underlying premise to collaboration is that shared power is becoming increasingly necessary . . . In order to move ahead as a society, we must devise ways to share power.'

Other authors base their prediction of increased stakeholder collaboration on a wider recognition of the advantages of collaborative approaches (Bacow and Wheeler 1984; Bingham 1986). Cormick et al. (1996: 17) predict that 'as consensus processes become more widely used and their benefits more widely known, more parties will adopt them'.

However, the use of collaborative processes is lower than many authors predicted or desired (Amy 1987; Wondolleck 1988; Cormick 1989; DuPraw 1993). Susskind et al. (2000) note that most participants in environmental conflicts continue to 'seek all-out victory through litigation or political manoeuvring'. They argue that, because they 'have seen so many examples of the approach applied successfully', they reject the idea that collaborative approaches do not work, and insist their use could be more widespread (Susskind et al. 2000: 8).

Potential obstacles to the use of collaborative approaches were explored in the early 1980s by Cormick and others who argued that, for such processes to be selected, two conditions must be fulfilled: '(1) there is a relative balance of power between the disputants; and (2) an impasse has been reached in the controversy' (as cited by Amy 1987: 80). Amy (1987: 92) argues that, 'after it is clear that adversarial approaches cannot satisfy the disputants, only then can the qualitative shift to a new and more desirable form of political relationship take place'. This seems to imply that, in each case of conflict, the parties must try adversarial approaches first.

9.2 The research

To determine if companies felt that it really was necessary to use adversarial approaches first to addresses conflict with stakeholders before collaborative ones could successfully be used, 20 senior executives from 14 companies were interviewed (see Table 9.1).[3] The scope of the research was restricted to the experiences of Canadian companies in industries dependent on natural resources (i.e. power, forestry, mining, manufacturing), because they are often the focus of conflicts with external stakeholders over environmental and social issues. The companies reflect a diversity of natural resources sectors. The majority of the companies either are based in or have operations in British Columbia,

---

3 The study is intentionally one-sided. No attempt was made to interview non-company personnel such as members of local communities, governments or non-governmental organisations. While it would be useful to canvass the perspectives of such stakeholder groups, it was beyond the scope of this study.

Company	Primary sectors	Operations
A	Mining, metals	Canada, international
B	Natural gas utility	Canada
C	Power utility	Canada
D	Metals	Canada
E	Mining	Canada, international
F	Mining	Canada
G	Oil, chemicals	Canada, international
H	Power generation (nuclear, hydro)	Canada
I	Mining	Canada, international
J	Oil	Canada
K	Oil	Canada
L	Oil, natural gas	Canada, international
M	Natural gas	Canada
N	Forestry	Canada, international

Table 9.1 **Participating companies**

Alberta, Ontario or Quebec, and some operate outside Canada. All participants had played key roles in deciding how to address conflict with external stakeholders.[4] Participating companies self-identified as already having had some experience with collaborative processes of conflict management. This was not a comprehensive cataloguing of all cases of collaboration, but rather a reflection of several companies' perspectives on their experiences with this approach to conflict and stakeholder management. Throughout the project, the participants themselves decided what was 'effective' and 'useful', and the project's results and recommendations reflect this business perspective.

9.3 Conflicts with stakeholders

The majority of the conflicts[5] identified had at their root stakeholder concern about the impacts, environmental and/or social, of the companies' activities on the communities

---

4 Participants' areas of responsibility vary and include: public, government, regulatory, aboriginal, and/or community affairs or relations, communications, sustainable development, corporate social responsibility, ethics, environment and other operational areas.

5 A subjective definition of conflict was employed. Conflict 'occurs when one or more parties perceive incompatible goals and then equally perceive interference from the other in their desire to obtain their goal' (Tidwell 1998: 31). Participants were asked to identify conflicts; they were not provided with a definition of 'conflict', except to the extent that relevant conflicts were

in which they operate. Conflicts most often arose when companies wished to expand or construct facilities such as pipelines, wells or power-generating stations, for which approval by a regulatory authority was required. In a smaller number of cases, participants cited conflicts arising from the lobbying efforts of non-governmental advocacy groups concerned with the environmental and social impacts of existing operations. While environmental issues most often sparked controversy, underlying concerns over social issues, aboriginal rights and public participation in general were closely linked and, in most cases, inseparable, from the original conflict.

9.4 How companies collaborated

All participants professed to be 'more collaborative' than they were in the past.[6] Using Arnstein's 'Ladder of Citizen Participation' (Arnstein 1969), there were few cases of 'non-participation' many of 'tokenism (informing, consultation, placation)' and several good examples that fit in the range of 'degrees of citizen power (partnership, delegated power, citizen control)' (as cited by Rahn 1996: 95). In its most limited form, participants cited various examples of 'collaboration' that could also be termed 'consultation'. Some involved open houses at which the company presented its plans or explained its operations. Others held or participated in town hall-style meetings at which people argued their cases. Some of the companies with overseas operations cited their establishment of foundations for local community development as collaborative, as the local community has input into how the money is spent. For all the companies, the movement towards recognising outside interests was the important element in defining 'greater collaboration'.

The vast majority of the companies interviewed had been involved in some full collaborative efforts with stakeholders. Many companies employing collaboration did so through complex, third party-facilitated, multi-stakeholder bodies formed to address sustainable development concerns around new projects or ongoing operations. The time-frames of these processes ranged from several months to years. Several became permanent, multi-company, non-governmental organisation (NGO), community advisory bodies on ongoing operations. In general, the companies report they abide by the decisions or recommendations made by these multi-stakeholder groups.

As noted below, some companies exceeded the legislated requirements of public input into environmental assessment. In several cases, companies were involved with other stakeholders in developing resource management plans. Other companies developed in-

---

to be those with external actors not internal ones, such as those involved in labour–management disputes. Several of the participants who worked in communications departments objected to the use of the word 'conflict'; however, further probing revealed that what they called 'issues' or 'controversies' were comparable with what others labelled 'conflicts' or 'disputes'.

6 However, their definitions of what constituted a 'collaborative' approach varied. Some of what the participants called collaboration did not meet the criteria of parties actively seeking a solution, but were, instead, limited to greater provision of information through limited consultation exercises. On a practical level, throughout the interviews, the concept of increased collaboration implied all forms of opening the company to meaningful outside inputs.

depth, mainly bilateral, agreements with local or aboriginal communities, to govern the establishment and longer-term operation of facilities.

9.5 Patterns of first use of collaborative approaches

This section considers the first conflicts cited by participants. These are the ones that led to the use of more collaborative methods to address conflict with stakeholders.[7] What follows are not case studies, but rather an overview of several cases organised into five basic patterns of conflict and attempts at resolution (see Table 9.2).[8] These are the primary types of situation that participants encountered.

Company	Tried to assert their rights	Pushed by regulators	Pressured by NGOs	Took more than their fair share of blame	Learned from others about collaboration
A	✔				
B		✔			✔
C		✔			✔
D				✔	
E					
F					✔
G					✔
H					✔
I			✔		
J				✔	
K				✔	
L			✔		
M		✔			
N	✔		✔		

Table 9.2 *First use of collaborative approaches*

7   To respect the companies' needs for confidentiality, many of the details are omitted here. Note that, while no dates are included, most of the cases took place in the late 1990s.
8   Note that, for three companies, two of these primary patterns occurred in the same conflict, so the number of cases cited equals more than the number of participating companies.

9.5.1 *Tried to assert their rights*

Two of the companies experienced great frustration in trying to assert their legal rights through the regulatory and legal systems. Both had the right to use a particular resource and encountered difficulties in exercising those rights. Collaborative approaches were employed when rights-based mechanisms failed to resolve the conflict.

One company, over a period of decades, faced numerous obstacles. Some members of the public objected to the expansion of its operations, initially on environmental grounds. The scientists could not agree on an assessment of the environmental impacts of expansion, and the company eventually took the government to court. Despite a court judgement in the company's favour, the provincial government intervened to halt the expansion and ordered a public inquiry. Although the inquiry recommended that the project proceed, a political decision was made to halt the project. Again, the company returned to court. The government was not likely to win, and grudgingly agreed to try a negotiation process with the company, other government bodies, NGOs and other stakeholders. This collaborative process involved two dozen stakeholder groups and lasted two years, and, in the company's opinion, resulted in a satisfactory agreement.

Another company faced protests and attempted to use the court system to have protestors removed. This was, however, ineffective in the long term as protesters returned, the company's reputation was clouded and its markets were negatively affected. The government was unwilling to intervene to defend the company's resource rights in the face of such visible protest. Eventually, a multi-stakeholder, consensus-based process on resource management was established and an agreement reached.

9.5.2 *Pushed by regulators*

As noted above, many of the companies experienced conflicts precipitated by the need for regulatory approval. In three of these cases, the regulatory agencies themselves were the catalysts that pushed companies to involve outside stakeholders. One company had not had occasion to seek approval for new development for some time. The application it prepared was rejected repeatedly by the regulator. Eventually, the company realised the regulator required more assurances that the public interest would be served by the project. The regulator instructed the company to consult the community; the company did and the project proceeded. Another company's project failed to receive approval: the company had conducted an informational open house and, to its great shock, many people objected strongly to its plans. Public pressure led to a commission of inquiry; public fear led to a refusal to approve the project. In another case, the regulator not only told the company to consult, but also whom to consult, and would not accept the application until it was satisfied that public concerns and inputs had been considered. Their initial use of collaboration was essentially forced on these companies.

9.5.3 *Pressured by NGOs*

Non-governmental organisations (NGOs) had a significant impact on at least three of the participating companies. They objected to company operations based primarily on concerns about sustainable development. They used their influence to inflict damage on the companies' reputations and markets, and also conducted public protests and awareness campaigns against the companies, making it difficult for business to continue. Two of the companies have begun to talk to such NGOs about common issues of concern, such as the long-term impacts of their businesses on society. Another company completed a successful multi-stakeholder consensus-based process that led to significant changes in the company's operations and expressions of public support for the company by the NGOs. In all three cases, participants cited NGO pressure as the reason they began to at least recognise the legitimacy of the concerns expressed and began to act on them, rather than attempt to prevent protests.

9.5.4 Took more than their fair share of blame

Three of the companies characterised the conflicts that led to the first use of collaboration as cases in which they had been wrongly blamed for pollution issues for which they were only partially responsible. One company received complaints about such an issue and determined that the pollution probably did not come from its facilities. However, as one of the largest companies in the community, the public perception was such that the regulatory agency required it to respond. The company then took the initiative to form a group of similar local companies, and involved the governmental regulators and key community members in a joint effort to investigate the sources of pollution and determine what all the companies could do to minimise such problems. That group continues to exist, senior operational personnel participate and the company's operational plans are subject to its scrutiny. Two other companies faced a similar situation, with the added motivation to work together provided by a common need for approval from a regulator for expansion of their operations. In those cases, too, a multi-company body was formed with other stakeholders to develop a common information base about environmental impacts and to devise joint solutions to their management. In all cases, the complexity of issues facing the companies required them to seek out others with whom to look for solutions to joint problems.

9.5.5 Learned from others about collaboration

Two of the companies that had been pushed by regulators to involve the public went beyond the minimal requirements of basic consultation to create much more participatory processes. Both had heard of such processes and decided to attempt them. Now they have ongoing multi-stakeholder groups that develop resource management plans that the company implements.

The remaining companies used collaborative methods in their first attempts to resolve conflicts. One had created a community advisory body but, as one participant stated, 'it had no teeth' and the company's credibility was suffering in the face of continued environmental concerns. Attempts are now under way to increase the advisory body's power; however, the results are as yet inconclusive. Another company had operated for many years without much interaction of any kind with outsiders, but, when faced with the prospect of applying for approval from a regulatory agency, undertook a successful extensive campaign to develop relations with the community and involve them more in company operations. A senior executive at another company had had experience with multi-stakeholder collaborative processes and insisted from the beginning on developing such processes to guide operations. Recognition of collaboration as a tool for addressing complex issues drove all these companies.

9.6   Adversarial approaches not required

As the patterns noted above indicate, only two of the participating companies could be said to have exhausted adversarial methods of conflict resolution before resorting to collaborative methods. The others were responding to the pressures of a more complex environment in which public expectations for corporate responsibility have increased. Of these, some were largely pressured to involve stakeholders either by regulatory authorities or by NGO campaigns that were damaging their ability to conduct business. This increased public expectation of their rights to participate in decisions that affect them is forcing more companies to incorporate outside input into decisions. A few of the companies turned to collaborative measures as a result of increased complexity of their business environment. When accused of causing environmental impacts for which they were only partially to blame, co-operation with other stakeholders was required. Many of the companies responded collaboratively or used outside pressures as an opportunity to employ collaborative measures, without using adversarial ones at all. These companies had been aware of the benefits of collaboration, tried it, and found it to be a successful approach for them to manage conflict.

The majority view of successful conflict management expressed was a pragmatic one: whatever process that allows a company to go forward with its basic objectives without stakeholder obstruction. Based on that understanding of success, all but two of the participants considered that greater collaboration had led to successful outcomes; both of the exceptions are continuing their attempts to collaborate in the hope that it will eventually prove successful.

9.7   A corporate shift to collaboration

The more salient finding was that, in general, once participating companies experienced a successful collaborative experience, they switched to using collaborative measures as a first tactic when faced with other controversies and conflicts (see Table 9.3). This was true even among many of those that had been forced into using collaboration the first time. Companies have not rejected other methods, but rather have made a corporate shift towards developing better relations with stakeholders in an effort to avoid the negative effects of conflicts with them. Instead of allowing a conflict to reach extreme proportions, relations with stakeholders have taken on greater importance throughout their operations. Collaboration has become for them the pragmatic response that will allow businesses to conduct themselves in a sustainable, responsible way. As values shift, companies that develop this awareness of the broader environments in which they operate will be better prepared to address complex issues and adapt to those shifts.

Company	Experience was a turning point for the company.	There is more collaboration now with stakeholders.
A	'We realised we were naïve about the political implications of our activities—we used to think having the rights to the resource and doing due diligence was enough.' 'It doesn't matter who is right; it matters that we have neighbours we need to get along with in the long term.'	'The locals had never been properly consulted—opposition had formed in a vacuum that we created.' 'We learned it wasn't the facts that get into people's hearts and minds.' 'Other parts of the company and other locations have learned from this too.'
B	'It was my personal Bay of Pigs experience, but it was also the experience that made others in this company understand that they couldn't use old templates.'	'We all understand now the need for front-end processes with the communities. They are the experts in what is important in their community.' 'We've used the model successfully ever since.'
C	'We're a big company still going through a paradigm shift—some parts are moving faster than others.'	'We've used the model again.' 'We've got a big project coming up in a few years—there may be opposition. We've already started putting our [community relations] people in early.'
D	'This is now just part of managing our business well; it just so happens that it helps us avoid conflicts.'	'The highest levels of decision-makers are on our community advisory panels—they run all major decisions past them.'
E	'I think we're raising the bar.'	'Our reputation precedes us—and it gets us more business.'
F	'It's the new reality, but I still have questions about the legitimacy of outside participation in our decisions.'	'We're going to abide by the community board's recommendations.'
G	'You have to be personally convinced that these things matter.'	'We changed our corporate structure to go beyond our legal responsibilities.'
H	'It was our big awakening. We realised we had virtually ignored the community through benign neglect.'	'Other sites are now being handled in the same way, even though there are no major events brewing.'
I	'We realised stakeholder engagement is key, but are still working on how it fits.'	'Most of the company is starting to get more comfortable with it.'
J	'It's been the agenda all along.'	'We've created positions, got a relations manual—it's ongoing.'

Table 9.3 **Selected comments on the impacts of participants' first collaborative experiences** (continued over)

Company	Experience was a turning point for the company.	There is more collaboration now with stakeholders.
K	'We eased our way into this thing.'	'We're still moving towards joint decision-making, but we share lots of information and consultation is now fully integrated into planning ever step of the way.'
L	'What we are being asked to do goes way beyond what we are capable of doing.'	'We've put lots of resources into this and worked with everyone.'
M	'We're in a culture change process.'	'Our applications certainly are more thorough now.'
N	'The genetic code of the company has been changed . . . we've moved into new relationships that allow us to deal with complexity.' 'It inspired us . . . We came to see discord in a less negative light . . . as long as it was not totally destabilising, we came to see diversity between all the different interests as being a good thing.'	'We moved toward an adaptive management system, away from a prescriptive system with an emphasis on rules and compliance.'

Table 9.3 (continued)

Following the first cases as outlined above, most of the participating companies made significant changes in the way they managed stakeholder relations. The failure of a project to go forward, and the concomitant financial losses, prompted one participant to characterise it as 'the learning experience that showed the rest of the company how not to do things'. Thereafter, stakeholder relations was given much greater prominence. The company now always involves outside stakeholders meaningfully in new projects. Some companies noted their successes in having projects approved without being required to face a hearings process, because the regulator acknowledged that they had already addressed stakeholder concerns through collaborative processes.

The experience, for some, generated a model on which they now base other relationships. Some processes resulted in codes of conduct or operating practices that are raising the standards in various industries. Many of the participants' planning processes now include public consultation and input at much earlier stages and throughout the project's development. Others noted that they reviewed, or are reviewing, how they relate to stakeholders at other locations where they have operations.

Several participants remarked that the collaborative experience made them realise that facts do not necessarily change people's minds, and that companies need to build relationships and trust if they want outsiders to understand and respect business interests. Opposition, in some cases, had 'formed in a vacuum' caused by companies' failure to inform and involve the public. A few participants noted that they no longer trusted the government or legal system to protect their rights to resources; they would not reject using such methods in future but, in general, try to resolve issues collaboratively first.

For a few, that first case was a formative experience that fundamentally changed the company's view of its responsibilities. Shifting the corporate culture towards greater respect for stakeholder input was cited either as having been accomplished, in a few cases, or as something senior leadership was strongly promoting in many others. A few of the participants who had been involved in extensive multi-stakeholder processes remarked on the influence they had on moving the company from its old system of management based on compliance and rules to one that emphasised results and the creativity required to achieve them. They are also starting to look beyond their legal and fiduciary responsibilities when making decisions, to consider the full social, economic and environmental implications of their activities.

These changed attitudes can be seen in many of the participants' responses when asked the research question of whether it is always possible to collaborate, or necessary to try other methods of conflict resolution first. Few answered specifically about trying other approaches. Most asserted that collaboration is now the best option, no matter what the case (see Table 9.4).

9.8 Advantages of collaboration

The reasons participants remained committed to collaborative processes were numerous. The primary reason many cite is that, in order to have sustainable business practices, involving stakeholders is essential. It allows companies to 'do business better, longer, and more sustainably'. This supports the majority view in current conflict management literature.[9]

Many participants (including those forced to collaborate that first time) feel that collaboration is worth trying, because its inherent advantages make it the best approach. Most participants argued that it was preferable to collaborate first and avoid courts wherever possible. Most participating companies have found that increasing stakeholder input in general is beneficial. Some have begun to see stakeholders as 'experts' in their communities. Greater outside input at earlier planning stages allows companies to anticipate concerns. Others have found that, because they nurture relationships on an ongoing basis, they receive a fair hearing when issues arise. Some collaborative efforts with communities have convinced regulators that companies have done all they can to

---

9   Collaborative approaches are seen by many conflict management practitioners as the best way to address conflicts (Gray 1989; Svendsen 1998; Isenhart and Spangle 2000; Susskind *et al.* 2000). Collaboration's touted advantages are multiple. It is seen as more legitimate and long-lasting because participants are directly involved in settlement (Amy 1987; Gray 1989; Swanson 1995; Kaner 1996; Susskind *et al.* 1999; Isenhart and Spangle 2000). 'Through participation in the negotiation process, a party may come to a more complete understanding of its interests, both as a result of becoming more informed, but also because of changes in its assessment of risk, including the risk of not reaching a settlement' (Sigurdson 1987: 4). In general, collaboration allows parties to address complex issues more effectively by promoting creative solutions (Hair 1984; Fisher *et al.* 1991).

Company	'Is it possible to collaborate always, or do you have to use other methods of conflict resolution first?'
A	'When you use a public resource you have lots of stakeholders, so you need to look at them collaboratively from the start.'
B	'Collaboration is a good, logical start.' 'It's hard to convince the lawyers and accountants—if they dominate your organisation you'll have to suffer through the bad stuff first.'
C	'It has to make business sense; it's not worth it for small projects where compensation or pay-outs will suffice.' 'Generational change will help—an attitude change with new awareness of corporate social responsibility.'
D	'If you have a short-term view there's no need to collaborate—you just pay more in legal bills and bad publicity; if your goal is long-term presence and ease of operations, there is no alternative to always collaborating.'
E	'It takes time, but it would take longer if you didn't communicate and collaborate.'
F	'It is now the new reality.'
G	'Perhaps you can learn from others' experiences (Bhopal, *Exxon Valdez*), but you have to be convinced that the public does have a legitimate right to participate in decisions that affect them.'
H	'It not a case thing, it's an attitude thing. You don't need an extreme catalytic event to shift to collaborating, but it often happens that way.'
I	'It's a more complex environment now; we have to involve others.'
J	'We still arrest protestors if they put us or themselves in physical danger, but we are talking with them too.' 'You need at least some common ground to collaborate.'
K	'It's the way to go.'
L	'Fundamental differences can preclude the use of collaborative processes.'
M	'I think now you have to do it.'
N	'We will not give up on some legal or government methods, but our first approach is now to attempt to collaborate.'

Table 9.4 *'Is it possible to collaborate always, or do you have to use other methods of conflict resolution first?'*

reach agreement. Collaboration can also increase the sense of ownership and let companies both share responsibility and give credit to others for resolving conflicts.

Participants have found that working with stakeholders can improve their reputations and even enhance business opportunities. In at least one case, a company's reputation as a good corporate citizen led to it being invited into another community. Sometimes the very act of agreement will help to minimise the perception of conflict: one company found that, after agreement to resolve a pollution issue was reached, local residents reported a decrease in pollution, even though the measures to control the problem had not yet been taken. As one participant stated, 'collaboration just works better than adjudication; it's less costly and much less damaging in the long term'.

The specific benefits of more formal, multi-stakeholder problem-solving group processes were repeated by multiple participants. While not all such processes in which participants had experience required decisions to be made by consensus, most did. Processes in which multiple stakeholders meet together, with the purpose of addressing a conflict collaboratively, are ideal for addressing the inherently complex nature of sustainable development conflicts.

The nature of multi-stakeholder processes is conducive to developing sustainable business practices. Before stakeholders can discuss solutions, these processes necessitate various clarifications and the development of a common understanding of the players and issues. They can involve research into the facts of a case, increasing the scientific understanding of the impacts of all stakeholder actions. One of the first activities is often the identification of stakeholders and their interests. It forces each party to identify its values and interests, and move beyond specific positions on how to protect those interests. This education process in a neutral setting can help stakeholders to understand each other's interests and their own core values better. Identification of common concerns is then possible.

Because not all self-identified stakeholders share the same concerns, a multi-stakeholder process helps to determine who really has a stake. One of the most often-cited benefits was the tendency of such groups to self-discipline, and to bring discussion to a reasonable level by downplaying rhetoric. Hard-line positions increase volatility and make it difficult for resolution to emerge; a multi-stakeholder group process is a valuable method to decrease such extremism and increase understanding of different groups. Such diverse views can be made productive by raising a range of options to address the situation. They can result in genuine innovation, if all parties can agree on basic objectives. The process focuses on results more than on how to reach them and it can be quite creative. All parties tend to see themselves as responsible for part of the solution. In contrast, adversarial approaches to conflict management force each side to take an extreme position, knowing that what often results will be a compromise somewhere between those extremes.

Collaboration is an ongoing method of conflict management. Companies are in a better position to deal with future controversy. It keeps lines of communication open, whether or not permanent bodies are established. Because better relationships are developed and stakeholders are familiar with how to successfully resolve a conflict, in future, multi-stakeholder collaborative processes can be repeated if necessary. Overall, collaborative methods provide companies with tools to better address conflicts and anticipate them before they arise.

A strong theme emerged from participants' reasons for adopting greater collaboration: in order to conduct business in a sustainable way, collaboration is essential. If a company's goal is long-term presence and ease of operations, collaboration with stakeholders is vital. It helps businesses to integrate different ecological, economic and social perspectives to make sustainable decisions. The alternative is always to be 'playing catch-up' and conducting 'damage control'. As one participant said, collaborating with stakeholders 'is just part of managing our business well; it just so happens that it helps us avoid conflicts'.

9.9 Limitations of collaboration

Despite the participants' and conflict analysts'[10] strong support of it, it is important to have a realistic view of the impacts that taking a more collaborative approach to stakeholder relations can have on a company. Collaboration does not necessarily minimise the controversy to which a company is exposed. It could even increase it, as greater scrutiny is possible. As expectations are raised, there is a risk to a company's reputation if it fails to follow through or to manage its involvement in a collaborative process successfully. There is also the risk that some dissident stakeholders will refuse to participate, and generate future controversy or conflict. Indeed, defining who is a 'legitimate stakeholder' can prove difficult. Overall, there is no guarantee that collaboration will always result in a workable agreement.

The money and resources involved in collaborative processes can be considerable. In addition to expenses associated with the process itself, agreements reached through such processes could require greater expenditure than originally envisioned. Often, significant human and financial resources are devoted to collaborative processes themselves, resources that could have been devoted to other activities. In some industries, the profit margins are narrower than in others. Some of the participants involved in large-scale, capital-intensive projects considered several million dollars spent on collaboration worth the extra effort, given that their profits were measured in hundreds of millions. In contrast, others had little financial room in which to manoeuvre. Two companies noted that they could no longer afford the old way of merely providing financial compensation to affected parties as the number of parties had increased exponentially. Collaboration in those cases led to fewer monetary payments.

Collaboration processes can be slow and frustrating. All participants noted the long time it takes to approach issues collaboratively. The process can often engender tension between short-term or shareholder interests and long-term timing requirements of a collaborative approach. (However, most participants argued that this time spent early on in addressing the process helped to decrease the overall time of a project's completion.)

10   The problems cited most frequently in conflict management literature are: increased complexity as more people become involved, lengthy and sometimes costly processes, and the risk of unfulfilled or unrealistically raised stakeholder expectations (Bacow and Wheeler 1984; Amy 1987; Cormick *et al* 1996). There are some case studies that attempt to evaluate collaborative processes (e.g. Bacow and Wheeler 1984; Bingham 1986; Dorcey and Riek 1989; Susskind *et al.* 1999), but in general the literature tends to downplay the negative aspects of collaboration.

Initially, collaboration usually creates more complexity. Plainly put, many participants complained that it was just harder to get things done quickly with more people involved.

The type of company also affects the likelihood of collaboration taking hold. Companies such as power utilities with a virtual monopoly have tended to take what one participant called 'an arrogant, "trust us", approach' to relating to stakeholders. With increased privatisation, collaboration becomes more necessary and more common. Several participants commented on a greater client focus in 'new industries', such as services, than exists in older, resource extraction ones. The general shift towards increased customer focus has also had an impact on the way companies relate to all stakeholders.

Collaboration works best when basic values conflicts are recognised and not allowed to prevent co-operation. While Hair (1984: 532) argues that collaboration's utility is limited primarily to 'local resource disputes that can be brokered; not values, which cannot', the study findings indicate a wider applicability. A danger of collaboration is that the external stakeholders might question the basic premise of the company's operations, not just the manner in which they are carried out. Sometimes, clashes over basic values impede progress, or prevent parties from communicating. There will probably continue to be stakeholders who object to what they perceive to be unsustainable natural resource practices, including the basic premise of wealth creation through natural resource development. However, those participants more experienced with collaboration argue that the challenge is to recognise differences, and focus on common ground. One cited a case in which a representative of an NGO said that he disagreed with the project, but that, as a result of increased understanding and respect gained through the collaborative process, would no longer prevent it from proceeding.

9.10 Conclusions

This project asked whether it is possible to avoid or minimise the use of adversarial approaches and instead use collaborative approaches as a first tactic, not a secondary 'alternative' to be tried after all adversarial approaches have failed. Based on both the patterns of conflict resolution as experienced by the participating companies and on the participants' responses to that question, it can be concluded that it is possible to do so.

More significantly, the companies that have employed collaborative approaches to relations with stakeholders have become committed to it. The importance of making a shift to greater collaboration outweighs the importance of approaching each potential conflict separately. Collaboration has allowed them to make decisions that address the needs for sustainable development. Despite collaboration's challenges, this study has shown that, once companies experience a successful collaborative experience, they prefer to use collaborative measures as a first tactic when faced with other controversies and conflicts, and as a way of managing ongoing relations with their stakeholders. If businesses want to operate in a sustainable way, this study has found that collaborative relations with stakeholders are vital.

This is also likely to be true for companies outside the natural resources sector that are also trying to achieve their corporate social responsibility mandates. In the 1980s, companies strove to achieve those mandates mainly by making donations and meeting environmental standards set by governments. In the 1990s, corporate social responsibility became about investing in communities, with the expectation of a return on that investment. Now, socially responsible companies are taking a holistic approach to sustainable development and attention has shifted towards accountability, transparency and verified reporting. The project's findings and recommendations reflect this shift in attention towards the need for greater relationship building, trust and openness with stakeholders.

9.11 Recommendations

This study of the use of collaborative approaches in conflict resolution found that this conflict management technique was being applied more broadly to ongoing stakeholder relations. Building collaborative stakeholder relations better manages conflict and minimises the destructive effects of conflicts when they arise. Developing ongoing good relations with stakeholders is the best conflict management approach a company could take.

The following recommendations were based on inputs from the study participants themselves, and are directed at all companies interested in better managing stakeholder relations by incorporating collaborative approaches to conflict management into their operations.

- **Accept that conflict is inevitable**. Do not expect to avoid conflict. However, you can minimise the destructive effects of conflict by being more collaborative with outside stakeholders. Doing so often results in a better resolution than if you relied on adversarial methods.

- **Adopt a longer-term view**. If you want your business to be sustainable, merely ensuring that you meet your fiduciary and legal responsibilities is not enough. Whether you like it or not, outside stakeholders demand a greater voice in the decisions that affect them. Collaboration with stakeholders can help you to address the complex problems associated with operating sustainably. Have the courage to stand up for long-term timelines instead of short-term quick fixes.

- **Put a face on your company**. It is not enough to do the right thing anymore; people have to know about it, too. However, to rely solely on impersonal communication methods is a mistake; you need face-to-face contact with the people who could help or hinder your interests. Talking about your commitment to sustainable development is not sufficient to convince most stakeholders of your credibility. You cannot just hire an outside public relations firm to show your integrity. It is important to know all your stakeholders, assess community opinion, identify leaders and talk to them.

- **Communicate early**. Get ahead of conflict by analysing and talking to communities as early as possible. Involve the community in your business before you have trouble; establish lines of communication, build trust, so that when you need public approval, the groundwork will have been laid. When undertaking a new project, try to talk to stakeholders early enough in the process so that their input really can change how a project proceeds. Remember that your stakeholders sometimes may want more than just facts. You can avoid or decrease the negative effects of conflict by keeping lines of communication open. It may raise more public controversy in the short term, but should help to reach sustainable solutions in the longer term.

- **Get the whole company on board.** It is important to align all your communications at all levels with corporate values because the public can see inconsistencies between what employees say and what the CEO says to shareholders. Incorporating a more collaborative approach may require considerable leadership within your company to shift employee values towards recognition of the need to deal with outside stakeholders and to truly respect their opinions and input. When you show them the benefits of collaboration, even stereotypically 'stubborn' engineers and accountants can change their attitudes. Some companies choose incentives that are more concrete: for example, bonus systems tied to demonstrated ability to work with stakeholders.

- **Don't pretend to collaborate.** The major risk to engaging outside stakeholders is that your company lacks credibility when it does not respond to their input. Collaboration does not mean giving in to every 'demand'. Through a collaborative approach you can stand up for your interests, be honest and accept trade-offs. At its fullest application, it can imply that you should be willing not to go ahead with a project if a collaborative process shows that it is not in the best interests of many stakeholders. As one participant put it, 'I'd rather have us wrong and not go ahead'.

- **Keep trying—a collaborative approach is worth the effort.** Collaboration is a difficult, but valuable, path. Once you start being open and transparent, you cannot really go back. You will need to continue to collaborate, as your reputation will always precede you. Through collaboration you can recognise fundamental differences, then move beyond them and say to stakeholders, 'given our differences, how will we work together on the rest of the agenda?' Collaborating is a pragmatic way of alleviating the negative effects of conflict and dealing with the complexities inherent in managing a business in a sustainable, responsible manner.

MANAGING CORPORATE STAKEHOLDERS

Subjecting Miles's 1987 data-collection framework to tests of validation*

James Weber
Duquesne University, USA

David M. Wasieleski
University of Pittsburgh, USA

The challenge of managing corporate stakeholders—understood as individuals or groups who are affected by or affect the organisation (Freeman 1984)—has been a long and arduous task for business executives. Never was this challenge greater in the history of American business than in the 1960s and 1970s. During these decades social activists from nearly every venue challenged managers and business practices with regards to product safety, employment practices, environmental responsibility and other issues affecting the firm's operations and profitability. Managers attempted to develop successful strategic responses to these challenges, often turning to academics or consultants for support.

One promising development from this petition for help was the concept of corporate social performance (CSP) and its more recent incarnation, corporate citizenship. These notions have received much attention in the business and society literature (Altman and Vidaver-Cohen 2000; Wartick and Cochran 1985). Primarily, the CSP movement gained momentum as stakeholders, such as consumers and social activists, voiced their disapproval of business's lack of responsiveness to societal issues and needs. Ironically, despite this attention, a comprehensive definition of CSP was lacking until the early 1990s (Wood 1991).

Unfortunately, the maturation of the field was slow due to conflicting and independent research ideas developed through scattered research efforts (Wood 1991). Few attempts were made to harness the individual theories proposed to analyse facets of a company's

---

* An earlier version of this chapter was presented at the national annual Academy of Management meeting, August 2000, under a different title.

responsiveness to its social environment. One of the most profound and comprehensive efforts was described in Robert Miles's book, *Managing the Corporate Social Environment* (1987).[1] Miles's framework and resulting model were designed to aid executives in the diagnosis of their organisation's performance and ultimately help them to intervene and improve their company's social performance and corporate citizenship.

Although an important contribution to the fields of CSP and corporate citizenship, Miles's framework was not without shortcomings. We found four weaknesses in his framework, which severely question the framework's internal and external validity. First, Miles did not validate whether the multiple overall business exposure measures in his framework were **essential** for an understanding of managing corporate stakeholders. Second, Miles did not consider whether additional overall business exposure measures were necessary to guarantee the **comprehensiveness** of this dimension in his framework. Third, Miles did not subject the **strength of the interrelationships** between the key components of his framework to rigorous analysis. And, fourth, the external validity of Miles's framework was suspect since Miles used only a limited number of firms from the insurance industry in his initial sample. Thus, it was unknown whether Miles's framework was **generalisable** across multiple industries with potentially widely varying stakeholder relationships.

The purpose of this research was to verify and expand on the framework that Miles used to construct his grounded theory of corporate stakeholder management. By subjecting the key components in Miles's framework to path analysis regression and correlation analysis and by analysing a larger database of field-based corporate case studies, we were able to:

- Test the necessity of the multiple overall business exposure measures included in Miles's framework

- Identify any new, critical components to be added to the overall business exposure measures in Miles's framework

- Measure the strength of the interrelationships between the key components in Miles's framework

- Generalise the applicability of Miles's framework across multiple industries

Systems management and philosophy of science literatures provided the logic for focusing our efforts on these four tests of validation. Essentialist philosophers 'argue that the term cause should only be used to refer to variables that explain a phenomenon in the sense that these variables, when taken together, are both necessary and sufficient for the effect to occur' (Cook and Campbell 1979: 14). These authors believed that it was important to completely understand all the determining factors causing an effect so as to 'be explicit about the factors that necessarily and inevitably produce the effect' (Cook and Campbell 1979: 18). We sought to verify and be explicit about the determining variables

---

1   We acknowledge that, in Miles's book, the author presented both a framework for data collection (in Chapter 1) and a grounded theory model based on his findings (in Chapter 13). Since we were seeking to replicate and validate the data-collection framework used by Miles, we used the same framework, with little modification, for our data collection and analysis to test the validity of Miles's earlier findings.

in Miles's original framework that affect a firm's stakeholder management and corporate citizenship.

C. West Churchman posited in his seminal work on systems and organisation (1971) that one of the main problems with designing a system was the determination of its basic components. The boundaries of the system became profoundly important. The designer of the system or framework must 'identify the whole relevant system and its components . . . and their interrelationships' (Churchman 1971: 8). Thus, Churchman was speaking of the essentiality and comprehensibility of the components of a system and the inter-relationships of these components.

Moreover, Churchman claimed that one aim in designing a system for research was the 'goal of generality'. Thus, when 'another designing mind faced with similar problems' used the model, the design was generalisable to a 'broader class of problems' (Churchman 1971: 6). We wanted to see if Miles's original framework was applicable to other industries beyond insurance that may have differing stakeholder relationships.

Generalisations from convenience samples in business ethics research are common-place (Randall and Gibson 1990: 463). In their study on the methodology of business ethics literature, Randall and Gibson advocated the use of random samples rather than convenience samples in research. Since Miles's original framework concentrated only on the insurance industry, a verification of his framework to other industries is warranted. Our study attempted to provide this verification of Miles's original design.

If significant research is interested in the 'desire for understanding and explanation' (Daft 1984: 12), then it is completely valid to verify the usefulness of a framework's dimensions and design. Prior to our study, Miles's original framework explained only the management of corporate stakeholder relationships with regard to the insurance industry. We wanted to expand his study to test the framework's validity, this being defined as 'the degree to which inferences from scores on tests or other assessments are supported or justified on the basis of actual evidence' (Schoenfeldt 1984: 74). Thus, validity demonstrates the 'degree of relatedness between inferences and actual events' (1984: 74). We wanted to discover how 'valid' Miles's original framework was in deter-mining how managers assess their corporate stakeholder relationships and corporate citizenship.

10.1 Literature background

10.1.1 Stakeholder theory

Scholars generally recognise R. Edward Freeman's classic work, *Strategic Management: A Stakeholder Approach* (1984), as the formal, academic beginning of stakeholder theory. While choosing not to engage in the accuracy of this claim, we acknowledge that Free-man provides for scholars and managers a clear picture of a turbulent environment demanding a system or framework to managing the various relationships contained within this dynamic environment. According to Freeman, the demands from owners, customers, employees and suppliers—those stakeholders traditionally understood by management models or theories as seeking change from the organisation—are accompanied by the demands from new, emerging stakeholders with powerful potential to influence the organisation—governments, competitors, consumer advocates, environmentalists, special-interest groups and the media (see Part 1: 'The Stakeholder Approach' in Freeman 1984).

Freeman criticises the traditional models that describe these organisational relationships, referred to as the 'managerial view' of business, and warns, 'the Managerial View of the firm simply provides no cohesive way of understanding the changes that have and will occur' (1984: 22). The 'stakeholder view of the firm', developed by Freeman and elaborated on by subsequent scholars, presents a more systematic and complete representation of the organisation and its stakeholders. In addition, the stakeholder view enables managers and others to evaluate each stakeholder relationship at any point in time in terms of its importance to the organisation, potential to benefit or harm the organisation, and its stability or instability as a change agent within the organisation's environment.

The richness of Freeman's contribution may be in recognising what follows his classic book, in addition to what is contained in his work. Managers continued to struggle with managing the expanding list of organisational stakeholders. Scholars began to investigate more deeply the nature and impact of these stakeholders on organisations. Evolutionary reformulations of Freeman's stakeholder view emerged as managers sought to strategically control their organisation's stakeholder relations and as scholars attempted to model, dissect and predict organisations' stakeholder relationships. The modern conception of stakeholder management can be seen in the notions of CSP and corporate citizenship.

10.1.2 *Corporate social performance/corporate citizenship*

The general understanding of business and society relationships has a nomadic history, evolving through many different names and emphases to its present-day understanding as corporate social performance (CSP) and corporate citizenship. Through its development, the field has modified what the business and society relationships are and has used various framework structures from which to evaluate a firm's performance.

The term 'corporate social responsibility' was first introduced in the 1950s. Carroll examined the social responsibility of business by integrating economic, legal, ethical and discretionary expectations of society towards businesses (Carroll 1979). Corporate social responsibility has been defined as 'the firm's consideration of, and response to, issues beyond narrow economic, technical, and legal requirements of the firm . . . [to] accomplish social benefits along with the traditional economic gains which the firm seeks' (Davis 1973: 312).

This term gradually gave way to 'corporate social responsiveness'. Frederick (1994, originally 1978) coined the term CSR2, or corporate social responsiveness, as opposed to CSR1, where the 'R' means 'responsibility'. Corporate social responsiveness research influenced many business and society models. Freeman (1984) argued that stakeholder[2] management gave rise to corporate social responsiveness, while Cochran and Wood

---

2   While many definitions of 'stakeholder' can be found in the literature, we understand a stakeholder to be 'any group or individual who can affect or is affected by the achievement of the organisation's objectives' (Freeman 1984: 46).

(1984) credited issues management with affecting the social responsiveness of firms. Finally, Frederick illustrated that social responsiveness had several shortcomings, the most significant of which deals with the absence of value theory in the field.

In retrospect, Wood (1991) characterised these developments into a broader category of CSP. Sethi (1979) relied on work by Ackerman and Bauer (1976) and Frederick (1994, originally 1978) to create categories for assessing CSP. Archie Carroll (1979) went a step further by formulating a three-dimensional model comprising mapping of various social issues, philosophies of social responsiveness, and social responsibility categories separated in terms of economic, legal, ethical and discretionary responsiveness (Carroll 1979).

In 1985, Wartick and Cochran recognised the transformation of the term CSP and discussed the evolution of the CSP model. From their historical account, they devised their own CSP model that integrated the principles of social responsibility, social responsiveness and social issues. Their definition of CSP was born from this model and simply involved the interaction of the three factors. Next, by focusing on the dynamics of social responsiveness, Wood was able to build on Wartick and Cochran's model and composed a current and viable definition of CSP. Wood defined CSP as

> A business organisation's configuration of principles of social responsibility, processes of social responsiveness, and policies, programs and observable outcomes as they relate to the firm's societal relationships (1991: 693).

According to Mitnick (1993: 15), 'Wood's work represents a very significant advance in our understanding of corporate social behaviour'. Mitnick went on to say that, since Wood's landmark piece in 1991, 'hers is easily the most successful encompassing attempt' to integrate earlier work (Mitnick 1993: 15).

Swanson (1995) reoriented the CSP model devised by Wood by injecting a normative element. She sought to integrate the economic and duty-aligned perspectives that drive human behaviour. These two perspectives were linked across the principles of social responsibility, the processes of social responsiveness and the outcomes, or social impacts, of corporate behaviour (Swanson 1995: 43). Her work marked a critical moment in CSP development in that shortcomings were acknowledged in the existing framework and future research directions were outlined.

The final progression of this notion into its current-day version emphasises the citizenry responsibilities of a business organisation to society. Corporate citizenship refers 'to businesses acting responsibly toward their stakeholders' (Post et al. 2002b: 81). This notion encompasses businesses proactively addressing business and society issues, building partnerships with stakeholders, seeking benefits through social strategic goals and integrating financial performance with social performance (Altman and Vidaver-Cohen 2000). Additional conceptual and applied descriptions of corporate citizenship have been forthcoming in The Journal of Corporate Citizenship.

10.1.3 Managing the corporate social environment

Embedded in business and society explorations and relevant to our research is Robert Miles's 1987 study of the insurance industry in its effort to manage the corporate stakeholders within the firm's social environment. Miles noted:

Executive leaders of America's largest corporations have been confronted during the past two decades with an unprecedented increase in social issues impinging upon their business policies and practices (1987: 1).

These 1960s and 1970s social issues included the emergence of consumer advocates, spearheaded by Ralph Nader's fight against the US automobile industry; environmentalists calling for businesses to be accountable for water and air quality; anti-Vietnam activists attacking the military industrial complex's manufacturing of conventional and chemical weapons; African-American groups organised under the civil rights movement and calling for an end to discriminatory employment practices; women's groups accusing businesses of gender bias and discrimination; labour unions demanding safer working conditions; and communities seeking an end to the use and transport of toxic materials needed by nuclear energy plants.[3]

Miles borrowed from strategic management and organisation theory to create a strategic approach for the management of corporate stakeholders. (His framework is described in the next section of this chapter.) However, we challenged Miles's work in terms of the essentiality, comprehensiveness and strength of the interrelationships of key components, as well as the framework's generalisability across industries.

Besides the potential weaknesses cited in this chapter, Miles's framework and model had other critics. Donna Wood (1991) mentioned that Miles concentrated too much on corporate responsiveness, since it was only one part of social performance (Wood 1991). Bhambri and Sonnenfeld (1988) called Miles's procedure for assessing CSP simple, since it narrowly interfaced with the public in that it only examined the insurance industry. Their 1988 field study focused on two industries—insurance and forest products—to analyse CSP and organisational structure.

Steve Brenner (1988: 633) reviewed Miles's 1987 book favourably overall, yet admitted that it was not clear 'how other scholars' work influenced the research design or final conclusions'. He also questioned the obtuse definitions of key factors used in the general framework. Specifically, he pointed out that no mechanisms were provided for firms to be categorised into high- or low-performance groups. Even more problematic may have been Miles's assumption that high ratings on CSP functions were indicative of the contributions that a firm makes to society. This could be the result of using only insurance firms in his research.

Despite their reservations, most scholars recognised the potential for Miles's framework to become an important and useful contribution to the quest of measuring an organisation's management of stakeholders and the pursuit of corporate citizenship. Therefore we propose the following research tests:

- **Test 1: Essentiality.** Is each of the multiple measures in Miles's overall business exposure component necessary?

- **Test 2: Comprehensiveness.** Are there measures missing from Miles's framework that would significantly contribute to explaining an organisation's business exposure to the social environment?

- **Test 3: Strength of the interrelationships.** Are the relationships between the key components in Miles's framework significantly correlated?

---

3 Adapted from Post *et al.* 2002b: 81.

■ **Test 4: Generalisability**. Are the interrelated patterns of the key components in Miles's framework applicable to other industry groups?

10.2 Miles's framework

In response to the new challenges placed on businesses to manage corporate stakeholders, Robert Miles devised a data-collection framework (see Fig. 10.1) to help executive leaders understand and manage the social turbulence. In the midst of this upheaval, it was assumed that managers recognised the importance of behaving as a good corporate citizen.

With CSP improvement as the goal, his framework was designed to facilitate organisational diagnosis and intervention of a firm's stakeholder management. More specifically, his framework identified key factors that affected corporate citizenship and the stakeholder relationships that existed among those factors. A summary of the main

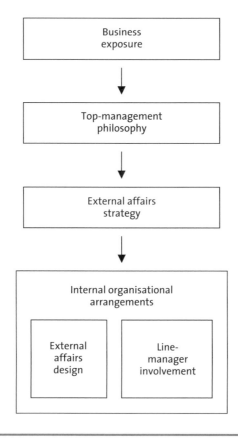

Figure 10.1 *Miles's data-collection framework for managing the corporate stakeholders*

components of the original framework is provided in Table 10.1. Each component lies on a continuum (see Tables 10.2–10.5). While firms may lie somewhere between the extremes, Miles believed that most companies could be characterised as one type or the other.

Key factor	Measurement dimensions	Tool characteristics	Postulated linkage
Overall business exposure	Product mix	Availability, affordability, safety	no linkage
	Customer mix	Industrial versus consumers	
	Geographic mix	Urban versus rural	
Top-management philosophy	Institution-oriented belief systems	Concerned with consequences to industry	Overall business exposure
	Enterprise-oriented belief systems	Concerned with firm-centred consequences	
External affairs strategy	Collaborative/problem-solving	Strategies focus on society's needs	Top-management philosophy
	Individualistic/adversarial	Strategies focus on economic self-interest of firm	
Internal organisational arrangements	External affairs design	Breadth, depth, and integration of employees devoted to external affairs activities	External affairs strategies
	Line-manager involvement	Staff sophistication in organising external affairs activities	

Table 10.1 ***Miles's (1987) original framework summary chart***

10.2.1 *Overall business exposure*

Miles begins his four-tiered framework with **overall business exposure**. Business exposure simply shows to what extent the organisation is vulnerable to unwelcome influences from the social environment. Exposure is measured on a continuum from high to low, based on a firm's product, customer and geographic mixes (see Tables 10.1 and 10.2 for additional description of these measures).

Measurement dimension	High-exposure company	Low-exposure company
Product mix	Necessity goods; negative contingencies	Luxury goods; few contingencies
Customer mix	Public	Commercial/industrial
Geographic mix	Urban	Rural

Table 10.2 **Continuum of Miles's (1987) measure of overall business exposure**

Characteristic value, intention or goal	Institution-oriented company	Enterprise-oriented company
Integration with society	High	Low
Strategic outlook	Long-term	Short-term
Strategic orientation	Adapts	Preserves status quo

Table 10.3 **Continuum of Miles's (1987) measure of top-management philosophy**

Characteristic of company actions and programmes	Collaborative and problem-solving company	Individualistic and adversarial company
Interaction with stakeholders	Open	Minimal and legal
Interests	Social and economic	Economic only
Strategic implementation	Long-term	Short-term
External affairs staff	Sophisticated	None

Table 10.4 **Continuum of Miles's (1987) measure of external affairs strategies**

Measurement dimension	Sophisticated	No or little sophistication
External affairs design	Extensive breadth, depth, integration of personnel	Few or no workers devoted to external affairs activities
Line-manager involvement	High	Low

Table 10.5 **Continuum of Miles's (1987) measure of internal organisational arrangements**

10.2.2 Top-management philosophy

Next in Miles's framework is **top-management philosophy**. Given the exposure to the social environment, it is necessary to determine how the corporation chooses to deal with society. This philosophy is deeply rooted in the executives' underlying values and beliefs regarding their firm's role in society: that is, its corporate citizenship. The philosophy also derives from the corporation's character and political orientation of the managers. Part of the underlying reason for being concerned about this component in the framework is the fact that many of the top executives in the corporate world were born and educated in an era when societal pressures did not exist on a wide scale. Miles found it necessary to create a framework for these executives to understand the new context in which business operates in the modern era. He created a continuum for explaining managerial philosophies, with institution-oriented philosophy occupying one end and enterprise-oriented philosophy at the other extreme. High overall business exposure is linked to an institutional top-management philosophy, while low overall business exposure is linked to an enterprise type of top-management philosophy in his framework (see Tables 10.1 and 10.3).

10.2.3 External affairs strategy

The third component in Miles's framework, **external affairs strategy**, is significantly linked to top-management philosophy (see Table 10.1). Miles terms this relationship the 'philosophy–strategy connection' because he sees the relationship as extremely strong and pervasive. There are two external affairs strategies described in the Miles framework. Collaborative/problem-solving strategies are based on 'trust and open communications with a variety of external constituencies' (Miles 1987: 8). This type of strategy is common with companies having an institution-oriented top-management philosophy (see Table 10.4). Short-term profit-making is often sacrificed for societal needs, demonstrating a key characteristic of corporate citizenship.

At the other extreme are individualistic or adversarial strategies. These strategies are common with companies manifesting an enterprise-oriented top-management philosophy. Executives of these companies believe that their 'principal responsibility . . . is to protect the company's self interest and to defend or buffer its core business policies and practices against social threats' (Miles 1987: 10). External affairs staff functions are often lacking in these types of company and, thus, they are unable to cope with their social exposure effectively.

10.2.4 Internal organisational arrangements

The final component in Miles's framework is the corporation's **internal organisational arrangements**, which focus on how corporations organise their business activities to manage stakeholder relations within the corporate social environment. This can be broken into two parts: external affairs design and line-manager involvement (see Table 10.1). Miles defines the former term further in terms of an **exposure–design contingency**. He posits that 'the sophistication of the corporate external affairs function must correspond to the degree of business exposure of the firm in order to achieve high levels of corporate social performance' (Miles 1987: 11).

Line-manager involvement is also included in the last major component of the framework. Miles stresses the importance of striving to get high levels of line-manager involvement and staff sophistication, which are related to executive philosophy and the sophistication of the core staff function. The continuum of the measure of internal organisational arrangements is summarised in Table 10.5.

10.3   Research methods

10.3.1 Sample

Graduate business students enrolled in two MBA programmes from 1988 to 1995 obtained the data from field research of organisational information. Each graduate researcher was trained in the concepts of stakeholder management and corporate citizenship, as well as the specifics of Miles's framework. In addition, examples of prior research using Miles's framework and research supervision by an experienced scholar were part of the training. The experienced scholar validated the researchers' interpretation of information from executive interviews and secondary sources for consistency across the data-collection period.

In total, there were 391 CSP case studies, significantly more observations than Miles's original set of seven. These organisations were selected by the experienced scholar and graduate researcher based on the availability of data and diversity of the organisation's demographics to the overall sample. Only 27 case studies were dropped from the dataset due to data-quality questions. The final sample represented a geographical cross-section of corporate America, evidenced by the regional distribution of organisations across the United States as shown in Table 10.6. In addition, the organisations sampled varied in size and industry membership. As shown in Table 10.7, of the companies analysed 58 were classified as small organisations based on number of employees (7–500 employees), 160 were mid-sized organisations (501–9,999 employees) and 173 were large organisations (10,000–400,000 employees). Expanding on Miles's original analysis of the insurance industry, our dataset, detailed in Table 10.8, comprised organisations from manufacturing ($n = 102$), financial services ($n = 86$), healthcare ($n = 66$), retail sales ($n = 63$), utilities ($n = 39$) and transportation ($n = 35$).

Region	Number of firms	Percentage of sample
West and north-west	70	18
Mid-west	106	27
South and south-west	66	17
North-east	149	38

Table 10.6 **Distribution of corporate headquarters, by region**

Source: authors' survey

Organisation size*	Number of firms	Percentage of sample
Small	58	15
Mid-sized	160	41
Large	173	44

* Small: 7–500 employees; mid-sized = 501–9,999 employees; large = 10,000 or more employees.

Table 10.7 **Distribution of organisations, by size**

Sector	Number of firms	Percentage of sample
Manufacturing	102	26
Financial services	86	22
Healthcare	66	17
Retail sales	63	16
Utilities	39	10
Transportation	35	9

Table 10.8 **Distribution of organisations, by sector**

10.3.2 Measures

In this section, we present the Corporate Social Performance Assessment Guide, which was based on components found in Miles's framework. This guide was used to measure a company's position along continua focusing on product mix, customer mix, geographic mix, overall business exposure, top-management philosophy, external affairs strategy, external affairs design and line-manager involvement. Once these positions were found, then correlations among the components were assessed.

10.3.2.1 Overall business exposure

Overall business exposure was determined by examining a company's product mix, customer mix and geographic mix along a continuum from high to low. This research project measured two additional components: organisational size and industry membership.

Products were classified as either necessities or luxury goods. Necessity items were products that the public purchased regularly for everyday use and continued to consume despite their modest price fluctuations, such as toiletries, energy providers, property or accident insurance, or staple food products. Luxury products, on the other hand, were those goods that did not enter the public arena as often because their purchase was contingent on higher income levels and vast consumer research, such as a yacht, high-fashion retailing or specialised financial consulting.

Miles postulated that products with negative contingencies were more highly exposed to the public. 'In addition, of the products . . . [possessing] potential contingencies that might adversely affect the consuming public, the corporation's business exposure will normally increase' (1987: 3). For example, airline travel initially might be regarded as a luxury since it is a relatively expensive mode of transport. But the possibility of consumer harm due to a mishap dramatically increases an airline carrier's overall business exposure.

The second major component included in Miles's overall business exposure dimension was **customer mix**. A customer, either a consumer or a commercial and industrial buyer, factored into a company's level of exposure to the social environment. According to Miles, 'consumer-products companies tend to be more exposed to the corporate social environment than are companies producing commercial or industrial products' (1987: 3). In addition, 'commercial and industrial customers have more sophisticated purchasing functions and are staffed by professionals who are technically trained to make informed purchase decisions' (1987: 4). Thus, customer products such as televisions tend to have high overall business exposure, whereas commercial/industrial products such as grinding wheels usually have low overall business exposure.

The next component of overall business exposure, **geographic mix**, was concerned with where a business entered the market. Urban areas were more highly exposed to the public than were rural areas because of population density and effectiveness of regulatory agencies. 'Corporations marketing consumer products regarded as necessities in urban areas are far more exposed to the corporate social environment than are those that sell similar products in non-urban areas' (Miles 1987: 4). Regulators in urban areas had 'far more resources and much more sophisticated regulatory agencies than their counterparts in non-urban states' (1987: 4; see also Miles and Bhambri 1983).

10.3.2.2 Additional components

Although Miles did not discuss additional components within his framework, it is reasonable to assume that **organisation size** is a potential factor in determining the overall business exposure for companies. Larger organisations (categorised according to the number of employees[4]) are bigger targets for social groups than are small firms, thereby allowing greater opportunity for publicising social issues.

The final factor, **industry membership**, like organisation size, was not included in Miles's original framework. We speculated, however, that different industries might have varying degrees of exposure to the social environment, naturally exposing some industries to more regulatory activity than others, such as extensive governmental scrutiny by regulatory watchdog agencies. For example, the computer industry was found to have 'significantly more environmental turbulence and discretion than the natural gas

---

4   We attempted to solicit other measures of firm size, such as sales volume and annual income, but found smaller firms reluctant to provide this 'competitive' information. As privately held firms, this information was unavailable via secondary sources. Number of employees was the most readily available measure of firm size provided by our respondents.

industry' in one study (Haleblian and Finkelstein 1993: 853). Or, the healthcare industry experiences high levels of regulatory control; thus, this industry may be under a higher level of public scrutiny than other industries.

10.3.2.3 Top-management philosophy

When looking at the first two major components of Miles's framework, it is logical to deduce a correlation between overall business exposure and top-management philosophy. Miles explained 'my experience in highly exposed industries shows that member firms tend to move toward the extremes of [top-management philosophy types]' (1987: 5-6). This study did not explicitly test this prediction, but it seemed more reasonable to us that high overall business exposure leads to institution-oriented philosophy and low overall business exposure leads to enterprise-oriented philosophy.

The variations of companies' top-management philosophy rested within a continuum according to Miles, with institution-oriented firms lying at one extreme and enterprise-oriented firms occupying the other end-point. We acknowledge that it is possible that these two orientations do not rest along the same continuum, but on separate and distinct continua. Despite the fact that other factors could contribute to a firm's philosophy, this study simply tried to replicate Miles's original framework using his same constructs. It was not our intention to revise his data-collection framework without testing it first.

Corporate documents provided a 'window in' to businesses to elicit top management's philosophical orientation. Specifically, these took the form of mission statements, corporate policies, letters from the CEO to stockholders or other constituencies, employee handbooks, etc. While it must noted that these documents may be prepared as publicity tools for the firm's owners or other stakeholder groups, they do give researchers a glimpse into what is deemed important for top management. Despite their potential for social desirability bias, firms have been found to exhibit a wide range of top-management philosophy perspectives, as shown later in our results section. Content analysis of corporate documentation, using the criteria found in Miles's framework, enabled researchers to classify a firm's top-management philosophy.

10.3.2.4 External affairs strategy

External affairs strategy can be described along a continuum, with collaborative strategies and adversarial strategies as the extremes.[5] It was believed that corporate strategies might vary according to a firm's interactions with the external environment. Thompson (1967) said that firms use boundary-spanning units 'to reduce environmental uncertainty' (quoted in Meznar and Nigh 1993: 32). Boundary-spanning units were seen to possess a 'bridging role' in an organisation (Meznar and Nigh 1993: 33).

Miles once again uses two extremes: at one extreme, a collaborative or problem-solving external affairs strategy focused on society's needs; at the other extreme, the adversarial or individualistic external affairs strategy, focused entirely on the economic self-interests of the firm. To discover a firm's external affairs strategy, corporate documentation describing programmes or actions was assessed. For example, corporate

---

5   Miles's external affairs strategy continuum may be contrasted with the typology of public affairs strategies developed by Meznar and Nigh (1993).

reports to stockholders, employee newsletters, press releases, policies and procedures, and employee handbooks were considered.

10.3.2.5 Internal organisational arrangements

The last component that Miles considered was the internal organisational arrangements, ranging from a sophisticated arrangement to no arrangement at all. Within this component were two dimensions: (1) **external affairs design**, in which extensive arrangements led to sophisticated internal organisational arrangements and little or no arrangement led to a company with no internal organisational arrangements; and (2) **line-manager involvement**, in which several 'formal devices' were used to measure line managers' involvement in the corporate social environment. These included establishing top-management steering committees, designating specific roles that link external affairs units to line operations, and rotating line managers through temporary and full-time job assignments in external affairs units.

Greening and Johnson (1997) studied the characteristics of the top-management team related to the ability of the team to deal with environmental crises effectively. They claimed that the best teams in handling environmental crises were 'creative, flexible, and adaptable' (Greening and Johnson 1997: 339). To deal with external crises effectively, they suggested that top-management teams must be heterogeneous: that is, they advocated diverse teams with a variety of functional backgrounds. Thus, the design of the external affairs team is quite important. Since the 'organisation of public affairs activities varies from highly centralised to comparatively decentralised' (Post *et al.* 1983: 135), Miles believed that most firms could be classified as one extreme or the other.

10.3.2.6 Testing the validity of Miles's framework

In order to test the validity of Miles's data-collection framework, we measured overall business exposure (its five components independently), top-management philosophy, external affairs strategy and internal organisational arrangements (comprising external affairs design and line-manager involvement). Each of these components lies on a continuum as described earlier in this section. Taken together, relationships and correlations between the framework's components became evident. A summary of the responses when applying Miles's data-collection criteria is shown in Table 10.9.

10.3.3 Data analysis

Initially, regression analysis was used to determine the necessity of each of the components of overall business exposure. A t-statistic enabled us to determine the statistical contribution made by each variable within a group of variables.

To perform the next analysis in this research, a path analysis using a regression statistic was implemented. Since the framework flows from an initial point to a final point with assumed relationships in between, a path analysis was the most relevant method for testing statistical significance. Path analysis enables researchers to examine the pattern of relationships between three or more variables. According to Bryman and Cramer (1999), 'the aim of path analysis is to provide quantitative estimates of the causal connections between sets of variables'. Thus, by evaluating the strength of the connec-

	Point on continuum*		
	HIGH	MEDIUM	LOW
Overall business exposure	64	9	27
Product mix	58	12	30
Customer mix	53	10	37
Geographic mix	69	11	20
Top-management philosophy	47	19	34
External affairs strategy	54	11	35
Internal organisational arrangements			
External affairs design	30	38	32
Line-manager involvement	24	25	51

* For overall business exposure, the continuum moves (from left to right in this table) from high to low; for top-management philosophy, it ranges from institution-oriented to enterprise-oriented; for external affairs strategy, it ranges from collaborative and problem-solving to individualistic and adversarial; for internal organisational arrangements, it ranges from sophisticated to none.

Table 10.9 **Responses when applying Miles's (1987) framework**

tions proposed in Miles's original data-collection framework, we were able to observe distinct paths of interconnected variables.

10.4 Results

In our first test of validity, we explored whether each of the three measures of Miles's overall business exposure component was essential to determine a firm's exposure to the social environment. As shown in Table 10.10, when using our dataset, product mix and geographic mix were statistically significant influences of overall business exposure ($t = 2.13$, $p = 0.036$; $t = 12.96$, $p = 0.001$; respectively) but customer mix was not ($t = 1.74$, $p = 0.176$).

Our second test of validity explored whether additional measures were needed for a more comprehensive account of Miles's business exposure. Analysing our results shown in Table 10.10 we found that an additional business exposure measure, organisation size (as determined by number of employees), had a statistically significant influence in determining the firm's business exposure ($t = 7.53$, $p = 0.009$). Industry membership was not found to exhibit a statistically significant influence on a firm's business exposure in this dataset ($t = 0.96$, $p = 0.537$).

Figure 10.2 shows the path direction and flow in order to test the strength of the interrelationships in Miles's framework, our third test of validity. Each interrelationship in the framework, except the 'overall business exposure–top-management philosophy' connection ($r = 0.267$), was found to be statistically correlated when using our dataset.

Variable	t-statistic	Significance
Geographic mix	12.96	0.001 *
Number of employees	7.53	0.009 *
Product mix	2.13	0.036 *
Customer mix	1.74	0.176
Industry membership	0.96	0.537

* significant at 0.05 level

Table 10.10 **The essentiality of business exposure variables as determined by path analysis regression**

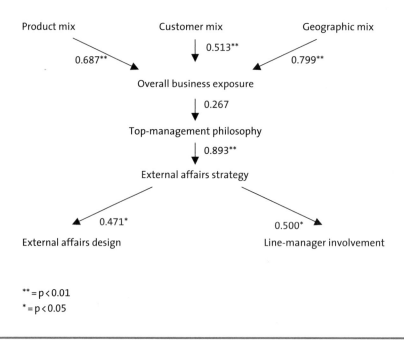

Figure 10.2 **Correlation analysis of Miles's original framework**

All three measures of overall business exposure in Miles's original framework were correlated with such exposure: product mix ($r = 0.687$), customer mix ($r = 0.513$) and geographic mix ($r = 0.799$). Top-management philosophy correlated with external affairs strategy ($r = 0.893$) and external affairs strategy correlated with both external affairs design ($r = 0.471$) and line-manager involvement ($r = 0.500$). All correlations, except that between overall business exposure and top-management philosophy (see Fig. 10.2), were significant at the $p = 0.05$ level, with all three measures of overall business exposure and the relationship between top-management philosophy and external affairs strategy significant at the $p = 0.01$ level. Thus, we were successful in replicating the relationships described in Miles's original framework.

In addition, these relationships could be separated into two distinct patterns of related variables. For example, as shown in Figure 10.3, a high product mix and a high geographic mix resulted in a high overall business exposure, which related to institutional-oriented top-management philosophy. Institutional-oriented top-management philosophy was correlated with collaborative external affairs strategy, which in turn was related to a sophisticated external affairs design.

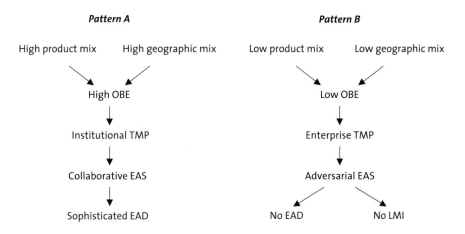

OBE = overall business exposure; TMP = top-management philosophy; EAS = external affairs strategy; EAD = external affairs design; LMI = line-manager involvement

Figure 10.3 **Relationship patterns found using entire (new) dataset**

Conversely, in 'relationship pattern B', we found components at the other end of the continuum also interrelated. For example, low product mix and low geographic mix resulted in a low overall business exposure, which correlated with enterprise top-management philosophy. Miles's framework was supported further in that enterprise-oriented top-management philosophy was related to an adversarial external affairs strategy, with no external affairs design or line-manager involvement.

This led us to our fourth test of validity: generalisability across industries. Miles discovered a path direction and strength of interrelationships among framework components when analysing seven firms from the insurance industry. The fact that we found the same path direction and component interrelationships (shown in Fig. 10.2) when studying 391 firms from six different industries supports the validity test of generalisability.

Additional within-industry analysis was explored and is shown in Figure 10.4. While some consistency was seen across industries, only limited relational patterns were discovered.[6] For example, high overall business exposure was related to institutional-

---

6 By grouping firms into various industry groups, some statistical rigour was lost and this may partially explain the lack of significant patterns in managing the corporate social environment.

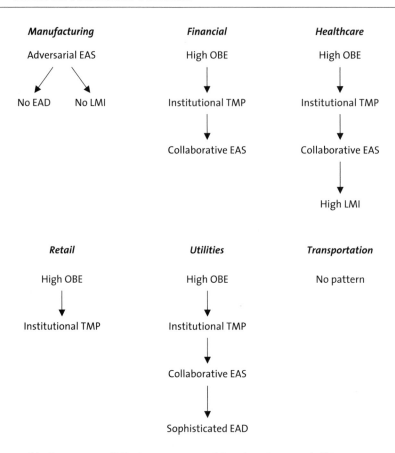

OBE = overall business exposure; TMP = top-management philosophy; EAS = external affairs strategy;
EAD = external affairs design; LMI = line-manager involvement

Figure 10.4 *Relationship patterns found by industry type*

oriented top-management philosophy for firms in the financial, healthcare, retail and utilities industries, but not for firms in the manufacturing and transportation industries.

The most developed patterns were found in the healthcare and utilities industries where high overall business exposure linked with institutional top-management philosophy which linked with collaborative external affairs strategy. In the healthcare industry collaborative external affairs strategy linked with high line-manager involvement, whereas in the utilities industry collaborative external affairs strategy linked with a sophisticated external affairs design. The other four industries failed to demonstrate any patterns of such magnitude; the transportation industry showed no interrelational patterns at all. The implications of these findings are discussed in the following section of this chapter.

10.5 Conclusions and implications

The results of the regression and correlation analyses conducted in this study provide general confirmation regarding our efforts to validate Miles's framework for managing corporate stakeholders and exhibiting characteristics of corporate citizenship. In addition, the broader dataset used in this research provided a critical, additional variable not included in Robert Miles's original framework: organisation size. The major conclusions drawn from our analysis of 391 corporate social performance case studies offer a direction for future research.

First, not all of the three original business exposure measures developed by Miles (product mix, customer mix and geographic mix) were critical influences in determining a company's overall business exposure. While product mix and geographic mix were found to be statistically significant in their influence on a firm's overall business exposure when using this dataset, customer mix could be dropped from our analysis for determining the degree of overall business exposure without losing significant explanatory power.

Therefore, scholars or executives concerned with determining critical corporate stakeholder relationships should focus on whether the public views the firm's product as a necessity or a luxury and whether it has the potential to cause serious harm. However, we acknowledge that the generalisation in Miles's original framework that necessities are necessarily viewed as having greater business exposure than luxuries may be suspect in some cases. For example, the fur industry markets a luxury item but it has high business exposure owing to public protests.

In addition, if a firm distributes its product or service in an urban setting, the firm is more vulnerable to interventions from stakeholders found in the social environment. Yet the emergence of electronic business exchanges and the Internet may significantly reduce the importance placed on the firm's geographic mix. In a high-tech, e-commerce world, geographic location is less critical. Our dataset was collected before the emergence of e-commerce and thus geographic mix was seen as an important element in determining a firm's overall business exposure at that time.

Second, the addition of organisation size to the list of measures influencing a company's business exposure is an important discovery in this study. Specifically, it was found that large and mid-sized firms tend to be more highly exposed than small organisations (with size determined by number of employees). Therefore, scholars should consider organisation size in their corporate stakeholder management investigations when considering corporate citizenship. In addition, executives employed by large or mid-sized organisations should be more wary of potential challenges from their social stakeholders than managers of small organisations. It appears that the organisation's size, not its industry membership, is a critical factor in assessing threats from corporate stakeholders.

Third, this research also explored the strength of the interrelationships among the variables found in Miles's framework. Notably, every relationship that was posited in Miles's original framework was significantly correlated using our expanded dataset, except one. Thus, the grounded theory approach taken by Miles—where a framework is constructed from the data gleaned from field-based research—appears to be a robust technique, withstanding the test of replication using our new dataset.

However, the one interrelationship not found to be statistically supported using our dataset is worthy of consideration. Why was overall business exposure not related to top-management philosophy? One explanation may lie in the discovery of a new overall business exposure measure: organisation size. When using our dataset, considering only the three overall business exposure measures identified by Miles was insufficient to statistically explain a firm's business exposure. Scholars should be acutely aware of the need to include organisation size when exploring the 'overall business exposure–top-management philosophy' relationship.

We should note that, like Miles, our lack of support for an overall business exposure–top-management philosophy linkage challenges the proposed relationships in Miles's original framework found in Chapter 1 of his book. But this lack of a statistically significant relationship does lend support to Miles's grounded model, presented later in his book in Chapter 13, where the influence of overall business exposure was depicted differently in his Figure 13-1 (Miles 1987: 274).

Last, now that the essentiality and comprehensiveness of the overall business exposure component has been validated, scholars and executives can now turn to the issue of relational patterns to further their understanding of how firms might manage their corporate stakeholders. As found in Miles's original work, the two patterns of variables found at the extremes of the corporate social performance measure continua were discovered when using our expanded dataset.

Firms that were highly exposed to the social environment tended to have an institutional-oriented top-management philosophy, collaborative external affairs strategy and well-developed internal organisational arrangements. Conversely, firms with minimal social environment exposure exhibited enterprise-oriented top-management philosophy, adversarial external affairs strategy and little or no internal organisational arrangements.

Both patterns appear reasonable when considering a firm's strategic management of stakeholder relationships. Firms highly exposed to social stakeholders' challenges are best served by a corporate philosophy that is highly integrated with society and long-term in its outlook, with an integration of the firm's economic interests with its social goals: characteristic of strong corporate citizenship. Firms not experiencing this degree of vulnerability to social environment challenges can afford to exhibit a corporate philosophy that envisions little integration with society and takes a short-term outlook, leading to a preference for legal interaction with social stakeholders and the strategic pursuit of predominantly economic interests: a less aggressive attention to corporate citizenship.

Thus, the framework provides both a **descriptive** view of how firms manage their corporate stakeholders and attend to corporate citizenship, and a **prescriptive** guide for executives seeking to understand how best to manage their corporate stakeholders and pursue corporate citizenship.

Limitations of this research should be noted. First, research was conducted by hundreds of different evaluators in acquiring the corporate social performance assessment data for our firms. While inconsistencies could occur since more than one researcher was used to collect the data, each researcher received consistent training in how to conduct a corporate social performance assessment and used the same guidelines regarding data collection and measurement. In addition, a single experienced researcher supervised each new researcher collecting the data. For control purposes and to maintain data quality, if there was any question raised regarding the validity of the case study data, the experienced researcher removed the case study from the final dataset of 391 firms and did not include the observation in the data analysis. In total only 27 case studies were removed from the dataset before the analysis was conducted.

Second, secondary corporate documentation was often used, along with corporate interviews, to determine a firm's top-management philosophy, external affairs strategy and internal organisational arrangements. This documentation could be biased, projecting the firm in a more positive light than that which accurately reflects the operations of the firm. What 'really occurs at the firm' may be different from what a firm states in its documentation. Nonetheless, we were pleased with the fairly random distribution of the classification of the firms across the criteria measure continua. If this was a serious bias in our dataset, more firms would have been classified in a more favourable light: that is, as having an institutional-oriented top-management philosophy, collaborative external affairs strategy, and extensive internal organisational arrangements. We did not find this to be the case with our dataset.

Third, the external environment may dramatically change the type and degree of influences on the corporate stakeholder relationships and some factors were not considered in Miles's or our data-collection phases. For example, exogenous factors, such as stock market fluctuations, recession or inflationary times, or publicly visible events, were not explicitly considered in the analysis.

Miles's framework and resulting model preceded the advent of wide public use of the Internet. Modern technological advances have complicated the operationalisation of the external affairs function. New issues regarding market size and business exposure have developed, as the world marketplace has become global. Future research may wish to examine the effects of the new economy and e-business environment.

Finally, future research may also want to continue the efforts begun in this study and expand on the results discovered herein. While our expanded dataset found Miles's framework to be a robust and generalisable framework for measuring corporate citizenship, more detailed industry data is needed to explore within-industry relationships. It may be desirable to integrate work done on top-management design and firm performance (Haleblian and Finkelstein 1993) and work done on the relationship between corporate social performance and corporate financial performance (Griffin and Mahon 1997). Since much work has been done on the effects of structure and design on firm profitability (Post *et al.* 1983; Meznar and Nigh 1993) and also on the effects of organisational structure on corporate social performance (Bhambri and Sonnenfeld 1988), a bridge between the two literatures may be a worthwhile task in gaining a better understanding of how managers assess their corporate stakeholder management and citizenship.

In conclusion, we believe that Robert Miles's framework for evaluating and managing the corporate stakeholders provides a systematic and valuable direction for scholars and executives interested in discovering how firms might best manage their corporate stakeholder relationships and pursue a strategy of corporate citizenship.

Part 2
STAKEHOLDER PERFORMANCE
AND REPORTING

APPROACHES TO STAKEHOLDER PERFORMANCE AND REPORTING: AN INVESTOR'S PERSPECTIVE

Investigating how sustainable companies deliver value to shareholders

Michael J. King

Innovys, UK

These are difficult times for the corporate organisation. Volatility and uncertainty are increasing within their markets, as customers demand greater choice and performance combined with greater value. We see the pharmaceutical companies facing fundamental challenges regarding the patent protection afforded to their products across the globe, when those products can save the lives of people who cannot afford them. At the same time, pharmaceutical companies are merging to create global behemoths that are able to fund future developments.

Within telecommunications, huge amounts have been paid for third generation (3G) licences, which have left many of the buyers with crippling levels of debt. However 3G applications have the *potential* to revolutionise the way individuals, groups and organisations interact with each other. In this world owning the customer relationship will be more valuable than owning the assets of production.

The energy sector within the UK has seen an outcry by sections of society at the perceived unfairness of fuel taxation levels and the profits made by companies. At the same time there is general acknowledgement of the need to reduce the levels of carbon-based emissions in the environment. In the USA there have been power outages, as supply has proved to be unable to meet demand.

The experience of the dot.com bubble has demonstrated that the capital markets are far from perfect soothsayers. The bubble has burst and only the companies with robust business models remain in business. It has highlighted a weakness of the capital markets, however: when uncertainty becomes too high, the science of corporate valuation struggles to keep up and intuitive analysis often takes over. Option thinking helped conceptually but struggled practically—a company such as eBay may be able to sell additional goods and services to its customer base, creating a future option or opportunity for growth, but this is difficult to quantify.

Environmental uncertainty may be increasing but it is not a new phenomenon for business. Lawrence and Lorsch (1967) had this to say based on their research: 'In successful firms, both differentiation and integration increased as environmental complexity increased. These findings suggest that organisational failure in the face of environmental complexity probably results from a combination of high differentiation and inadequate integration.'

In other words, the corporate organisation can adapt itself to environmental change and those organisations that do not adapt will be more likely to fail. Differentiation and integration create opposing forces within an organisation, based on the need for specialisation to compete successfully and the need for co-ordination, in order to direct all of the organisation's resources towards the same goals.

The experiences of companies such as Shell and Nike, described by Herkströter (1996), Mcintosh *et al.* (1998) and Elkington (1997), highlight new challenges from within the corporate environment. Herkströter (1996) described these challenges as 'a ghost in the global system'. This 'ghost' is a manifestation of the new expectations of corporate organisations, as their role has increased in significance in the lives of people across the globe. Based on the work of Lawrence and Lorsch (1967), these integrative measures need to incorporate external stakeholders more than ever before. Those organisations that are unable to adapt their strategy and structure to significant changes in their environment will fail.

11.1 The focus of this work

This report builds on previous work (King 2001), which sought to find out whether organisations were disadvantaged over rivals by their sustainability performance. This work found that a portfolio of companies with superior sustainability performance were also able to deliver excellent financial returns to their shareholders. There was no apparent disadvantage.

This previous work did not prove causation, however. It cannot be stated categorically that, if a company improves its sustainability performance, then there will be a corresponding increase in financial performance. To understand how these 'sustainable' companies delivered returns to their shareholders, it is necessary to go a level below the share price to understand the underlying financial drivers of shareholder value.

In this previous study Suncor was studied further, as an example of a company that was given the top rating for its sustainability performance within the energy sector, but also gave superior returns compared with market indices and a basket of large competitors. This is shown in Figure 11.1.

This study remains focused on the shareholder but will seek to understand how Suncor creates the superior level of returns identified in Figure 11.1.

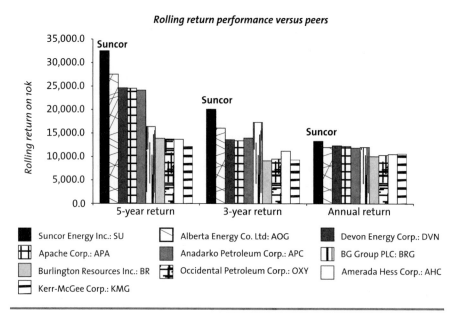

Figure 11.1 **Suncor returns performance**

Source: King 2001

The analysis takes an investor's perspective on sustainability. For readers who are interested in learning more about the technical approaches to this work and gaining a greater depth of knowledge of investment finance, references will be made to relevant literature.

11.2 Analytical approach

11.2.1 Building the sample set

Dow Jones has a hierarchical classification structure for companies, which consists of economic sectors, market sectors, industry groups and sub-groups. Suncor is classified within the Dow Jones industry group called 'Secondary Oil Companies', which is in turn within the energy economic sector. The other industry groups within the energy sector include coal, oil drilling, oilfield equipment and services, pipelines and major oil companies.

The components[1] of the Dow Jones Sustainability Index (DJSI World) are reviewed regularly and include companies from all of the economic sectors. Within each economic sector the company with the leading corporate sustainability score is identified.

1   www.sustainability-index.com/djsi_world/components.html

Within the 'Secondary Oil Companies' industry group there are over 100 companies. At the time of the study, three of these companies are members of the DJSI World Index:

- BG Group PLC (UK)

- Sasol Ltd (South Africa)

- Suncor Energy Inc. (Canada)

As members of the index, these companies have some of the leading corporate sustainability scores within their sector. For the purposes of this report we will use this as a mechanism to differentiate 'sustainable' or 'stakeholder' companies from their peers. We can then compare their performance relative to others.

The other companies within the industry group were tested for availability of share price and financial data over the period January 1998 to December 2000. There were 39 companies in the final set, as shown in Table 11.1.

11.2.2 Assessing performance

As with the previous study (King 2001), performance will be assessed using the total shareholder return (TSR) measure. TSR is defined as the total return for the shareholder in the form of dividends and share price appreciation. This is an external measure, in the sense that it relates to the share price of the company and indirectly to internal measures, such as margins, revenues or market share.

From 1 January 1998 to 31 December 2000, there are over 700 annual periods: for example, 1 January 1998 to 31 December 1998, 2 January 1998 to 1 January 1999, etc. These returns form a distribution as shown in Figure 11.2. The average value of this distribution is used to assess performance. This gives an indication of the return that a typical investor would have made and smoothes out any chance gains or losses.

The standard deviation of annual returns is used as the measure of risk for the purpose of this analysis. There are alternative measures but this metric gives an indication of the volatility within the share price that investors would be exposed to. Further information on the calculation of average annual returns and measures of risk can be found in Brealey and Myers 1981 and Higson 1995.

The analysis will then go a level below TSR to understand the key financial values that have driven the creation of shareholder returns. For the purpose of this report the key drivers to be assessed are limited to revenues, margins and risk. Further information on the relationship between company performance and superior shareholder returns can be found in Copeland *et al.* 1990 and McTaggart *et al.* 1994.

The time-scale of this study is the period from January 1998 to December 2000. This period has been used to allow for companies with different accounting year-ends. It would be possible to assess TSR performance up to the current date; however, at the time of this study financial accounting data was unavailable for 2001 for all companies.

Alberta Energy Co.	Canada
Amerada Hess Corp.	USA
Anadarko Petroleum Corp.	USA
Anderson Exploration Ltd	Canada
Apache Corp.	USA
Ashland Inc.	USA
BG Group PLC	United Kingdom
Bonavista Petroleum Ltd	Canada
Burlington Resources Inc.	USA
Cabot Oil & Gas Corp. Cl A	USA
Caltex Australia Ltd	Australia
Canadian Hunter Exploration Ltd	Canada
Canadian Natural Resources Ltd	Canada
Chieftain International Inc.	Canada
Cosmo Oil Co.	Japan
Devon Energy Corp.	USA
Encal Energy Ltd	Canada
Enterprise Oil PLC	United Kingdom
EOG Resources Inc.	USA
Japan Energy Corp.	Japan
Kerr-McGee Corp.	USA
Murphy Oil Corp.	USA
Nexen Inc.	Canada
Nippon Mitsubishi Oil Corp.	Japan
Occidental Petroleum Corp.	USA
Origin Energy Ltd	Australia
Pancanadian Petroleum Inc.	Canada
Paramount Resources Ltd	Canada
Penn West Petroleum Ltd	Canada
Petroleos (Compania Española De)	Spain
Rio Alto Exploration Ltd	Canada
Santos Ltd	Australia
Sasol Ltd	South Africa
Showa Shell Sekiyu K.K.	Japan
Suncor Energy Inc.	Canada
Talisman Energy Inc.	Canada
Teikoku Oil Co.	Japan
Vermilion Resources Ltd	Canada
Woodside Petroleum Ltd	Australia

Table 11.1 *Companies analysed from the Secondary Oil Companies industry group*

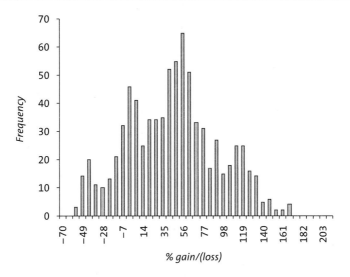

Figure 11.2 *Example distribution of annual returns*

11.3 Findings

The first place to start is to examine shareholder returns.

11.3.1 Total shareholder return (TSR) performance

The results for the companies in this study are shown in Figure 11.3. The average returns for every company in the test universe are ranked and plotted on the chart.

Over the period January 1998 to December 2000, the average annual returns for BG Group, Suncor and Sasol were 2.09%, 15.64% and 27.22%, respectively. Suncor and Sasol both achieved above average returns for this sample universe. Sasol achieved upper-quartile performance. This analysis reinforces previous work (King 2001) that 'sustainability' does not appear to damage TSR performance—none of the companies is in the bottom quartile.

Next we will consider the key financial drivers that created these returns.

11.3.2 The underlying financial drivers

To some it may appear that a firm's share price has no rhyme or reason to it. However, there is a science behind corporate valuation. A share price traded in an open market can be thought of as the expected future benefits that an investor can expect to receive—in the form of dividends and capital gain (i.e. selling the share for more than you paid). The

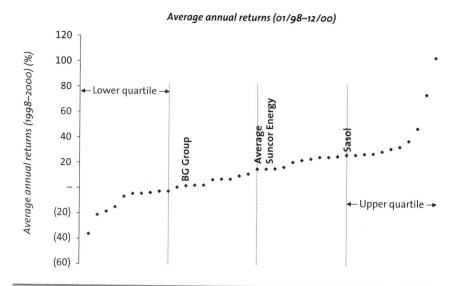

Figure 11.3 ***Average annual returns for the test universe***

critical word in the last sentence was 'expected', as different investors will have different views on how the stock will perform. If a company manages to beat the market's expectations then the share price will increase based on new information, and the current holders of the share will have a capital gain. Investors will then decide whether they think the company will continue to outperform relative to other investment opportunities. Further information on the underlying analysis of a company's share and the expectations of the capital markets can be found in Copeland *et al.* 1990.

Therefore, the underlying financial performance of a company and the implications for expected future performance drive the current price of the shares. This analysis will stay at a basic level and focus on three key variables: revenues, margins and risk. Revenues give an indication of how the company is growing and performing in its markets. Margins give an indication of efficiency in extracting profits from its operations, as well as how valuable the product or service is to customers and consumers. Risk is a key factor affecting future expectations. If a company is perceived as high-risk, then expected future returns from the company would be worth less, as they may not be achieved at all.

Obviously different industries and companies will have a different focus for their business and so the importance of the financial drivers will vary. For example, the steel industry is characterised by global oversupply and subsidised national industries in some countries. Typically, the critical driver for this industry would be margin, as companies strive to ensure their operations are efficient and that they are able to deliver profits, as prices are pushed down because of oversupply. For other industries sales growth is the key, as there is a battle to capture share in a new market.

Changes in the key financial drivers of the three companies from the Dow Jones Sustainability Index are shown in Figure 11.4.

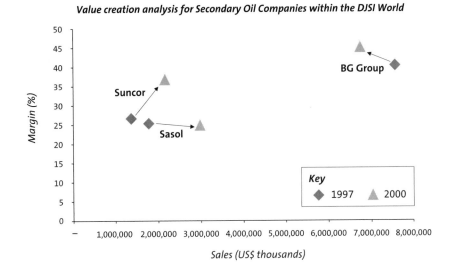

Figure 11.4 **Key financial measures driving shareholder returns**

Source: Datastream

Financial data for 1997 is used as the base level and then performance is assessed relative to this point, as share price movements are based on changes in future performance expectations. Therefore, if you had bought shares in these companies at the start of 1998, you would know how the companies had performed in 1997 and would have your own expectations of future performance. The performance of the company during the years 1998–2000 would be a critical factor for the performance of your shares.

Sasol delivered the best average annual returns and it appears to have delivered this primarily through sales growth as margins have deteriorated slightly from 25.4% to 24.9%. Suncor delivered the next best returns of this group, through a combination of sales growth and increasing margins (from 26.6% to 36.8%). Finally, BG Group delivered average annual returns of 2.09%—less than the average of the test universe of stocks. BG Group's sales have reduced over the period. For this report, it is not intended to go to the level below the financials; however, this reduction in sales would appear to be due to a refocusing of the business as certain parts were spun off and sold. This may be with a goal of achieving higher margins, as BG Group's margins have increased from 40.3% to 45.1%.

We can combine the results shown in Figures 11.3 and 11.4 into one diagram, Figure 11.5.

The bubble size indicates the average annual return performance stated earlier, with Sasol delivering the best returns of the three companies. The horizontal axis gives the compound annual growth rate (CAGR) in sales over the period. The growth rate is used as it is *changes* that are key to changes in shareholder returns. Sasol has delivered the best performance, with sales growth of more than 18% per annum over the period. BG Group has seen negative sales growth as it has disposed of parts of its business.

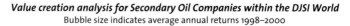

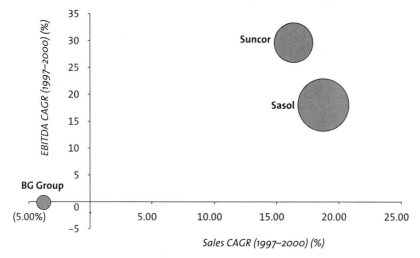

CAGR = compound annual growth rate; EBITDA = earnings before interest tax, depreciation and amortisation

Figure 11.5 *The relationship between key financial drivers and TSR performance*

Source: Datastream, Dow Jones

The vertical axis gives the growth (CAGR) in earnings before interest tax, depreciation and amortisation (EBITDA). This can be considered as analogous to profit but it is a cash measure rather than an earnings measure. The capital markets prefer cash measures such as this, as they are seen as providing a cleaner way of comparing company performance. Further information on the use of cash measures, such as EBITDA, over accounting measures of performance, such as earnings, can be found in Copeland *et al.* 1990.

Suncor has achieved the greatest increase in EBITDA, at more than 29% per annum. BG Group has seen virtually no increase in EBITDA; the increase in margins shown in Figure 11.4 are offset by the reduced absolute levels of EBITDA resulting from reduced sales. Through refocusing on higher margin operations, BG Group may be looking to improve this performance in the future.

11.3.3 Risk

If a company's share price is based on future expectations, higher risk reduces the value of any future benefits. Risk is a difficult concept to capture but the variability in the share price can act as a proxy for the market's perception of the risk associated with a company. For the purpose of this report, the standard deviation of annual returns (as shown in Fig. 11.2) is used as the measure of risk. Further information on approaches to quantifying risk can be found in Brealey and Myers 1981 and Bessis 1998.

For the universe of companies within this report the risk measures are shown in Figure 11.6.

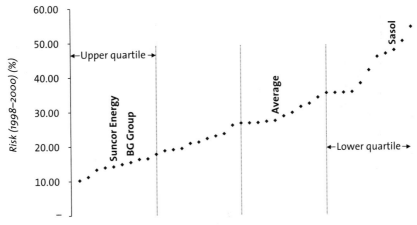

Figure 11.6 **Risk levels for the test universe**

Source: Dow Jones

The figure shows Suncor and BG Group achieving upper-quartile performance within the universe of companies for this report. Sasol exhibits higher volatility in its share price and this is reflected in lower-quartile performance.

If we combine this analysis with the analysis of returns in Figure 11.3, we can see the risk–return trade-off performance for the test universe of companies (Fig. 11.7). The risk–return data is calculated for each company as the average annual return divided by the standard deviation of annual returns (the chosen measure of risk). Organisations with lower risk scores (less volatility in their share price) may actually deliver good returns relative to this lower risk involved. Conversely, organisations that deliver higher absolute returns may achieve this with a relatively high level of risk. Although there is generally a correlation between risk and return, investors would place a higher value on organisations that can deliver returns at a lower level of risk.

Suncor delivers upper-quartile performance in terms of risk and return, while BG and Sasol deliver mid-quartile performance.

11.3.4 Analysis of returns: the industry level

Of the three aspects of sustainability performance—social, environmental and economic—this report focuses on how 'sustainable' companies deliver economic value. Companies can employ various strategies to drive economic performance for investors, as described by Porter (1980). However, analysis at the industry level can help us to understand the key value drivers.

Figure 11.8 confirms the relationships between the average annual returns and the growth in sales and EBITDA (similar to profits). The coefficient of determination (R^2) for average annual returns relative to growth in sales and EBITDA is 0.52 and 0.56,

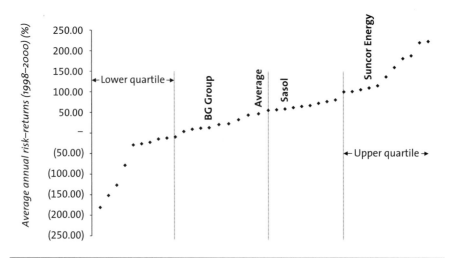

Figure 11.7 **Risk–return performance for the test universe**

Source: Dow Jones

respectively. The r-squared (R^2) value can be interpreted as the proportion of the variance in the average annual returns attributable to the variance in sales growth or EBITDA growth.

If companies within the energy sector are to deliver increasing returns for investors, then they need to grow sales and the cash flowing from those sales. Increasing margin without increasing EBITDA does not deliver returns to investors—as is shown in Figure 11.9.

There is almost no correlation ($R^2 = 0.04$) between increases in margin and increases in average annual returns for this industry and test universe.

11.4 Conclusion

11.4.1 Exploring further

Sustainability is not mutually exclusive to creating returns for shareholders. However, there is no straight line of causation from sustainability to superior performance for shareholders. To understand the impact of sustainability on shareholder returns we need to apply principles from corporate finance and valuation. This is illustrated in Figure 11.10.

If sustainable companies are to drive greater returns for shareholders, then they must be able to increase the levels of free cash flow over time and, more importantly, to manage

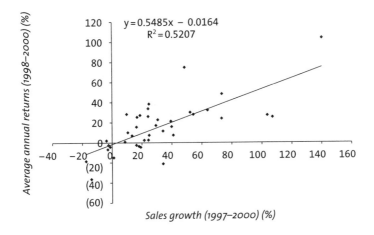

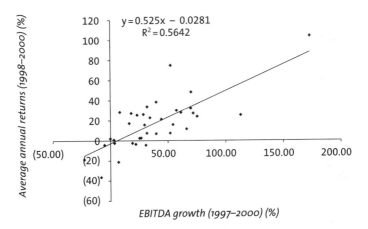

EBITDA = earnings before interest tax, depreciation and amortisation

Figure 11.8 **Correlation between annual returns, sales growth and EBITDA growth**

Source: Datastream, Dow Jones

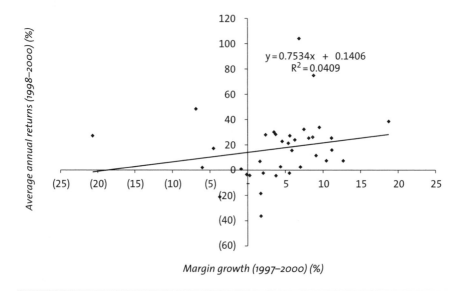

Figure 11.9 ***Increasing margin has almost no correlation to increasing returns***

Source: Datastream, Dow Jones

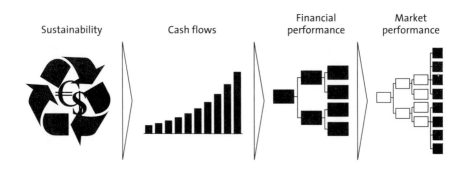

Figure 11.10 ***Sustainability needs to be understood in terms of its impact on competitive performance***

and ideally beat the expectations of the markets. This requires the ability to manage financial performance in terms of growing sales, managing costs and improving margins. This in turn will depend on market performance, measured by market shares, brand premium, advertising spend and other measures. This study has sought to analyse the performance of 'sustainable' companies in terms of key value drivers—revenues, margins and risk.

11.4.1.1 Products and service

Below the financial drivers of performance is the performance in the company's markets. Driving revenues there will be an increase in the penetration of existing markets and the development of new markets. Underlying increases in profits there will be an improvement in the efficiency of an organisation, as well as an increase in the price charged through more effective marketing.

This is an area that touches on intangibles such as trust and empathy, as described by Fukuyama (1995). Companies that can deliver psychological as well as functional value potentially have a competitive edge. Customers are willing to pay a premium for this psychological value and are less likely to switch to a cheaper functional alternative. This is the nirvana of marketing as it allows for the development of a true relationship, rather than a superficial, price-based buyer–supplier relationship.

Investigating this area is very difficult using publicly available data. However, it is possible to examine some related areas for evidence. For example, the Fairtrade movement often involves products that are priced at a premium to similar goods on the same shelf in a supermarket. Consumers are still willing to buy the products, however, in exchange for the psychological values associated with the purchase. A similar process can be seen with 'green' electricity provision.

11.4.1.2 Capital market reputation

In addition to the relationship with the buyers of the company's products or services, there is another party that is critical to a company's success—the investor community. Companies have different reputations in the capital markets, based on past performance. Some companies, such as GE, have consistently managed to exceed investor expectations and consequently delivered excellent returns to investors. Other companies, such as 3M, have aligned their performance management processes to ensure that they are always seeking new growth opportunities and not relying solely on existing products.

Sustainability, with a focus on managing the expectations of a wider group of stakeholders, will enable companies to reduce the risk of unexpected shocks—which will be of value to investors.

This could be examined through an event analysis. This process looks at critical events, such as Brent Spar, and examines the market's reaction. The hypothesis to be tested would be that a 'sustainable' company would be:

- Less prone to such shocks

- Given more credit by the markets that this would not happen again: i.e. this was a one-off, chance event, rather than a sign of poor management within the organisation

11.4.2 *Summary*

The three companies from the Dow Jones World Sustainability Index (DJSI) demonstrate the challenges of delivering on a sustainable agenda. As members of the index, they have been independently rated as superior performers in corporate sustainability relative to their peers. Suncor and British Gas have both been rated the leading company within the energy sector at different points in time.

The economic aspect of the DJSI corporate sustainability assessment[2] measures opportunities and risks relating to strategic, management and industry-specific issues. It does not directly measure the returns delivered to investors.

One of the leading corporate sustainability companies, Sasol, is able to deliver upper-quartile returns comparable to some of the best in the industry, and Suncor also achieves a very respectable 15% per annum average return for their investors. BG Group appears to have performed less well in terms of returns, as it has reduced its sales generated through an apparent refocusing process.

Both Suncor and BG Group exhibit some of the lowest levels of risk associated with their share price. Suncor's strong returns performance translates this into upper-quartile performance in terms of risk–return.

This report demonstrates further that sustainability and shareholder returns are not mutually exclusive. However, it is not simply the case that leading-edge sustainability companies automatically produce superior returns for investors. Shareholder returns are driven by the underlying economic characteristics of the business.

Leading-edge companies will integrate their strategy, processes and people across the three domains (social, environmental and economic), or the triple bottom line as described by Elkington (1997). From an investor's perspective this offers the potential to create an organisation with excellent returns and a lower risk profile—all of the thrills and none of the spills!

A link from sustainability to increasing shareholder returns will not be a one-to-one relationship; rather, it will be a link from initiatives and projects within the company through to increasing revenue, profit, margin and reduced risk. The leading companies will be those that are able continuously to create opportunities for growth that exceed the expectations of their investors. These projects will be appraised in a framework that considers the social, environmental and economic characteristics of each opportunity.

---

2 www.sustainability-index.com/djsi_world/methodology.html

TOP MANAGERS AND INSTITUTIONAL STAKEHOLDERS
A test of two models of adaptation and performance*

Michael V. Russo   *Frank C. Schultz*

University of Oregon, USA   Michigan State University, USA

The array of stakeholders interacting with the modern organisation is always in flux. Shareholders protest by instigating proxy campaigns, unions co-operate by approving new contracts and regulators intrude by launching inquiries. In the cases where a stakeholder asserts itself, theorists have argued that the organisation takes responsive actions for both normative (Clarkson 1991) and instrumental (Jones 1995) reasons.

The empirical literature on stakeholder theory has always assumed that stakeholder actions elicit organisational outcomes. But, in reviewing contributions to this body of literature, Mitchell *et al.* (1997) criticise most studies for being concerned less with change than with the analysis of static relationships. For example, a number of empirical studies find relationships between organisational outcomes and stakeholder management, but generally rely on tests performed on cross-sectional data. Thus, although at points in time connections between stakeholders and organisations have been found, the precise methods by which they influence each other across time remain vague. Even less well understood is whether or not organisational initiatives lead to positive outcomes in the eyes of either a focal stakeholder or even the organisation itself (Fleisher 1993). Given the clear attention to longitudinal issues in Freeman's (1984) seminal work in stakeholder management, this intellectual gap is especially frustrating.

In this chapter, we address this need for more refined analysis by examining shifts in stakeholder relations, how the top-management teams of firms subsequently reflected their new external context, and whether or not organisational outcomes were influenced by the make-up of top-management teams. Our specific empirical context for addressing

* The authors thank Greg Hundley and participants at a seminar at the University of Minnesota for valuable suggestions and guidance with earlier versions of this chapter.

this question is the US electric utility industry from 1974 to 1984. This period witnessed a dramatic increase in the saliency of a key stakeholder—state regulatory commissions—that demanded a response from utilities.[1] We focus on how the top-management teams of utilities are increasingly populated by lawyers, and whether or not greater legal training at the highest levels of firms has resulted in positive organisational outcomes.

We craft theories about relationships among our variables of interest by drawing on two distinct theories from the organisational sciences: resource dependence theory and institutional theory. Both of these theories can be applied directly to the phenomena under study. But, as we show below, each provides its own set of expectations about relationships between external influences, top-management teams and firm performance. In building a bridge from organisation theory to stakeholder theory, we will ascertain which of the perspectives from the former domain has the most promise for enriching the latter.

12.1 Organisational responses to stakeholder influences

The stakeholder theory literature that has been developed to date has several important foci. According to Donaldson and Preston (1995), three strands of stakeholder theory have been developed: descriptive, instrumental and normative. Our contribution is in the descriptive and instrumental domains, because we describe stakeholder-related actions and test for their influence on corporate outcome variables.

Descriptive work to date has explored whether or not managers believe that shareholders are the sole constituency that they should serve (Baumhart 1968; Brenner and Molander 1977; Posner and Schmidt 1984) and what actions organisations take in response to stakeholder pressures (Post *et al.* 1983; Miles 1982; Clarkson 1991; Greening and Gray 1994). A number of important studies in the instrumental area have explored how social performance influences dimensions of organisational performance, chiefly profitability. In broad surveys, Wood and Jones (1995) and Griffin and Mahon (1997) assembled and reviewed studies on the relationship between a number of stakeholder performance areas (e.g. labour issues or environmental performance) and profits, finding that considerable equivocality exists.

One key issue shared by the vast majority of these empirical studies is that despite the implicit assumption of causality, most of them are cross-sectional in terms of data collection and analysis. This lack of research tracking the broad causal system across time may be due to the data collection constraints or the methodological challenges presented by such analysis. In any case, what is largely missing from the body of research in this area are empirical studies that trace (1) changes in stakeholder dimensions, (2) organisational responses to these changes, and (3) multi-dimensional outcomes.

---

1 Despite the growing literature on stakeholders, a single, widely accepted definition of the term does not exist. Although definitions of stakeholders can be broad or narrow (Mitchell *et al.* 1997), government regulators would appear to fit with any definition chosen. For example, this central role is illustrated by Schuler and Rehbein (1997: 130) who describe government as 'the major determinant of policy salience'.

We focus on top managers in our analysis. Although executives are central to stakeholder management theory (Freeman 1984), empirical analysis has given pride of place to major structural elements used to address stakeholder influences: for example, corporate boards (Jones 1986), public affairs functions (Fleisher 1993) or committees (Greening 1992). We believe that a focus on the top-management team can provide considerable insight in explaining firm responses and outcomes. Jones (1995: 407) spotlighted the importance of managers as 'contracting agents' for the firm because they '(a) contract with all other stakeholders either directly or indirectly though their agents and (b) have "strategic position" (Herman 1981) regarding key decisions of the firm'. If stakeholder management is conducted by executives, knowledge of the relationships between top-management teams and stakeholders should be further explored.

A focus on senior executives also responds to several calls in the literature to target these individuals for another reason. Gray and Allen (1987), Kreiner and Bhambri (1991) and, most recently, Mitchell *et al.* (1997) argued that managerial perceptions and cognitive processes play a key role in organisational actions. There are indications that the training received by individuals is a determinant of the perceptual lenses utilised by managers in dealing with stakeholders. In studying the electric utility industry, Roberts and Bluhm (1981: 35) argued that:

> Professional training may be especially important because of its impact on people's mental processes. There is some justice to the popular impression that lawyers 'think like lawyers' and that engineers 'think like engineers'. Legal training emphasises the need for general rules, which are nonetheless ambiguous when applied to specific cases. It is based on the legitimacy of divergent interests, which in turn legitimates bargaining and compromise as ways of settling disputes—especially in light of ambiguously applicable principles and different goals. Engineering, in contrast, focuses on the need to reduce problems to numerical form; the existence of 'right' (or at least 'best') answers to problems thus defined; the importance of a non-rhetorical, objective approach; and the importance of vigorously implementing the 'right' answer. Thus, organisations whose personnel practices tend to put lawyers in top management jobs may act quite differently from those whose recruitment and advancement systems turn key tasks over to engineers.

In this sense, our study provides a point of contact with previous research on the cognitive perspectives employed by top managers. Many studies in that body of literature analyse how the past experiences of top managers influence their detection and processing of environmental cues, in the tradition of Dearborn and Simon (1958). In contrast, however, we will emphasise the role of external factors in eliciting the make-up of the top-management team itself.

It is here where our study can contribute most directly to the growing interest in top managers and top-management teams. While this literature has broadened, it has tended to focus on how top-management teams influence organisational process and outcomes (e.g. Bantel and Jackson 1989; Wiersema and Bantel 1992; Smith *et al.* 1994; for a review, see Finkelstein and Hambrick 1996). But little research on the antecedents of change in top-management team composition has materialised, even though this was identified as a key area by Hambrick and Mason (1984). More recently, Finkelstein and Hambrick (1996: 130) state that 'the proposition that top managerial characteristics and actions are greatly affected by [environmental, organisational and CEO forces] is not a new one . . .

yet adequate research attention has not been devoted to it'. One study in this area, by Wiersema and Bantel (1993), tested for linkages between environmental complexity and several management team demographic variables, such as heterogeneity and tenure. But no significant results were found, and other studies have explored the environment–top-management team relationship only obliquely (Finkelstein and Hambrick 1996). Thus, our study will help to bridge a serious gap in this literature.

Ours is a dynamic theory, and in its development we utilise several perspectives from the organisation sciences. Such theories are beginning to inform stakeholder theory research (e.g. Hill and Jones 1992; Greening and Gray 1994; Rowley 1997). This intellectual synthesis has numerous bases, including the tendency in organisation science research to use open systems approaches to model organisation–environment linkages, its general eschewing of strict optimising frameworks and its dynamic perspective.

We provide two distinct theoretical perspectives on the relationship between top-management teams and changing stakeholder influences on the corporation, based on resource dependence theory and institutional theory. These theories, which employ an open systems framework (Scott 1992), are ideal for studies focusing on organisation–environment relationships. We focus on the rapid rise to saliency of state electric utility regulators in the early 1970s, and how the 'conflictual' relationship (Gormley 1983) between regulators and utilities may have elicited a rise in legal expertise among top-management teams. This historical context thus provides a rich proving ground for our theories, as it provides an important shift in stakeholder relations, organisational actions and outcomes before and after this shift. Both of the theories we develop suggest that individuals with legal training would rise in utilities during this period, but for contrasting reasons. The theories also differ substantially in their expectations of how such skills in top-management teams would affect organisational effectiveness and efficiency. We begin by providing a brief survey of electric utility regulation during the study period.

12.2 The research setting: the US electric utility industry, 1974–84

Prior to the OPEC (Organisation of the Petroleum Exporting Countries) oil embargo of late 1973, the US electric utility industry enjoyed decades of munificence. Demand for electricity rose constantly and, driven by the exploitation of scale economies, its price steadily declined. During this period, regulators, responsible for permitting reductions to existing rates and for approving new generating stations that would deflate rates further, found their job quiet and painless. Remarking on what he thought regulators might have done in these past years, a California regulator in the 1980s mused that 'they probably played a lot of golf' (Gormley 1983: 6). Not surprisingly, the pre-embargo regulatory climate in the electricity industry is often used to illustrate theories arguing that, over time, regulated firms 'capture' their regulatory agencies (Bernstein 1955; Kolko 1963). But such a portrayal simply cannot be squared with the subsequent events that occurred in the industry.

The sharp increases in oil prices following the OPEC embargo had a profound impact on the electric utility industry. Their primary effect was to produce a spike in electricity rates. A second, related, effect was that regulatory delays in changing electric rates, which benefited utilities when fuel prices were falling, now hurt them if they could not raise rates in time to cover higher fuel prices. The financial impact on utilities was immediate and profound (Navarro 1985). Both of these effects worsened regulatory relations, and this reversal of fortune was aggravated by the fact that procedural hearings, once pro forma rubber-stamping sessions, now became intense, controversial and legalistic (Anderson 1980). Meanwhile, state regulatory staffs were expanded and urged to take strong stands against politically unpopular rate increases. However, within this overall sea change, there were variations. This was due to differences across states in terms of the difficulty of state-wide utility regulation. In some, activism and the attendant uncertainty were more frequently seen. In others, a more accommodating posture was struck.

Changed industry-wide conditions persisted until the end of our study period. By the mid-1980s, a number of positive national trends combined to reduce the turbulence felt by the industry. Fuel price increases relented, construction schedules ebbed and interest rates dipped. The net result of these changes was that the nature of regulation, though changed permanently after the oil embargo, did become more predictable and some sense of stability returned to regulatory relations.

It is important to note that, during the study period, the role of regulators is consistent with Rowley's (1997) network analysis of stakeholders. Following the OPEC embargo, a fundamental transformation in the complexity of regulation took place. In more placid times, the simple, dyadic regulator–utility relationship functioned well, but post-embargo regulation became an arena entered by numerous outside constituencies to fight commissions, utilities and each other. Manufacturing interests waged war with consumer groups over cross-subsidies to residential customers, environmentalists were at odds with low-income advocates over the use of high-cost renewables and utilities fought all comers over the issue of folding construction costs into rates. Thus, regulation became characterised by multiple and generally conflicting voices; in this sense, it can be appreciated as a complex amalgam of stakeholder relationships. Given that the regulatory commission is the point where players with few other links come to adjudicate conflicts, in Rowley's (1997) schema, commissions could be said to exhibit high centrality in a low-density network. As a result, post-embargo regulators enjoyed a high level of control over the other stakeholders (i.e. a 'commander' role), demanding the attention of utilities and their top managers.

We believe that, if organisations are held to respond to changes in the constellation of stakeholders and their relative influence, then the top management of firms can be expected to be reshaped in response to the new imperatives facing the organisation. In particular, the professional training necessary for executive leadership in a new context is likely to change. The causal mechanisms by which this change transpires and influences organisational efficiency and effectiveness is distinct from theory to theory, providing an opportunity to compare and contrast their predictive powers. In conducting our tests, we can begin to appreciate which ideas from the organisation science literature deserve closer examination as stakeholder theorists deepen their body of knowledge.

12.3 Regulation, top managers and firm performance: two theoretical perspectives

12.3.1 Resource dependence theory: lawyers as acquirers of resources

The resource dependence approach to the value of legal training within top-management teams is based on Pfeffer and Salancik's (1978) conceptualisation, in which an organisation is intimately tied to its environment. The primary aim of organisational initiatives is to acquire and maintain resources, a problem that is complicated by the fact that no organisation has complete control of its environment, where the resources on which it depends are embedded. In this framework, the key performance criterion is not efficiency; organisational effectiveness, defined as 'the ability to create acceptable outcomes and actions' (Pfeffer and Salancik 1978: 11), is of prime importance. Securing a stream of critical resources from the environment ranks very high among acceptable outcomes.

Thus, resource dependence theory provides a clear point of contact with stakeholder theory. Mitchell *et al.* (1997) argue that managers should respond to the increasing salience of a stakeholder. If this is so, and if executive selection is a mechanism for addressing stakeholder concerns (Jones 1995), then analysis should be able to uncover significant links between the two. But resource dependence theory is unique by virtue of its strong focus on critical resources, the nature of control over them and various organisational actions to reduce dependence. As such, it can be viewed in relatively utilitarian terms, where stakeholder theory considers also the normative issues that face organisations (Donaldson and Preston 1995). Stakeholder theory would consider stakeholders that control resources to be worthy of managerial attention, but it would also see value in giving voice to less powerful external groups, because of the importance of being responsive to legitimate questions that they may raise. Thus, questions raised by resource dependence theory might be viewed as more narrow than those raised by stakeholder theory.

In resource dependence theory, the purpose of much boundary-spanning is to improve organisational effectiveness through purposive actions that confront environmental uncertainties. One way organisations can stabilise a turbulent environment is to seek regulation of their industrial sector. In this way, resource dependence views regulation in the same way as Stigler (1971), for whom regulation is sought out by the industry, not imposed over its protests. Even if the original intent of regulation is purposive, over time firms can come to dominate regulators (Bernstein 1955). However, when regulatory conditions become more acrimonious, the result of renewed public support for more active regulation, organisations must adapt to the new environment in order to remain effective.

One tool for doing so is executive selection. In a resource dependence view, top managers are selected when environments change if they are 'appropriate for coping with that context' (Pfeffer and Salancik 1978: 342). For example, if mergers and acquisitions become more central to the continued survival of an organisation, then executives with financial training would be more likely to ascend the corporate ranks. Pfeffer and Salancik (1977) provide some evidence that this training–selection link is true for hospitals: the medical training of top managers tends to be greater as the need to acquire resources from health insurers (as opposed to philanthropic sources) increases.

A straightforward extension of this thinking would suggest that appropriately trained individuals in the top-management team would enhance organisational effectiveness. When the regulatory environment shifts to a more turbulent and legalistic environment, we would expect the value of legal training to be enhanced. In the industry we study, electric utilities, Pfeffer and Salancik (1978: 242) cited Pacific Gas & Electric Company as an example of a firm where 'most of the engineers who populated the high administrative positions are gone, replaced by lawyers who can deal with the increasingly complex legal and regulatory environment'.

Although on a national basis, the regulatory environment became convulsive and less munificent following OPEC's embargo (Anderson 1980; Gormley 1983), differences in regulatory state climates arose which allow us to examine the rise in lawyers in this industry. In keeping with resource dependence theory, we would expect that lawyers would be more likely to rise within environments where state regulatory climates were more difficult for firms. Here, the translation of national trends into local regulatory activism was stronger, and here the value of legal talent would be greater. It is important to note that, within resource dependence theory, the role of lawyers does not change across time within a difficult regulatory climate. Thus, this theory suggests in a straightforward manner the following hypotheses:

H1

> The number of top managers with legal training in regulated organisations will be greater the more difficult the organisation's regulatory climate.

H2

> Within difficult regulatory climates, the greater the level of legal training in top-management teams of regulated organisations, the higher the level of effectiveness of those organisations.

12.3.2 Institutional theory: lawyers as symbols of conformity

A distinct perspective on the rise of lawyers in regulated sectors is based on institutional theory (Meyer and Rowan 1977; DiMaggio and Powell 1983). In this theory, regulation is an institutional cornerstone, intended to constrain and, perhaps more importantly, standardise the behaviour of regulated organisations. Although electric utilities operate in a strong technical environment, they are also subject to a highly institutionalised environment (Scott 1992: 133). As with resource dependence, organisations succeed by acquiring resources and, in institutional theory, organisations are rewarded by conforming to institutional expectations. To fall out of conformity is to risk sanctions and declining prospects for resource acquisition.

Under such conditions, the key route to success in such endeavours is so-called 'mimetic isomorphism' (DiMaggio and Powell 1983), wherein the organisation responds to pressure for conformity by adopting structures and behaviours that are prevalent in the field and, thus, patterning itself in accordance with norms set by the institutional environment. In this schema, top managers can be portrayed as elements by which organisations can achieve and maintain isomorphism with their organisational fields, and may relate to general perceptions about what is proper in a particular industrial environment (Fligstein 1987). Thus, the rise of lawyers in a heavily regulated industry during turbulent times is seen as a way to comply with pressures to formalise and legalise relationships with regulators, when procedural formality replaced the more casual pre-embargo regulatory conditions.

Imitation plays a critical role in institution theory. This tendency, however, is non-uniform. It is more likely to materialise in environments that are highly institutionalised: that is, full of cognitive, normative and regulative structures that guide social behaviour (Scott 1995). Within such environments, forces promoting imitation vary directly with the level of uncertainty prevalent (DiMaggio and Powell 1983: 151). To the extent that the surrounding environment becomes less predictable and the old recipes for operation cease to be effective, organisations survey their environments to pick up cues about what changes are being instituted by their cohorts.

According to institutional theory, the simple spread of practices across organisational fields does not, in and of itself, indicate institutionalisation. Rather, the tendency for practices to be imitated is not apparent at first, but materialises later in institutional processes. If the pattern of imitation changes across time, then this would support institution theory over so-called 'simple imitation' (Zucker 1987). Tolbert and Zucker (1983) demonstrated that practices are first established by organisations within the institutional environment that take actions for rational, purposive reasons. After a threshold is met, such actions are imitated by other organisations in the field, whether or not they have rational bases. Thus, late movers, in contrast, institute such changes more to imitate perceived best practices than for rational, calculated motives. For example, Tolbert and Zucker (1983) argue that the spread of civil service across a sample of cities was driven by perceptions that it was the legitimate way to provide governmental services.

What Tolbert and Zucker infer, but do not show, is that behaviour in later periods was in fact due to imitative behaviour (Scott 1995). Given that asymmetries across regulatory climates emerged after the OPEC embargo (in fact, it was only after the embargo that ratings of regulators began to be developed), we can assume that a rise of lawyers where regulation was most difficult represents a rational response to a changed and intensified regulatory environment. But we can further institution theory by exploring patterns of imitation explicitly. Several studies (Davis 1991; Haveman 1993) have considered whether industry adoptions of innovative behaviours were connected to focal organisation adoptions, with mixed results. But, in both cases, the effect of imitation across the study period was assumed constant. In this study, we explore whether patterns of imitation vary across the study period, to get closer to the intent of institution theory (DiMaggio and Powell 1983).

We pause here to underscore the point that, like resource dependence theory, there is affinity between stakeholder theory and institutional theory. Given that stakeholder theory stresses the importance of being proactive and anticipatory (Freeman 1984), it is consistent with the early spread of best practices in an institutional field. Where it differs from institutional theory is in the role of best practices at a later date. Here, actions are taken less to be proactive than to react to external pressures. A key difference between institutional theory and stakeholder theory emerges here: there is no strong role for imitation within the latter. Furthermore, stakeholder theory views being a late mover as a distinct negative, while institutional theory ascribes value to such behaviour.

As noted above, in our research setting, after the onset of regulatory turbulence nation-wide, the regulatory demands facing utilities, while rising very quickly, were not equal in all jurisdictions. In some states, regulation proved more difficult for firms than in other states. It is in these states where institutional theory would predict an increase in the numbers of lawyers in the early years of the turbulent nationwide environment. This rise would be a rational response to pressing stakeholder concerns. And, in these early years, imitation would not be prevalent. In later years, in contrast, imitation would be prevalent and the impact of a difficult state regulatory environment would cease to influence the number of lawyers in top-management slots in these organisations. This leads to our first set of hypotheses concerning institution theory. For these and those that follow, for the sake of brevity, we have removed reference in the hypotheses to the idea that the hypothe-sised relationships depend on a clear starting point, and that starting point is the OPEC-originated onset of regulatory turbulence in the industry.

H3

The relationship between the number of top managers with legal training in a regulated organisation and its being in a difficult regulatory climate will be positive initially and weaken with time.

H4

The relationship between the number of top managers with legal training in a regulated organisation and the number of top managers industry-wide with legal training will become positive with time.

As with resource dependence theory, institutional theory suggests that organisational innovations can enhance organisational effectiveness. As noted above, the mechanism for securing these advantages differs across time, as early, rational changes are sup-planted by changes undertaken to seek legitimacy by conforming to institutional norms. It is here where we can test the relationship of legal talent and effectiveness across the study period. If differing motivations lie behind the acquisition of legal talent within top-management teams, then the differences in their impact on effectiveness should arise over time. Specifically, within difficult regulatory climates, early movers act to add law-yers to proactively address pressing stakeholder contingencies.

Later, with the same regulatory climate, although the value of lawyers is still positive, proactivity is lost and the impact diminishes. The situation outside of difficult regulatory climates is different. There, the value of legal talent early in the process is minimal, because early in the institutional process, norms have yet to be established. Rather, it is only later in the process that having lawyers on a top-management team has a salutary effect on resource acquisition. This is because, later in the process, having lawyers is seen as conforming to industry-wide norms about what is a proper top-management team make-up. In this way, by considering not only the top-management teams, but the time position within an unfolding process of institutionalisation, we can ascertain whether resource dependence theory or institution theory carries greater explanatory power.

H5

> Within difficult regulatory climates, the relationship between the level of legal training in top-management teams of regulated organisations and the organisation's effectiveness will be positive initially, and then weaken with time.

H6

> Outside of difficult regulatory climates, the relationship between the level of legal training in top-management teams of regulated organisations and the organisation's effectiveness will become positive with time.

An additional point of differentiation between the resource dependence theory and institutional theory arises from examining the impact of lawyers on organisational efficiency. Whereas resource dependence theory considers efficiency as an internal dimension that is not essential to organisational resource acquisition (Pfeffer and Salancik 1978), institutional theory is more aggressive in its portrayal of efficiency.

Because organisations protect their technical activities by decoupling them from external elements in institutional environments (Meyer and Rowan 1977), influences on efficiency and effectiveness do not parallel one other. It is also more likely that organisations situated in highly institutionalised fields are buffered from pressure for efficiency by strong fiscal and legal barriers (DiMaggio and Powell 1983). To quote Zucker (1987: 445), 'organisational conformity to the institutional environment simultaneously increases positive evaluation, resource flows, and therefore survival chances, *and* reduces efficiency' [italics in original]. Given that institutionalisation takes place across time, and that early changes are undertaken to address instrumental reasons rather than seek conformity, we can test Zucker's ideas by ascertaining whether later adopters experienced efficiency losses. These arguments lead directly to the next hypothesis:

H7

> The relationship between the level of legal training in top-management teams of regulated organisations and the organisation's efficiency will become negative with time.

12.4 Methods

12.4.1 Sample

We drew a sample from the set of US, privately owned electric utilities. This industry is regulated, providing the necessary proving ground for our hypotheses. We began with the 182 companies that were designated as 'Major' by the US Federal Energy Regulatory Commission (FERC) in 1986, a category containing all electric utilities selling to more than a very small number of customers. Eighty-five utilities that were members of federally registered holding companies, and therefore subject to a number of special regulations (Hawes 1986), were excluded. These firms have a separate corporate management level lying above the top-management team (TMT) of the utilities, which suggests that they would not be appropriate for the tests being considered here.

Of the 97 remaining firms, we removed 10 that were exempted from annual filings by the Securities and Exchange Commission, since this produced a major data gap. Also removed were 19 utilities that are generating subsidiaries of utilities or aluminium companies, since they have distinct organisational forms from those retained in the sample. Finally, 14 companies that had less than 75% of their 1986 sales in their home state were excluded. Drawing this line balanced the need for a viable sample size with the need to isolate state regulation. TMT biographical information was taken from various issues of *Dun and Bradstreet's Reference Book of Corporate Managements*. Data on TMT backgrounds were incomplete or missing for 13 firms. Thus, our total sample size was 97 − (10 + 19 + 14 + 13), or 41 firms.

The sample consists of firms that are generally larger than the population average; this is because a number of very small utilities were excluded from the set. The size effect may also be increased owing to the tendency for smaller utilities that were present in the population before 1986 to fall below the size that requires reporting to FERC by 1986, when the sample was developed. Information on mergers was incomplete, but suggests that a small number (e.g. one or two per year) took place as well. Thus, our sample can be viewed as representative of larger, publicly held utilities during the study period, but our results may not be generalisable to very small utilities.

Our study period runs from 1974 to 1984, when the industry was beset by turbulence. The onset of turbulence in regulatory relations is relatively sharply defined, commencing in 1974, the first post-embargo year. It is from this point that a new institutional framework was erected in the industry. A review of the industry suggests that the return of stability can be placed roughly at the end of 1984. First, mid-year costs of capital, a critical variable for an industry engaged in construction, fell by five full percentage points (16.0% to 10.9%) between 1984 and 1985. Second, for the first time since the embargo, many utilities began to earn the target rates of return set by regulators. Third, the average level of diversification within the sampled firms doubled from 1984 to 1985. As this diversification was typically driven by free cash flows (Russo 1992), it is another sign of financial health. Finally, in 1985, both oil and gas prices, prime inputs for many utility plants, declined by double digit rates.

12.4.2 *Measures*

Difficult state regulatory climate. As we discussed above, although national trends clearly defined a period of regulatory turbulence, the state-wide regulation to which utilities were subject varied. Some states struck a relatively accommodating posture towards utilities, while others were more aggressive in questioning expenditures, trimming rates and generally raising the uncertainty faced by utilities. To capture differences in regulatory environments, we used assessments produced by the Value Line Investment Survey. The assessment process places each state regulatory commission into one of three categories: above average, average or below average, in order of increasing difficulty for utilities. Initial analyses suggested that a clear delineation appeared between the first category and the last two categories. Model fit was best when the last two categories were combined into a single dummy variable, coded 1 if the state's commission was rated below average or average, and 0 for the above average category. We term this variable 'difficult regulatory climate', to contrast it with the less difficult conditions represented by an above-average regulatory climate. This allowed for a more parsimonious model than if more than one dummy variable was used, as we also used the regulatory variable to form interactions with other variables.

Professional training. Members of the TMT were defined as those reporting to the firm's CEO directly, generally the senior vice-president level and above. Legal training was coded 1 when the individual in question had a law degree, and 0 otherwise. We felt that using TMT members rather than the CEO was the proper choice for several reasons. First, top managers rather than CEOs are specifically discussed in several theoretical contributions: for example, Pfeffer and Salancik (1978) and DiMaggio and Powell (1983). Second, top-management teams are relatively fluid, unlike CEOs, which change only infrequently (and less so in this sample than the broader set of American firms). Third, the choice of CEOs is likely to be restricted to a much smaller set of individuals than those chosen to enter TMTs in this industry, in which firms almost never promote from without (four instances in our data).

It could be argued that simply possessing legal credentials does not guarantee that an individual engaged in legal practice. We were confident that possession of a law degree covaried with professional experience. We tested this proposition with a limited sample of firms for which we had professional experience. The number of executives with law degrees correlates with the years of legal experience of TMT members at a 0.85 level, suggesting that little is added by reducing the sample size in order to include years of legal experience. We had data for the years 1969 to 1986 for this data for studying the rise of those with legal credentials. Thus, for analyses of the professional training of top managers, we had 18 years × 41 firms, or 738 observations.

Industry-wide TMT lawyers. In order to test hypothesis 3, we needed to develop an industry-wide measure of the number of lawyers in TMTs. We considered a utility's referent group to consist of all utilities in the sample, excluding the focal utility. Thus, for a given year, we aggregated figures for the 41 firms in the sample to obtain industry-wide figures, and then removed the figure for the focal utility. In this way, we avoid the possibility that a spurious finding might emerge. Also, by removing the focal utility's number—an internal measure—the industry-wide figure can be viewed as truly external to the organisation.

Organisational performance. Organisational effectiveness has been defined as 'the ability to create acceptable outcomes and actions' (Pfeffer and Salancik 1978: 11). The construct of effectiveness has been subject to some controversy, primarily because there are multiple models of how to define and measure effectiveness (Cameron and Whetten 1983), and because some effectiveness measures represent organisational means, not ends (Quinn and Rohrbaugh 1983). We obtained measures of effectiveness that match the types of model that were described in resource dependence and institutional theories, which deploy an open systems approach. Of the eight models of organisational effectiveness described by Cameron (1986), the 'system resource model' would appear to apply here. In the open systems model, resource acquisition and external support represent ends; flexibility and readiness represent means (Quinn and Rohrbaugh 1983: 374). We sought measures that would represent ends, not means, and therefore looked for those that captured resource acquisition and external support.

One likely candidate, profitability, could not be used for two reasons. The first is that profits are constrained in this industry such that an upper bound on the rate of return is set by regulators. The second is that profits in this industry for much of the period were strongly influenced by an accounting practice wherein utilities credited themselves for expected cash flows from construction work in progress. Such 'phantom' earnings varied from firm to firm, necessitating caution in making inter-firm comparisons (Chandy and Davidson 1983).

We located two other measures of effectiveness in this industry that reflect resource acquisition and external support. Obtaining borrowed funds at favourable rates is critical for utilities, as they were continually engaged in facility expansion during this period. Thus, organisational effectiveness can be measured by the ability of a firm to upgrade its bond rating, or to avoid downgrades. Although it might be argued that this measure is not directly related to the regulatory relationship, in reality financial markets are tightly linked to the nature of regulation. Speaking of this derivative relationship, one observer stated that 'When you buy the securities of a utility, you're buying the public utilities commission' (*Business Week* 1979). We tracked the ability of utilities to improve bond ratings by assigning a numerical scale to Moody's bond ratings, and then measured change by considering this scale in linear terms. For example, if a firm moved from an Aaa rating (coded 40) to Aa (coded 36.66), its change would be coded as −3.33. For the majority of years, no change took place and the variable was coded 0. This operation-alisation is a simplification, but surely captures a sense of how the company's financial stature was viewed by financial decision-makers. We had figures for bond ratings and a control variable, stock beta, from 1974 to 1984 for 39 firms, so that the number of observations for these analyses is 11 years × 38 firms, or 418.

Because the utility also depends on favourable treatment by its regulators to improve its financial health, we used a measure of its ability to obtain resources and support through the regulatory apparatus. As a public utility, each company must petition its state commission for approval before raising its rates. The proposed increases in electric rates are then scrutinised by regulators, who determine a fair level of increase. We used the percentage increase granted by regulators as a percentage of the requested rate increase, which we term 'rate case disposition'. The data we used came from annual reports compiled by regulators (e.g. NARUC 1974). Because rate increase requests are not made every year, we only had 225 such instances within the turbulent period.

We were fortunate to have quite detailed information on organisational efficiency. To measure efficiency, we used total factor productivity, accepted by economists as the best efficiency measure (Cowing 1981). Figures for 1972 to 1985 were prepared by the National Association of Regulatory Utility Commissioners (NARUC 1987), and are expressed in kilowatt-hours per dollar of input (kWh/US\$).[2] As with the other performance analyses, we focus on the turbulent years from 1974 to 1984. The number of observations for analyses of efficiency is 11 years × 41 firms, or 451.

---

2 Total factor productivity expresses the ratio of outputs to inputs for a particular firm. Speci-fically, outputs are measured as the number of kilowatt-hours sold and inputs are the expenses associated with labour, fuel, capital, purchased power and other costs of production. The figures thus provide an estimate of the number of kilowatt-hours produced per dollar of input, the average being 41.29 kWh/US\$. Over time, the measure captures the change in the firm's ability to yield outputs as compared to inputs.

Control variables. Two variables were used in all analyses to capture basic organisational dimensions. The firm's growth rate was defined as the annual percentage change in kilowatt-hour sales. For firm size, the total net assets of the firm, expressed in billions of constant 1986 dollars was used. Data for these measures came from the annual *Financial Statistics of Selected Electric Utilities* (e.g. FERC 1988). We also included the 'difficult regulatory climate' variable in runs to estimate organisational efficiency, to explore whether difficult state regulation militates against productive efficiency in the industry. Also, we include the stock beta for each of the firms in regressions of bond rating changes, in order to control the effect of risk on those changes. Both of these variables came from the Value Line Investment Survey for the years used in this analysis.

We also included variables to control the effect of TMT members with other than legal backgrounds. Although our theory is focused on legal training, we felt that the inclusion of variables for other backgrounds would be of interest to readers. So in regressions of organisational performance we include the number of engineers and generalists in the TMT of firms. The former included those with technical degrees and the latter included those with non-technical degrees and MBAs. In the case of multiple degrees, the final degree determined the coding of an individual. For example, those with BS and MBA degrees were coded as generalists. For any firm, the sum of individuals coded as lawyers, engineers and generalists is equal to the size of the top-management team.

12.4.3 Data analysis

For our analyses, we employed pooled, cross-sectional time-series analysis, with all variables except inter-year growth lagged one year. We made a statistical correction to remove the possibility of spurious significance and to account for trends in the data. In our estimations, we included fixed effects for firms when initial analyses indicated that such corrections were necessary (Hsiao 1986). This was true of all regressions, except for those estimating rate case disposition. Rather than include a string of dummy variables for each firm, we 'de-meaned' each variable by subtracting the mean for all observations for a firm from the value for each of the firm's observations. This is computationally equivalent to adding dummy variables (Hsiao 1986).

In two cases we had full panel data—observations for all firms for all time periods. This occurred for the analysis of the rise of lawyers with TMTs, and for productivity. In these cases, we used the statistical package PROC AUTOREG, which includes a correction for serial correlation.[3] For the studies of bond ratings and rate case outcomes necessary to test hypotheses 4 and 5, the situation was more complex. We could have pooled all observations and used 3-way interaction variables (e.g. difficult regulatory climate × TMT lawyers × time) to test hypotheses 3–7, or we could have separated the data on one of those measures and used a simpler 2-way interaction. Because of the cumbersome nature of 3-way interactions, we chose to conduct separate analyses for firms operating in difficult regulatory climates and in less difficult regulatory climates. We could not, however, conduct a balanced analysis with either set, because a small number of states

---

3 In practice, inserting a blank record after the block of data corresponding to each individual (here, firm) will allow PROC AUTOREG to change its autoregressive parameter to employ a separate number for each individual (K. Meyer, personal communication, 16 September 1999).

changed from one regulatory climate to another during the study. Because we could not locate a statistical package that can accommodate such imbalanced panels, we used OLS analysis. In the case of bond rating changes, the fixed effects model should act to mitigate autocorrelation.

Several of our hypotheses require the assessment of interaction terms in regression analysis. Analysis and evaluation of interaction terms lead to several methodological issues. It is often the case that interaction terms can be correlated with their constituent terms, which can yield problems associated with multicollinearity. This can cause estimates to move around from equation to equation. Thus, assessing overall model fit statistics is important in this setting. In OLS regressions, we assessed the value of hierarchical regressions with familiar F tests. For runs using PROC AUTOREG, however, this approach is not appropriate, because that program transforms the variables themselves as part of an analysis. Thus, the actual values of variables that enter regression routines are not the same from specification to specification. Because this routine uses maximum likelihood techniques, we used a statistic formed by taking twice the difference in log-likelihood ratios to assess hierarchical regressions. This approach was recommended as the preferred approach by the provider of the software.[4] The resulting statistic has a χ-square distribution, and can be so evaluated.

12.5 Results

Table 12.1 provides correlations for the study. Figures suggest that the number of top-management team members with legal training is correlated most with firm size. The larger the firm, the greater the number of TMT members with legal training. And the industry-wide number of lawyers rises with time, as shown by the strong correlation between industry-wide lawyers and years since the onset of turbulence in the industry. Time is also negatively correlated with productivity and stock beta, indicating time trends apparent in those variables. Higher growth is correlated with higher productivity, as growth means fuller usage of existing facilities and, therefore, greater efficiency. The performance variables, on the other hand, display no correlation, suggesting that they may be picking up different tendencies.

Table 12.2 provides the results of regressions to test hypotheses 1, 3 and 4 regarding the make-up of the TMT. Model A tests hypothesis 1 by testing whether or not lawyers were more likely to ascend the ranks of utilities located in states where the regulatory climate was difficult. Although acting in the expected direction, the regulatory variable is not significant. Thus, no support for hypothesis 1 was found. In this equation, only the impact of firm size is significant, indicating that larger firms are more likely to have greater numbers of lawyers in their top echelons. This is likely to be a result of the propensity of larger firms to have larger TMTs. The direct effect of industry-wide TMT lawyers is not significant, which suggests that imitative tendencies were not apparent within the study period. Finally, no general time trend is apparent in this model.

4   K. Meyer, personal communication, 16 September 1999.

Correlation coefficients

	Mean	Std Dev.	1	2	3	4	5	6	7	8	9	10	11
1 Firm-wide TMT members with legal training	0.88	1.15											
2 Difficult regulatory climate	0.70	0.46	06*										
3 Industry-wide TMT members with legal training	34.32	5.38	-11*	01									
4 Sales growth rate (%)	2.87	6.64	-06	-05	-04								
5 Firm size ($ billion)	2.44	2.67	60*	06	-10*	-11*							
6 Years since OPEC embargo	6.00	3.17	08	01	91	-09*	02						
7 Bond rating change[a]	-0.61	3.72	02	-03	-12*	08	-04	02					
8 Rate case disposition[b] (%)	61.45	25.89	-14*	-14*	-29*	-04	-18*	14*	08				
9 Total factor productivity[c]	42.17	12.99	07	-20*	-43*	25*	-15*	-26*	-07	09			
10 Firm-wide TMT members with technical training	2.58	1.59	17*	-22*	12*	-06	42*	16	-07	-02	-17*		
11 Firm-wide TMT members with general training	1.23	1.18	11*	10*	08*	01	17*	10	—	07	05	-07	
12 Stock beta	0.69	0.11	07	-29*	-40*	10*	20*	-43*	00	01	30*	17*	05

Decimals omitted. Significance levels based on two-tailed tests $* p < .05$
Number of observations is 225 to 451.   Std Dev. = Standard Deviation   TMT = top-management team   OPEC = Organisation of the Petroleum Exporting Countries

a   Units are 3.33 per bond rate increment (see text)
b   Allowed rate increase divided by firm requested increase, expressed as percentage
c   Units are kilowatt-hours per dollar (see text)

Table 12.1 *Descriptive statistics and correlation coefficients*

	(A)	(B)
Intercept	0.589*** (0.134)	0.350*** (0.038)
Difficult regulatory climate	0.262 (0.222)	0.100 (0.080)
Industry-wide TMT members with legal training	−0.008 (0.014)	−0.042*** (0.008)
Sales growth rate	0.0003 (0.004)	0.0003 (0.004)
Firm size	0.070*** (0.027)	0.533*** (0.039)
Years since OPEC embargo	0.017 (0.024)	−0.025 (0.039)
Difficult regulatory environment × years since OPEC embargo	−0.040*** (0.010)	
Industry-wide TMT members with legal training × years since OPEC embargo	0.003*** (0.001)	
Log likelihood	−372.1	−346.3
−2 × Δ Log likelihood		51.6***

TMT = top-management team   OPEC = Organisation of the Petroleum Exporting Countries

Standard errors in parentheses. Significance levels based on one-tailed tests.

*** $p < .01$ ** $p < .05$ * $p < .10$

Table 12.2 ***Regression results: top-management team study.***
Dependent variable: firm-wide TMT members with legal training

Model B tests hypotheses 3 and 4 by adding interaction terms for time and the regulatory climate and for time and industry-wide TMT lawyers. For hypothesis 3 to be supported, the direct effect of the difficult regulatory climate would need to be positive, while the interaction term is negative. This does not occur, however. Instead, the direct term, while in the expected direction, is not significant. So lawyers were not more likely to be promoted in difficult regulatory conditions in the years just after the onset of regulatory turbulence, but were less likely to be promoted with time. The coefficient on industry-wide TMT lawyers becomes significant, as its effect is brought into focus with the inclusion of the interaction term. Hypothesis 4 is assessed by viewing the interaction term for time and industry-wide TMT lawyers. The variable of interest, the number of industry-wide TMT members with legal training, has a negative overall effect on TMT lawyers in focal firms. However, this negative effect diminished with time, as shown by the interaction term. Thus, there is support for the notion that, during turbulent periods, cues are taken from prevalent practices from the referent group of organisations, supporting hypothesis 4. Finally, it is important to note that the test for the increased explanatory power of model B over model A is highly significant, indicating that the interaction terms adds new value to the regression analysis.

Table 12.3 includes regressions to ascertain the effects on bond rating changes of legal training within TMTs during the turbulent period. Models C and D report findings for the sub-sample of utilities in difficult regulatory climates; models E and F report findings for the sub-sample of utilities in more accommodating regulatory climates.

Model C provides results for direct effects for bond ratings of utilities in difficult regulatory climates. Here, we test hypothesis 2, which suggests that legal training will positively influence bond ratings. In our results, however, the only type of training that has a significant impact on bond rating changes is that of the generalist, and the negative coefficient suggests that the greater the number of generalist within the TMT, the greater the chance of a lower bond rating. Thus, no support for hypothesis 2 was found. Of the controls, sales growth has a positive effect on bond ratings, indicating that the impact of

	(C) Difficult regulatory climate	(D) Difficult regulatory climate	(E) Less difficult regulatory climate	(F) Less difficult regulatory climate
Intercept	−0.393* (0.250)	−0.414** (0.247)	−0.550** (0.279)	−0.535** (0.277)
Firm-wide TMT members with legal training	0.308 (0.439)	1.943*** (0.739)	0.527 (0.660)	−0.520 (0.917)
Firm-wide TMT members with technical training	−0.216 (0.282)	−0.350 (0.283)	−0.587** (0.261)	−0.522** (0.262)
Firm-wide TMT members with general training	−0.687* (0.377)	−0.568* (0.375)	1.560*** (0.649)	1.307** (0.663)
Sales growth rate	0.066** (0.035)	0.066** (0.034)	−0.012 (0.050)	−0.016 (0.050)
Firm size	−1.907*** (0.591)	−1.825*** (0.585)	−1.731** (1.014)	−1.959** (1.017)
Years since OPEC embargo	0.408*** (0.094)	0.550*** (0.107)	0.048 (0.138)	−0.044 (0.149)
Stock beta	6.011* (3.718)	5.417* (3.677)	−2.222 (4.932)	−1.554 (4.914)
Firm-wide TMT members with legal training × years since OPEC embargo		−0.182*** (0.066)		0.152** (0.093)
Adjusted R^2	.08	.10	.06	.07
Model F	4.59***	5.04***	2.10**	2.20**
F Test for ΔR^2		7.47***		2.66*
N	294	294	124	124

TMT = top-management team   OPEC = Organisation of the Petroleum Exporting Countries
Standard errors in parentheses. Significance levels based on one-tailed tests.

*** $p < .01$ ** $p < .05$ * $p < .10$

Table 12.3 **Regression result: bond rating changes**

growth on profits is noted by external assessors of these firms. Firm size has a negative influence on bond ratings. During this period, this may have reflected the propensity for larger companies to take leading roles in major construction projects and acquire greater risk. The stock beta, a measure of risk, has a weak positive effect on bond rating, an unexpected result that does not carry through to the subset of firms in less difficult regulatory climates. Finally, a positive time trend is shown, indicating that within this sub-sample, the trend in bond ratings was positive during the study period. Model D adds the interaction term and time trend variable to test hypothesis 5. For this hypothesis to be confirmed, the coefficient on the law degree would need to be positive, and the coefficient on the interaction term would need to be negative. This is what occurs in the regressions, which show that the effect of legal training depends on the time since the onset of regulatory turbulence. The F test statistic for the increase in explanatory power (Kleinbaum *et al.* 1988) is significant, bolstering confidence in the results.

Models E and F repeat the analysis of models C and D, but for firm-years in which the utility faces a less difficult regulatory climate. In model E, the direct effects of the training variables show a different pattern, with engineering and generalist training being negative and positive, respectively. The result for the former may be due to the ability of technical training to be put to use on engineering problems, not regulatory issues. For the latter, this may be due to an ability to deal productively with multiple stakeholders in this environment. The direct effect of legal training, while positive, does not reach significance. Sales growth does not affect bond ratings in this group, which may mean that regulators are seen as cushioning utilities even under poor sales conditions. And the coefficient on firm size is significant and negative, mirroring the results shown for difficult regulatory climates. Model F, where we add the interaction term and time trend, can be used to test for support for hypothesis 6. The addition of this variable improves the model at a moderate degree of significance. The significance of the interaction term indicates that the value of lawyers in this environment became increasingly positive across the study period, confirming hypothesis 6 for our first measure of organisational effectiveness.

Our analysis of rate case disposition uncovered very little explanatory power for our variables of interest (see Table 12.4). In all models, the downward time trend is responsible for the model's significance. Neither in the case of utilities in difficult regulatory climates nor in the case of less difficult climates was any support for hypotheses 5 or 6 found.[5] The fact that results for rate case disposition are not consistent with our model is worthy of some comment. Some gamesmanship may be involved in these rate cases, which is difficult to predict and may not always be present in a given observation. But, more importantly, the lack of significant results may be due to other factors that our theories do not address. For example, external assessment by those rating bonds may be done at a less fine-grained level and thus be more susceptible to the type of symbolic actions that institution theory places at its centre. In contrast, rate cases involve situations where much more data is presented, sometimes in confidence. While there is no doubt that utilities are opportunistic in data given in support of their cases, utility commissions

---

5   We also attempted to estimate a separate measure of rate case performance, which compared the approved rate increases to the existing rate base of the utility. This analysis was similar to that presented for rate case disposition, but not all models converged when subjected to our statistical analysis.

	(G) Difficult regulatory climate	(H) Difficult regulatory climate	(I) Less difficult regulatory climate	(J) Less difficult regulatory climate
Intercept	72.997*** (5.632)	77.120*** (6.465)	86.618*** (8.913)	91.243** (10.136)
Firm-wide TMT members with legal training	−0.163 (2.062)	−5.682 (4.749)	3.469 (4.406)	−2.645 (7.743)
Firm-wide TMT members with technical training	1.212 (1.471)	1.163 (1.468)	0.894 (2.406)	1.167 (2.424)
Firm-wide TMT members with general training	−0.428 (1.833)	−0.633 (1.836)	2.055 (3.867)	2.331 (3.880)
Sales growth rate	−0.165 (0.296)	−0.166 (0.295)	−0.155 (0.531)	−0.096 (0.535)
Firm size	−1.789* (0.920)	−1.616* (0.920)	−2.793 (2.724)	−3.222 (2.763)
Years since OPEC embargo	−1.793*** (0.645)	−2.400*** (0.797)	−3.337*** (1.029)	−4.201*** (1.368)
Firm-wide TMT members with legal training × years since OPEC embargo		0.752 (0.583)		1.055 (1.099)
Adjusted R^2	.05	.05	.08	.08
Model F	2.35**	2.24**	1.93**	1.78*
F Test for ΔR^2		1.60, ns		.91, ns
N	163	163	62	62

TMT = top-management team   OPEC = Organisation of the Petroleum Exporting Countries
Standard errors in parentheses. Significance levels based on one-tailed tests.

*** $p < .01$ ** $p < .05$ * $p < .10$

Table 12.4 **Regression results: rate case disposition**

depend less on incomplete data than do bond rating agencies. Thus, their decisions may reflect less judgemental considerations.

Table 12.5 provides regression estimates of analyses of total factor productivity, our measure of efficiency. Model K provides direct effects estimates. Factor productivity appears to be driven by sales growth, reflecting more efficient use of facilities. Finally, the presence of scale economies in the form of a size–productivity link is not shown in the equations. But location within a difficult regulatory climate appeared to hinder factor productivity. Thus, complaints that difficult regulation acts against one aspect of a utility's wellbeing appear to have some support. The number of TMT members with engineering training, which might be expected to positively influence productive efficiency, instead has a negative effect. However, greater numbers of TMT members with general training improve efficiency. These results are puzzling, but might indicate that

	(K)	(L)
Intercept	39.762***	39.746***
	(2.550)	(2.548)
Firm-wide TMT members with legal training	-1.536**	-1.569**
	(0.662)	(0.866)
Firm-wide TMT members with technical training	-0.978***	-0.981***
	(0.236)	(0.236)
Firm-wide TMT members with general training	1.290***	-1.291***
	(0.432)	(0.451)
Difficult regulatory environment	-3.403**	-3.376**
	(1.796)	(1.863)
Sales growth rate	0.192***	0.192***
	(0.028)	(0.028)
Firm size	-0.536	0.575
	(0.562)	(0.563)
Years since OPEC embargo	-1.735***	-1.738***
	(0.059)	(0.071)
Firm-wide TMT members with legal training × years since OPEC embargo		0.004
		(0.070)
Log likelihood	-1548.2	-1548.1
-2 × Δ Log likelihood		0.2, ns

TMT = top-management team   OPEC = Organisation of the Petroleum Exporting Countries

Standard errors in parentheses. Significance levels based on one-tailed tests

*** p < .01   ** p < .05   * p < .10

Table 12.5 **Regression results: total factor productivity**

engineer-laden TMTs may have lacked the innovative capacities to create efficiency in a greatly changed environment. The coefficient of the number of TMT members with legal training is significant and negative. That is, during the study period generally, the greater the number of TMT lawyers, the poorer the efficiency. Model L adds the variable necessary to test hypothesis 7, an interaction term formed by multiplying TMT lawyers by the time trend. This term is insignificant, showing that the impact of lawyers on efficiency was constant across the study period.

To summarise, while there was no support for hypotheses generated from resource dependence theory in our study, our results were relatively consistent with institution theory. Although location in more difficult regulatory climates did not prompt a rise in TMT lawyers, as time passed, in difficult regulatory climates, there was a tendency for TMTs to be less populated by lawyers. Across time, we did find a pronounced rise in mimetic behaviour, consistent with institution theory. There is also some support for institution theory in the analysis of one of our organisational effectiveness variables, bond rating changes. There, we find that, in keeping with hypotheses 5 and 6, lawyers were an aid to effectiveness early in the study period for utilities in difficult regulatory climates, with that effect fading with time. In contrast, lawyers in less difficult climates only became valuable after time had passed. Finally, although lawyers had a negative impact overall on productive efficiency, this effect was unchanged across time, meaning that, as institutionalisation proceeded, a more negative impact was not perceived.

Support for an institutional theory world-view makes sense in this industry, as it is one of the most institutionalised in America. Even so, there are reasons why even institution theory does not perfectly the explain the phenomenon we studied. For example, in studying the ascendance of CEOs, sociological processes (Cannella and Lubatkin 1993) or power (Allen and Panian 1982) have been stressed in other studies. To the extent that those theories apply to top-management teams, perhaps when succession processes are dominated by such influences, the linkage between top-management teams and outcome variables is attenuated. Another explanation may be the choice of lawyers as the topic of study, because there may be a built-in tendency for top managers with legal training to underperform. Magee *et al.* found evidence that, at the national level, lawyers produce a drag on the economy (1989: 118). They attributed this underperformance to the fact that lawyers have become too numerous, and focus attention on empty legal issues rather than organisational capabilities. Jones (1986) found that the number of lawyers on corporate boards was positively correlated to the number of shareholder lawsuits, and suggested that rather than being experts in avoiding litigation, they may have pushed some boards into risky legal undertakings. Finally, we could not measure whether top-management teams tended towards bridging behaviour rather than buffering behaviour, or vice versa. This variable might have accounted for further variance in our models (Meznar and Nigh 1995).

While outside the scope of our analysis, it is also worth noting that the concept of institutional environment is worthy of further scrutiny. While authors have noted that organisations view their institutional environment through different eyes and through a lens coloured by experience (Scott 1995), this study addressed an important additional element: institutional environments frequently can be viewed as 'layered'. For utilities, this layering was hierarchical, consisting of institutional actors in two key strata. At the national level, actors included federal regulators, industry-wide lobbying groups and other federal players. At the state-wide level, institutional environments are strongly influenced by state public utility regulators, the state-wide political apparatus and groups called interveners that intercede in rate cases. While it is valuable to concentrate on the national level, our study shows that a type of institutional 'micro-climate' surrounded each utility. Such layering is also evident in other settings, such as for professions that are subject to multiple institutional environments. College educators, for example, are immersed in the institutional framework of their home campus, while also subject to the institutional norms of their home discipline.

12.6 Conclusion

12.6.1 *Top managers as stakeholder coping mechanisms*

The chapter demonstrates that the nature of top-management teams is influenced by changing stakeholder pressures, and that top managers influence organisational outcomes. The idea that behavioural explanations for the phenomena under study were supported gives currency to the idea that managers are chosen and perform in ways that balance instrumental and non-instrumental needs. Our results also indicate that cross-influences between stakeholders and organisations affect the very top executive levels of those organisations. This is an important finding, because it has the potential to widen the applicability of stakeholder theory.

The central role of top managers in a stakeholder framework resonates with Jones's (1995: 408) assertion that 'top managers are at the centre of a "hub and spoke" stakeholder model of the firm because they contract with all other stakeholders'. Further evidence of the centrality of top managers in a stakeholder model was found by Waddock and Graves (1997), who established that the perceived quality of management was tied not only to financial performance but also to performance with respect to other stakeholders. Our study thus contributes to a limited, but potentially significant, set of studies on the topic of top managers and other stakeholders. As noted above, a number of other stakeholder studies have focused on the rise of sub-units as a structural response to stakeholder issues. What we and others show, however, is that the stakeholder model can be applied at the highest levels of organisations. Clearly, more research on this vital topic is warranted.

Research can also explore further the backgrounds of TMTs and external conditions. Given our theoretical focus, we spotlighted legal training, which was critical to the phenomenon of interest. However, it would be interesting to see whether or not firms in other fields under regulatory change experienced changes in TMT make-up and ensuing performance impacts. It may turn out that long-distance telecommunications saw the management of firms move away from a legal focus to a technical, and possibly even a marketing, focus as its industry experienced deregulation and subsequent competitive pressure.

Such work would join ours in contributing knowledge to the area of how environmental change elicits change in top-management teams. Wiersema and Bantel (1993) did not find a link between environmental variables and top-management team demographics, and we did not find a straightforward link between regulatory climate and the number of TMT lawyers. Instead, however, we found that industry-wide actions influenced TMT change, in a process that unfolded over time. This implies that the relationships between environments and TMT change may be more subtle than indicated by theories that strip the causal system down to simple, direct linear relationships. Inter-temporal change further complicates the situation. Thus, research that untangled this complex web of causality would be of great value.

12.6.2 *Institutions and stakeholder theory*

Judging from our results, stakeholder theory has much to learn from the organisational sciences. Others have observed that organisation theory can add value to the study of trust

(Hosmer 1995), legitimacy (Greening and Gray 1994) and contracting (Jones 1995) within the rubric of stakeholder theory. Thus, this chapter adds to a growing attempt to draw from related fields and synthesise a more complete knowledge of stakeholder management.

Given the value of institutional theory in explaining the phenomena under study, it is valuable to pause and consider how other ideas from institutional theory might be woven into stakeholder theory. One provocative notion involves the idea of normative pressures for conformity (DiMaggio and Powell 1983; Scott 1992). These pressures can be generalised, and not necessarily articulated through easily identifiable persons or organisations that are typically identified as stakeholders. Does their presence fall outside the topic area of stakeholder management? What if those normative pressures consist of broadly based societal calls for more socially responsible management? Is this why organisations are often judged as ignoring such pressures? In general, normative pressures appear to fall outside of even broad definitions of stakeholders (Clarkson 1995; Mitchell *et al.* 1997). A major challenge in reproaching institutional and stakeholder theories will be the resolution of this issue.

Of course, stakeholder theory can offer much to the organisation sciences. In the empirical context that we addressed, a quite sharply defined event took place which energised regulatory commissions, but changes in the influence of stakeholders can occur slowly and be heavily dependent on changing societal morals and expectations. The study of these gradual changes certainly can bring to organisation theory valuable new ideas about how institutions evolve. For example, Suchman (1995: 574) defines legitimacy as 'a generalised perception or assumption that the actions of an entity are desirable, proper, or appropriate within some socially constructed system of norms, beliefs, values, and definitions'. In describing several broad types of legitimacy, Suchman provides some background on one type, moral legitimacy, which rests on judgements as to whether a particular activity promotes social welfare as perceived by its referent audience. The discussion that follows, however, includes no references to the stakeholder literature, which could add value by providing a sense of where the moral dimension of legitimacy is derived and, more importantly, how it might evolve across time (Freeman 1984). Thus, rather than taking societal perceptions as given, the study of how they are formed and take root could be inspired by stakeholder theory. To put it another way, the organisation sciences have provided a great body of literature on how organisations deal with changing environments, but in many cases, have not been occupied with appreciating why environments change in the first place.

Of prime value would be the addition of an ethical component to the broader set of theories of organisation and environment. We have focused more on the instrumental aspect of stakeholder management in this chapter, but other governance issues that stress the wider set of issues confronting corporations might offer other opportunities for stakeholder theory to inform the organisation sciences. For example, just as the composition of top-management teams can be portrayed as a tool for confronting stakeholder issues, so too can another mechanism for corporate governance, the board of directors. Here, board membership by external constituents has an instrumental effect (Pfeffer and Salancik 1978), but it also often has an ethical component. For example, within the electric utility industry, several firms at later dates added environmental representatives to their corporate board. This may be seen as an effort to co-opt these groups, a more instrumental interpretation. But if inclusion and provision of a voice is seen as a legitimate moral responsibility that can be proved empirically, then such actions would demonstrate the value-added of the stakeholder theory.

Our results are consistent with the basic idea that organisations react to changes in their constellation of stakeholders in ways that do not conform to optimising behaviour. Once the intellectual constraint of optimisation is relaxed, considerable worth can be found in tying organisational outcomes to internal changes that reflected the shifting imperatives of stakeholders. To that end, we hope to have contributed to a more informed stakeholder theory.

13

A COMPARATIVE STUDY OF STAKEHOLDER-ORIENTED SOCIAL AUDIT MODELS AND REPORTS

Jane Zhang

University of Sunderland, UK

Ian Fraser and Wan Ying Hill

Glasgow Caledonian University, UK

The concept of social audit is well established and it is now over 20 years since the first social audits were carried out by organisations such as Social Audit Ltd in the UK. While social audit has gone through various phases since then—and an extended period of significant disinterest—it has attracted an unprecedented level of interest since the early 1990s (Geddes 1992).[1] Social accounts and reports published by Traidcraft plc, the New Economics Foundation (NEF) and The Body Shop in the UK, and the SbN Bank in Denmark and Ben & Jerry's in the USA have all attracted widespread publicity (Gray *et al.* 1997). The resurgence of interest in social audit reflects increasing pressure from the public for a greater degree of social accountability. It is increasingly recognised that accountability requires disclosure of a broad array of economic and social information to society at large, not just to shareholders (Coy and Pratt 1998). However, recent developments of social audit may also reflect an increasing realisation on the part of corporations of their responsibilities in terms of social, ethical and environmental performance. Further, there is the suggestion that social responsibility and reporting may improve the corporate bottom-line performance (Waddock and Smith 2000). Even more radical is the growing belief that, for capitalism itself to be sustainable, it must focus on more than just the financial results. This is arguably encapsulated in the triple-bottom-line approach of SustainAbility: economic prosperity, environmental quality and social justice (Elkington 1997).

---

1 The concept of 'social audit' is discussed in Section 13.1. Social audit is understood here as a generic term that refers to the process that an organisation undertakes when assessing and reporting on its social performance and stakeholder involvement. The term 'social audit' may be perceived as implying restriction to the 'do good' activities of the firm. This perspective would regard the term 'responsibility audit' as more comprehensive, embracing the organisation's negative as well as positive activities.

Social audit has also attracted considerable attention in the research literature (e.g. Brooks 1980; Heard and Bolce 1981; Filios 1986; Wokutch and Fahey 1986; Dennis *et al.* 1998; Ostapski and Pressley 1992; Ostapski and Isaacs 1992; Hill *et al.* 1998; Sillanpää 1998; Cotton *et al.* 2000; Owen *et al.* 2000; Gao and Zhang 2001). However, most of those studies involve either a single case study or surveys of current practice, which offer little insight into the common characteristics of social audit models (Gao and Zhang 2001). While there is no common generally accepted method of social audit and report, it may be worthwhile to analyse the praxis of established models of social audit. The purpose of this chapter is to compare and contrast the social audit approaches adopted by seven different organisations in the British Isles. It attempts to identity the similarities and differences among these accounts/reports.

At the time of writing, however, there are multiple *types* of social audit in use and there are ever more alternative foci for social audits than before. Many contemporary examples are designed to improve company profitability through more responsible social practice. The fundamental premise underlying such social audits is that profitability and social responsibility are not only complementary but also synergistic. Thus, unlike many early social audits, contemporary social audits are not antagonistic to capitalism per se, but are consistent with a more rounded and sympathetic capitalism appropriate to the 21st century. These new social audits (or social responsibility audits) are internally generated and implemented by management and are at the opposite end of the spectrum of social audit from the early 'confrontational' exercises. The early social audits were criticised for their failure to establish dialogue with the organisation, while contemporary social audits seek explicitly to engage with all stakeholders, including the auditee organisation. It is with such contrasting social audit approaches that this chapter is explicitly concerned.

Seven social audit models that focus on stakeholder interests are selected for this comparative study: Beechwood; The Body Shop; Traidcraft; Liverpool Housing Trust's Directions (LHTD); The Co-operative Bank; Agency for Personal Service Overseas (APSO); and New Economics Foundation (NEF). The case study has therefore included different types of organisation, from banking and fair-trade retailing to NGOs and the public sector. This study attempts primarily to compare social audit models in the UK service (banking and retailing), public and charity sectors because these have faced increasing public pressure for public accountability and social responsibility.[2]

The chapter is organised as follows: Alternative concepts of social audit are discussed in Section 13.1 through a literature review. In Section 13.2, the main characteristics of the seven social audit models are described. Section 13.3 compares and contrasts the social audit models, examining the essential differences and similarities between these models. The final section contains our conclusions.

---

2   An exception is APSO, which is an Irish-based government agency. APSO is included in the study since the APSO social accounts follow the Traidcraft model (Traidcraft Exchange acted as a consultant) and adopt the NEF social accounting methodology.

13.1 The concept of social audit

Social audit and social accounting are by now relatively familiar concepts; the term 'social audit' was first used in the 1950s. Initially, social audits were used as a form of external investigation to assess the impact of large corporations on their workforce, consumers and the community. In the 1970s, the measurement of social performance by accountants was the major focus in the literature (e.g. Spicer 1978; Pomeranz 1978).[3] The investigative type of social audit continued into the 1980s. The literature predominately saw social audit as an approach to examining the impact of plant closures and of investment or relocation decisions and, increasingly, uncovering the ethical behaviour and environmental impact of business communities (e.g. Harte and Owen 1987). In the 1990s, broader developments of social audit have emerged, driven by wide recognition of stakeholder interests and involvement, and by public pressure for accountability. Accordingly, companies increasingly disclose their social performance through published social accounts or reports.

In the literature, social audit has been defined in various ways with different emphases. Social audit is sometimes a synonym for social accounting (see Dey *et al.* 1995; Gray *et al.* 1997). Buchholz (1982: 499) defines social audit as:

> an attempt by an individual corporation to measure its performance in an area where it is making a social impact . . . an attempt to identify, measure, evaluate, report and monitor the effects a corporation is having on society that are not covered in the traditional financial reports.

This definition gives prominence to the measurement of social impact. According to the author, 'audit' is a precise term in accounting terminology because it has an 'attestation' function, indicating that financial information and data are fairly and truly reported in financial statements according to generally accepted accounting principles. Social audit refers more to attempts made to measure and report social performance and impact of an organisation.

Murphy and Burton (1980) define social audit as a technique that attempts to document the activities of a firm in regard to such issues as the hiring and promotion of women and minorities, corporate donations, etc. Such a definition, however, suggests a relatively limited purpose for social audit. More recent definitions offer broader perspectives. For instance, Cotton *et al.* (2000) define social audit as 'the process which an organisation undertakes when assessing and reporting on its social performance'. The focus has shifted from external investigation to internal review.

Most importantly, social audit has moved towards a more systematic assessment of the social performance of an organisation, often including a wider dialogue with its stakeholders and external verification, disclosure and accreditation. For example, Traidcraft Exchange, the development non-profit organisation and sister organisation of Traidcraft plc, produced its first set of externally verified social accounts in 1996. There were two innovations in the system:

---

3   Accountants, however, were not in general very supportive of social accounting at this time. Murphy and Burton (1980), in a survey of three professional accounting associations, found an absence of strong support in the accounting community for the use of social accounting techniques.

1. The structure of the reporting, which included:
   - 'Basic description': statistical and qualitative data describing the stakeholder category and the organisation
   - 'Accountability information': generally quantitative data describing the extent to which the organisation has met stakeholders' and society's expectations, measured against the organisation's objectives, legal and quasi-legal regulations and social norms

2. The inclusion of stakeholder voices, quotations, results of stakeholder questionnaires and analytical commentary from the consultation process (Traidcraft Exchange 1996)

There are no generally accepted principles for social accounting and auditing practice. Zadek and Raynard (1995) present a range of examples of social accounting that are broadly similar in orientation. However, there are some differing emphases among the approaches examined by them. Zadek (1998) notes that there are clear signs of a convergence of standards taking place in the practice of social and ethical accounting, auditing and reporting, and proposes eight quality principles for the development of social and ethical accounting and auditing: inclusivity, comparability, completeness, regularity and evolution, embeddedness, externally verified, communication and continuous improvement. Gray *et al.* (1997) consider social accounting as the generic term. Zadek (1998) analyses some of these terms, such as 'ethical accounts', 'social audits', 'human accounting', 'intellectual capital', 'ethical audits', 'social performance reports' and 'social balances', and finds that in many aspects they are quite similar to each other. In this chapter social audit is used as a generic term for social accounting, social auditing, ethical accounting, ethical audit, etc.

Researchers in the social audit arena have suggested a variety of categorical classifications of approaches. Buchholz (1982: 502-10) puts together a shopping list of types including the following:

- Inventory approach: a simple listing and short description of programmes that the firm has developed to deal with social problems

- Programme management approach: a more systematic effort to measure costs, benefits and achievements. It is 'an extension of a traditional management audit to social programmes'.

- Process audit: similar to the above approaches, but with more information over four phases (history and background, objectives, operations and evaluation)

- Cost–benefit approach: an attempt to list all social costs and benefits with a common (monetary) denominator

- Social indicator approach: utilising social criteria (e.g. suitable housing, good health, job opportunities) to clarify community needs and then evaluating corporate activities in the light of these community indicators

Steiner and Steiner (1991: 178) believe that virtually all audits of voluntary programmes are of the inventory type: that is, a general description of what a company has done. The NEF (1996) categorises areas to be measured with social audit, including: **core aims** of the organisation, generally reflected in a mission statement, and **specific stakeholder aims**, identified during a consultation process with identified stakeholder groups.

Zadek (1998) argues that reporting on social and ethical performance is not only a matter of disclosure; it is an integral element of the process of communication between the company and key stakeholders. In this sense, reporting is a way by which stakeholders can see if the company 'listened' to their concerns and, over time, whether it has responded in practical terms. Reporting is essentially an element of the communication, dialogue, learning and decision-making process, rather than the endpoint in a retrospective analysis. Mackenzie (1998) comments that current practice places considerable emphasis on data collection, but very little on analysis, theory building and experimental testing in the area. There are also some more narrowly focused definitions of social audit, including 'ethical checklist' and quality audit (Natale and Ford 1994).

The models or frameworks of social audit have been approached differently (e.g. Pearce 1996; Gray *et al.* 1997; Hill *et al.* 1998; Sillanpää 1998). Gray *et al.* (1997) discuss the 'organisation-centred', the 'stakeholder-centred' and the 'polyvocal citizenship perspective (PCP)' approaches to social audit. Hill *et al.* (1998) and Sillanpää (1998) advocate a dialogue-based approach. Sillanpää argues that 'a dialogue-driven approach is needed to nurture empowered stakeholder relationships'. Sillanpää believes that it is possible to link processes of stakeholder dialogue and inclusion with management systems designed to secure continuous improvement in product quality, human resource and safety management as well as individual learning and development. Hill *et al.* (1998) view the active involvement of stakeholder groups as central to the operation of the social audit exercise. The objectives are to encourage dialogue and sharing of information in order to cope with the tensions and demand on services. However, both the stakeholder-centred and PCP approaches require that the issues of identification of 'stakeholders' and 'citizens' are addressed, and particularly their representation. Informal dialogue and a consultation process have been emphasised by Hill *et al.* (1998).

Dawson (1998) argues that the role of social audit should be examined based on different groupings of organisations. A social audit framework may offer broad-based methodological underpinning and application value across all sectors of human organisation (Hill *et al.* 1998). In effect, social audit aims to make an organisation more transparent and accountable (Zadek and Raynard 1995).

Increasing numbers of corporations now accept the notion of 'corporate social responsibility' (e.g. The Body Shop International,[4] BT, The Co-operative Bank), and have developed substantial community support programmes. Subsequently many organisations in private sector and in non-profit organisations and government agencies have adopted social audit concepts in managing their business and activities. 'There is a growing body of experiences in corporate social and ethical accounting, auditing, and reporting, partic-

---

4   For the case of The Body Shop International, see Arkin 1996. The company decided to carry out a social audit after establishing programmes for environmental protection and health and safety at work. The starting point for this latest exercise, which has taken about three years to research, plan and implement, was the view that all stakeholders should have a say in shaping a company's behaviour. 'The Body Shop has a strong belief in accountability and transparency,' says David Wheeler, former general manager for ethical audit, '. . . Business will only be legitimate in the eyes of stakeholders in the 21st century if it behaves in an accountable way. So companies cannot continue to behave as if they operate in a moral vacuum.'

ularly across Europe and North America. Associated with this development has been the emergence of varied terminology and differing approaches' (Zadek 1998).[5]

However, the social audit approaches and programmes discussed so far largely envisage corporate responsibility without reference to impacts on stakeholders that result from day-to-day operating practices. Waddock and Smith (2000: 75) argue that a social (or, to use their terminology, *responsibility*) audit of a company's core operating practices provides an opportunity for a company to assess its overall performance against its 'core values, ethics, internal operating practices, management systems, and, most importantly the expectations of key stakeholders'. It is argued that this type of social audit facilitates high performance by companies, both financially and socially. Other recent writing on social audit (e.g. Gonella *et al.* 1998; SustainAbility 1999) emphasises the efficacy of social audits in strengthening an organisation's strategic management procedures.

It is consistent with such thinking that several recent initiatives highlight what may be argued to be the emergence of 'a new age capitalism appropriate to a new millennium, in which the boundary between corporate and human values is beginning to dissolve . . . The argument is now about what kind of capitalism we want' (Elkington and Burke 1987). One expression of this thinking is the Global Reporting Initiative (GRI),[6] which was established in late 1997 with the mission of developing globally applicable guidelines for reporting on economic, environmental and social performance, initially for corporations and eventually for any business, governmental or non-governmental organisation.[7] The GRI guidelines represent the first global framework for comprehensive sustainability reporting, encompassing the 'triple bottom line' of economic, environmental and social issues. The GRI guidelines have been adopted as a framework for corporate responsibility reporting by a significant number of household name companies including KLM Royal Dutch Airlines, General Motors, Procter & Gamble and Siemens. This 'managerial turn' in the new wave of social audit is not without its critics. Humphrey and Owen (2000) raise the question of whether stakeholder *management* rather than stakeholder *accountability* is increasingly driving developments.

In this chapter, however, we are more concerned with the type of contemporary social audit that specifically addresses stakeholder concerns. These might usefully be designated as stakeholder responsibility audits. More specifically, our focus in this chapter is on one particular type of responsibility audit: those concerned with stakeholder *perceptions* of the organisation. We address this issue in the context of several different types of organisation to illustrate its broad applicability and importance.

---

5   According to Simon Zadek of the NEF, 90% of *Fortune* 500 companies already have codes of conduct covering a range of social and environmental issues, although they do not necessarily seek external verification of their compliance with these codes.

6   Several other voluntary initiatives complement the GRI. These include ISO 14000 (focusing on corporate environmental management systems and practices), AA 1000 (aimed at increasing the quality of social and ethical accounting, auditing and reporting) and SA 8000 (aimed at improving labour conditions around the world through a humane workplace standard).

7   www.globalreporting.org

13.2 Social audit models and reports

Many organisations across the world have gone through a process of social auditing irrespective of the nature of their business and size. These range from the small community enterprise to the large local development trust, or non-profit organisation; from a workers' collective to the large co-operative with a more traditional management structure; and from the voluntary organisation to the small firm with social objectives. Section 13.1 indicated the diversity of possible approaches to social audit. We restrict our analysis here to seven different social audit models, well established in the UK or Ireland (along with their respective reports), all of which have as a primary focus an engagement with stakeholder concerns.

This type of social audit is an organisational-based process influenced both by the identification of stakeholders and their interests in an organisation and by the particular missions and objectives of the organisation. The models of social audit with which we are concerned here are those of the following organisations: Beechwood College, The Body Shop, Traidcraft, The Co-operative Bank, Liverpool Housing Trust's Directions (LHTD), the Agency for Personal Service Overseas (APSO) and the New Economics Foundation (NEF). The selection of these seven models[8] fairly represents different types of organisation from charitable agency, retailer, bank, through to public services.

13.2.1 The Beechwood model

The Beechwood model was developed in the late 1970s in connection with social audit at Beechwood College in Leeds. The model was designed for community organisations to plan, manage and measure non-financial activities and to monitor both the internal and the external consequences of the organisations' social and commercial operations. The Beechwood model consists of four main elements: statement of purpose; aims and targets; the internal view; and the external view. This covers all stakeholders associated with an organisation and includes wider issues such as environmental impact analysis, ownership rights and trading partners.

Beechwood College, in the later 1970s and early 1980s, pioneered social audit for industrial co-operatives and community enterprises, reflected in a booklet, *Social Audit: A Management Tool for Co-operative Working*, authored by Spreckley and published by Beechwood College in 1982. The Beechwood model focuses on the inclusion of social audit in the constitution of an organisation, and developed a detailed set of clauses for the memorandum and articles of association of a company's constitution. This provides a legally binding constitutional foundation for undertaking social audit. These clauses consist of the four elements of social audit in the memorandum of association and a detailed description of how social audit is to be carried out in the articles of association.

The Beechwood model argues that social audit can be used to manage change:

> As a result of applying social audit many organisations need to make changes, both in their structures and in their interaction with the wider community. The system is designed to enable organisations to plan and manage change both

---

8 The term 'model' is used for convenience of description rather than to suggest entirely distinct paradigms.

during the process of applying social audit and as part of the following year's
target (Spreckley 1997: 11).

The procedure of social audit (i.e. the way in which social audit is planned and carried
out follows a sequence) is presented in Box 13.1 (see Spreckley 1997: 10).

Preparation for management
- Set up audit team
- Prepare working schedule
- Agree terms of reference

Define the scope
- Analyse previous year's social audit targets
- Identify shortfalls
- Prepare this year's social audit agenda

Practical application: the social audit toolkit
- Annual target sheets
- Statement of purpose
- Internal view
- External view

Monitoring and measurement
- Present findings and future targets
- Carry out quarterly accumulative, progressive and tabulated (APT) reporting
- Audit annual evaluations

Box 13.1 *The Beechwood social audit model*

Source: Spreckley 1997: 10

The Beechwood model comprises two main themes when measuring performance:
monitoring and evaluation. Monitoring is undertaken by quarterly accumulative,
progressive and tabulated (APT) reporting. Evaluation (end-of-year auditing which relies
to a great extent on variance analysis) is a review of the current year's plans, conclusions
and recommendations, which sets the following year's social audit agenda. It uses
participative methods for determining criteria and strategy, planning detailed schedules
and for evaluating outcomes. Though an audit team is constituted to handle the day-to-
day management of the social audit, involvement by all stakeholders is also required.
Shared responsibility for an organisation's actions is one of the main objectives in
employing participative techniques.

However, the Beechwood model does not put stakeholders as the core of social audit;
rather, it relies principally on the audit team which is appointed by the management
board. Although community and stakeholders are involved in the audit, the involvement
is just treated as part of 'the external view'. It defines social audit as 'a method for

organisations to plan, manage and measure non-financial activities and to monitor both the internal and external consequences of the organisations' social and commercial operations' (Spreckley 1997: 1). Its foundation is based 'within the concept of viability', and 'it is dynamic and responsive to the wider social and environmental milieu' for the purpose of managing change. The Beechwood model also emphasises that 'social audit aims to complement financial accounting and integrate financial and non-financial factors into a unitary accounting procedure' (Spreckley 1997: 5).

13.2.2 The Body Shop model

The Body Shop commenced its first social audit in 1993. Its social audit methodology aims at ensuring continuous improvement in the company's stakeholder relations as well as ensuring greater external accountability and transparency for its social performance and wider societal impact. The Body Shop's commitment to social audit followed successful experience in implementing audit programmes for environmental protection and health and safety at work, as well as ingredient monitoring programmes for animal protection. Table 13.1 presents The Body Shop's main social statements, their characteristics and underlying foundations.

Statements	Main characteristics	Foundations
Environmental Statement (1992)	▪ Environment protection is the main theme of the statement ▪ Products-focus approach, rather than stakeholder-focus approach	The European Union Eco-management and Audit Scheme (EMAS)
The Values Report 1995, published in January 1996. It contains three separate statements concerning: ▪ Performance on environmental issues ▪ Animal protection ▪ Social issues	▪ The report comprised of three statements on the company's performance on environmental, animal protection and social issues. ▪ Each statement has an element of independent verification in line with established best practice. ▪ Included in the publication is a paper, *The Body Shop Approach to Ethical Auditing*, describing the methods underpinning the three reports. ▪ A verification statement indicates an external verification process.	▪ Mission statement ▪ Trading chart ▪ Managers' and employees handbooks ▪ Community trade programme
The Values Report 1997, published in January 1998	▪ Single statement covering these three aspects: environmental performance; animal protection; social issues	▪ Mission statement ▪ Trading chart ▪ Managers' and employees handbooks ▪ Community trade programme

Table 13.1 *The Body Shop's social statements and their foundation*

The Body Shop's audit cycle consists of ten key components: policy review, determination of audit scope, agreement of performance indicators, stakeholder consultation and survey, internal management systems audit, preparation of accounts and internal report, agreement of strategies and local targets, verification, publication of statement and internal reports, and follow-up dialogue with stakeholders (see Fig. 13.1).

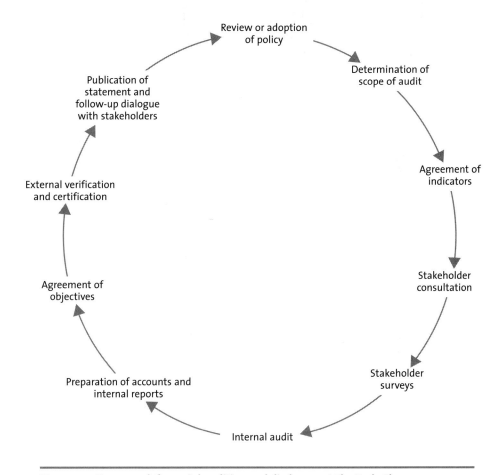

Figure 13.1 *Framework for social auditing and disclosure at The Body Shop*

Source: Sillanpää 1998

There are three types of performance measurement in The Body Shop's approach to social audit:

- **Performance against standards (performance indicators)** set up internal benchmarks and external benchmarks, both quantitative and qualitative, and reflect nationally and internationally available information on best practices for activities and policies that describe the organisation's social performance.

- **Stakeholder perception of performance against core values (the Mission Statement and Trading Charter).** The stakeholder groups of The Body Shop include: staff employed directly by The Body Shop International; international head franchisees; UK and US local franchisees; UK and US customers; suppliers; community trade suppliers; shareholders; local community (Littlehampton); UK non-governmental organisations; foundation applicants.

- **Stakeholder perception of performance against specific needs of stakeholders** identified as salient through consultation with stakeholders in focus groups and measured in anonymous and confidential surveys of opinion.

The approach to stakeholder involvement in The Body Shop model comprises focus group meetings and a large-scale survey. Following the focus groups, when specific issues have been identified as salient or of particular interest to stakeholders, questionnaires are designed to measure more wide-scale opinion. These questionnaires are intended to capture perceptions of the company's performance against both stakeholder-specific needs and core values articulated by the company (Sillanpää 1998). Sillanpää believes that focus groups and large-scale confidential surveys of opinion (where the questions themselves are co-designed in focus groups with stakeholder representatives) can be applied to almost any relationship. Engaging stakeholders in direct dialogue is one of the most important and sensitive processes in social auditing. It is especially important to identify salient issues for each group in face-to-face conversation before conducting wide-scale surveys of opinion. The Body Shop's first social audit engaged stakeholder groups in focus groups to explore specific stakeholder needs and to allow stakeholder views and concerns to be expressed. To ensure open dialogue in the discussion, it was considered important, especially for the initial stages of the process, that the verifiers had access to the process as observers.

There were three main sources of information for The Body Shop's first audit process:

1. The results of the focus groups and survey

2. The documentary information provided by departments which had agreed quantitative and qualitative standards

3. The output from confidential internal audit interviews with staff and managers

The format chosen for The Body Shop's first Social Statement was based on a stakeholder approach with each group with its own heading in the report. An introductory section gave a general explanation about the scope of the social audit and how the information had been compiled and what assumptions were used. A foreword by the company founders gave their overview of the statement.

Because of the complex nature of social audit and the variety of stakeholder needs for information, a multi-tier approach was adopted for the publication of The Body Shop's first Social Statement. The full statement was published based on the approved, verified accounts and made available to all stakeholder groups. Following publication of the results of the company's first social audit, stakeholders were invited to engage in follow-up dialogue in order to obtain feedback on how they reacted to the findings presented in the Social Statement. The departments responsible for specific stakeholder relations were encouraged to enter into direct dialogue with stakeholder representatives.

13.2.3 The Traidcraft model

Traidcraft plc is a UK-based trade organisation that commenced in 1979. In about 20 years, Traidcraft has grown into a public limited company with annual sales of over £7 million. In 1993, Traidcraft issued its first Social Audit Report 1992–1993 and in 1994 the second Social Audit Report 1993–1994. In each subsequent year, 'social accounts' have been issued.[9]

Traidcraft Exchange, its sister company, also issued its Social Accounts 1995/96 in 1996. In its 1995/96 social accounts, the accounts were audited, for the first time, to the same level of rigour as a financial audit using the auditing standards developed by the Auditing Practices Board. Traidcraft Exchange is the first organisation to have used financial auditors to audit their finished accounts.[10] As Raynard (1998) comments, there are two innovations in the accounts: the structure of the reporting and the use of financial auditors. The Traidcraft model covers social audit of both Traidcraft plc and its sister organisation, Traidcraft Exchange.

Traidcraft and the NEF jointly developed the social accounting methodology. The key elements of the methodology (as shown in Table 13.2) include: objective and values identification, defining stakeholders, establishing social performance indicators and benchmarks, accounting and measuring performance against objectives and benchmarks, independent verification, and reporting the results to the stakeholders and public. There have been some slight adjustments in terms of wording in 1995–96 from the previous year, but the very last items highlight the importance of the reporting function and 'independent audit'. Social Accounts 1995/96 specifically states that generally accepted

Social Accounts 1994–95	Social Accounts 1995–96
1. Identify the social objectives and the ethical values	1. Identify the social objectives and the ethical values
2. Define the stakeholders	2. Define the stakeholders
3. Establish social performance indicators	3. Establish social performance indicators
4. Accounting	4. Measure performance
5. Auditing	5. Keep records
6. Comprehensive	6. Prepare accounts
7. Regular	7. Submit the accounts to independent audit
	8. Report the results

Table 13.2 **Social accounting methodology used in Traidcraft's social accounts**

9   The 1992–93 and 1993–94 reports were entitled 'Social Audit', whereas in the following years they were called 'Social Accounts'. These titles reflect substantial differences in their format, subheadings, contents and length. For example, the 1993–94 social audit report has a total of 23 pages whereas social accounts 1995–96 has only 15 pages.

10   The social accounts were audited by Rainbow Gillespie, a firm of Chartered Accountants with offices in Newcastle-upon-Tyne and Hexham. The firm also audited Traidcraft Exchange's financial accounts.

accounting principles (GAAP) of relevance, understandability, reliability, completeness, objectivity, timeliness and consistency should apply in preparing social accounts.[11]

In the Traidcraft model, social accounting is based on the perceptions and evaluation of the company's performance made by its stakeholders, and comparative benchmarks established by the company. Traidcraft adopts the stakeholder approach in presenting its social accounts. This provides each stakeholder group with a separate section in the accounts.[12] Traidcraft believes that stakeholders are key groups who are affected by, or can affect, the activities of the company. The company is committed to accountability to its stakeholders by its foundation principles, which state that it seeks 'to establish a just trading system which expresses the principles of love and justice fundamental to the Christian faith; it will foster . . . an inclusive community of purpose and relationships' (Traidcraft *Social Accounts* 1994/95). Its stakeholder groups include: producers, customers, public, employees, shareholders and managers. Each group of stakeholders has a section within its social accounts, which begins by stating a clear objective for the group, and goes on to explain the objective, scope of accounts and consultation process.

Traidcraft uses indicators to measure its performance against key objectives (see Traidcraft's *Social Accounts* 1994/95). It also conducts structured interviews 'based on a list of topics identified by producers as key determinants of fair trade' (p. 4). Producers identify 'continuity of their relationship with the company and continuity of orders as the key factor in assessing Traidcraft's performance' (p. 5). The approach to stakeholder involvement is based on interviews and on a questionnaire survey. Zadek (1998) comments that Traidcraft's social accounts have set a standard in the British context, as evidenced by the companies that have sought to draw from, and be measured against, Traidcraft's standards of quality.

13.2.4 *Liverpool Housing Trust's Directions (LHTD) model*

The Liverpool Housing Trust's Directions ('Directions') is a grant-funded public service under Section 16 of the Housing and Planning Act 1986. 'Directions' is a small team that is a part of Liverpool Housing Trust's external services section. They work with local-authority housing tenants to promote tenant participation in housing management and estate regeneration. In 1998, LHTD published its first social audit report called *A Report of Directions' Social Audit Pilot Project September 1997–March 1998*. The report is based on the six key principles shown in Box 13.2.

The LHTD social audit pilot project includes: staff training and awareness raising; establishing a performance monitoring system; carrying out surveys of key stakeholder groups; data analysis and production of the social audit report; and external verification. Its social audit process consists of the following components:

- ▪ **Ongoing data collection:** the ongoing collection of data utilising pro forma. This information is collated on a monthly basis in the form of a summary sheet

---

11 The use of GAAP in social reports, as discussed by Gray *et al.* (1997), raises the contentious issue of whether social audit functions in essentially the same way as traditional financial reporting.

12 Another common approach in presenting social audit reports or accounts is based on themes (the theme reporting model), i.e. a report is presented according to themes, each theme has its own heading/section and only the stakeholders concerned are addressed within the section.

- **Multi-perspective:** reflect the views of all those involved with or who are affected by the organisation (the 'stakeholders')

- **Comprehensive:** aim ultimately to embrace all aspects of an organisation's social, environmental, cultural and community benefit performance

- **Comparative:** offer a means whereby the organisation can compare its own performance over time, make comparisons with other organisations engaged in similar work and relate performance to appropriate benchmarks

- **Regular:** undertake regularly, not just be an occasional or one-off exercise

- **Verification:** be verified (audited) independently

- **Disclosure:** available to all stakeholders and to the wide community

Box 13.2 *Key principles of the LHTD social audit*

- **Monthly team meetings.** Team meeting records form a core part of the social audit process.

- **Focus group meetings.** A programme of focus group meetings is to be facilitated by a trained quality auditor from elsewhere in the Trust with the aim of obtaining systematic feedback on group perceptions of the Directions team's performance.

- **Objectives questionnaire.** An annual objectives questionnaire has been developed inviting a scored response on the Directions team's performance on each of its stated objectives and actions, with space for additional comments.

- **Employee survey.** On the performance of the team and to highlight any shortcomings.

LHTD identifies stakeholders as individual groups, such as: groups it is currently working with; founders/overseers; employees; partners; and others. It defines seven key objectives for the team and, for each objective, actions undertaken towards achieving that objective are listed. These objectives are presented together with the methods of social bookkeeping adopted to ensure that Directions is able to measure and report on its performance both quantitatively and qualitatively.

One main characteristic of the LHTD model is the emphasis on actions against its objectives. Social audit focuses on the measures of these individual actions from the stakeholder perspective using mainly postal questionnaires and focus group meetings.

13.2.5 *The Co-operative Bank model*

The Co-operative Bank is a UK high-street bank that most prominently markets financial services based on ethical trading and investment practice. In 1998 it published its first social report called the Partnership Report disclosing its social and partnership performance. The Co-operative Bank used the partnership approach to design its social audit model with the corporate objective of delivering benefits to all its partners in a socially responsible and ecologically sustainable manner. The partnership model has evolved over a decade with three key developments associated with the publication of the Mission Statement, Ethical Policy and Ecological Mission Statement of the Bank.[13] The model categorises all its stakeholders into seven partners and the 'interdependence' of these partners is fully recognised and considered in the establishing of values, social responsibility objectives and performance indicators. A distinguishing feature of the partnership approach is that it clearly recognises a conflict of interest among different partners. As a result, organisations should try to achieve the best possible balance of interests. This is regarded as the most critical aspect of making the partnership approach work.

The Co-operative Bank model requires the establishment of a Partnership Development Team whose responsibility is to undertake a detailed assessment of the bank's performance in relation to each of the seven stakeholder groups. The team prioritises the areas for each partner and their relationship with the bank, and determines to what extent the bank delivers value in a socially responsible and ecologically sustainable manner. The model concentrates on the assessment of three areas: 'delivering value', 'social responsibility' and 'ecological sustainability'. Subsequent to the assessment in relation to each area, new goals for the next reporting year are planned with managers taking personal responsibility for performance. The bank adopts the 'triple bottom line' criteria, embracing economic, environmental and social issues (see e.g. Elkington 1997).

In terms of reporting, the bank adopts a stakeholder approach. Each stakeholder has a separate section in the report with the assessment of objectives against 'Delivering Value', 'Social Responsibility' and 'Ecological Sustainability'. The Partnership Report was verified independently and used to provide information on the impact on each of the partners. The Partnership Ballot was used to gather data and to assess stakeholder opinion on individual issues. The Partnership Report is different from other social audit reports in that the report gives the name of the responsible person/persons for each area of social responsibility together with their personal comments. It puts accountability and responsibility at the centre of the report and sets up future objectives.

13.2.6 The APSO model

The Agency for Personal Service Overseas (APSO) was established in the Republic of Ireland in the early 1970s as a state-sponsored body with a view to promoting and sponsoring temporary personal service in developing countries. Its mission is 'to contribute to sustainable improvement in the living conditions of poor communities in developing countries by enhancing human resources, skills and local capacities in the interests of development, peace and justice' (APSO 1998).

To obtain the views and the perceptions of stakeholders on the quality and effectiveness of its service, APSO published its first social accounting report in 1998. The report

---

13 A central theme of the Mission Statement of the Bank is the principle of inclusion (i.e. The Co-operative Bank should take account of the interests of all parties affected by its activities, not just shareholders). The Ethical Policy, developed in close consultation with its customers, sets out clearly who The Co-operative Bank will (and will not) do business with. The Ecological Mission Statement aims at maintaining the minimum conditions for an ecologically sustainable society.

was based on social accounting methodology with the input from various stakeholders. The methodology focuses on the input from all stakeholder divisions into the process of identifying the parameters against which the organisation's performance is measured. APSO uses a social accounting team consisting of its own employees and external social audit consultants. Seven stakeholder groups were identified by the social accounting team. Each stakeholder group was asked to distinguish all the stakeholders groups within APSO and these were checked off against the groupings suggested by the social accounting team.[14] In addition, each stakeholder group was invited to map each stakeholder's relationship with APSO and with the other stakeholders. Each stakeholder group was then asked to consider APSO's mission statement and APSO's stated values and to decide which were the key criteria by which they would judge APSO. During the process, stakeholders were also consulted about the most appropriate method of collecting data.

APSO uses structured questionnaires to collect data from its main stakeholder groups (overseas partner organisations, sending agencies, development workers, APSO field staff and APSO's staff in Dublin). The questionnaires cover both a common set of general issues in regard to APSO's development objectives and a specific set of questions pertaining only to points raised by that particular stakeholder group. A member of the research staff at the Equality Studies Department at University College Dublin assisted with the (independent) data processing and analysis. The results were passed back to the APSO social accounting team for the preparation of the social accounts.

In APSO's social accounts, four mini case studies were presented to illustrate how APSO's objectives were measured. Uniquely among the social reports covered in this study, such case studies were shown in the report. Like those of Traidcraft, APSO's social accounts were audited by a firm of chartered accountants. The auditors' report states that the auditors extracted what they considered to be relevant auditing standards from those issued by the Auditing Practices Board.

13.2.7 The NEF model

The New Economics Foundation (NEF) was founded in 1984 as an independent, non-profit, research, education and consultancy institution, dedicated to promoting approaches to economics that are sensitive and responsive to critical social and environmental issues. NEF's aim is to promote social responsibility in the corporate, not-for-profit and public sectors. NEF is one of the leading organisations in the development of social auditing. NEF works nationally and internationally across a number of programme areas, including social auditing, sustainable development indicators, community economics and value-based organisations. Examples of the influence of NEF were seen above in the cases of Traidcraft and APSO. Currently, NEF also acts as Secretariat to the Institute of Social and Ethical Accountability (AccountAbility), an international professional body formed in 1995 to establish standards in the area of social auditing.

The key principles for social audit practice defined by the NEF include (see NEF 1997):

---

14   Note that the concept of 'social accountants' was used in APSO's social accounts. Although there is no explanation of this terminology, it seems that social accountants refer to the members of the social accounting team.

- **Multi-perspective:** to reflect the views of all those (i.e. stakeholders) involved with or affected by the organisation, including their world-views, concerns, interests, needs and perceptions

- **Comparative:** to offer a means whereby the organisation can compare its own performance over time, make comparisons with other organisations engaged in similar work, and relate its performance to appropriate social norms

- **Comprehensive:** to embrace all aspects of an organisation's social and environmental performance

- **Regular:** to take place regularly, and not just be a one-off exercise or done occasionally as the mood takes

- **Verification:** to use social accounts to 'prove' what the organisation has achieved; social accounts should be verified (audited) by one or more persons who have no vested interest in the results

- **Disclosure:** to make social audit reports available to all of those people involved in the organisation. Through this, everyone becomes more involved in the fortunes of the organisation by seeing what it has achieved. People are empowered to comment further on what the organisation is saying about itself.

The NEF model emphasises the organisational perspective to a large extent, and that it is for the organisation and its stakeholders to determine the social objectives and the indicators used to assess performance. It differs from other evaluations (which tend to be imposed from outside) with respect to the terms of reference; the latter are determined by whoever is commissioning the evaluation. Social auditing involves stakeholders not only in the assessment of the organisation but also in ways forward in terms of the significant issues raised in the assessment. The NEF model covers: policy or document review; management systems; stakeholder dialogue; performance indicators and benchmarks; disclosure and verification. The audit cycle is reproduced in Figure 13.2. Clearly, the NEF model, which considers social audit as 'a way to improve the social performance of organisations' (NEF 1998), is different from the Beechwood concept. The Beechwood model provides a different focus in that social audit is used by an organisation as a means to plan, manage and measure non-financial activities in response to the challenge of social and environmental concerns. The NEF social audit model has been adopted by a number of organisations across the world.

13.3 Comparison

The above models reflect different organisational perspectives and objectives of social audit. Considerations of whether the social audit process is intended primarily for an internal management system (i.e. as a management tool: the Beechwood model); whether it is a means of strengthening public accountability (as for Traidcraft, The Body Shop and The Co-operative Bank); or whether it is used to obtain the views and the

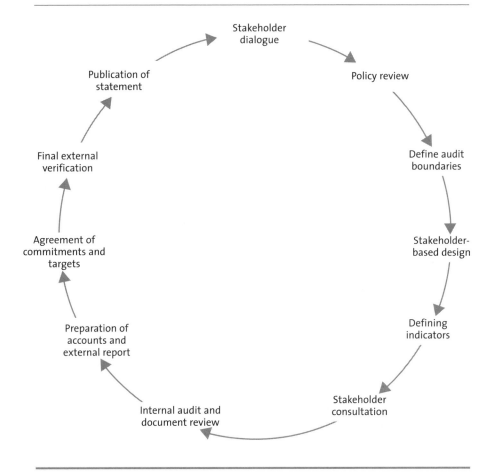

Figure 13.2 ***The New Economics Foundation's social audit cycle***

Source: NEF 1998

perceptions of stakeholders (the NEF model and the APSO model) do create tensions that raise questions regarding both the reasons why organisations engage in the process, and the way processes are implemented. Clearly, the exclusive focus on internal management obviates any need to verify and disclose the results to the public, or even perhaps within the organisation beyond the management and board. Emphasis on strengthening the organisation's legitimacy in the public domain may require verification and some sort of disclosure. On the other hand, the need for external verification concerns again the relative emphasis between social audit as a management tool and a means of strengthening accountability and legitimacy. Clearly, an emphasis on the latter may imply the need for external verification of some kind (for example The Body Shop, Traidcraft, The Co-operative Bank, NEF and APSO).

Table 13.3 provides a summary of these seven social audit models. While the positive role of social audit has been recognised in all models, the focus varies. Approaches to social audit and stakeholder inclusion in the process of social audit differ. All seven models recognise the role and involvement of stakeholders in the audit process. However, only The Co-operative Bank model explicitly considers possible conflicts of interest between stakeholder groups.

As far as the social audit process is concerned, the seven models reflect the following general features:

- Determining objectives, goals and benchmarks for assessment and evaluation (policy determination or review)

- Identifying stakeholders or partners and their interests

- Taking stakeholders' interests and views as the core of social audit (the Beechwood model is an exception)

- Conducting internal (management) audit and reporting against the organisation's objectives and stakeholders' interests

- Verification either internally or externally and independently

- Disclosure of performance assessments to the stakeholders and the public

- Setting up the goals or actions for the next reporting year

Clearly, the approach to stakeholder involvement (called either inclusion or dialogue) comprises focus group meetings (interviews) and questionnaire surveys (including feedback). While all the models call for the involvement of stakeholders in the auditing process, only the APSO model provides an opportunity for stakeholders to identify stakeholder groups against the groupings set up by the social audit team (social accountants). In other models, stakeholders are mainly engaged in completing questionnaires and interviews.

In several cases (e.g. The Body Shop, APSO), mission statements and ethical statements are the underlying documents for setting up social audit policy and objectives. These documents are then used to formulate criteria and benchmarks for measuring performance.

The cases analysed in this chapter highlight two broadly different approaches to social reporting: the stakeholder approach and the theme (topic-based) approach.[15] The stakeholder approach provides information for each stakeholder group presented in separate sections in the report. These cover, in turn, objectives, performance assessment and future goals. Sillanpää (1998) advocates that a stakeholder model/approach should follow a common format which includes:

---

15 In the wider literature other approaches to social and stakeholder responsibility audits are evident: for example, those drawing from traditional concepts of financial accounting-based audit. This is evident even in the Traidcraft approach, which involves the production of an arm's-length, independent audit report by the company's financial auditors. Wilson and Gatward (1998) see this as a positive step forward in developing the rigour of the standard financial audit methodology. This may be a moot point, however; such approaches may unnecessarily close down stakeholder dialogue.

Organisation	Report title	Reporting headings*	Focus	Methods of stakeholder involvement	Social audit process
Beechwood	Social Audit Report	Thematic	Constitution foundation / Manage change / Viability	Representative of stakeholders in the audit team and stakeholder survey	Preparation for management → define the audit scope → practical application of social audit toolkit → monitoring and measurement
The Body Shop	Social Statement	Stakeholder groups	Stakeholder relations, accountability and transparency	Focus group followed by questionnaires	Review or adoption of policy → determination of scope of audit → agreement of indicators → stakeholder consultation and survey → internal audit → preparation of accounts and internal reports → agreement of objectives → external verification and certification → publications of statement and follow-up dialogue with stakeholders
Traidcraft	Social Audit Report / Social Accounts	Stakeholder groups	Accountability / Stakeholders' evaluation of company performance	Stakeholder interview followed by questionnaire survey	Objective and value identification → defining stakeholders → setting performance indicators → accounting and measuring performance → independent verification → reporting the accounts
LHTD	Social Audit Report	Thematic	Objectives and actions	Questionnaires followed by focus meeting	Staff training and awareness-raising → establishing a performance monitoring system → survey → data analysis → production of social audit report → external verification
The Co-operative Bank	Partnership Report	Stakeholder (partnership) groups	Accountability and responsibility	Partnership ballot	Partnership development team → performance assessment → determining priority area and relationship → agreement of objectives and responsibility → assessment of three defined areas → sets new objectives and goals for next reporting year → verification and reporting of assessments.
APSO	Social Accounts	Mixed (first thematic then stakeholder groups) and case study	Views and perceptions of stakeholders on the quality and effectiveness of the service	Questionnaire and field visit interviews	Social accounting team → identification of stakeholders → stakeholders map each stakeholder's relationship with APSO and with other stakeholders → confidential structures questionnaires → questionnaires analysis → verification and reporting of social accounts
NEF	n/a	n/a	Social objectives and indicators	n/a: in general, stakeholder dialogue through various approaches, depending on the nature of stakeholder group and resources available	Stakeholder dialogue → policy review → define audit boundaries → stakeholder-based design → defining indicators → stakeholder consultation → internal audit and document review → preparation of accounts and external report → agreement of commitment and targets → final external verification → publication of statement

Table 13.3 *A comparison of the social audit models*

- The basis for the company's approach and aims for each stakeholder group (with reference to relevant policies, etc.), and basic information about the stakeholder group (e.g. size, structural/contractual relationship to the company)

- The methodology used for each consultation process (i.e. what combination of focus groups, surveys and discussions was used to capture stakeholder perceptions)

- The results of stakeholder consultation with perception surveys described as even-handedly and neutrally as possible in order to avoid premature interpretation, together with direct quotations from stakeholders selected in an independent fashion

- Quantitative and qualitative standards of performance where these existed

- A company response in the form of a quote from a board member or senior manager setting out his or her reaction to the audit results and noting where progress is already being made and/or where improvements were clearly required ('Next Step')

Under the theme approach, a social audit report is structured according to major themes (such as equal opportunity, environmental protection or training). Each theme is dealt with in its own section and so only those stakeholders involved in the activities and performance of the particular theme or those with interests that are deemed to be related to the theme are addressed within the section. Here, stakeholder groups and their interests are inherently mixed. Those two approaches have their advantages and limitations. The difficulty with the stakeholder approach is the identification and classification of stakeholders (particularly external/indirect stakeholders), and there could be the possibility of stakeholder exclusion from the report. Also, under the stakeholder approach, the conflict of interests among stakeholders is generally difficult to address. The theme approach has the advantage of overcoming these difficulties. However, social audit reports under the theme approach may not give stakeholder groups a specific section in the report.

However, there is no consensus about the particular criteria or principles for social audit reports. Generally accepted accounting principles (relevance, understandability, reliability, completeness, objectivity, timeliness and consistency) were recommended in the Traidcraft model. Other models do not specify any detailed criteria. There is perhaps a danger for social audit that financial reporting principles and procedure are used to misplace the foundation of social audit reports. Frederick *et al.* (1992: 119) report that, by 1990, the pressure for greater disclosure of social performance information had led 90% of the top 500 corporations to include information about their social activities in the company's annual report. As generally argued, social audit is different from the traditionally perceived '(financial) audit' in its objectives, methodology and focus (Gray *et al.* 1997). The disclosure of social performance information is part of the social audit process, but is not social audit per se. The inclusion of social performance information in the company's annual report is an expansion of financial reporting. Gray *et al.* (1997) argue that this cannot be regarded as a replacement for social audit reports. In Dierkes and Berthoin's (1986) view, the criteria essential to the institutionalisation of any social reporting system include: (1) the reliability and credibility of the reporting process; (2) the use of information to affect change; and (3) an easy integration of methodological progress. Woodward (1998) considers 'objectivity or freedom from bias, understandability or clarity, and comparability of results' as the most popular features required in social reports. Filios (1995) suggests that a government-sponsored agency should be set up to be responsible for collecting social accountability reports (social audit reports), overseeing social-economic accounting procedures, and setting standards for social effectiveness. However, institutionalisation of both social reporting systems and social accounting standards setting have been critically examined by Gray *et al.* (1997).

The development of the GRI in 2001 and similar initiatives has taken corporate social reporting into a new phase. The proponents of these new 'managerial' social audits appear keen to bring the social audit process into the mainstream of current business thinking (see e.g. Elkington 1997; SustainAbility 1999).

13.4 Concluding remarks

Social audit has evolved from the early external investigation stage to the process of internal review, assessment and reporting on the social performance of an organisation. It has shifted from an early information gathering, data measurement and disclosure foci to an open dialogic and participatory approach. Such innovative practice has extended from the corporate sector in the early stage to all types of organisation.

This study aims to analyse the key features of established social audit models with a view to identifying their similarities and differences. Through a comparison of the seven cases selected, our analysis shows that there are various interesting similarities and differences in the theoretical perspectives as well as general applicative design, with universal emphasis on the inclusion of stakeholders in the audit process. The stakeholder approach and the theme (topic-based) approach are mainly used in presenting social reports. External verification is a common phenomenon although verifiers are not necessarily qualified accountants. In several cases, social reports are audited by social auditors from other accreditation or consultancy agencies (such as the NEF). There are clear benefits to the use of external verification. It can be argued that the impact of social audit will partly reflect how well it is evaluated. Wilson and Gatward (1998) see the use of external verification as a positive step forward in exploiting the rigour of standard financial audit methodology. However a cautionary note may be called for. An overly 'independent' approach to social audit with a strict dichotomy between the roles of accountant and auditor may compromise the 'dialogic' benefits of more interactive and informal approaches.

There is still a long way to go in the development of social and ethical accounting, auditing and reporting. As Raynard (1998) comments, there is ongoing research which seeks to integrate social, environmental and financial accounting processes, as well as bringing together the range of methodologies that have been developed in non-profit organisations. To encourage social audit and the wide practice of social reporting, more tangible benefits derived from such a process may have to be identified. It may be difficult for an organisation to quantify the value and impact of social audit on its business performance, because there is no systematic accounting (measurement) system that can separate social audit from the rest of the management of the organisation.[16] At the same time, however, some degree of standardisation is beginning to become evident in systems such as those developed under the aegis of the GRI as well as in the models developed by the international accounting firms. It is unclear, however, how robust these systems will prove to be. Further research addressing these issues would be helpful to the development and expansion of social audit.

16 For example, before their takeover, Ben & Jerry's, the US ice cream company, found it difficult to quantify the impact of social auditing on profits. The firm has been producing 'social performance reports' for the past seven years and has now adopted the more systematic accounting approach developed by NEF. Explaining the philosophy behind these social accounting activities, Alan Parker, Ben & Jerry's director of investor relations and social accounting, said: 'We have publicly expressed a desire to be the kind of company that measures its success as much by its social contribution as by its financial success. We have undertaken all kinds of initiatives, both in the way in which we run the workplace and in the kind of innovative supplier relationships that we get involved in. We've been active in progressive political and social issues on several fronts and, given that we are undertaking those initiatives, we need to assess how well we are performing in those areas' (Arkin 1996).

BIBLIOGRAPHY

Ackerman, R.W. (1973) 'How Companies Respond to Social Demands', *Harvard Business Review* 51.4: 88-98.

Ackerman, R.W., and R.A. Bauer (1976) *Corporate Social Responsiveness: The Modern Dilemma* (Reston, VA: Reston Publishing).

Action Aid (1999) *Good Business: Evaluating the Impact of Business–Community Partnership in India* (www.actionaid.org).

Adams, J.S. (1965) 'Inequity in Social Exchange', in L. Berkowitz (ed.), *Advances in Experimental Social Psychology* 2: 267-99.

Alba, R.D. (1982) 'Taking Stock of Network Analysis: A Decade's Results', in S.B. Bacharach (ed.), *Research in the Sociology of Organizations. Vol. I* (Greenwich, CT: JAI Press): 39-74.

Alkhafaji, A.R. (1989) *A Stakeholder Approach to Corporate Governance: Managing in a Dynamic Environment* (New York: Quorum Books).

Allen, M.P., and S.K. Panian (1982) 'Power, Performance, and Succession in the Large Corporation', *Administration Science Quarterly* 27: 538-47.

Alliance for Environmental Innovation (1999) *Catalyzing Environmental Results: Lessons in Advocacy Organization–Business Partnerships* (www.edfpewalliance.org).

Altman, B.W., and D. Vidaver-Cohen (2000) 'A Framework for Understanding Corporate Citizenship', *Business and Society Review*, Spring 2000: 1-7.

Amnesty International and Program and Prince of Wales Business Leaders Forum (2000) *Human Rights: Is It Any of Your Business?* (London: Amnesty International and Program and Prince of Wales Business Leaders Forum).

Amy, D.J. (1987) *The Politics of Environmental Mediation* (New York: Columbia University Press).

Anderson, D.D. (1980) 'State Regulation of Public Utilities', in J.Q. Wilson (ed.), *The Politics of Regulation* (New York: Basic Books): 3-41.

Andriof, J. (2001) 'Patterns of Stakeholder Partnership Building', in J. Andriof and M. McIntosh (eds.), *Perspectives on Corporate Citizenship* (Sheffield, UK: Greenleaf Publishing): 215-38.

APSO (Agency for Personal Service Overseas) (1998) *Annual Report 1998* (Dublin: APSO).

Arkin, A. (1996) 'Open Business is Good for Business', *People Management* 2.1: 24-26.

Arnstein, S. (1969) 'Ladder of Citizen Participation', *Journal of the American Institute of Planners*, July 1969.

Asghar (2000) 'It's a harsh reality in Pakistan, but poor children must work', *Asghar*, 23 January 2000.

Axley, S. (1985) 'Managerial and Organizational Communication in Terms of the Conduit Metaphor', *Academy of Management Review* 9.3: 428-37.

Bacow, L.S., and M. Wheeler (1984) *Environmental Dispute Resolution* (New York: Plenum Press).

Banerjee, S.B. (2000) 'Whose Land is it Anyway? National Interest, Indigenous Stakeholders, and Colonial Discourses', *Organization and Environment* 13: 3-38.

Bantel, K.A., and S.E. Jackson (1989) 'Top Management and Innovations in Banking: Does the composition of the top team make a difference?', *Strategic Management Journal* 10 (special issue): 107-24.

Barley, S. (1986) 'Technology as an Occasion for Structuring: Evidence from Observations of CT Scanners and the Social Order of Radiology Departments', *Administrative Science Quarterly* 31: 78-108.

—— (1990) 'The Alignment of Technology and Structure though Roles and Networks', *Administrative Science Quarterly* 35: 61-103.

Barney, J. (1991) 'Firm Resources and Sustained Competitive Advantage', *Journal of Management* 17.1: 99-120.

Baumhart, R. (1968) *An Honest Profit: What Businessmen Say about Ethics in Business* (New York: Holt, Rinehart & Winston).

Bavelas, A. (1948) 'A Mathematical Model for Group Structures', *Human Organization* 7: 16-30.

Beloe, S. (1999) 'Globalisation and the Environment: Exploring the Connections', in P. Newell (ed.), *IDS Bulletin* 30.3 (July 1999): 1-8.

Bendell, J. (ed.) (2000) *Terms for Endearment: Business, NGOs and Sustainable Development* (Sheffield, UK: Greenleaf Publishing).

Benjamin, M. (1999) *What's Fair about the Fair Labor Association?* (www.globalexchange.org/economy/corporations/sweatshops/fla.html).

Bennett, S.J., R. Freierman and S. George (1993) *Corporate Realities and Environmental Truths: Strategies for Leading your Business in the Environmental Era* (New York: John Wiley).

Berko, R., A. Wolvin and R. Ray (1997) *Business Communication in a Changing World* (New York: St Martin's Press).

Berman, S.L. (1998) 'Managerial Opportunism and Firm Performance: An Empirical Test of Instrumental Stakeholder Theory' (unpublished dissertation; Seattle, WA: University of Washington).

Berman, S.L., A.C. Wicks, S. Kotha and T.M. Jones (1999) 'Does Stakeholder Orientation Matter? The Relationship between Stakeholder Management Models and Firm Financial Performance', *Academy of Management Journal* 42.5 (October 1999): 488-506.

Bernheim, B.D., and M.D. Whinston (1986) 'Common Agency', *Econometrica* 54: 923-42.

Bernstein, M.H. (1955) *Regulating Business by Independent Commission* (Westport, CT: Greenwood Press).

Bessis, J. (1998) *Risk Management in Banking* (New York: John Wiley).

Bhambri, A., and J. Sonnenfeld (1988) 'Organization Structure and Corporate Social Performance: A Field Study in Two Contrasting Industries', *Academy of Management Journal* 31.3: 642-62.

Bhargava, S., and R. Welford (1996) 'Corporate Strategy and the Environment: The Theory', in R. Welford (ed.), *Corporate Environmental Management: Systems and Strategy* (London: Earthscan Publications).

Bingham, G. (1986) *Resolving Environmental Disputes: A Decade of Experience* (Washington, DC: The Conservation Foundation).

Brass, D.J. (1995) 'A Social Network Perspective on Human Resources Management', in G.R. Ferris (ed.), *Research in Personnel and Human Resources Management. Vol. XIII* (Greenwich, CN: JAI Press).

Brealey, R.A., and S.C. Myers (1981) *Principles of Corporate Finance* (New York: McGraw–Hill).

Brenner, S.N. (1988) 'Book Review: Managing the Corporate Social Environment: A Grounded Theory', *Administrative Sciences Quarterly* 33.4: 632-34.

—— (1993) 'The Stakeholder Theory of the Firm and Organizational Decision Making: Some Propositions and a Model', in J. Pasquero and D. Collins (eds.), *Proceedings of the Fourth Annual Meeting of the International Association for Business and Society* (San Diego: IABS): 205-10.

Brenner, S.N., and P. Cochran (1991) 'The Stakeholder Theory of the Firm: Implications for Business and Society Research', paper presented at the International Association for Business and Society [IABS] conference (Sundance, UT: IABS).

Brenner, S.N., and E.A. Molander (1977) 'Is the Ethics of Business Changing?', *Harvard Business Review* 58.1: 54-65.

Brinberg, D., and J.E. McGrath (1985) *Validity and the Research Process* (Beverley Hills, CA: Sage).

Brooks, L.J. (1980) 'An Attitude Survey Approach in the Social Audit: The Southern Press Experience', *Accounting, Organisations and Society* 5.3: 341-55.

Brown, A.D. (1994) 'Politics, Symbolic Action and Myth Making in Pursuit of Legitimacy', *Organization Studies* 15: 861-78.

Brunsson, N. (1989) *The Organization of Hypocrisy* (Chichester, UK: John Wiley).

Bryman, A., and D. Cramer (1999) *Quantitative Data Analysis with SPSS Release 8 for Windows* (London: Routledge).

Buchholz, R. (1982) *Business Environment and Public Policy* (Englewood Cliffs, NJ: Prentice Hall).

Business Week (1979) 'A Dark Future for Utilities', 28 May 1979: 108-22.

Calton, J. (1996) 'Legitimizing Stakeholder Voice: The Normative Argument for Institutionalizing Institutional Discourse', paper presented at the International Association for Business and Society [IABS] conference (Santa Fe, NM: IABS).

—— (2001) 'Dialogue and the Art of Thinking Together: A Pioneering Approach to Communicating in Business and in Life by William Isaacs', *Business and Society* 40.3: 343-48.

Calton, J., and N. Kurland (1996) 'A Theory of Stakeholder Enabling', in D. Boje, R. Gephart and T. Thatchenkery (eds.), *Postmodern Management and Organization Theory* (Thousand Oaks, CA: Sage): 154-77.

Cameron, K.S. (1986) 'Effectiveness as Paradox: Consensus and Conflict in Conceptions of Organizational Effectiveness', *Management Science* 32: 539-53.

Cameron, K.S., and D.A. Whetten (1983) *Organizational Effectiveness: A Comparison of Multiple Models* (New York: Academic Press).

Cannella, A.A., Jr, and M. Lubatkin (1993) 'Succession as a Sociopolitical Process: Internal Impediments to Outsider Selection', *Academy of Management Journal* 36: 763-93.

Carroll, A.B. (1979) 'A Three-dimensional Conceptual Model of Corporate Social Performance', *Academy of Management Review* 4: 497-505.

—— (1993) *Business and Society: Ethics and Stakeholder Management* (Cincinnati, OH: South-Western).

Cartwright, D., and F. Harary (1956) 'Structural Balance: A Generalization of Heider's Theory', *Psychological Review* 63: 277-93.

Cavanagh, G.F., D.J. Moberg and M. Velasquez (1981) 'The Ethics of Organizational Politics', *Academy of Management Review* 6.3: 363-74.

Center for Research and Advanced Study (1987) 'Tables 1 and 3', in S. Hasbrouck and S. Vezie (eds.), *The Forests of Maine: Statistical Supplement* (Orono, ME: University of Southern Maine and Land and Water Resources Center).

Chandy, P.R., and W.N. Davidson (1983) 'AFUDC and Its Impact on the Profitability of Electric Utilities', *Public Utilities Fortnightly* 121 (4 August 1983): 34-36.

Cheney, G., and L.T. Christensen (2001) 'Organizational Communication: Linkages between Internal and External Communication', in *The New Handbook of Organizational Communication: Advances in Theory, Research, and Methods* (Thousand Oaks, CA: Sage): 231-69.

Cheney, G., and G.N. Dionisopoulos (1989) 'Public Relations? No, Relations with Publics: A Rhetorical-Organizational Approach to Contemporary Corporate Communication', in C.H. Botan and V. Hazleton, Jr (eds.), *Public Relations Theory* (Hillsdale, NJ: Lawrence Erlbaum): 135-58.

Child, J. (1972) 'Organizational Structure, Environment and Performance: The Role of Strategic Choice', *Sociology* 6: 1-22.

Christensen, L.T. (1995) 'Buffering Organizational Identity in the Marketing Culture', *Organization Studies* 16.4: 651-72.

Christensen, P. (1997) 'Pitfalls in Implementing Environmental Management in Industry', paper presented at the 1997 Business and the Environment Conference, University of Leeds, UK, 18–19 September 1997 (Leeds, UK: ERP Environment).

Churchman, C.W. (1971) *The Design of Inquiring Systems: Basic Concepts of Systems and Organization* (New York: Basic Books).

Clancy, T. (2000) *The Bear and the Dragon* (New York: G.P. Putnam's).

Clarkson Centre for Business Ethics (1999) *Principles of Stakeholder Management* (Toronto: Rotman School of Management, University of Toronto).

Clarkson, M.B.E. (1991) 'Defining, Evaluating, and Managing Corporate Social Performance: The Stakeholder Management Model', *Research in Corporate Social Performance and Policy* 12: 331-58.

—— (1994) 'A Risk Based Model of Stakeholder Theory', in *Proceedings of the Second Toronto Conference on Stakeholder Theory* (Toronto: Centre for Corporate Social Performance and Ethics, University of Toronto).

—— (1995) 'A Stakeholder Framework for Analysing and Evaluating Corporate Social Performance', *Academy of Management Review* 20.1: 92-117.

Clemens, B.W., and Y. Lin (1995) 'Stakeholder Commitment to Recycle 2000: An Analysis of Efforts by the Department of Energy', in *Waste Management Conference Proceedings* (Knoxville, TN: US Department of Energy).

Cochran, P.L., and R.A. Wood (1984) 'Corporate Social Responsibility and Financial Performance', *Academy of Management Journal* 27: 42-56.

Cook, T., and D. Campbell (1979) *Quasi-Experimentation: Design and Analysis Issues for Field Settings* (Boston, MA: Houghton-Mifflin).

Coolidge, P.T. (1963) *History of the Maine Woods* (Bangor, ME: Furbush-Roberts).

Copeland, T., T. Koller and J. Murrin (1990) *Valuation: Measuring and Managing the value of Companies* (New York: John Wiley).

Cormick, G.W. (1989) 'Commentary II', in Canadian Environmental Assessment Research Council, *The Place of Negotiation in Environmental Assessment* (Hull, Canada: Canadian Environmental Assessment Research Council): 39-43.

Cormick, G.W., N. Dale, P. Emond, S.G. Sigurdson and B.D. Stuart (1996) *Building Consensus for a Sustainable Future: Putting Principles into Practice* (Ottawa: National Round Table on the Environment and the Economy).

Cotton, P., I.A.M. Fraser and W.Y. Hill (2000) 'The Social Audit Agenda: Primary Health Care in a Stakeholder Society', *International Journal of Auditing* 4.1: 3-28.

Cowing, T.G. (1981) *Productivity Measurement in Regulated Industries* (New York: Academic Press).

Coy, D., and M. Pratt (1998) 'An Insight into Accountability and Politics in Universities: A Case Study', *Accounting, Auditing and Accountability Journal* 11.5: 540-61.

Cramer, J. (1998) 'Environmental Management: From "Fit" to "Stretch" ', *Business Strategy and the Environment* 7: 162-72.

Crane, A. (1998) 'Culture Clash and Mediation: Exploring the Cultural Dynamics of Business–NGO Collaboration', *Greener Management International* 24 (Winter 1998): 61-76.

Crowfoot, J.E., and J.M. Wondolleck (1990) *Environmental Disputes: Community Involvement in Conflict Resolution* (Washington, DC: Island Press).

Czarniawska, B. (2000) 'Identity Lost or Identity Found? Celebration and Lamentation over the Postmodern View of Identity in Social Science and Fiction', in M. Schultz, M.J. Hatch and M.H. Larsen (eds.), *The Expressive Organization* (Oxford, UK: Oxford University Press).

Daft, R. (1984) 'Antecedents of Significant and Not-so-significant Organizational Research', in T. Bateman and G. Ferris (eds.), *Method and Analysis in Organizational Research* (Reston, VA: Reston Publishing): 3-14.

Dahl, R.A. (1957) 'The Concept of Power', *Behavioral Science* 2: 201-15.

Davis, G.F. (1991) 'Agents without Principles? The Spread of the Poison Pill through the Intercorporate Network', *Administrative Science Quarterly* 36: 583-613.

Davis, J.H., D.F. Schoorman and L. Donaldson (1997) 'Toward a Stewardship Theory of Management', *Academy of Management Review* 22.1.

Davis, K. (1973) 'The Case for and against Business Assumption of Social Responsibilities', *Academy of Management Journal* 16: 312-22.

Dawson, E. (1998) 'The Relevance of Social Audit for Oxfam GB', *Journal of Business Ethics* 17.13: 1,457-69.

Dearborn, D.C., and H.A. Simon (1958) 'Selective Perception: A Note on the Departmental Identification of Executives', *Sociometry* 21: 140-44.

Deetz, S. (1995) *Transforming Communication Transforming Business: Building Responsive and Responsible Workplaces* (Cresskill, NJ: Hampton Press).

Dennis, B., C.P. Neck and M. Goldsby (1998) 'Body Shop International: An Exploration of Corporate Social Responsibility', *Management Decision* 36.10: 649-53.

Dess, G.G., and D.W. Beard (1984) 'Dimensions of Organizational Task Environments', *Administrative Science Quarterly* 29: 52-73.

Dey, C., R. Evans and R.H. Gray (1995) 'Towards Social Information Systems and Bookkeeping: A Note on Developing the Mechanisms for Social Accounting and Audit', *Journal of Applied Accounting Research* 2.3: 36-69.

Dierkes, M., and A. Berthoin (1986) 'Whither Corporate Social Reporting: Is it Time to Legislate?', *California Management Review* 28.3: 106-21.

DiMaggio, P.J., and W.W. Powell (1983) 'The Iron Cage Revisited: Institutional Isomorphism and Collective Rationality in Organizational Fields', *American Sociological Review* 48: 147-60.

DOE (US Department of Energy) (2000) 'Secretary Richardson suspends release of materials from DOE facilities', *DOE News* R-00-182.

Doherty, G., and C.T. Ennew (1995) 'The Marketing of Pharmaceuticals: Standardization or Customisation?' *Journal of Marketing Practice: Applied Marketing Science* 1.3: 39-50.

Donaldson, T., and T.W. Dunfee (1999) *Ties That Bind: A Social Contracts Approach to Business Ethics* (Boston, MA: Harvard Business School Press).

Donaldson, T., and L.E. Preston (1995) 'The Stakeholder Theory of the Corporation: Concepts, Evidence and Implications', *Academy of Management Review* 20.1: 65-91.

Dorcey, A.H.J., and C.L. Riek (1989) 'Negotiation-Based Approaches to the Settlement of Environmental Disputes in Canada', in Canadian Environmental Assessment Research Council, *The Place of Negotiation in Environmental Assessment* (Hull, Canada: Canadian Environmental Assessment Research Council): 7-36.

Doreian, P., and K.L. Woodard (1992) 'Fixed List versus Snowball Selection of Social Networks', *Social Science Research* 21: 216-33.

Driscoll, C. (1996) 'Fostering Constructive Conflict Management in a Multi-Stakeholder Context: The Case of the Forest Round Table on Sustainable Development', *International Journal of Conflict Management* 7.2: 156-72.

DuPraw, M.E. (1993) 'From Theory to Practice in Environmental Dispute Resolution: Negotiating the Transition', in D.J.D. Sandole and H. van der Merwe (eds.), *Conflict Resolution Theory and Practice: Integration and Application* (Manchester, UK: Manchester University Press): 232-47.

Ecologist (1993) *Whose Common Future? Reclaiming the Commons* (Philadelphia: New Society Publishers).

Edwards, M. (2000) *Future Positive* (London: Earthscan Publications).

Eisenhardt, K.M. (1989) 'Agency Theory: An Assessment and Review', *Academy of Management Review* 14.1: 57-74.

Eisenhardt, K.M., and L. Bourgeois (1988) 'Politics of Strategic Decision-making in High-Velocity Environments: Toward a Mid-range Theory', *Academy of Management Journal* 31.4: 737-70.

Elkington, J. (1997) *Cannibals with Forks: The Triple Bottom Line of 21st Century Business* (Oxford, UK: Capstone Publishing).

Elkington, J., and T. Burke (1987) *The Green Capitalists* (London: Victor Gollancz).

Elkington, J., and S. Fennell (1998) 'Partners for Sustainability', *Greener Management International* 24 (Winter 1998): 48-60.

Ellul, J. (1973) *Propaganda: The Formation of Men's Attitudes* (New York: Vintage Books).

Elsbach, K.D. (1994) 'Managing Organizational Legitimacy in the California Cattle Industry: The Construction and Effectiveness of Verbal Accounts', *Administrative Science Quarterly* 39: 57-88.

Emerson, R.M. (1962) 'Power–Dependence Relations', *American Sociological Review* 27: 31-40.

English, M.R., A.K. Gibson, D.L. Feldman and B.E. Tonn (1993) *Stakeholder Involvement: Open Processes for Reaching Decisions about the Future Uses of Contaminated Sites* (Knoxville, TN: University of Tennessee Press).

Environment Council (1999) *Guidelines for Stakeholder Dialogue: A Joint Venture* (London: The Environment Council and Shell International).

Environment Reporter (1993) 'Report on Naturally Occurring Radiation to Determine Need for Rules', *Environment Reporter* 23.3: 3225.

EPA (US Environmental Protection Agency) (1998) *The National Report Card on Environmental Knowledge, Attitudes and Behaviors* (Washington, DC: EPA).

Erickson, B.H. (1988) 'The Relational Basis of Attitudes', In B. Wellman and S.D. Berkowitz (eds.), *Social Structures: A Network Approach* (Cambridge, UK: Cambridge University Press): 99-121.

Evan, W.M., and R.E. Freeman (1988) 'A Stakeholder Theory for the Modern Corporation: Kantian Capitalism', in T.L. Beauchamp and N.E. Bowie (eds.), *Ethical Theory and Business* (Englewood Cliffs, NJ: Prentice Hall).

—— (1993) 'A Stakeholder Theory of the Modern Corporation: Kantian Capitalism', in T.L. Beauchamp and N.E. Bowie (eds.), *Ethical Theory and Business* (Englewood Cliffs, NJ: Prentice Hall, 4th edn): 97-106.

FERC (Federal Energy Regulatory Commission) (1988) *Financial Statistics of Selected Electric Utilities* (Washington, DC: Government Printing Office).

Filios, V.P. (1985) 'Assessment of Attitudes toward Corporate Social Accountability', *Journal of Business Ethics* 4.3: 155-73.

—— (1986) 'Review and Analysis of the Empirical Research in Corporate Social Accounting', *Journal of Business Ethics* 5.4: 291-306.

Fineman, S., and K. Clarke (1996) 'Green Stakeholders: Industry Interpretations and Response', *Journal of Management Studies* 33.6: 715-30.

Finkelstein, S., and D. Hambrick (1996) *Strategic Leadership: Top Executives and their Effects on Organizations* (Minneapolis, MN: West).

Fisher, R., B. Ury and B. Patton (1991) *Getting to Yes: Negotiating Agreement Without Giving In* (New York: Houghton-Mifflin, 2nd edn).

Fleisher, C.S. (1993) 'Public Affairs Management Performance: An Empirical Analysis of Evaluation and Measurement', *Research in Corporate Social Performance and Policy* 14: 139-63.

Fligstein, N. (1987) 'The Intraorganizational Power Struggle: Rise of Finance Personnel to Top Leadership in Large Corporations, 1919–1979', *American Sociological Review* 52: 44-58.

Forrest, C.J., and R. Hix Mays (1997) *The Practical Guide to Environmental Community Relations* (New York: John Wiley).

Frederick, W.C. (1978) 'From CSR1 to CSR2: The Maturing of Business and Society Thought' (working paper no. 279; Pittsburgh, PA: Graduate School of Business, University of Pittsburgh).

—— (1987) 'Theories of Corporate Social Performance', in S.P. Sethi and C.M. Falbe (eds.), *Business and Society* (Lexington, MA: Lexington Books).

—— (1994) 'From CSR1 to CSR2: The Maturing of Business and Society Thought', *Business and Society* 33.2 (August 1994): 150-64.

Frederick, W.C., J. Post and K. Davis (1992) *Business and Society* (New York: McGraw–Hill).

Freeman, L.C. (1978/79) 'Centrality in Social Networks: Conceptual Clarification', *Social Networks* 1: 215-39.

Freeman, R.E. (1984) *Strategic Management: A Stakeholder Approach* (Boston, MA: Pitman).

—— (1994) 'The Politics of Stakeholder Theory: Some Future Directions', *Business Ethics Quarterly* 4: 409-21.

—— (1999) 'Divergent Stakeholder Theory', *Academy of Management Review* 24.2: 233-36.

Freeman, R.E., and D.R. Gilbert (1988) *Corporate Strategy and the Search for Ethics* (Englewood Cliffs, NJ: Prentice Hall).

Freeman, R.E., and D.L. Reed (1983) 'Stockholders and Stakeholders: A New Perspective on Corporate Governance', *California Management Review* 25.3: 88-106.

Freidkin, N.E. (1980) 'A Test of the Structural Features of Granovetter's "Strength of Weak Ties" Theory', *Social Networks* 2: 411-22.

French, H. (2000) *Vanishing Borders: Protecting the Planet in the Age of Globalization* (New York: W.W. Norton).

Frisch, M., L. Solitare, M. Greenberg and K. Lowrie (1998) 'Regional Economic Benefits of Environmental Management at the US Department of Energy's Major Nuclear Weapons Sites', *Journal of Environmental Management* 54: 23-37.

Frooman, J. (1999) 'Stakeholder Influence Strategies', *Academy of Management Review* 24.2: 191-205.

Fukuyama, F. (1995) *Trust: The Social Virtues and the Creation of Prosperity* (New York: Free Press).

Gao, S.S., and J.J. Zhang (2001) 'A Comparative Study of Stakeholder Engagement Approaches in Social Accounting', in J. Andriof and M. McIntosh (eds.), *Perspectives on Corporate Citizenship* (Sheffield, UK: Greenleaf Publishing): 239-55.

Geddes, M. (1992) 'The Social Audit Movement', in D. Owen (ed.), *Green Reporting* (London: Chapman & Hall): 215-41.

Gerde, V. (2000) 'Stakeholders and Organization Design: An Empirical Test of Corporate Social Performance', in J. Logsdon, D. Wood and L. Benson (eds.), *Research in Stakeholder Theory, 1997-1998: The Sloan Foundation Minigrant Project* (Toronto: Clarkson Centre for Business Ethics): 7-20.

Ghemawat, P., and H. Stander (1999) 'Nucor at Crossroads in Ghemawat', in *Strategy and the Business Landscape* (Reading, MA: Addison Wesley).

Giddens, A. (1976) *New Rules of Sociological Method* (London: Hutchinson).

—— (1982) *Profiles and Critiques in Social Theory* (Berkeley, CA: University of California Press).

Gilbreath, K. (ed.) (1984) *Business and the Environment: Toward Common Ground* (Washington, DC: The Conservation Foundation, 2nd edn).

Gilly, M.C., and M. Wolfinbarger (1998) 'Advertising's Internal Audience', *Journal of Marketing* 62.1 (January 1998): 69-88.

Gioia, D.A. (1999) 'Response: Practicability, Paradigms and Problems in Stakeholder Theorizing', *Academy of Management Review* 24.2 (April 1999): 228-32.

Gladwell, M. (2000) *The Tipping Point: How Little Things Can Make a Big Difference* (Boston, MA: Little, Brown).

Glynn, M., C. Bhattacharya and H. Rao (1995) 'Understanding the Bond of Identification: An Investigation of its Correlates among Art Museum Members', *Journal of Marketing* 59: 46-57.

Gonella, C., A. Pilling and S. Zadek (1998) *Making Values Count: Contemporary Experience in Social and Ethical Accounting, Auditing and Reporting* (London: Association of Chartered Certified Accountants).

Gormley, W.T., Jr (1983) *The Politics of Public Utility Regulation* (Pittsburgh, PA: University of Pittsburgh Press).

Granovetter, M. (1973) 'The Strength of Weak Ties', *American Journal of Sociology* 78: 1,360-80.

—— (1982) 'The Strength of Weak Ties Revisited', in P.V. Marsden and N. Lin (eds.), *Social Structure and Network Analysis* (Beverly Hills, CA: Sage): 105-30.

—— (1985) 'Economic Action and Social Structure: A Theory of Embeddedness', *American Journal of Sociology* 91.3: 481-510.

Gray, B. (1989) *Collaborating: Finding Common Ground for Multiparty Problems* (San Francisco: Jossey-Bass).

Gray, B., and R.G. Allen (1987) 'Cognitive and Group Biases in Issues Management: What You Don't Know Can Hurt You', in A.A. Marcus, A.M. Kaufman and D.R. Beam (eds.), *Business Strategy and Public Policy* (New York: Quorum): 195-208.

Gray, E.R., and J.M. Balmer (1998) 'Managing Corporate Image and Corporate Reputation', *Long Range Planning* 31.5: 695-702.

Gray, R., C. Dey, D. Oen, R. Evans and S. Zadek (1997) 'Struggling with the Praxis of Social Accounting: Stakeholders, Accountability, Audits and Procedures', *Accounting, Auditing and Accountability Journal* 10.3: 325-64.

Greenall, D., and D. Rovere (1999) *Engaging Stakeholders and Business–NGO Partnerships in Developing Countries: Maximizing an Increasingly Important Source of Value* (Ottawa: Centre For Innovation in Corporate Responsibility).

Greening, D.W. (1992) 'Organizing for Public Issues: Predictors of Structure and Process', *Research in Corporate Social Performance and Policy* 13: 83-117.

Greening, D.W., and B. Gray (1994) 'Testing a Model of Organizational Response to Social and Political Issues', *Academy of Management Journal* 37.3: 467-98.

Greening, D.W., and R.A. Johnson (1997) 'Managing Industrial and Environmental Crises: The Role of Heterogeneous Top Management Teams', *Business and Society* 36.4: 334-61.

Greenpeace (1995) AES: *Dirty Deeds for Dirty Energy* (www.greenpeace.org/~usa/reports/energy/AES. html).

Gresalfi, M. (2001) personal communication with B.W. Clemens and S.R. Gallagher.

GRI (2000) Global Reporting Initiative, www.globalreporting.org.

Griffin, J.J., and J.F. Mahon (1997) 'The Corporate Social Performance and Corporate Financial Performance Debate: Twenty-five Years of Incomparable Research', *Business and Society* 36.1: 5-31.

Grunig, J.E. (1975) 'A Multisystems Theory of Organizational Communication', *Communication Research* 2: 99-136.

—— (1984) 'Organizations, Environments, and Models of Public Relations', *Public Relations Research and Education* 1.1: 6-29.

—— (ed., with D.M. Dozier, W.P. Ehling, L.A. Grunig, F.C. Repper and J. White) (1992) *Excellence in Public Relations and Communication Management* (Hillsdale, NJ: Lawrence Erlbaum).

Grunig, J.E., and L.A. Grunig (1992) 'Models of Public Relations and Communication', in J.E. Grunig (ed., with D.M. Dozier, W.P. Ehling, L.A. Grunig, F.C. Repper and J. White), *Excellence in Public Relations and Communication Management* (Hillsdale, NJ: Lawrence Erlbaum): 285-325.

Grunig, J.E., and C. Hunt (1984) *Managing Public Relations* (New York: Holt, Rinehart & Winston).

Hair, J.D. (1984) 'Winning through Mediation', in K. Gilbreath (ed.), *Business and the Environment: Toward Common Ground* (Washington, DC: The Conservation Foundation, 2nd edn): 527-33.

Haleblian, J., and S. Finkelstein (1993) 'Top Management Team Size, CEO Dominance, and Firm Performance: The Moderating Roles of Environmental Turbulence and Discretion', *Academy of Management Journal* 36.4: 844-63.

Hambrick, D.C., and P. Mason (1984) 'Upper Echelons: The Organization as a Reflection of its Top Managers', *Academy of Management Review* 9: 193-206.

Hannan, M.T., and J. Freeman (1989) *Organizational Ecology* (Cambridge, MA: Harvard University Press).

Harary, F. (1959) 'Graph Theoretic Methods in the Management Sciences', *Management Science* 5: 387-403.

Hardi, P., and S. Barg (1997) *Measuring Sustainable Development: Review of Current Practice* (Ottawa: Industry Canada).

Harrison, J.S., and R.E. Freeman (1999) 'Stakeholders, Social Responsibility, and Performance: Empirical Evidence and Theoretical Perspectives', *Academy of Management Journal* 42.5: 479-85.

Harte, G.F., and D.L. Owen (1987) 'Fighting De-industrialisation: The Role of Social Government Social Audits', *Accounting, Organizations and Society* 12: 123-41.

Hartman, C.L., and E.R. Stafford (1997) 'Green Alliances: Building New Business with Environmental Groups', *Long Range Planning* 30.2: 184-96.

Hashemi, S. (1997) 'Building up Capacity for Banking with the Poor: The Grameen Bank in Bangladesh', in *Microfinance for the Poor?* (Paris: Organisation for Economic Co-operation and Development).

Hassler, D. (1999) 'Flat-rolled steel price rise seen', *American Metal Market*, 6 May 1999: 6.

Haveman, H.A. (1993) 'Follow the Leader: Mimetic Isomorphism and Entry into New Markets', *Administrative Science Quarterly* 38: 564-92.

Hawes, D.W. (1986) *Utility Holding Companies* (New York: Clark Boardman).

Heap, S. (ed.) (2000) *NGOs Engaging Business: A World of Difference and a Difference to the World* (Oxford, UK: INTRAC).

Heard, J.E., and W.J. Bolce (1981) 'The Political Significance of Corporate Social Reporting in the United States of America', *Accounting, Organisations and Society* 6.3: 247-55.

Hellriegel, D., and J.W. Slocum, Jr (1996) *Management* (Cincinnati, OH: South-Western College Publishing, 7th edn).

Hemphill, T. (1999) 'The White House Apparel Industry Partnership Agreement: Will Self-regulation be Successful?', *Business and Society Review* 104.2.

Herkströter, C. (1996) *Dealing with Contradictory Expectations: The Dilemmas Facing Multi-nationals* (Amsterdam: Shell International Ltd, 11 October 1996).

Herman, E.S. (1981) *Corporate Control, Corporate Power* (Cambridge, UK: Cambridge University Press).

Hickson, D., C.R. Hinings, C.A. Lee, R.E. Schneck and J.M. Pennings (1971) 'A Strategic Contingencies Theory of Intraorganizational Power', *Administrative Science Quarterly* 14: 378-97.

Higson, C. (1995) *Business Finance* (London: Reed Elsevier).

Hill, C.W.L., and T.M. Jones (1992) 'Stakeholder-Agency Theory', *Journal of Management Studies* 29.2: 131-54.

Hill, W.Y., I.A.M. Fraser and P. Cotton (1998) 'Patients' Voices, Rights and Responsibilities: On Implementing Social Audit in Primary Health Care', *Journal of Business Ethics* 17.13: 1,481-97.

Hillary, R. (1999) *Evaluation of Study Reports on the Barriers, Opportunities and Drivers for Small and Medium Sized Enterprises in the Adoption of Environmental Management Systems* (London: Department of Trade and Industry, Environmental Directorate): 3-53.

—— (ed.) (2000) *Small and Medium-Sized Enterprises and the Environment: Business Imperatives* (Sheffield, UK: Greenleaf Publishing).

Hillman, A.J., and M. Hitt (1999) 'Corporate Political Strategy Formulation: A Model of Approach, Participation, and Strategy Decisions', *Academy of Management Review* 24.4: 825-42.

Hillman, A.J., and G.D. Keim (2001) 'Shareholder Value, Stakeholder Management, and Social Issues: What's the Bottom Line?', *Strategic Management Journal* 22.2 (February 2001): 125-40.

Hoffman, A., J. Smith and S. Soukup (1999) *Molten Metal Technology (A) and (B)* (Boston, MA: Boston University).

Hoffman, B. (1993) *Win–Win Competitiveness Made in Canada: How to be Competitive Using the Consensus Approach* (North York/Ontario: Captus Press).

Hooghiemstra, R. (2000) 'Corporate Communication and Impression Management: New Perspectives Why Companies Engage in Corporate Social Reporting', *Journal of Business Ethics* 27.1–2: 55-70.

Hosmer, L.T. (1995) 'Trust: The Connecting Link between Organizational Theory and Philosophical Ethics', *Academy of Management Review* 20: 379-403.

Hosseini, J., and S.N. Brenner (1992) 'The Stakeholder Theory of the Firm: A Methodology to Generate Value Matrix Weights', *Business Ethics Quarterly* 2.2: 99-119.

Hsiao, C. (1986) *Analysis of Panel Data* (New York: Cambridge University Press).

Humphrey, C., and D. Owen (2000) 'Debating the "Power" of Audit', *International Journal of Auditing* 4.1: 29-50.

Hunt, C.B., and E.R. Auster (1990) 'Proactive Environmental Management: Avoiding the Toxic Trap', *Sloan Management Review*, Winter 1990: 7-18.

Huselid, M. (1995) 'The Impact of Human Resource Management Practices on Turnover, Productivity, and Corporate Financial Performance', *Academy of Management Journal* 38: 635-72.

IAEA (International Atomic Energy Agency) (1992) *Application of Exemption Principles to the Recycle and Reuse of Materials from Nuclear Facilities* (Vienna: IAEA).

Ice, R. (1991) 'Corporate Publics and Rhetorical Strategies: The Case of Union Carbide's Bhopal Crisis', *Management Communication Quarterly* 4.3: 341-62.

Inside EPA (2000) 'Industry Goes on Global Offensive against Environmentalist: Targeting Funding, Internet Activities', *Inside EPA Weekly Report* 21.37 (15 September 2000).

Isaacs, W.N. (1999) *Dialogue and the Art of Thinking Together* (New York: Currency).

ISEA (Institute for Social and Ethical Accountability) (1999) *AA 1000* (London: ISEA).

ISEAL (International Social and Environmental Accreditation and Labelling Alliance) (1999) *Safeguarding Environmental and Social Issues in Trade* (public statement, 20 December 1999; Kaslo, BC, Canada: ISEAL).

Isenhart, M.W., and M. Spangle (2000) *Collaborative Approaches to Resolving Conflict* (Thousand Oaks, CA: Sage).

ISRI (Institute of Scrap Recycling Industries) (1992) *Radioactivity in the Scrap Recycling Process* (Washington, DC: ISRI).

Japanese Center for International Exchange (1999) *Corporate–NGO Partnership in Asia Pacific* (Tokyo: Japanese Center for International Exchange).

Jawahar, I.W., and G.L. McLaughlin (2001) 'Toward a Descriptive Stakeholder Theory: An Organizational Life Cycle Approach', *Academy of Management Review* 26.3 (July 2001): 397-414.

Jensen, M.C. (2000) *Value Maximization and the Corporate Objective Function* (Boston, MA: Harvard Business School Press).

Jensen, M.C., and W.H. Meckling (1976) 'The Theory of the Firm: Managerial Behavior, Agency Costs, and Ownership Structure', *Journal of Financial Economics* 3: 305-60.

Johnson-Cramer, M. (2001) *Antecedents of Organization Set Conflict: A Private Government Approach* (Boston University Working Paper; Boston, MA: Boston University).

Jones, T.M. (1980) 'Corporate Social Responsibility Revisited, Redefined', *California Management Review* 22.3: 59-67.

—— (1986) 'Corporate Board Structure and Performance: Variations in the Incidence of Shareholder Suits', *Research in Corporate Social Performance and Policy* 8: 345-59.

—— (1995) 'Instrumental Stakeholder Theory: A Synthesis of Ethics and Economics', *Academy of Management Review* 20.2: 404-37.

Jones, T.M., and A.C. Wicks (1999) 'Convergent Stakeholder Theory', *Academy of Management Review* 24.2 (April 1999): 206-21.

Judd, R.W. (1988) 'Reshaping Maine's Landscape: Rural Culture, Tourism, and Conservation, 1890–1929', *Journal of Forest History*, October 1988: 180-90.

Kaner, S. (1996) *Facilitator's Guide to Participatory Decision-making* (Gabriola Island, BC: New Society Publishers).

Kapferer, B. (1969) 'Norms and the Manipulation of Relationships in a Work Context', in J.C. Mitchell (ed.), *Social Networks in Urban Situations: Analyses of Personal Relationships in Central African Towns* (Manchester, UK: Manchester University Press): 181-244.

Kilduff, M. (1992) 'The Friendship Network as a Decision-making Resource: Dispositional Moderators of Social Influences on Organizational Choice', *Journal of Personality and Social Psychology* 62.1: 168-80.

King, M.J. (2001) 'Sustainability: Advantaged or Disadvantaged?', *Journal of Corporate Citizenship* 3 (Autumn 2001): 99-125.

Kleinbaum, D.G., L.L. Kupper and K.E. Muller (1988) *Applied Regression Analysis and other Multivariable Methods* (Boston, MA: PWS-KENT Publishing Company).

Kochan, T., and S. Rubenstein (2000) 'Toward a Stakeholder View of the Firm: The Saturn Partnership', *Organization Science* 11.4: 367-86.

Kolko, G. (1963) *The Triumph of Conservatism* (New York: The Free Press).

Konig, D. (1936) *Theorie der Endlichen und Unendlich Graphen* (New York: Chelsea).

Kotler, P., G. Armstrong, J. Saunders and V. Wong (2001) *Principles of Marketing* (Harlow, UK: FT–Prentice Hall, 3rd European edn).

Kreiner, P., and A. Bambri (1991) 'Influence and Information in Organization–Stakeholder Relationships', in J.E. Post (ed.), *Research in Corporate Social Performance and Policy. Vol. XII* (Greenwich, CT: JAI Press): 3-36.

Kuster, T. (1994) 'Danger: Radioactive Scrap', *New Steel* 10: 30-42.

Lansky, M. (1992) *Beyond the Beauty Strip* (Gardiner, ME: Tilbury House).

Lawrence, P., and J.W. Lorsch (1967) *Organisation and Environment: Managing Differentiation and Integration* (Boston, MA: Division of Research, Harvard Business School).

Lincoln, J.R. (1982) 'Intra- (and Inter-) Organizational Networks', in S.B. Bacharach (ed.), *Research in the Sociology of Organizations. Vol. I* (Greenwich, CN: JAI Press): 1-38.

Livesey, S.M. (1999) 'McDonald's and the Environmental Defense Fund: A Case Study of a Green Alliance', *Journal of Business Communication* 36.1: 5-39.

Long, F.J., and M.B. Arnold (1995) *The Power of Environmental Partnerships* (Fort Worth, TX: Dryden Press).

Lubenau, J.O., and J.G. Yusko (1995) 'Radioactive Materials in Recycled Metals', *Health Physics* 68: 440-51.

Luoma, P., and J. Goodstein (1999) 'Stakeholders and Corporate Boards: Institutional Influences on Board Composition and Structure', *Academy of Management Journal* 42.5: 553-63.

Mackenzie, C. (1998) 'Ethical Auditing and Ethical Knowledge', *Journal of Business Ethics* 17.13: 1,395-1,402.

Madsen, H., and J.P. Ulhøi (1996) 'Environmental Management in Danish Manufacturing Companies: Attitudes and Actions', *Business Strategy and the Environment* 5.1: 22-29.

Madsen, H., K. Sinding and J.P. Ulhøi (1997) 'Sustainability and Corporate Environmental Focus: An Analysis of Danish Small and Medium-Sized Companies', *Managerial and Decision Economics* 18.6: 443-53.

Magee, S.P., W.A. Brock and L. Young (1989) *Black Hole Tariffs and Endogenous Policy Theory* (Cambridge, UK: Cambridge University Press).

Maignan, I., O.C. Ferrell and G.T.M. Hult (1999) 'Corporate Citizenship: Cultural Antecedents and Business Benefits', *Journal of the Academy of Marketing Science* 27.4: 455-69.

Maine Department of Conservation Land Use Regulatory Commission (1997) *Comprehensive Land Use Plan* (Augusta, ME: Department of Conservation).

Maine Forest Service (1995) *An Evaluation of the Effects of the Forests Practices Act* (Augusta, ME: Department of Conservation).

Maine Forest Service State Planning Office (1996a) *Economic Impact of the Citizens' Initiative to Promote Forest Rehabilitation and Eliminate Clearcutting* (Augusta, ME: Maine Department of Conservation).

—— (1996b) *Comparison of the Forest Practices Act, the Citizens' Initiative to Promote Forest Rehabilitation and Eliminate Clearcutting, and the Competing Measure to Implement the Compact for Maine's Forests* (Augusta, ME: Maine Department of Conservation).

Malandri, A. (1999) 'Culture, Organisation and the Environment: The Eco-preneurial Logic', paper presented at the 1997 Business and the Environment Conference, University of Leeds, UK, 18–19 September 1997 (Leeds, UK: ERP Environment).

Marsden, C., and J. Andriof (1998) 'Towards an Understanding of Corporate Citizenship and How to Influence It', *Citizenship Studies* 2.2: 329-52.

Marsden, P.V. (1990) 'Network Data and Measurement', *Annual Review of Sociology* 16: 435-63.

Mazlish, B., and R. Buultjers (1993) *An Introduction to Global History* (Boulder, CO: Westview Press).

McIntosh, M., D. Leipziger, K. Jones and G. Coleman (1998) *Corporate Citizenship: Successful Strategies for Responsible Companies* (London: FT Pitman).

McTaggart, J.M., P.W. Kontes and M.C. Mankins (1994) *The Value Imperative: Managing for Superior Shareholder Returns* (New York: The Free Press).

Merritt, J.Q. (1998) 'EMS into SME Won't Go? Attitudes, Awareness and Practices in the London Borough of Croydon', *Business Strategy and the Environment* 7: 90-100.

Meyer, J.W., and B. Rowan (1977) 'Institutionalized Organizations: Formal Structure as Myth and Ceremony', *American Journal of Sociology* 83: 340-63.

Meznar, M.B., and D. Nigh (1993) 'Managing Corporate Legitimacy: Public Affairs Activities, Strategies and Effectiveness', *Business and Society* 32.1: 30-43.

—— (1995) 'Buffer or Bridge? Environmental and Organizational Determinants of Public Affairs Activities in American Firms', *Academy of Management Journal* 38.4: 975-96.

Miles, R.H. (1982) *Coffin Nails and Corporate Strategies* (Englewood Cliffs, NJ: Prentice Hall).

—— (1987) *Managing the Corporate Social Environment* (Englewood Cliffs, NJ: Prentice Hall).

Miles, R.H., and A. Bhambri (1983) *The Regulatory Executives* (Beverly Hills, CA: Sage).

Mitchell, R.K., B.R. Agle and D.J. Wood (1997) 'Toward a Theory of Stakeholder Identification and Salience: Defining the Principle of Who and What Really Counts', *Academy of Management Review* 22.4 (October 1997): 853-86.

Mitnick, B.M. (1993) 'Organizing Research in Corporate Social Performance: The CSP System as Core Paradigm', *Proceedings from International Association of Business and Society (IABS) Conference, 1993*.

Monge, P.R., and E.M. Eisenberg (1987) 'Emergent Communication Networks', in F.M. Jablin, L.L. Putman, K.H. Roberts and L.W. Porter (eds.), *Handbook of Organizational Communication: An Interdisciplinary Perspective* (Newbury Park, CA: Sage): 304-42.

Moore, M. (1998) 'Coalition Building between Native American and Environmental Organizations in Opposition to Development: The Case of the New Los Padres Dam Project', *Organization and Environment* 11: 287-313.

Morris, S. (1997) 'Internal Effects of Stakeholder Management Devices', *Journal of Business Ethics* 16: 413-24.

Murphy, D.F., and J. Bendell (1997) *In the Company of Partners: Business, Environmental Groups and Sustainable Development Post-Rio* (Bristol, UK: The Policy Press).

—— (1999) *Partners in Time?* (discussion paper 109; Geneva: United Nations Research Institute for Social Development [UNRISD]).

Murphy, P.E., and E.J. Burton (1980) 'Accountants Assess the Social Audit', *Business* 30.5: 33-38.

NARUC (National Association of Regulatory Utility Commissioners) (1974) *Annual Report on Utility and Carrier Regulation* (Washington, DC: NARUC).

—— (1987) *Electric Utility Performance Study, 1972–1985* (Washington, DC: NARUC).

Natale, S.M., and J.W. Ford (1994) 'The Social Audit and Ethics', *Managerial Auditing Journal* 9.1: 29-36.

National Research Council (1998) *A Review of Decontamination and Decommissioning Technology Development Programs at the Department of Energy* (Washington, DC: National Academy Press).

Navarro, P. (1985) *The Dimming of America: The Real Costs of Electric Utility Regulatory Failure* (Cambridge, MA: Ballinger).

Neal, M., and C. Davies (1998) *The Corporation under Siege* (London: Social Affairs Unit).

NEF (New Economics Foundation) (1996) *Value-Based Organisation: Organising NGOs for Value-Based Effectiveness* (London: NEF).

—— (1997) *Social Auditing for Small Organisations: A Workbook for Trainers and Practitioners* (London: NEF).

—— (1998) *Briefing Paper on Social Auditing* (London: NEF).

Nelson, R.E. (1989) 'The Strength of Strong Ties: Social Networks and Intergroup Conflict in Organizations', *Academy of Management Journal* 32: 377-401.

Newton, T., and G. Harte (1997) 'Green Business: Technicist Kitsch?', *Journal of Management Studies* 34.1: 752-98.

O'Donnell, F.R., S.J. Cotter, D.C. Kocher, E.L. Etnier and A.P. Watson (1978) *Potential Radiation Dose to Man from Recycle of Metals Reclaimed from a Decommissioned Nuclear Power Plant* (Oak Ridge, TN: Oak Ridge National Laboratory).

Ogden, S., and R. Watson (1999) 'Corporate Performance and Stakeholder Management: Balancing Shareholder and Customer Interests in the UK Privatized Water Industry', *Academy of Management Journal* 42.5: 526-38.

Oliver, C. (1991) 'Strategic Responses to Institutional Processes', *Academy of Management Review* 16: 145-79.

Ostapski, S.A., and C.N. Isaacs (1992) 'Corporate Moral Responsibility and the Moral Audit: Challenges for Refuse Relief Inc.', *Journal of Business Ethics* 11.3: 231-40.

Ostapski, S.A., and D.G. Pressley (1992) 'Moral Audit for Diabco Corp.', *Journal of Business Ethics* 11.1: 71-81.

Owen, D.L., T.A. Swift, C. Humphrey and M. Bowerman (2000) 'The New Social Audits: Accountability, Managerial Capture or the Agenda of Social Champions?', *European Accounting Review* 9.1: 81-98.

Pearce, J. (1996) *Measuring Social Wealth: A Study of Social Audit Practice for Community and Co-operative Enterprises* (London: New Economics Foundation).

Pearce, J., P. Raynard and S. Zadek (1997) *Social Auditing from Small Organisations* (London: New Economics Foundation).

Pellow, D.N. (1999) 'Negotiation and Confrontation: Environmental Policymaking through Consensus', *Society and Natural Resources* 12: 189-203.

Peters, G. (1999) *Waltzing with the Raptors: A Practical Roadmap to Protecting your Company's Reputation* (Chichester, UK: John Wiley).

Pfeffer, J. (1981) *Power in Organizations* (Marshfield, MA: Pitman).

Pfeffer, J., and G.R. Salancik (1977) 'Organizational Context and the Characteristics and Tenure of Hospital Administrators', *Academy of Management Journal* 20: 74-88.

—— (1978) *The External Control of Organizations: A Resource Dependence Perspective* (New York: Harper & Row).

Philips, A., and J. Reichart (2000) 'The Environment as a Stakeholder? A Fairness-Based Approach', *Business Ethics* 23.2: 185-97.

Phillips, R. (1997) 'Stakeholder Theory and a Principle of Fairness', *Business Ethics Quarterly* 7.1: 51-66.

Pires, M.A. (1988) 'Building Coalitions with External Constituencies', in R.L. Heath (ed.), *Strategic Issues Management: How Organizations Influence and Respond to Public Interests and Policies* (San Francisco: Jossey-Bass): 185-98.

Pomeranz, F. (1978) 'Social Measurement: A Primer for Implementation', *Journal of Accounting, Auditing and Finance* 1.4: 385-96.

Pondy, L.R. (1967) 'Organizational Conflict: Concepts and Models', *Administrative Science Quarterly* 12: 296-320.

Porter, M.E. (1980) *Competitive Strategy* (New York: The Free Press).

Porter, M.E., and V.E. Millar (1991) 'How Information Gives you Competitive Advantage', in *Michael E. Porter on Competition and Strategy* (Boston, MA: Harvard University Press).

Posner, B.Z., and W.H. Schmidt (1984) 'Values and the American Manager', *California Management Review* 20.3: 202-16.

Post, J.E., E.A. Murray, R.B. Dickie and J.F. Mahon (1983) 'Managing Public Affairs: The Public Affairs Function', *California Management Review* 26.1: 135-50.

Post, J.E., L. Preston and S. Sachs (2002a) *Redefining the Corporation: Stakeholder Management and Organizational Wealth* (Stanford, CA: Stanford University).

Post, J.E., A.T. Lawrence and J. Weber (2002b) *Business and Society: Corporate Strategy, Public Policy, Ethics* (New York: McGraw–Hill, 10th edn).

Prahalad, C.K., and G. Hamel (1990) 'The Core Competence of the Corporation', *Harvard Business Review*, May/June 1990: 79-91.

Quadrex (1993) *DOE Weapons Complex Scrap Metal Inventory* (Oak Ridge, TN: Quadrex).

Quinn, R.E., and J. Rohrbaugh (1983) 'A Spatial Model of Effectiveness Criteria: Towards a Competing Values Approach to Organizational Analysis', *Management Science* 29: 363-77.

Rachels, J. (1999) *The Elements of Moral Philosophy* (New York: McGraw–Hill).

Rahman, S.S. (2000) 'The Global Stakeholder's Message, the Firm's Response, and an Interpretation of the Ensuing International Dilemma: Moving Children from Tin Sheds to Brick Houses' (PhD dissertation; Fort Lauderdale, FL: Nova Southeastern University).

Rahn, T. (1996) 'Public Involvement and Consultation', in B. Ibbotson and J.-D. Phyper (eds.), *Environmental Management in Canada* (Toronto: McGraw–Hill Ryerson): 85-119.

Randall, D.M., and A.M. Gibson (1990) 'Methodology in Business Ethics Research: A Review and Critical Assessment', *Journal of Business Ethics* 9: 457-71.

Rands, G.P. (1991) 'The Corporate Social Performance Model Revisited', *International Association for Business and Society Proceedings* (Sundance, UT: IABS): 64-77.

Raynard, P. (1998) 'Coming Together. A Review of Contemporary Approaches to Social Accounting, Auditing and Reporting in Non-profit Organisations', *Journal of Business Ethics* 17.13: 1,471-79.

Redding, W.C., and P.K. Tompkins (1988) 'Organizational Communication: Past and Present Tenses', in G.M. Goldhaber and G.A. Barnett (eds.), *Handbook of Organizational Communication* (Norwood, NJ: Ablex).

Regelbrugge, L. (1999) 'Business and Civil Society: Reflections on Roles, Responsibilities, and Opportunities at the Dawn of a New Century', in *Promoting Corporate Citizenship: Opportunities for Business and Civil Society Engagement* (Washington, DC: CIVICUS).

Reilly, W.K. (1986) 'Foreword', in G. Bingham (ed.), *Resolving Environmental Disputes: A Decade of Experience* (Washington, DC: The Conservation Foundation): ix-xi.

Rein, M., and W. Gamson (1999) 'An Overview of Frame Critical Analysis' (Course Memo, 26 April Version).

Richardson, B. (2000) 'Release of Materials for Re-use and Recycle', *DOE Memorandum for all Departmental Elements* (Washington, DC: US Department of Energy).

Ring, P.S. (1994) 'Fragile and Resilient Trust and their Roles in Cooperative Interorganizational Relationships', in J. Pasquero and D. Collins (eds.), *Proceedings of the Fourth Annual Meeting of the International Association for Business and Society* (San Diego: IABS): 107-13.

Roberts, M.J., and J.S. Bluhm (1981) *The Choices of Power* (Cambridge, MA: Harvard University Press).

Rowley, T.J. (1997) 'Moving beyond Dyadic Ties: A Network Theory of Stakeholder Influences', *Academy of Management Review* 22.4: 887-910.

Rowley, T.J., and S. Berman (2000) 'A Brand New Brand of Corporate Social Performance', *Business and Society* 39.4: 397-418.

Ruben, B.D., and L.P. Stewart (1998) *Communication and Human Behavior* (Boston, MA: Allyn & Bacon, 4th edn).

Rugman, A., and A. Verbeke (1998) 'Corporate Strategies and Environmental Regulations: An Organising Framework', *Strategic Management Journal* 19: 363-75.

Russo, M.V. (1992) 'Power Plays: Regulation, Diversification, and Backward Integration in the Electric Utility Industry', *Strategic Management Journal* 13: 13-27.

Salancik, G.R. (1979) 'Interorganizational Dependence and Responsiveness to Affirmative Action: The Case of Women and Defense Contractors', *Academy of Management Journal* 22: 375-94.

Sanford Cohen & Associates (1992) *Scrap Metal Recycling of Norm Contaminated Petroleum Equipment* (Washington, DC: US Environmental Protection Agency).

Savage, G.T., T.H. Nix, C.J. Whitehead and J.D. Blair (1991) 'Strategies for Assessing and Managing Organizational Stakeholders', *Academy of Management Executive* 5.2: 61-75.

Schneidewind, U., and H. Petersen (2000) 'Change the Rules! Business–NGO Relations and Structuration Theory', in J. Bendell (ed.), *Terms for Endearment: Business, NGOs and Sustainable Development* (Sheffield, UK: Greenleaf Publishing).

Schoenfeldt, L.F. (1984) 'Psychometric Properties of Organizational Research Instruments', in T. Bateman and G. Ferris (eds.), *Method and Analysis in Organizational Research* (Reston, VA: Reston Publishing): 68-80.

Schuler, D.A., and K. Rehbein (1997) 'The Filtering Role of the Firm in Corporate Political Involvement', *Business and Society* 36: 116-39.

Schultz, D.E., S.I. Tannenbaum and R.F. Lauterborn (1993) *Integrated Marketing Communications* (Lincolnwood, IL: NTC Publishing).

Sciulli, L.M., and V. Taiani (2001) 'Advertising Content for the Global Audience: A Research Proposal', *Competitiveness Review* 11.2: 39-47.

Scott, J. (1991) *Social Network Analysis: A Handbook* (London: Sage).

Scott, S.G., and V.R. Lane (2000) 'A Stakeholder Approach to Organizational Identity', *Academy of Management Review* 25.1: 43-62.

Scott, W.R. (1992) *Organizations: Rational, Natural, and Open Systems* (Englewood Cliffs, NJ: Prentice Hall, 3rd edn).

—— (1995) *Institutions and Organizations* (Thousand Oaks, CA: Sage).

Sethi, S.P. (1979) 'A Conceptual Framework for Environmental Analysis of Social Issues and Evaluation of Business Response Patterns', *Academy of Management Review* 4.1: 63-74.

—— (1997) 'The Notion of the "Good Corporation" in a Competitive Global Economy', in S.P. Sethi, P. Steidemeier and C.M. Falbe (eds.), *Scaling the Corporate Wall: Readings in Business and Society* (Englewood Cliffs, NJ: Prentice Hall, 2nd edn).

Shapiro, R.B. (1999) Address to Greenpeace Business Conference London, 6 October 1999.

Sharfman, M.P., T.S. Pinkson and T.D. Sigerstad (2000) 'The Effects of Managerial Values on Social Issues Evaluation: An Empirical Examination', *Business and Society* 39: 144-82.

Sheppard, B., R. Lewicki and J.M. Minton (1992) *Organizational Justice* (New York: The Free Press).

Shimp, T.A. (1997) *Advertising, Promotion and Supplemental Aspects of Integrated Marketing Communications* (Fort Worth, TX: Dryden Press, 4th edn).

Sigurdson, S.G. (1987) 'Settling Environmental Disputes: Reflections on Two Cases', *Canadian Environmental Mediation Newsletter* 2.3: 1-5.

Sillanpää, M. (1998) 'The Body Shop Values Report: Towards Integrated Stakeholder Auditing', *Journal of Business Ethics* 17.13: 1,443-56.

Smircich, L., and C. Stubbart (1985) 'Strategic Management in an Enacted World', *Academy of Management Review* 10: 724-36.

Smith, A., R. Kemp and C. Duff (1998) *Small Firms and the Environment: Further Analysis of the 1998 Groundwork Survey* (Birmingham, UK: Groundwork Publications).

Smith, D.C. (1972) *A History of Lumbering in Maine 1861–1960* (Orono, ME: University of Maine Press).

Smith, K.G., K.A. Smith, J.D. Olian, H.P. Sims, D.P. O'Bannon and J.A. Scully (1994) 'Top Management Team Demography and Process: The Role of Social Integration and Communication', *Administrative Science Quarterly* 39: 412-38.

Sonnenfeld, J.A. (1981) *Corporate Views of the Public Interest: Perceptions of the Forest Products Industry* (Boston, MA: Auburn House).

Spicer, B.H. (1978) 'Accounting for Corporate Social Performance: Some Problems and Issues', *Journal of Contemporary Business* 7.1: 151-70.

Spreckley, F. (1982) *Social Audit: A Management Tool for Co-operative Work* (UK: Beechwood College).

—— (1997) *Social Audit Toolkit* (Willenhall, UK: Social Enterprise Partnership).

Stafford, E.R., and C.L. Hartman (1996) 'Green Alliances: Strategic Relations between Businesses and Environmental Groups', *Business Horizons*, March/April 1996: 50-59.

Stafford, E.R., M.J. Polonsky and C.L. Hartman (2000) 'Environmental NGO–Business Collaboration and Strategic Bridging: A Case Analysis of the Greenpeace–Foron Alliance', *Business Strategy and the Environment* 9.

Starik, M. (1994) 'Essay by Mark Starik: Pl. 89-95 of the Toronto Conference: Reflections on Stakeholder Theory', *Business and Society* 33: 82-141.

—— (1995) 'Should Trees Have Managerial Standing? Toward Stakeholder Status for Non-Human Nature', *Business Ethics* 14: 207-17.

Starik, M., G. Throop, J. Doody and M.E. Joyce (1996) 'Growing an Environmental Strategy', *Business Strategy and the Environment* 5: 12-21.

Steger, U., and R. Meima (1998) *The Strategy Dimensions of Environmental Management* (Basingstoke, UK: Macmillan).

Steiner, G., and J. Steiner (1991) *Business, Government and Society* (New York: McGraw–Hill).

Stigler, G.J. (1971) 'The Theory of Economic Regulation', *Bell Journal of Economics* 2.1: 3-21.

Stoel, T. (1981) 'Citizen Groups: A Creative Force', *EPA Journal* 7.2: 22-24.

Stoney, C., and D. Winstanley (2001) 'Stakeholding: Confusion or Utopia? Mapping the Conceptual Terrain', *Journal of Management Studies* 38.5: 603-26.

Suchman, M.C. (1995) 'Managing Legitimacy: Strategic and Institutional Approaches', *Academy of Management Review* 20: 571-610.

Susskind, L., S. McKearnan and J. Thomas-Larmer (1999) *The Consensus Building Handbook: A Comprehensive Guide to Reaching Agreement* (Thousand Oaks, CA: Sage).

Susskind, L., P.F. Levy and J. Thomas-Larmer (2000) *Negotiating Environmental Agreements: How to Avoid Escalating Confrontation, Needless Costs, and Unnecessary Litigation* (Washington, DC: Island Press).

SustainAbility (1999) *The Social Reporting Report* (London: SustainAbility).

Svendsen, A. (1998) *The Stakeholder Strategy: Profiting from Collaborative Business Relationships* (San Francisco: Berrett-Koehler).

Swanson, D.L. (1995) 'Addressing a Theoretical Problem by Reorienting the Corporate Social Performance Model', *Academy of Management Review* 20.1: 43-64.

Swanson, E. (1995) *Environmental Conflict and Alternative Dispute Resolution* (Edmonton, Canada: Environmental Law Centre).

Tennyson, R., and L. Wilde (2000) *The Guiding Hand: Brokering Partnerships for Sustainable Development* (New York: United Nations Department of Information).

Thompson, J.D. (1967) *Organizations in Action* (New York: McGraw–Hill).

Thompson, J.K., S.L. Wartick, and H.L. Smith (1991) 'Integrating Corporate Social Performance and Stakeholder Management: Implications for a Research Agenda in Small Business', *Research in Corporate Social Performance and Policy* 12: 207-30.

Tidwell, A.C. (1998) *Conflict Resolved? A Critical Assessment of Conflict Resolution* (London: Pinter).

Tilley, F. (2000) 'Small Firms and Environmental Ethics: How Deep Do They Go?', in R. Hillary (ed.), *Small and Medium-Sized Enterprises and the Environment: Business Imperatives* (Sheffield, UK: Greenleaf Publishing): 35-48.

Tolbert, P.S., and L.G. Zucker (1983) 'Institutional Sources of Change in the Formal Structure of Organizations: The Diffusion of Civil Service Reform, 1880–1935', *Administrative Science Quarterly* 30: 22-39.

Traidcraft (1993) *Social Audit Report 1992/93* (Gateshead, UK: Traidcraft).

—— (1994) *Social Audit Report 1993/94* (Gateshead, UK: Traidcraft).

—— (1995) *Social Accounts 1994/95* (Gateshead, UK: Traidcraft).

Traidcraft Exchange (1996) *Social Accounts 1995/96* (Gateshead, UK: Traidcraft Exchange).

Tulin, M.F. (1996) 'As We Talk So We Organize' (unpublished dissertation; Boston, MA: Boston University).

Tushman, M.L. (1977) 'Special Boundary Roles in the Innovation Process', *Administrative Science Quarterly* 22: 587-605.

TXU-Europe (2000) *Environmental and Social Report 2000* (London: TXU-Europe).

Ulhøi, J.P., and H. Madsen (1997) 'Environmental Decisions in Business and Stakeholder Influences' (working paper; Aarhus, Denmark: Aarhus School of Business).

UNEP (United Nations Environment Programme) and Prince of Wales Business Leaders Forum (1994) *Partnerships for Sustainable Development* (London: Flashprint Enterprises).

US Census Bureau (1999) *1997 Economic Census: Iron and Steel Mills* (Washington, DC: US Department of Commerce).

Vaughan, D. (1995) *The Challenger Launch Decision* (Chicago: University of Chicago Press).

Verstehen-Ryan, L. (1995) 'Stakeholder Theory: In Search of the Normative Core', in D. Nigh and D. Collins (eds.), *Proceedings of the Sixth Annual Meeting of the International Association for Business and Society* (IABS): 141-45.

Waddell, S. (2000) 'The Win–Win Rationale for Engaging with NGOs', in J. Bendell (ed.), *Terms for Endearment: Business, NGOs and Sustainable Development* (Sheffield, UK: Greenleaf Publishing): 193-206.

Waddock, S.A. (2002) *Leading Corporate Citizens: Vision, Values, Value Added* (New York: McGraw–Hill).

Waddock, S.A., and S.B. Graves (1997) 'Quality of Management and Quality of Stakeholder Relations: Are They Synonymous?', *Business and Society* 36.3 (September 1997): 250-79.

Waddock, S.A., and N. Smith (2000) 'Corporate Responsibility Audits: Doing Well By Doing Good', *Sloan Management Review* 41.2 (Winter 2000): 75-84.

Wall, J., and R. Callister (1995) 'Conflict and its Management', *Journal of Management* 21.3: 515-58.

Wartick, S.L., and P.L. Cochran (1985) 'The Evolution of the Corporate Social Performance Model', *Academy of Management Review* 10.4: 758-69.

Wartick, S.L., and J.F. Mahon (1994) 'Toward a Substantive Definition of the Corporate Issue Construct', *Business and Society* 33: 293-311.

WCED (World Commission on Environment and Development) (1987) *Our Common Future* (Oxford, UK: Oxford University Press).

Weddle, R.L. (1995) 'Preparing Tailored Fact Books and Prospect Proposals', *Economic Development Review* 13.1: 32-36.

Weiman, G. (1980) 'Conversation Networks as Communication Networks', abstract of PhD dissertation, University of Haifa, Israel.

Weitzman, E.A., and P.F. Weitzman (2000) 'Problem Solving and Decision Making in Conflict Resolution', in M. Deutsch and P.T. Coleman (eds.), *The Handbook of Conflict Resolution: Theory and Practice* (San Francisco: Jossey-Bass): 185-209.

Welcomer, S.A., D. Gioia and M. Kilduff (2000) 'Resisting the Discourse of Modernity: Rationality and Emotion in Hazardous Waste Siting', *Human Relations* 53.9: 1,175-1,206.

Welford, R. (1995) *Environmental Strategy and Sustainable Development: The Corporate Challenge for the 21st Century* (London: Routledge).

Werner, J.D., and D.W. Reicher (1992) *Testimony on Behalf of the Natural Resources Defense Council (NRDC) before the Subcommittee on Energy and the Environment of the House Interior Committee on Establishment of National Standards for the Cleanup of Radiologically Contaminated Sites* (Washington, DC: NRDC).

Westley, F., and H. Vredenburg (1991) 'Strategic Bridging: The Collaboration between Environmentalists and Business in the Marketing of Green Products', *Journal of Applied Behavioural Science* 27.1: 65-90.

Wheeler, D., H. Fabig and R. Boele (2002) 'Paradoxes and Dilemmas for Stakeholder Responsive Firms in the Extractive Sector: Lessons from the Case of Shell and the Ogoni', *Journal of Business Ethics* 39: 297-318.

Wiersema, M.F., and K.A. Bantel (1992) 'Top Management Team Demography and Corporate Strategic Change', *Academy of Management Journal* 35: 91-121.

—— (1993) 'Top Management Team Turnover as an Adaptation Mechanism: The Role of the Environment', *Strategic Management Journal* 14: 485-504.

Wilde, T.G. (1998) 'Public Participation in the Environmental Assessment of the Jumbo Glacier Ski Area Proposal' (MRM thesis report no. 224; Burnaby, BC: Simon Fraser University, School of Resource and Environmental Management).

Williamson, O.E. (1981) 'The Economics of Organization: The Transaction Cost Approach', *American Journal of Sociology* 87.3: 548-77.

Wilson, M., and M. Gatward (1998) 'Auditing Social Accounts: What it is and how to do it', *Accountancy*, January 1998: 140-41.

Wilson, S.R., and L.L. Putnam (1990) 'Interaction Goals in Negotiation', in J.A. Anderson (ed.), *Communication Yearbook 13* (Newbury Park, CA: Sage): 374-406.

Windsor, D. (1992) 'Stakeholder Management in Multinational Enterprises', in. S.N. Brenner and S.A. Waddock (eds.), *Proceedings of the Third Annual Meeting of the International Association for Business and Society* (Leuven, Belgium: IABS): 121-28.

—— (2002) 'Stakeholder Responsibilities: Lessons for Managers', in J. Andriof, S. Waddock, B. Husted and S. Sutherland Rahman (eds.), *Unfolding Stakeholder Thinking: Theory, Responsibility and Engagement* (Sheffield, UK: Greenleaf Publishing): 137-54.

Winer, M., and K. Ray (1994) *Collaboration Handbook: Creating, Sustaining, and Enjoying the Journey* (St Paul, MN: Amherst H. Wilder Foundation).

Winn, M.I. (2001) 'Building Stakeholder Theory with a Decision Modelling Methodology', *Business and Society* 40.2: 133-66.

Winter, M., and U. Steger (1998) *Managing Outside Pressure: Strategies for Preventing Corporate Disasters* (Chichester, UK: John Wiley).

Wokutch, R.E., and L. Fahey (1986) 'A Value Explicit Approach for Evaluating Corporate Social Performance', *Journal of Accounting and Public Policy* 5.3: 191-214.

Wondolleck, J.M. (1988) *Public Lands and Conflict Resolution: Managing National Forest Disputes* (London: Plenum Press).

—— (1996) 'Teetering at the Top of the Ladder: The Experience of Citizen Group Participants in Alternative Dispute Resolution Processes', *Sociological Perspectives* 39: 249-73.

Wood, D.J. (1991) 'Corporate Social Performance Revisited', *Academy of Management Review* 16.4: 691-718.

Wood, D.J., and R.E. Jones (1995) 'Stakeholder Mismatching: A Theoretical Problem in Empirical Research on Corporate Social Performance', *International Journal of Organizational Analysis* 3: 229-67.

Woodward, D.G. (1998) 'An Attempt at the Classification of a Quarter of a Century of (Non-critical) Corporate Social Reporting', paper presented at the *British Accounting Association Annual Conference*, April 1998, Manchester, UK.

WRI (World Resources Institute) (1992) *The AES Corporation (B)* (Washington, DC: WRI).

—— (1994) *Corpomedina* (Washington, DC: WRI).

Yin, K.R. (1994) *Case Study Research: Design and Methods* (Thousand Oaks, CA: Sage).

Yoxon, M. (1997) 'Sense or Nonsense: An Antidote to the Environmental Review for SMEs', paper presented at the 1997 Business and the Environment Conference, University of Leeds, UK, 18–19 September 1997 (Leeds, UK: ERP Environment).

Yuthas, K.D., and J.F. Dillard (1999) 'Ethical Development of Advanced Technology: A Postmodern Stakeholder Perspective', *Journal of Business Ethics* 19: 19-49.

Zadek, S. (1998) 'Balancing Performance, Ethics, and Accountability', *Journal of Business Ethics* 17.13: 1,421-41.

Zadek, S., and P. Raynard (1995) 'Accounting Works: A Comparative Review of Contemporary Approaches to Social and Ethical Accounting', *Accounting Forum* 19.2–3: 164-75.

Zohah, D. (1997) *Rewiring the Corporate Brain* (New York: Berrett-Koehler).

Zucker, L.G. (1987) 'Institutional Theories of Organizations', *Annual Review of Sociology* 13: 443-64.

ABBREVIATIONS

3G	third generation
AAFLI	Asian-American Free Trade Labor Institute
AFL–CIO	American Federation of Labor–Congress of Industrial Organisations
APSO	Agency for Personal Service Overseas
APT	accumulative, progressive and tabulated (reporting)
ARMR	Association of Radioactive Metal Recyclers
ATA	Appropriate Technology Association
BASF	Bangladesh Shishu Aadhikar Forum
BGMEA	Bangladesh Garment Manufacturers' Exporters' Association
BS	bachelor of science
CAGR	compound annual growth rate
CAT	computerised axial tomography
CCI	corporate community involvement
CEO	chief executive officer
CERCLA	Comprehensive Environmental Response, Compensation, and Liability Act of 1980 (USA)
CI	Conservation International
CIDESA	Fundación de Capacitación e Investigación para el Desarrollo Socioambiental
CLC	Child Labor Coalition
CO_2	carbon dioxide
CSP	corporate social performance
CSR1	corporate social responsibility
CSR2	corporate social responsiveness
DJSI	Dow Jones Sustainability Index
DM	deutsche mark
DNA	deoxyribonucleic acid
DOE	Department of Energy (USA)
EBITDA	earnings before interest tax, depreciation and amortisation
EDF	Environmental Defense Fund
EMAS	Eco-management and Audit Scheme
EPA	Environmental Protection Agency
ETI	Ethical Trading Initiative
FERC	Federal Energy Regulatory Commission (USA)
FLA	Fair Labor Association
FP	for-profit
FSC	Forest Stewardship Council
GAAP	generally accepted accounting principles
GLP	good laboratory practice
GM	genetically modified
GMP	good manufacturing practice
GRI	Global Reporting Initiative
H&S	health and safety
HR	human resources
IAEA	International Atomic Energy Agency

ILO	International Labour Organisation
IMF	International Monetary Fund
IPO	initial public offering
ISCT	Integrative Social Contracts Theory
ISEA	Institute of Social and Ethical Accountability
ISEAL	International Social and Environmental Accreditation and Labelling Alliance
ISO	International Organisation for Standardisation
ISRI	Institute of Scrap Recycling Industries
IUF	International Union for Food and Agricultural Workers
LHTD	Liverpool Housing Trust's Directions
LURC	Land Use Regulation Commission
MBA	Master of Business Administration
MNC	multinational corporation
MO	mixed-objective
MOU	Memorandum of Understanding
MSC	Marine Stewardship Council
NARUC	National Association of Regulatory Utility Commissioners (USA)
NEF	New Economics Foundation
NGO	non-governmental organisation
NORM	naturally occurring radioactive material
NPB	non-profit business
NPL	non-profit labour
NRC	Nuclear Regulatory Commission (USA)
OLS	ordinary least squares
OPEC	Organisation of the Petroleum Exporting Countries
PANP	Poverty Alleviation and Nutrition Program
PCP	polyvocal citizenship perspective
PiC	Partners in Change
PPF	Paria Project Foundation
RSM	radioactive scrap metal
SACCS	South Asian Coalition on Child Servitude
SAI	Social Accountability International
SEAAR	social and ethical accounting, auditing and reporting
SEED	Sound Environment Enterprise Development (CI)
SITRABI	Sindicato de Trabajadores Bananeros de Izabal
SKOP	Sramik Karmachari Oikkya Parishad (United Front of Workers and Employees, Bangladesh)
SMA	Steel Manufacturers' Association
SME	small or medium-sized enterprise
SOPS	standard operating procedures
SRB	socially responsible business
TMT	top-management team
TNC	transnational corporation
TSR	total shareholder return
UN	United Nations
UNEP	United Nations Environment Programme
UNICEF	United Nations Children's Fund
UNITE	Union of Needletrades, Industrial and Textile Employees
WCED	World Commission on Environment and Development
WTO	World Trade Organisation
WRI	World Resources Institute
WWF	World Wide Fund for Nature

BIOGRAPHIES

Jörg Andriof works in the corporate centre of Celanese. His competence areas are corporate development, strategy and stakeholder management. He received a PhD from Warwick Business School, UK, and studied business and engineering in Berlin and Leicester, UK. Previously, he held a position at KPMG Corporate Finance. He has also worked for Daimler-Benz and BMW Rolls-Royce. Jörg was one of the founding members of the Warwick Corporate Citizenship Unit, where he is an Associate Fellow. He is a member of the editorial board of *The Journal of Corporate Citizenship*. joerg@andriof.de

Jem Bendell has been involved in a variety of voluntary corporate responses to social and environmental challenges since 1995. He is an author of two books and a columnist on corporate responsibility, holds a PhD on the topic, and teaches at Nottingham University Business School, UK, where he is a Visiting Fellow. He founded the progressive careers network Lifeworth.com and works as a consult on corporate responsibility issues in developing countries, for example with the United Nations. His ideas have helped to inspire novel responses to sustainability issues, such as the Marine Stewardship Council and the UN Global Compact. www.jembendell.com

Shawn L. Berman is an assistant professor of management and organisational analysis at Santa Clara University, USA. He received his PhD in strategic management from the University of Washington. His research interests include empirical examinations of firm–stakeholder relationships, issues of inter-organisational trust, and corporate governance. sberman@scu.edu

Bruce W. Clemens has a PhD in strategy from the University of Tennessee in Knoxville, an MPA in economics from Harvard University and a BS in civil and environmental engineering from Cornell University, USA. Bruce is currently carrying out research on the relationships between environmental policies, business strategies, environmental performance and financial performance. He has held various positions in academia, government and industry. He is an assistant professor at James Madison University. clemenbw@jmu.edu

Philip L. Cochran is the Thomas W. Binford Chair in Corporate Citizenship at Indiana University's Kelley School of Business Indianapolis, USA. He holds a PhD in business, government and society from the University of Washington. Professor Cochran is the author of articles on corporate social performance, issues management, crisis management and business ethics. He was the first President of the International Association for Business and Society (IABS) and is a past Chair of the

Social Issues in Management Division of the Academy of Management. Professor Cochran also serves on the editorial boards of several journals.

plc@psu.edu

Jonathan Cohen is the Programme Manager at AccountAbility responsible for the AA 1000 Series. He is the founding Content Manager of the news link of the United Nations (UN) Global Compact website, and also manages an e-mail list concerning socially responsible business. He has served as a member of national NGO committees on the UN International Year of Volunteers in 2001, the Five-Year Review of the UN Beijing Women's Conference in 2000, the UN International Year of Older Persons in 1999, and the Universal Declaration of Human Rights 50th Anniversary in 1998. He has taught classes as an Assistant Adjunct Professor at New York University's School of Continuing and Professional Studies concerning NGOs. He has volunteered extensively with NGOs and on political campaigns at national, state and local levels. Mr Cohen has an MA in The Relationship between Non-profit Organisations and Socially Responsible Business from New York University.

jonathan@accountability.org.uk

Andrew Crane is a Senior Lecturer in Business Ethics at the International Centre for Corporate Social Responsibility (ICCSR) at the University of Nottingham, UK. He has a PhD from the University of Nottingham and a BSc from the University of Warwick. His current research interests include business ethics and organisation, social construction of morality, theoretical approaches to corporate citizenship, stakeholder communication, and organisational greening. He has published articles on these subjects in various journals, including *Academy of Management Review, The Journal of Business Ethics, The Journal of Business Research* and *Organization Studies*. His latest book, *Business Ethics: Managing Corporate Citizenship in the Global Economy* (co-authored with Dirk Matten) is due to be published by Oxford University Press in 2003.

Andrew.Crane@nottingham.ac.uk

Aharon Factor is a lecturer in organisational behaviour and business strategy. His key research focus is toward corporate greening and stakeholder management. Currently he is a guest lecturer at the university of New England, Australia. With previous management consultancy experience, he is also developing stakeholder management strategies for industry.

afactor@une.edu.au

Ian Fraser is a chartered accountant and Reader in Accounting and Finance at Glasgow Caledonian University, UK. His research interests cover financial reporting, audit, corporate governance, and social audit and accountability. He has published in various academic and professional journals. He is currently working on research into the future of corporate governance funded by the Institute of Chartered Accountants of Scotland.

i.a.m.fraser@gcal.ac.uk

Scott R. Gallagher earned his PhD from Rutgers University, USA. He received a MPP from Harvard University and a BBA from the University of Texas at Austin. He is currently an assistant professor at James Madison University.

gallagsr@jmu.edu

Virginia W. Gerde researches and teaches in the area of business ethics, corporate social performance, corporate governance, and business and society. She has published in *Business and Society, Teaching Business Ethics* and *The Journal of Corporate Citizenship*. After graduating with engineering degrees from Princeton University and the University of Virginia, USA, she received her PhD in Management from Virginia Polytechnic Institute and State University. She has management experience in environmental engineering and the military.

gerde@mgt.unm.edu

Wan Ying Hill is a senior lecturer in accounting at Glasgow Caledonian University, UK. Her main research and teaching interests are in the areas of social accounting and corporate accountability. She has published in a range of academic journals, including *Critical Perspectives in Accounting*, *The Journal of Business Ethics* and *The International Journal of Auditing*.
w.y.hill@gcal.ac.uk

Bryan W. Husted is a Professor of Management at the Instituto Tecnológico y de Estudios Superiores de Monterrey (Mexico) and Alumni Association Chair of Business Ethics at the Instituto de Empresa (Spain). His research focuses on cross-cultural business ethics and corporate social and environmental performance. His work has appeared in such publications as *The Journal of International Business Studies*, *Business Ethics Quarterly*, *The Journal of Environment and Development*, *Business and Society* and *The Journal of Business Ethics*. He is currently a member of the editorial board of *The Journal of International Management*.
bhusted@egade.sistema.itesm.mx

Michael E. Johnson-Cramer is a doctoral candidate in the Department of Organisational Behavior in the School of Management at Boston University, USA. He is also affiliated with the Human Resources Policy Institute. His research focuses on the political and institutional forces that shape firm–stakeholder relationships, especially the occurrence of stakeholder conflict.
mejc@bu.edu

Michael King is a management consultant focused on the business case for sustainability. He is interested in how organisations, at different points in the sustainability learning curve, develop strategy and implement this within their business. Different approaches are needed, depending upon the context of the business. A particular specialism within Innovys is the innovative use of mobile communications technology, which will increase the spotlight still further on corporate sustainable performance. Leading organisations will recognise this as an opportunity to deliver superior triple-bottom-line performance.
michael.king@innovys.co.uk

Sharon M. Livesey is Associate Professor of communication at Fordham University Graduate School of Business in New York. Her research interests focus on the reciprocal effects of language and institutional practice, especially concerning sustainable development. Her prior research focuses on discourses and discursive practices that have evolved in tandem with new understandings of corporate social responsibility. She has published papers in *Management Communication Quarterly*, *The Journal of Business Communication* and *Organization and Environment* and was the winner of the 1999 Distinguished Publication on Business Communication Award of the Association for Business Communication.
livesey@fordham.edu

James E. Post is Professor of Management and Faculty Director of the doctoral programme in the School of Management at Boston University, USA. His most recent book, *Redefining the Corporation: Stakeholder Management and Organizational Wealth*, co-authored with Lee Preston and Sybille Sachs, was published recently by Stanford University Press.
jepost@bu.edu

Sandra Sutherland Rahman is an Assistant Professor in the Economics and Business Administration Department at Framingham State College, USA. She has published on international firm–stakeholder discourse regarding labour conditions in developing countries. She has presented her work at international conferences on stakeholder responsibility, on firm–stakeholder collaborations in developing countries and on MNCs enriching employee work life in their manufacturing facilities in Bangladesh.
srahman@frc.mass.edu

Julia Robbins (née Grossman) is a former Canadian diplomat. She holds an MA in conflict analysis and management from Royal Roads University (Victoria, Canada) and a BA in international relations from the University of Toronto. She became interested in the relationships between business and society while posted to the Canadian Embassy in Bogotá, Colombia. Now a Vancouver-based consultant, she provides policy development, facilitation and advisory services. Her practice focuses on corporate responsibility, sustainability and conflict management.
julia.robbins@telus.net

Michael V. Russo is Professor of Management at the Lundquist College of Business, University of Oregon, USA. His current research interests include national and international political influences on corporate strategy, corporate environmental management, organisational economics and collaborative strategies. Recent publications include 'The Emergence of Sustainable Industries: Building on Natural Capital' (*Strategic Management Journal*, forthcoming), 'Institutional Environments in Flux: The Impact of Regulatory Change on CEO Succession and Performance', with H. Haveman and A. Meyer (*Organization Science*, May/June 2001), 'Institutions, Exchange Relations, and the Emergence of New Fields: Regulatory Policies and Independent Power Production in America, 1978–1992' (*Administrative Science Quarterly*, March 2001) and *Environmental Management: Readings and Cases* (Houghton-Mifflin, 1999). He received his PhD in Business and Public Policy from the Hass School of Business, University of California at Berkeley.
mrusso@lcbmail.uoregon.edu

Frank C. Schultz is a Visiting Assistant Professor at Michigan State University, USA. He received his PhD in Strategic Management from the University of Minnesota. His research interests include methods of balancing stakeholder interests, cognitive decision-making processes of CEOs and senior managers and the integration of generic business-level strategies. In addition to having taught a wide variety of courses such as Strategic Management, International Management, Accounting, Finance, Marketing, Economics and Statistics, his work experience includes *Fortune* 500 companies such as IBM, Chevron and Pillsbury—as well as two entrepreneurial ventures of his own. He has also consulted with organisations such as a Swiss multinational manufacturer and a university-based academic health centre.
schultzi@msu.edu

Sandra Waddock is Professor of Management at Boston College's Carroll School of Management, USA, and Senior Research Fellow at Boston College's Center for Corporate Citizenship. She received her MBA (1979) and DBA (1985) from Boston University and has published extensively on corporate responsibility, corporate citizenship and inter-sector collaboration in journals such as *The Academy of Management Journal*, *Strategic Management Journal*, *The Journal of Corporate Citizenship*, *Human Relations* and *Business and Society*, among many others. Her book, *Not by Schools Alone*, was published by Praeger in 1995. Her 1997 paper with Sam Graves, entitled 'Quality of Management and Quality of Stakeholder Relations: Are They Synonymous?', in *Business and Society*, won the 1997 Moskowitz Prize. Her latest book is *Leading Corporate Citizens: Vision, Values, Value Added* (McGraw–Hill, 2002). She was Senior Fellow at the Ethics Resource Center in Washington, DC, from 2000–2002 and a founding faculty member of the Leadership for Change Program at Boston College.
waddock@bc.edu

David Wasieleski completed his MBA with a focus on business ethics while working as an independent marketing representative for manufactured building products. Currently, he is completing doctoral work in business at the Katz Graduate School of Business, University of Pittsburgh, USA.
Dmw723@aol.com

James Weber is a Professor of Management and Director of the Beard Center for Leadership in Ethics, Duquesne University, USA. His research interests include the assessment of values, moral

reasoning and ethical behaviour, corporate social performance and ethical issues in technology. He is the co-author of the 10th edition of *Business and Society* (McGraw–Hill, 2002).
weberj@duq.edu

Stephanie A. Welcomer is an assistant professor of management at the University of Maine Business School, USA. She received her PhD from the Pennsylvania State University and has published in *Human Relations* and other outlets as well. She is currently the Proceedings Editor for the International Association for Business and Society (IABS). Her research interests include stakeholder networks, organisation and natural environment issues, and the use of rhetoric to construct meaning.
welcomer@maine.edu

Jane Zhang is a senior lecturer in accounting and finance at Sunderland Business School, University of Sunderland, UK. She is doing a PhD (part-time) at Glasgow Caledonian University (UK) in the area of social audit in the National Health Service (NHS). Her current research interests include social audit in the NHS, long-term care finance and insurance, and dividend policy of Chinese listed companies. She has published articles in the area of social audit and financing long-term care in China.
jane.zhang@sunderland.ac.uk

INDEX